The Neolithic of Mainland Scotland

The Neolithic of Mainland Scotland

Edited by Kenneth Brophy, Gavin MacGregor and
Ian Ralston

EDINBURGH
University Press

Edinburgh University Press is one of the leading university presses in the UK.
We publish academic books and journals in our selected subject areas across the
humanities and social sciences, combining cutting-edge scholarship with high editorial
and production values to produce academic works of lasting importance. For more
information visit our website: www.edinburghuniversitypress.com

Edinburgh University Press Ltd
The Tun – Holyrood Road
12 (2f) Jackson's Entry
Edinburgh EH8 8PJ

Typeset in 10.5/12 Ehrhardt by
Servis Filmsetting Ltd, Stockport, Cheshire
and printed and bound in Great Britain by
CPI Group (UK) Ltd, Croydon CR0 4YY

A CIP record for this book is available from the British Library

ISBN 978 0 7486 8572 1 (hardback)
ISBN 978 0 7486 8573 8 (paperback)
ISBN 978 0 7486 8574 5 (webready PDF)
ISBN 978 0 7486 8575 2 (epub)

Edinburgh University Press would like to acknowledge the generous financial support
of Historic Scotland (Alba Aosmhor) towards the publication of this volume.

HISTORIC SCOTLAND
ALBA AOSMHOR

Contents

Part III   Pits, Pots and Practice

Tables and Figures

Tables

Figures

Notes on the Contributors

Kenneth Brophy is Senior Lecturer in Archaeology at the University of Glasgow. His research interests include the Neolithic and Bronze Age of Britain, with particular interest in settlement sites and ceremonial monuments. He has directed a series of excavations of cropmark sites in Perth and Kinross, and is co-director of the Strathearn Environs and Royal Forteviot (SERF) project.

Claire Christie, after graduating in archaeology from Aberdeen in 2012, achieved a Master's Degree with distinction from UCL, during which she researched Grooved Ware and Beaker pits from mainland Scotland. In 2014, she began doctoral research on the earlier prehistoric settlement systems of the west mainland of Shetland.

Gabriel Cooney is on the staff of the School of Archaeology, University College Dublin, where he has been a full professor since 2006. He was appointed Professor of Celtic Archaeology two years later. His wide interests in prehistory are particularly focused on the Neolithic period, and on the use of stone from the monumental to the object (especially axes) and the quarries where they were produced, particularly those on islands.

Vicki Cummings is Reader in Archaeology at the University of Central Lancashire. Her research interests include the Mesolithic and Neolithic of Britain and Ireland, with a particular focus on monuments and landscape.

Alex Gibson, Reader in British Prehistory at Bradford University, is currently President of the Prehistoric Society. A graduate of Newcastle and Leicester universities, where he took his doctorate with a thesis on Beaker domestic pottery, he worked for Leicester University, the Clwyd–Powys Archaeological Trust and English Heritage's Centre for Archaeology before joining Bradford in 2001.

Roy Loveday is a retired teacher. He completed a national survey of cursus monuments for his PhD at Leicester University where he is now an Honorary Research Fellow. His interests extend beyond the monuments to the underlying social dynamics that shaped and spread them, and their role in the Middle Neolithic transformation.

Gavin MacGregor is a Director at Northlight Heritage, Glasgow. His research interests include the value of archaeology and historic environment to society, integrated landscape research and creative practices in cultural heritage.

Ann MacSween is a graduate of the universities of Edinburgh and Bradford, where she completed her doctorate on Orcadian Neolithic pottery. She has maintained her interests in prehistoric pottery from Scotland throughout her career, during which she has worked for AOC Archaeology and the University of Dundee. She is currently Head of Strategic Heritage Management at Historic Environment Scotland.

Kirsty Millican is an established researcher with a particular expertise in remote sensing. She completed an AHRC-funded PhD at Glasgow University in 2009, on the topic of timber Neolithic monuments in Scotland. She currently works within Heritage Management for Historic Environment Scotland.

Gordon Noble is Senior Lecturer in Archaeology at the University of Aberdeen, which he joined in 2008 after postdoctoral research at the University of Glasgow. An active field archaeologist, he maintains wide interests in Scottish pre- and protohistory. A co-founder of the Strathearn and Royal Forteviot (SERF) project, he worked on the major Neolithic–Early Bronze Age complex at Forteviot from 2006 to 2011 and is now director of the University of Aberdeen Northern Picts project.

Emma Philip is presently a PhD student at Aberdeen University, having completed an M Litt in Archaeological Studies at Glasgow in 2008. Her interests lie in the later Mesolithic and earlier Neolithic of north-east Scotland, and span landscape, mobility and material culture.

Ian Ralston is Abercromby Professor of Archaeology and currently Head of the School of History, Classics and Archaeology at Edinburgh University. His interests include Scottish prehistory of all periods, applied archaeology and the European Iron Age, on which he has published widely.

Neil Wilkin is Curator, Bronze Age Collection in the Department of Britain, Europe and Prehistory at the British Museum. His research interests include socio-economic links between Bronze Age ceramics and metalwork; funerary practices and the material culture of death; and new approaches to the study and creation of classifications and typo-chronologies.

Rebecca K. Younger is an early career researcher based at the University of Glasgow whose research interests include the Neolithic and Early Bronze Age of Scotland, monument biography in the past and present, and the processes of commemoration and memory in prehistory. She completed her PhD on Scotland's henge monuments in 2015.

Acknowledgements

A wide range of people have helped in the writing of this book. Ian Ralston would like to acknowledge that his chapter benefited from informal chats and discussions down the years with Colvin and Moira Greig, Ian Shepherd, Roger Mercer, Kenneth Brophy and other colleagues across Scottish archaeology, some of whom are no longer here to put right any of the writer's recollections which may be faulty. Gavin MacGregor thanks Kenneth Brophy, Chris Dalglish, Helen Green, Benjamin Grahn-Danielson, Gerhard Emisher, Alan Leslie and Aphrodite Sorotou. Vicki Cummings acknowledges the benefit to her chapter of ongoing discussions with Colin Richards and Alasdair Whittle; Oliver Harris, Lesley McFadyen and Mick Wysocki who were kind enough to comment on an earlier draft of her chapter. Roy Loveday would like to express his deep gratitude to Gordon Barclay for his support over so many years, and to Kenneth Brophy and Angela Gannon. Rebecca Younger thanks Kenneth Brophy, Julian Thomas and Christine Younger for advice and comments on earlier versions of her chapter, and notes her sincere thanks also to the family of Sue Green for the generous award of the Susan Green Bursary which supported some of the research that her chapter draws on. The chapter by Kirsty Millican was based in part on doctoral research funded by an AHRC collaborative doctoral award between RCAHMS and the University of Glasgow; Gordon Noble and Kenneth Brophy read through and commented on early drafts of this chapter. Gordon Noble, Claire Christie and Emma Philip would like to thank Charlie and Hilary Murray for access to unpublished site data and to Alison Sandison for helping with illustrations. Kenneth Brophy would like to acknowledge his gratitude to Gordon Barclay for providing the list of settlement sites upon which this chapter his based; information on unpublished sites was provided by Gordon Noble and Alastair Becket. Finally, Neil Wilkin thanks Alexandra (Lekky) Shepherd, Kenneth Brophy, Gordon Noble and Stuart Needham for allowing sight of unpublished work. The late Ian Shepherd provided early encouragement in pursuing a number of lines of research concerning Beaker forms and decoration, while Paul

Garwood read and provided helpful comments on earlier drafts, and Louise Wheeler helped to improve the text, while Stephen Crummy assisted in preparing the illustrations.

Foreword:
'The prehistory of my own lands, the lowlands'

This volume consists of a series of contributions that reflect our current understanding of many aspects of the archaeology of *mainland* Scotland in the Neolithic period (that is, between *c*. 4000 and 2500 BC). The unusual geographical focus of the book stems from its origins: to honour the contributions to this subject of Gordon Barclay, an eminent scholar of the Scottish Neolithic, whose focus throughout his career where the Neolithic was concerned had a resolutely lowland gaze. Neolithic studies in Scotland have traditionally been dominated by the study of the spectacular Orcadian record, and have often been taken forward in the shadow of developments in southern England. It is evident that Gordon became very frustrated over the time, effort and resources spent on excavations and research on Orkney and Wessex (the 'luminous centres') relative to other parts of the country. Yet, rather than just complain, Gordon sought to re-balance this with his own work and, with the support of various colleagues and digging partners, he also developed a very important intellectual argument for the need to study what had often appeared marginal and peripheral – whether that be eastern lowland Scotland as a region, or cursus monuments, or Neolithic settlement sites or cropmarks. As a result, it would be fair to say that Gordon's contribution to the study of the field evidence for the British Neolithic is immense; in particular, he revolutionised our understanding of the Neolithic north of the Border while literally inspiring a generation of new researchers.

The contributors to this volume all owe a great debt of gratitude to Gordon: professionally, personally or both. This is reflected in the topics covered by the chapters, inspired by a comment, or challenge or words of wisdom from Gordon, or by the results of one of his excavations, or a paper he wrote or even whole research areas that he worked on. And each contributor was asked to prepare a chapter to this book written in a similarly tireless and enthusiastic spirit to that which Gordon has always shown in his work, hence the attention to detail and sheer depth to many of the following chapters. During the Neolithic phase of his career Gordon was a great

collator of lists of sites or other features that he often generously passed on
to fellow archaeologists, and some of that spirit is here too. The contributors
to the following pages, range across – and we hope no offence is caused – the
generations of Neolithic scholars, with the work of early career researchers
(including current postgraduate students) sitting alongside that of more
established colleagues. Gordon's approach to the Neolithic and his thoughtful contributions to its study continue to inspire researchers, and we hope
this book reflects this.

As well as celebrating Gordon's career to date, this book is also intended
to offer a rounded picture of what we know about the Neolithic of mainland,
lowland Scotland, and contributors have focused on settlement, monumentality, material culture, practices such as deposition and funerary rites. The
relatively manageable geographical scope of the volume, and the excellent
central archives of information we have in Scotland (from the National
Monuments Record of Scotland to the annual publication of *Discovery and
Excavation in Scotland*) mean that our contributors have a fair chance of
offering comprehensive overviews, of making connections and of offering
syntheses in ways that are probably much harder to achieve in, for instance,
England. Yet we are also in a position to identify clear strands of regional
variation, and interaction, within and beyond the mainland (including connections with Orkney and Ireland, for instance). Our excellent pottery chronologies, extensive dating programmes and the comprehensive Scottish
Archaeological Research Framework Neolithic (ScARF) document (which
went online[1] in 2012) have given us a strong frame upon which to hang our
interpretations.

As well as on the Scottish lowlands, however, the chapters that follow
focus on margins, fringes and neighbouring areas in order to contextualise
the Neolithic of mainland Scotland – whether this be Orkney, Ireland, the
islands off the west coast or Scotland's uplands. This perspective represents
a two-way exchange of knowledge and ideas; and the fluidity of the boundaries of Scotland in prehistory, which transcend modern political frontiers,
were again encouraged by Gordon's work. In other words: what we say
about the Neolithic here, and how we have gone about making sense of it,
should be of significance to studying the Neolithic in other parts of northern
Europe. Neolithic studies in Scotland are dynamic, and of wide interest, and
this volume, which reflects Gordon's passions, offers the first overview of its
kind for over a decade.

This book would not have been possible without the help and support of
many people, not least those who contributed to the volume. They have demonstrated a good deal of patience through this volume's relatively slow gesta-
tion. Thanks are due also to Historic Scotland (now Historic Environment
Scotland), Gordon's former employers, who have throughout been very
supportive of this project in various ways. And we thank in particular Liz
Goring and Adam Barclay, who kept the book a secret from Gordon for

years, and offered support, advice and help without hesitation when it was
sought. We hope that they, and he, are pleased with the outcome.

KB, GM, IR

Editorial notes

All individual radiocarbon determinations in this book are cited as calibrated
BC (cal. BC) dates, accompanied by their laboratory code and, unless stated,
are provided with a two sigma (95 per cent confidence) range. Date ranges
have also been given in cal. BC, with more generic time periods omitting the
inclusion of 'cal.', for example, 'second half of the third millennium BC'.

The boundaries of Scotland's local authorities have been redrawn twice
since the early 1970s, and in some instances their names have been changed.
The 'Aberdeenshire' of the current system, for example, is neither coter-
minous with 'Grampian Region' as set up in 1974, nor with the historical
county of 'Aberdeenshire', which preceded it. In general we have preferred
to use the current designations, such that the timber hall at Balbridie (once
in Kincardineshire, then in Kincardine and Deeside District of Grampian
Region) is now in Aberdeenshire. In some instances, it has made sense
to retain older designations, such as 'Tayside' in which much of Gordon
Barclay's own fieldwork took place. In the case of individual sites, clari-
fication of geographical attributions can readily be obtained by using the
Royal Commission on the Ancient and Historical Monuments of Scotland's
CANMORE system.

Note

1. Available at: http://www.scottishheritagehub.com/content/scarf-neolithic-
   panel-report.

This volume is dedicated to
GORDON BARCLAY
Prehistorian of the Scottish Lowlands

PART I

Scotland's Mainland Neolithic in Context

CHAPTER I

Gordon Barclay:
A Career in the Scottish Neolithic

Ian Ralston

Gordon Barclay (Figure 1.1), as many readers of this chapter will know, is a man of many interests and several passions. He spent most of his professional career in the service of archaeology within, latterly, the Scottish Government, and before that in a raft of state bodies and agencies of the Scottish Executive, and before that the Scottish Office all the way back to the old Department of the Environment of the mid-1970s. This contribution will, in keeping with the central concerns of the chapters by his friends and colleagues that are offered to him in the present volume, focus on 'early farmer' Gordon, as opposed to his other *personas*, although some of these will nonetheless, I am sure, emerge in this chapter, for several of them cross-cut with his Neolithic interests. My only qualifications for taking on this task are that I have known Gordon throughout his professional career, that I too am a lowland, east coast Scot who shares some of his mind-set, but also because I was the supervisor of Gordon's Edinburgh PhD thesis, submitted in 2001 and entitled *The First Farmers: The Neolithic of East-Central Scotland*. This was a doctorate awarded according to the Edinburgh rules on the basis of an extended justificatory essay setting his key research publications (over the ten years preceding 2000) on the Scottish Neolithic into wider context. It was – and readers who know the author will not be surprised to hear this – among the least troublesome theses I have ever been called on to oversee, with, in a reversal of what often happens, the supervisor being chivvied from time to time by the supervisee to hurry the administrative and other processes along. I hope the foregoing comments, however, will suffice to explain why a later prehistoric impostor pens these words. It is appropriate to note here that Gordon had intended since the early part of his professional career in the 1980s to undertake research as a part-time student with a view to submitting a doctoral dissertation on a cognate topic – initially the Neolithic of Perthshire – but had been stymied, despite the encouragement of Iain MacIvor, the then Chief Inspector of Ancient Monuments by – in Gordon's view – lukewarm, nay tepid, official support thereafter within the civil service.

Figure 1.1 Gordon Barclay (photograph: Adam Barclay, reproduced with permission).

Gordon is by birth an Aberdonian, brought up in the fine grey granite setting of the city's Westburn Road, where his parents were neighbours of Colvin and Moira Greig. In the 1960s and early 1970s, the Greigs, especially Colvin, played a seminal role in encouraging a whole series of north-east schoolchildren to develop an active interest in Scottish archaeology: several were in due course to become professional archaeologists in, and indeed beyond, the country. One key element of this engagement was Colvin's important excavations (1964–71) at the multi-period promontory fort of Castle Point, Troup (Cullykhan) (Greig and Greig 1990; Ralston 2006), on what was then the Banffshire (now Aberdeenshire) coast near Pennan, soon thereafter to become celebrated as a key setting for Bill Forsyth's *Local Hero*. Gordon worked at Cullykhan for some of his summers while an Aberdeen schoolboy at the city's Robert Gordon's College, which he left in the summer of 1972 to attend Edinburgh University, having decided to read Archaeology. At the university, in the old Department of Prehistoric Archaeology at 19 George Square, he was thus a member of the penulti-mate cohort of undergraduates to complete – in 1976 – their Master of Arts degrees under Professor Stuart Piggott, the second distinguished holder of the Abercromby Chair, who retired in 1977. The Edinburgh Archaeology Department at that time was in large measure focused in terms of practical work on the prehistory of Britain, as witnessed not only by the recruitment of Roger Mercer to the staff, and by Trevor Watkins' fieldwork in Fife and elsewhere in eastern Scotland, but also by Stuart Piggott's last excava-tion project (to 1972), at Dalladies, then in Kincardineshire (now too in

Aberdeenshire), which involved the first extensive excavation of a Scottish earthen long barrow, prior to its destruction through gravel quarrying (Piggott 1972).

From university, and already having acquired a range of supervisory experience in fieldwork within Britain and across the North Sea in Norway, Gordon was soon – in 1977 – recruited as a key member of the early intake into the Central Excavation Unit (CEU), the Scottish Inspectorate of Ancient Monuments' slightly tardy response to the series of regional archaeological field units established across much of England under the auspices of the then Department of the Environment. This was at a time when the concept of 'polluter pays' in relation to cultural resources lay far in the future, and where the need to respond to catastrophic threats to the archaeological record – and not simply natural ones such as coastal erosion – was still accepted as being a responsibility of the state. The creation of the CEU represented a significant upswing in the level of direct government support for rescue fieldwork across Scotland.

It was in the CEU, with its national responsibilities, and soon a part of the new Scottish Development Department (SDD), that Gordon spent the first seven years of his career (to 1983). On behalf of the SDD, he thus directed his first major rescue excavations, involving the management of substantial teams – in some cases based for several months in the field in rural settings between, on the one hand, the hinterland of Kirkcaldy and, on the other, the straths of Sutherland (Highland). Directing such projects involved Gordon not only in all aspects of the field archaeology itself, but also in arranging the feeding and housing – in essence providing pastoral care to – of the numerous staff recruited by a variety of means and initially largely maintained under the *ancien régime* of minimal daily 'volunteer' indemnities coupled with relatively generous accommodation allowances. *Autres temps, autres mœurs* indeed – and undoubtedly circumstances that immediately placed much responsibility on the shoulders of new young excavation directors such as Gordon. Others have told me that Gordon was to continue his generosity towards his field crews in the research phase of his digging career in terms both of the comfort of their accommodation and the quality of mealtime provisions.

Gordon's first published report appeared in 1980 and concerned the excavation of a cairn north of the Forth near Glenrothes in Fife (Barclay 1978). Leaving to one side his important fieldwork on later prehistoric settlements at Myrehead near Falkirk (Barclay 1983a) and at Upper Suisgill in the Strath of Kildonan, Sutherland in Highland (Barclay 1985), characteristically rapidly and fully reported, that decade marked Gordon's first substantial published contributions to the study of Neolithic archaeology – largely, but not exclusively, taking the form of major accounts of the examination of cropmark sites in the arable lands of, in particular, Tayside (essentially Angus and Perth and Kinross) and Fife. At this time, the impact of locally-based aerial photography, in terms of both the numbers and scale of lowland sites that were being discovered in the cereal fields, was beginning to be appreciated. It was assuredly propitious that the first season of the Royal Commission on the Ancient and Historical Monuments of Scotland's (RCAHMS) flying programme got underway in 1976, an excellent year for cropmark development, with pronounced soil moisture deficits over some of the key landscapes of the eastern Lowlands (Maxwell 1979). As we shall see, the doyen of Scottish aerial archaeologists, Gordon Maxwell of RCAHMS, who led these early indigenous aerial campaigns, in due course became one of Gordon's key collaborators in the field. Gordon's first major project in the lowland Scottish Neolithic series, again promptly published (1983b), was his late 1970s excavation at North Mains, Strathallan, in Perth and Kinross. This targeted a ceremonial complex threatened by a proposal to extend the runway there to accommodate the lumbering needs of a recommissioned Lancaster bomber, then recently acquired. In the event, the Lancaster never flew and the extension was not needed; but by the time that was evident the archaeological field project had been completed.

Fieldwork at North Mains involved the complete excavation of a cropmark henge monument and the examination of an upstanding and, as Gordon's team demonstrated, elaborately-constructed, barrow in close proximity to it as well as other, lesser, structures nearby. The disentangling of the complex sequence of mound construction at the North Mains barrow was a *tour de force* of interpretation that testified to Gordon's thoroughness at the trowel's edge. Strathallan was the second major mainland Scottish henge to be fully investigated in modern times, after Roger Mercer's extensive examination of Balfarg on the outskirts of Glenrothes in Fife (Mercer 1981); and these projects followed smaller-scale work in the preceding decade on Orkney by Colin Renfrew at the Ring of Brodgar (Renfrew 1979), and by the late Graham Ritchie (1976) at the Standing Stones of Stenness. A comparison of the scale of excavations apparent from my end-of-campaign aerial view of Stenness (Ritchie 1976, plate 4a) and Strathallan (Barclay 1983b, plate 12, and front cover of this book) demonstrates the changing ambitions of state-funded archaeology between the early 1970s and the late 1980s; but although the budget for Graham Ritchie's fieldwork at Stenness in 1972 was a then unheard-of £2,000, that sum would, of course, have been dwarfed by the funds deployed at Strathallan relatively shortly thereafter. In many ways, the Strathallan project exemplifies the Barclay approach not only in the thoroughness and completeness of the site's examination and the translation of that thoroughness into the report itself, but in the 'downstream', related activities that succeeded it: an account of the cultivation remains found stratified beneath the Strathallan barrow (Barclay 1989a); a joint paper reassessing the evidence for the atypical ditch circuit at Balfarg, written with Roger Mercer and others (Mercer *et al.* 1988); and – this time as a purely research excavation (undertaken with Myra Tolan), for which Gordon obtained the funding and which he directed during his summer leave – the sampling of a nearby cropmark enclosure on the edge of the terrace above the River Earn (Barclay and Tolan 1990), potentially a component of the wider later Neolithic complex around Strathallan, but in the event dated to the second millennium BC. All these were complemented by a more general rumination on the interpretation of henges, which appeared (Barclay 1989b) in the Prehistoric Society's *Proceedings* and, much later, his consideration of the relationship between henges and timber circles (2005a). This sequence of field activity and library research leading to prompt publication – as well as his dedication to digging in holidays from his official role – typified much of Gordon's career, which was marked also by his willingness to collaborate in order to extract as much value as possible from each site he tackled.

The second major Neolithic project, and the most extensive field undertaking for which Gordon was directly responsible, was the examination of further components of the important Neolithic and later complex on the outskirts of the expanding New Town of Glenrothes – at Balfarg – this time at the 'Riding School' site. The final publication of this, written with his main lieutenant, Chris Russell-White (Barclay and Russell-White 1993), formed a substantial part of volume 123 of the *Proceedings of the Society of Antiquaries of Scotland*; it was preceded by an award-winning popular account of the ceremonial complex, published under the auspices of the local authority, Fife (Barclay 1993a) (Figure 1.2). Another key innovation in the reporting of these excavations was the consideration of the *engineering* of these Neolithic structures, as well as their architecture. Of particular interest at the Riding School site was a pair of rectangular timber structures that predated the neighbouring henge enclosure. With another long-term collaborator, the illustrator David Hogg, these structures were carefully analysed and demonstrated not to have been roofed buildings, but rather light enclosures surrounding rebuilt platforms that could have served to expose the dead. Whether certain Neolithic structures could have been roofed has long been a contentious issue for some archaeologists (cf. Musson 1971), and Gordon here championed a new approach to this problem that would serve him well in his future excavations.

Before many of these publications had appeared, Gordon had moved on from the Central Excavation Unit. In 1983, he was appointed as an Inspector of Ancient Monuments in the Scottish Development Department, being promoted to Principal Inspector in the renamed Historic Scotland five years later. He remained in this post until 2006 before, for the final three years of his Historic Scotland career (to 2009), heading the agency's Heritage Policy Team. Gordon's initial responsibilities within the Inspectorate – for example, for scheduling ancient monuments, many of which were cropmarks – saw him still focused on his personal archaeological heartland, lowland eastern Scotland. As he became more senior within the agency, however, his responsibilities naturally widened; for much of the 1990s, for example, he

Figure 1.2 The front cover of Gordon Barclay's (1993a) award-winning booklet, which summarises the results of the Balfarg excavations, written to accompany the Balfarg heritage trail.

was in overall charge of the Archaeology Programme; and in the succeeding decade – alongside other roles – he had oversight of the archaeological and architectural research, fieldwork and restoration needed in advance of the construction at Holyrood (Edinburgh) of the new Scottish Parliament complex, as well as the subsequent stages of this project through to its final publication (Barclay and Ritchie 2008).

In the early years of Gordon's time in the Inspectorate, however, the maintenance of research interests and the tradition of active leadership of fieldwork by individual inspectors were both still encouraged, and thus Gordon was able to further progress his fieldwork and research on the eastern Scottish Neolithic. Latterly, however, the ethos within Historic Scotland changed, such that Gordon's subsequent field projects were pieces of pure research, undertaken during his leave from official duties. Between 2001 and 2003, he also had a temporary change of career. He was seconded to Stirling University as Principal Researcher on the Arts and Humanities Research Board-financed First Farmers Project,[1] which examined the evidence for early agricultural settlement in east-central Scotland and the outcomes of which – again expeditiously published – will be considered below; Gordon had been an Honorary Research Fellow in the then Department of Environmental Science at the university from 1997, and was Honorary Professor there from 2003 until 2009. In different circumstances than then prevailed financially and in other ways in the university sector, the initiatives built around the First Farmers Project might have led to archaeology as a discipline establishing a bridgehead at Stirling, but sadly this was not to be at that time.

On numerous occasions, Gordon worked alongside others in the field. With Gordon Maxwell, for example, he revisited earlier traces first identified during the campaigns of Sir Ian Richmond and Kenneth St Joseph within the great legionary fortress of Inchtuthil, Perth and Kinross, and economically defined these as the remains of a Neolithic long mortuary enclosure (1991), the first such site to be confirmed by the spade in Scotland. Later in the same decade, this collaboration of the two Gordons led, with the involvement of colleagues Donald Davidson and Ian Simpson from the Department of Environmental Science at Stirling, to the important intervention at the oft-misunderstood and misinterpreted Cleaven Dyke which, bisected by the modern main road north from Perth to Blairgowrie, marches through the lowland conifers on Meikleour Estate in Perth and Kinross; the extension of its flanking ditches into the adjacent cereal fields, where the bank itself has been ploughed out, is still apparent from the air in the correct circumstances. Careful, relatively modest, but analytical excavation (Figure 1.3), complemented by a well-thought-out programme of environmental analyses and detailed topographic survey, have made of the Cleaven Dyke Scotland's grandest earthen Neolithic monument, an Early Neolithic bank barrow/cursus monument with, as Gordon – never one shy to advance the claims of Scottish monuments – has suggested, a strong claim to the best preserved monument of this class anywhere in Europe. Any idea that the Dyke was, for example, a Roman forework for the nearby legionary establishment on the Inchtuthil plateau can no longer be entertained. The interim

Figure 1.3 One of Barclay's and Maxwell's trenches at the Cleaven Dyke, in this case investigating the central mound of the monument (photograph: Kenneth Brophy, reproduced with permission).

account of the project appeared remarkably quickly (Barclay *et al.* 1995); the definitive publication, setting the Dyke into wider context, particularly in relation to other Neolithic sites around the Tay–Isla confluence, appeared three years later (Barclay and Maxwell 1998), with the authors contributing a summary to an overview of the cursus monuments of Britain and Ireland in the following year (Barclay and Maxwell 1999). Thanks to a programme of localised removal of the conifers, again organised by Gordon, the Cleaven Dyke is now a monument that can be appreciated for what it is much more readily than was the case beforehand when it was largely concealed by trees.

Gordon also turned his attention to the post-built, potentially roofed, structures of the eastern Scottish Neolithic, following on from his examination and analyses of Balfarg Riding School. As part of the Cleaven Dyke project, a nearby cropmark site at Littleour was examined to assess its relationship to the Dyke, and indeed to determine whether it was a roofed building at all. Littleour proved to have been a few centuries later in date than the Dyke, a free-standing timber rectangular structure, which, for want of a better description, was a Late Neolithic 'ritual enclosure', with sherds from a fine Grooved Ware vessel recovered from a pit that post-dated the monument. This work (and that at Balfarg Riding School) foreshadowed an increasing interest of Gordon's in a range of rectangular and linear Neolithic structures. Subsequently, two further such structures were examined, both in concert with Kenneth Brophy of Glasgow University – at Carsie Mains

Figure 1.4 Excavations at Carsie Mains in 2002 showing Gordon Barclay deep
in conversation with co-director Kenneth Brophy (photograph: Kevin Kennie,
reproduced with permission).

(Figure 1.4) again near Meikleour in Perthshire (Brophy and Barclay 2004)
and at Claish Farm, near Callander in Stirling Council (Barclay *et al.* 2002).
Gavin MacGregor, then of GUARD, when it was still the applied field
unit housed within Glasgow University, also co-directed the Claish project.
At Claish a significant addition to the corpus of major Scottish Neolithic
timber halls was examined, in a structure that was demonstrated to conform
in substantial measure to the analysis of the architecture of this series that
Gordon had previously proposed. The identification of a shared architectural vocabulary across a range of such structures was a typically astute
Barclay observation presented in league with collaborator Hogg. These
excavations prompted re-evaluation of the chronology and significance of
further potentially Neolithic timber structures in Scotland, previously consigned to cropmark archive obscurity (e.g., Brophy 2007; Millican 2009).

   If Gordon's direct involvement in the archaeology of Neolithic Tayside
has primarily lain in the examination of the lowland zone of likely destruction (e.g., Barclay 1993b), and in the examination of the 'negatives' of pits,
ditches and the like, this has not been exclusively the case. In collaboration with Clive Ruggles, and as part of his wider interests in characterising the regional and sub-regional variations in the sites and monuments of
the Neolithic period, he also tackled the potential southern outliers of the
Recumbent Stone Circle tradition, a monument category focused on the
knuckle of north-east Scotland. At least one clear, if somewhat ruinous,

example was located at Colmeallie, south of the Mounth near Edzell in Angus (Barclay and Ruggles 1999). This interest then developed into a subsequent collaboration between Ruggles and Gordon, in which, in two contributions to *Antiquity* (Barclay and Ruggles 2000; 2002), they critically examined Euan MacKie's views on calendars and cosmologies in Neolithic Orkney. The intervention into problematic monuments of the north-east was foreshadowed by Barclay's earlier thoughtful attempt to synthesise available information on, and make sense of, the chronologically difficult Clava Cairns of the Inner Moray Firth area (Barclay 1992). Subsequent excavations by Richard Bradley (2000; 2005) on both of these classes of monuments has largely resolved these problems, with Bradley's fieldwork strongly encouraged and supported by Gordon.

Within Historic Scotland, the task of reassessing and presenting the important henge at Cairnpapple in the Bathgate Hills of West Lothian, a Guardianship monument presented to the public since its excavation by Stuart Piggott in the early years of his tenure of the Abercromby Chair at Edinburgh, fell to Gordon. Fifty years on from Piggott's initial report (1948), there was naturally – not least as a result of Gordon's own field examination of other sites – a much fuller range of local *comparanda* which could be brought to bear to rework the Cairnpapple sequence as initially set out in 1948; at that time Piggott had very largely to depend on analogies with geographically remote sites well to the south within Britain. In a particularly clear and cogent exposition published again in the *Proceedings of the Prehistoric Society* (1999a), Gordon set out the case for a revision of the sequence of use of some of the components of Cairnpapple from that which Piggott had initially proposed, in the process reducing the number of main phases in the site record from five to four. That account was accompanied by a new visitors' guidebook to the site for Historic Scotland, prepared in conjunction with his colleague, Doreen Grove (Barclay and Grove 1998). This, like the Balfarg booklet mentioned earlier (Barclay 1993a), is another excellent example of Gordon's facility as a populariser. In presenting his recasting of the Cairnpapple sequence, Gordon fully acknowledged the lucidity of Stuart Piggott's account of the site, which had made possible its reinterpretation. In a second paper (2000a), he approached another of Piggott's classic sites in the same vein, this time reinterpreting the excavation of the Strathtay stone circle at Croft Moraig (Perth and Kinross) in light of subsequent discoveries, which again foreshadowed renewed interest in this monument (Bradley and Sheridan 2005).

Mention of these two papers in which classic excavations were elegantly reinterpreted, naturally leads to a consideration of a further category of Gordon's contributions to the study of Neolithic Scotland. This was part of an ongoing data-gathering process that Gordon undertook, pulling together the fruits of many years of researching, visiting, scheduling and excavating a range of actual or potential Neolithic sites across lowland, mainland

Scotland. He compiled lists of cursus monuments, round mounds and barrows, henge monuments, timber halls and rectangular enclosures, and, later-
ally, possible settlement and occupation sites. This assembled data formed
the basis of a range of papers produced in the period just after 2000, which
saw him review and reassess monument categories and their distributions
at the national level. Of these, the most recent concerned the monument
category with which he perhaps most particularly identified: henges and
the smaller, related hengiform monuments (2005a). Earlier papers in the
same set allowed Gordon to develop his ideas on the nature of the record for
settlements (1996; 2003a), and enclosures (2001a). Gordon was also generous with these lists, passing the assembled information on to postgraduate
students; Gordon's data for instance directly inspired research into cursus
monuments (Brophy 1999), round mounds (Brophy 2010) and settlement
(Brophy 2006), and underlie several chapters in this book (e.g., Chapters 7,
8 and 10).

The publication of a *Festschrift* for John Coles in 1999 provided Gordon
with an opportunity to set out an overview of the Neolithic archaeology of
Tayside, on which so much of his own work had been concentrated. In this
he described how a 'hidden landscape' had been revealed, thus showing
a locally distinctive admixture of sites and monuments attributable to the
first farmers (Barclay 1999b). In a second contribution on the same theme
the following year, he was able to develop his argument further in a paper
given at the fiftieth anniversary conference of the Perthshire Society of
Natural Science (Barclay 2000b). This Perthshire connection was always a
strong feature of Gordon's work; he was a friend and colleague of Margaret
Stewart, Gordon Childe's only Edinburgh doctoral student, and her solici-
tor husband John, who were leading lights in the Perthshire archaeological community. He had a great commitment to community archaeology
in the county: local people were frequently part of his excavation teams,
and Gordon also encouraged campaigns of fieldwalking within the county,
in collaboration with the Perthshire Society of Natural Science and local
'stones and bones' fieldwalkers. Gordon was a great proponent of the need
for large-scale fieldwalking campaigns to shed light on Neolithic settlement
patterns (cf. 2003a) and some sites discovered by such local groups formed
targets for the Scotland's First Farmers Project excavations (Barclay and
Wickham-Jones 2002).

When, in the mid-1990s, Kevin Edwards and I were planning the contributions to an overview of the environment and archaeology of Scotland
between the country's initial human settlement (as then understood) and
the establishment of the medieval kingdom, the obvious candidate to ask
to provide the chapter on the Neolithic was Gordon. The brief synthesis (1997, revised 2003b) he presented very much had a fresh flavour to
it, highlighting some of the then new cropmark evidence and, perhaps as
significantly, giving proportionally less emphasis to the Orcadian record

and to chambered cairns than had previously been the norm in syntheses of the Scottish evidence for early farming communities. This chapter was followed in 1998 (reprinted in 2005) by Gordon's own contribution to the Canongate/Birlinn series on *The Making of Scotland*, which he conceived and edited. These highly accessible (both in content and price) and well-illustrated volumes (here colour was first deployed in a major way and to considerable effect in a Scottish archaeological series) remain, even now, in many instances the best introductions to their topics; and Gordon's *Farmers, Temples and Tombs: The First Farmers in Scotland*, with its elegant watercolour reconstructions again by David Hogg, certainly falls into this category (Barclay 1998). Thereafter, his contributions to two works he also edited demonstrate different sides of his involvement with the Scottish Neolithic, and with the developing archaeology of the country more generally. In the earlier publication, a special section in an issue of the journal *Antiquity* in 2002, the changing character and the new dynamism of Scottish archaeology were clearly demonstrated to colleagues internationally through a series of contributions commissioned by Gordon. Two years later, with the late Ian Shepherd, Gordon was responsible for the editing of the Society of Antiquaries of Scotland's *Scotland in Ancient Europe* conference papers as a monograph in the Society's series (Shepherd and Barclay 2004) – as indeed he was for the shape and content of that successful conference itself.

His own paper in that volume (Barclay 2004a), founded on a quotation from Gordon Childe, forms part of what will here be considered the last (to date!) strand of Gordon's contributions to the Scottish Neolithic. This very much has to do with cultural perceptions, primarily external, of Scotland's geography and resources and their value (particularly as applied to the Neolithic period); and of the adoption of certain regional archaeological traditions in an unreflective, *pars pro toto* way as almost totemic of the wider archaeological record of the country. Such attitudes thereby downplay, if not eliminate, at least by default, the regional diversity (and the different human strategies on the part of early farmers that underpinned these) that is really present in the archaeological record, and for which Gordon has proved a powerful advocate.

Gordon's major paper in this regard – it may not unreasonably be termed a manifesto – is that published in the *Proceedings of the Prehistoric Society* (Barclay 2001b), although it was preceded by a briefer excursus of a related theme as part of the *Neolithic Orkney in its European Context* conference published by the MacDonald Institute at Cambridge during the preceding year (Barclay 2000c). He subsequently published a further notable paper (2004b) in which, in the context of what was then increasingly being referred to as 'Four Nations History', in a nutshell the merits of presenting the history of Britain in ways other than from a southern, Anglocentric position (in part itself a reaction to the perspective on British history then being promulgated by Simon Schama on BBC TV), he considered the problems and issues that had arisen

from the adoption of a single 'acceptable' stance for the writing of earlier prehistories of Britain and Ireland. That such matters – and the need to consider
the worth of regional archaeological records on their own merits – continue
to be of interest to him, is shown by his most recent contribution to Neolithic
studies, the volume on *Regional Neolithics* he edited with Kenneth Brophy for
the Neolithic Studies Group (NSG) in 2009. In this volume (the proceedings
of a NSG conference organised in London by Gordon with Brophy) Gordon
continued, as he had done for decades, to promote the study of the Neolithic
in Scotland beyond the 'luminous' centre of Orkney (Barclay 2009).

We can thus see in the elements of Gordon's work considered above
(and, as has been said, other matters to which he has made significant contributions have here been set aside), one of the most coherent and sustained programmes of personal research into the archaeology of a particular
timespan across a major, and previously understudied, portion of the country that Scottish archaeology has seen in the last century. And, far from
simply gathering, as Stuart Piggott might have said, other men's flowers,
it is a programme underscored by many months in the field, collecting and
interpreting primary data, combined, of course, with the reinterpretation of
information already assembled by others, and leading to synthesis and reassessment at a variety of levels.

Across the published contributions reviewed here, Gordon has played
the central role in revitalising the study and understanding of the lowlands
of eastern Scotland north from the Forth to the north Esk, and sometimes
across the Mounth, during the Neolithic, the period now increasingly termed
the Chalcolithic, and the earlier part of the Bronze Age. His approach has
had a number of coherent strands to it. Major monument complexes have
been examined, a standard outcome being that the main sites he has engaged
with have been set into comprehensible hinterlands, both in terms of other
monuments of the period in their vicinities and, through the work of his
collaborators, into their environmental settings. Importantly, Gordon has
stressed how radiocarbon and other evidence has made plain the *longue durée*
over which some sites were used, reworked and altered, all the while remaining key places in the landscapes and doubtless in the minds of the nearby
communities of early agriculturalists. New categories of sites have been
examined, on the one hand, reassessing and generally extending the range of
the ritual and funerary architectures of these periods, but also, importantly,
complementing these with important work on the settlement record, in the
narrower sense of that term. Categories of sites – notably henges – have
been meticulously reassessed and mapped anew; it is salutary to recall that
the map of Scottish henges published when Gordon was at primary school
had only a dozen sites on the mainland identified on it (Piggott 1962: 71,
fig. 9). And, as befits the research of an Inspector of Ancient Monuments,
these academic objectives were matched by more prosaic, but nonetheless
key, aims, more especially identifying, and assessing the relative severity

of, threats to the diverse components of the earlier prehistoric archaeological record whose existence and extent Gordon had done so much to clarify. Their subsequent protection and management was as much a concern to him as the study of their cropmarks.

Beyond such matters, as we have seen, Gordon has made major contributions to the comprehension of Neolithic Britain, notably through his sustained arguments as to the importance of regional variation across the country, and his opposition to the recurrent trait of certain archaeologists to use a number of – one is tempted to say 'the same old' – preferred regions as the 'yardsticks' for the entirety of the British Isles and against which other regional traditions must be measured (Brophy and Barclay 2009). Perhaps Gordon's philosophical position in this regard is most cogently presented in his important 'Metropolitan and Parochial' paper published in the Prehistoric Society's *Proceedings* over a decade ago (Barclay 2001b), a paper likely to stand alongside his major excavation reports as an enduring contribution to Neolithic studies.

Over the last several years, Gordon's archaeological interests have shifted radically to much more recent times, to the anti-tank defences, the pill boxes and other features of the stop-lines across Scotland that were critical to defence plans had invasion occurred in the early years of the Second World War (Barclay 2005b; 2013). He has also turned his hand to the surviving physical remains of the previous Great War within Scotland. In a future nearer than we may care to think, direct oral testimony of the construction and intended uses of those 1940s constructions will disappear and these once urgent constructions, around which some of this volume's authors may have played in their childhoods, will begin the long passage to another kind of prehistory. Now they have an assiduous student in Gordon; and we wish him well in these important endeavours. But perhaps the chapters in this volume may encourage him not to tear himself entirely away from the earlier prehistory of his land; and we may not entirely forlornly anticipate a future contribution or two from his pen to the study of the Neolithic of the Scottish lowlands, which he has made so much his own.

Note

1. http://archaeologydataservice.ac.uk/archives/view/barclay_na_2003.

Bibliography

This is not a complete bibliography of Gordon's contributions, but simply a listing of those cited in this chapter.

Barclay, G. J. (1978), 'The excavation of a cairn at Pitcairn, Glenrothes, Fife', *Proceedings of the Society of Antiquaries of Scotland*, 109: 361–6.

Barclay, G. J. (1983a), 'The excavation of a settlement of the later Bronze Age at Myrehead, Falkirk District', *Glasgow Archaeological Journal*, 10: 41–71.

Barclay, G. J. (1983b), 'Sites of the third millennium BC to the first millennium AD at North Mains, Strathallan, Perthshire', *Proceedings of the Society of Antiquaries of Scotland*, 113: 122–281.

Barclay, G. J. (1985), 'Excavations at Upper Suisgill, Sutherland', *Proceedings of the Society of Antiquaries of Scotland*, 115: 159–98.

Barclay, G. J. (1989a), 'The cultivation remains beneath the North Mains, Strathallan barrow', *Proceedings of the Society of Antiquaries of Scotland*, 119: 59–61.

Barclay, G. J. (1989b), 'Henge monuments: reappraisal or reductionism?', *Proceedings of the Prehistoric Society*, 55: 260–2.

Barclay, G. J. (1992), 'Are the Clava "passage graves" really passage graves?: a reconsideration of the nature and associations of the Clava passage graves and ring-cairns', in N. Sharples and A. Sheridan (eds), *Vessels for the Ancestors*, Edinburgh: Edinburgh University Press, 77–82.

Barclay, G. J. (1993a), *Balfarg: The Prehistoric Ceremonial Complex*, Glenrothes: Fife Regional Council.

Barclay, G. J. (1993b), 'The Scottish gravels: a neglected resource?', in M. Fulford and E. Nichols (eds), *Developing Landscapes of Britain. The Archaeology of the British Gravels: A Review*, London: Society of Antiquaries of London, 106–24.

Barclay, G. J. (1996), 'Neolithic buildings in Scotland', in T. Darvill and J. Thomas (eds), *Neolithic Buildings in Northwest Europe and Beyond*, Oxford: Oxbow Books, 61–75.

Barclay, G. J. (1997), 'The Neolithic', in K. J. Edwards and I. B. M. Ralston (eds), *Scotland: Environment and Archaeology 8000 BC to AD 1000*, Chichester and New York: Wiley, 127–50.

Barclay, G. J. (1998), *Farmers, Temples and Tombs: The First Farmers in Scotland*, Edinburgh: Canongate (2005 edition published by Birlinn).

Barclay, G. J. (1999a), 'Cairnpapple re-visited: 1948–1998', *Proceedings of the Prehistoric Society*, 65: 17–46.

Barclay, G. J. (1999b), 'A hidden landscape: the Neolithic of Tayside', in A. Harding (ed.), *Experiment and Design: Archaeological Studies in Honour of John Coles*, Oxford: Oxbow Books, 20–9.

Barclay, G. J. (2000a), 'Croft Moraig reconsidered', *Tayside and Fife Archaeological Journal*, 6: 1–7.

Barclay, G. J. (2000b), 'The Neolithic of Tayside: a landscape revealed 1949–1999', in Anon. (ed.), *Dirt, Dust and Development: 50 Years of Perthshire Archaeology*, Perth: Perthshire Society of Natural Science Occasional Paper, 5–25.

Barclay, G. J. (2000c), 'Between Orkney and Wessex: the search for the regional Neolithics of Britain', in A. Ritchie (ed.), *Neolithic Orkney in its European Context*, Cambridge: McDonald Institute, 275–85.

Barclay, G. J. (2001a), 'Neolithic enclosures in Scotland', in T. Darvill and J. Thomas (eds), *Neolithic Enclosures in Atlantic Northwest Europe*, Oxford: Oxbow Books, 144–54.

Barclay, G. J. (2001b), '"Metropolitan" and "parochial"/"core" and "periphery": a historiography of the Neolithic of Scotland', *Proceedings of the Prehistoric Society*, 67: 1–16.

Barclay, G. J. (2002), 'Scotland 2002', *Antiquity*, 76: 777–83.

Barclay, G. J. (2003a), 'Neolithic settlement in the lowlands of Scotland: a preliminary survey', in I. Armit, E. Murphy, E. Nelis and D. D. A. Simpson (eds), *Neolithic Settlement in Ireland and Western Britain*, Oxford: Oxbow Books, 71–83.

Barclay, G. J. (2003b), 'The Neolithic', in K. J. Edwards and I. B. M. Ralston (eds), *Scotland After the Ice Age: Environment, Archaeology and History 8000 BC–AD 1000*, Edinburgh: Edinburgh University Press, 127–50.

Barclay, G. J. (2004a), '"… Scotland cannot have been an inviting country for agricultural settlement": a history of the Neolithic of Scotland', in Shepherd and Barclay (eds), *Scotland in Ancient Europe*, 31–44.

Barclay, G. J. (2004b), '"Four Nations Prehistory": cores and archetypes in the writing of prehistory', in H. Brocklehurst and R. Phillips (eds), *History, Nationhood and the Question of Britain*, London: Palgrave, 151–9.

Barclay, G. J. (2005a), 'The henge and hengiform in Scotland', in V. Cummings and A. Pannett (eds), *Set in Stone: New Approaches to Neolithic Monumentality in Scotland*, Oxford: Oxbow Books, 81–93.

Barclay, G. J. (2005b), 'The Cowie Line: a Second World War "stop line" west of Stonehaven, Aberdeenshire', *Proceedings of the Society of Antiquaries of Scotland*, 135: 119–61.

Barclay, G. J. (2009), 'Introduction: a regional agenda', in Brophy and Barclay (eds), *Defining a Regional Neolithic*, 1–4.

Barclay, G. J. (2013), *If Hitler Comes. Preparing for Invasion: Scotland 1940.* Edinburgh: Birlinn.

Barclay, G. J., Brophy, K. and MacGregor, G. (2002), 'Claish, Stirling: an Early Neolithic building in its context', *Proceedings of the Society of Antiquaries of Scotland*, 132: 65–137.

Barclay, G. J. and Grove, D. (1998), *Cairnpapple Hill*, Edinburgh: Historic Scotland guidebook.

Barclay, G. J. and Maxwell, G. S. (1991), 'Excavation of a Neolithic long mortuary enclosure within the Roman legionary fortress at Inchtuthil, Perthshire', *Proceedings of the Society of Antiquaries of Scotland*, 121: 27–44.

Barclay, G. J and Maxwell, G. S. (1998), *The Cleaven Dyke and Littleour: Monuments in the Neolithic of Tayside*, Edinburgh: Society of Antiquaries of Scotland.

Barclay, G. J. and Maxwell, G. S. (1999), 'The Cleaven Dyke Project: a summary account', in A. Barclay and J. Harding (eds), *Pathways and Ceremonies: The Cursus Monuments of Britain and Ireland*, Oxford: Oxbow Books, 98–106.

Barclay, G. J., Maxwell, G. S., Simpson, I. and Davidson, D. A. (1995), 'The Cleaven Dyke; a cursus monument/bank barrow in Tayside, Scotland', *Antiquity*, 69: 317–26.

Barclay, G. J. and Ritchie, A. (eds) (2008), *Scotland's Parliament Site and the*

Canongate: Archaeology and History, Edinburgh: Society of Antiquaries of Scotland.

Barclay, G. J. and Ruggles, C. L. N. (1999), 'On the frontier? Recumbent stone circles in Kincardine and Angus', *Tayside and Fife Archaeological Journal*, 5: 12–22.

Barclay, G. J. and Ruggles, C. L. N. (2000), 'Cosmology, calendars and society in Neolithic Orkney: a rejoinder to Euan MacKie', *Antiquity*, 74: 62–74.

Barclay, G. J. and Ruggles, C. L. N. (2002), 'Will the data drive the model? A response to Euan MacKie', *Antiquity*, 76: 668–71.

Barclay, G. J. and Russell-White, C. J. (eds) (1993), 'Excavations in the ceremonial complex of the fourth to second millennium BC at Balfarg/Balbirnie, Glenrothes, Fife', *Proceedings of the Society of Antiquaries of Scotland*, 123: 43–210.

Barclay, G. J. and Tolan, M. (1990), 'Trial excavation of a terrace-edge enclosure at North Mains, Strathallan, Perthshire', *Proceedings of the Society of Antiquaries of Scotland*, 120: 45–53.

Barclay, G. J. and Wickham-Jones, C. J. (2002), 'The investigation of some lithic scatters in Perthshire', *Tayside and Fife Archaeological Journal*, 8: 1–9.

Bradley, R. (2000), *The Good Stones: A New Investigation of the Clava Cairns*, Edinburgh: Society of Antiquaries of Scotland.

Bradley, R. (2005), *The Moon and the Bonfire*, Edinburgh: Society of Antiquaries of Scotland.

Bradley, R. and Sheridan, A. (2005), 'Croft Morag and the chronology of stone circles', *Proceedings of the Prehistoric Society*, 71: 269–81.

Brophy, K. (1999), 'The cursus monuments of Scotland', in A. Barclay and J. Harding (eds), *Pathways and Ceremonies: The Cursus Monuments of Britain and Ireland*, Oxford: Oxbow Books, 119–29.

Brophy, K. (2006), 'Rethinking Scotland's Neolithic: combining circumstance with context', *Proceedings of the Society of Antiquaries of Scotland*, 136: 7–46.

Brophy, K. (2007), 'From big houses to cult houses: Early Neolithic timber halls in Scotland', *Proceedings of the Prehistoric Society*, 73: 75–96.

Brophy, K (2010), ' "… a place where they tried their criminals": Neolithic round mounds in Perth and Kinross', in J. Leary, T. Darvill, T. and D. Field (eds), *Neolithic Mounds and Monumentality in the British Neolithic and Beyond*, Oxford: Oxbow Books, 10–27.

Brophy, K. and Barclay, G. J. (2004), 'A rectilinear timber structure and post-ring at Carsie Mains, Meikleour, Perthshire', *Tayside and Fife Archaeological Journal*, 10: 1–22.

Brophy, K. and Barclay, G. J. (eds) (2009), *Defining a Regional Neolithic: The Evidence from Britain and Ireland*, Oxford: Oxbow Books.

Greig, M. K. and Greig, C. (1990), 'Remains of a 12th century structure and other medieval features on the Knoll of Castle Point, Troup (Cullykhan), Banff and Buchan', *Proceedings of the Society of Antiquaries of Scotland*, 119: 279–96.

Maxwell, G. S. (1979), 'Air photography and the works of the Royal Commission on the Ancient and Historical Monuments of Scotland', *Aerial Archaeology*, 2: 37–43.

Mercer, R. J. (1981), 'The excavation of a Late Neolithic henge-type enclosure at Balfarg, Markinch, Fife, Scotland, 1977–78', *Proceedings of the Society of Antiquaries of Scotland*, 111: 63–171.

Mercer, R. J., Barclay, G. J., Jordan, D. and Russell-White, C. J. (1988), 'The Neolithic henge-type enclosure at Balfarg – a re-assessment of the evidence for an incomplete ditch circuit', *Proceedings of the Society of Antiquaries of Scotland*, 118: 61–7.

Millican, K. (2009), 'Contextualising the cropmark record: the timber monuments of the Neolithic of Scotland', unpublished PhD thesis, University of Glasgow.

Musson, C. R. (1971), 'A study of possible building forms at Durrington Walls, Woodhenge and The Sanctuary', in G. J. Wainwright and I. H. Longworth (eds), *Durrington Walls: Excavations 1966–1968*, London: Research Reports of the Society of Antiquaries of London, 363–77.

Piggott, S. (1948), 'The excavations at Cairnpapple Hill, West Lothian', *Proceedings of the Society of Antiquaries of Scotland*, 82: 68–123.

Piggott, S. (ed.) (1962), *The Prehistoric People of Scotland*, London: Routledge & Kegan Paul.

Piggott, S. (1972), 'Excavations of the Dalladies long barrow, Fettercairn, Kincardineshire', *Proceedings of the Society of Antiquaries of Scotland*, 104: 23–47.

Ralston, I. (2006), 'Colvin Greig (obituary)', *The Scotsman*, 11 July 2006.

Renfrew, A. C. (1979), *Investigations in Orkney*, London: Research Reports of the Society of Antiquaries of London.

Ritchie, J. N. G. (1976), 'The Stones of Stenness, Orkney', *Proceedings of the Society of Antiquaries of Scotland*, 107: 1–60.

Shepherd, I. A. G. and Barclay, G. J. (eds) (2004), *Scotland in Ancient Europe: The Neolithic and Early Bronze Age of Scotland in their European Context*, Edinburgh: Society of Antiquaries of Scotland.

CHAPTER 2

Neolithic Pasts, Neolithic Futures: The Contemporary Socio-politics of Prehistoric Landscapes

Gavin MacGregor

Introduction

In this chapter I wish to extend an exploration, which Gordon Barclay pioneered, into the landscapes of the Neolithic. While many others were intent on mapping the Neolithic landscapes of the past, Gordon commenced an important journey from the archaeology of the Neolithic to the heritage of Scotland by beginning to explore elements of the perception of the remnants of Neolithic landscapes in the present. This research manifested itself in a number of significant papers that reflected on the assumptions that had traditionally underpinned practices in relation to contemporary socio-political categories that affected the ways in which the Neolithic of Scotland (and indeed beyond) was represented. Thus, this chapter will comprise several sections: in the first, I shall reflect on the nature of Gordon's contribution to the critique of the contemporary socio-politics of the Neolithic through a synthesis of some of his key publications on this subject; and in the second, I shall consider how our current conceptions of landscapes and the nature of our practices may be affecting our interpretations of, and relationships with, those landscapes that have significant Neolithic components. In the final section, I shall begin tentatively to suggest some of the ways these themes may converge and explore what this potentially means for our practices in the future.

Historiographies of the Neolithic

In the first paper which I wish to consider, 'Between Orkney and Wessex', Gordon explored the regionality of the Neolithic in Scotland and beyond (Barclay 2000). It had long been recognised that there is regional variation in the character of evidence from the Scottish Neolithic, but this tended to privilege the upstanding stone monuments that predominated in the record; and many earlier commentators considered such variation as either a reflection of past patterns or the outcome of differences in survival or visibility

(Piggott 1954; Sharples and Sheridan 1992; see also Brophy and Barclay 2009). In this respect, Barclay stressed the radical contribution that the results of investigations over the previous couple of decades had made to our understanding of the character of the Neolithic in lowland contexts (Barclay 2000: 277). However, more importantly, he extended a critique of earlier accounts not simply in terms of the impact of new data revealing new patterns; rather he was concerned with the ways in which interpretative models affected the regional prehistories that up to that point had been constructed and narrated.

He developed his argument by investigating the ways in which well-studied regions of Britain (such as Orkney and Wessex) generated interpretative models that were in turn applied to other less well-studied regions, and argued that this redeployment of models from elsewhere resulted in a series of perceptual and political relationships which were problematic (Barclay 2000). One of these problems was the biasing tendency to accord chronological priority to the well-studied regions, noting that where monument types were first discovered did not necessarily represent where they first originated. Ultimately, Gordon was critical of universalising narratives and was aware that the value of each region's Neolithic was on its own terms. In the present context, one of the most important elements about our interpretative models, on which Gordon began to reflect, were the 'interesting parallels between archaeological perceptions and those of the Scottish landscape in general' (Barclay 2000: 277).

In a second paper, '"Metropolitan" and "parochial"/"core" and "periphery"', Gordon extended some of the themes he had previously tackled, but with a more overt concern for the political context of nationhood within the United Kingdom (Barclay 2001; 2004). He also extended his discussion on the ramifications for our interpretations of the relationship between archaeological landscapes and the history of the perceptions of landscapes more generally. This inter-relationship between landscape perception and archaeological interpretation was made with reference to other representations of Scottish landscape, as manifest in visual arts and literature, with the particular example of the different representations of 'Highlands' and 'Lowlands'. Gordon suggested that the perception of the nature of the archetypal landscapes, following Howkins (1986) (i.e., Scotland, Highland, largely deserted; England, cultivated landscapes, populated), had major ramifications on the ways in which both English and Scottish prehistories were written. Considered from this broader context, Gordon referred to the impact of the work of Fox (1932), in terms of his definitions of Lowland and Highland zones of Britain, which suggested a fundamental relationship between geography, geology, environment and archaeology. Gordon then went on to demonstrate that the work of Fox had a major impact on the writings of the prehistory of Britain certainly until the mid-1970s, as marked then by a significantly more nuanced definition of lowland/highland landscapes (Stevenson 1975). Gordon then explored other aspects of the inter-relationships between archetypal landscapes and regional variability in monument types and differential archaeological visibility in terms of models of core and periphery in the past (Barclay 2001; 2004).

These important papers on the ways in which the Neolithic had been defined, categorised and narrated (Barclay 2000; 2001; 2004) represented an important step in a wider reflection on the nature of Scottish prehistories and their political dimensions, which was particularly timely in terms of the establishment of a Scottish parliament in 1999 (see Chapter 1). Indeed, it is striking that, from their outset in his paper of 2000, Barclay's intellectual concerns were entangled with the practical outcomes of our perceptions of the past on contemporary practices. For example, Gordon explicitly noted that some of his thinking derived from his engagement in the nomination of the Heart of Neolithic Orkney as a World Heritage Site in 1998; and he recalled that the process of establishing the Archaeolink Prehistory Park, Aberdeenshire, was in the face of perceptions that there were more important centres of prehistory elsewhere in the country (Barclay 2000: 275–6). I now want to build on this socio-political aspect of Gordon's thinking by considering the ways in which our perceptions of the different Neolithic traditions within Scotland are actually manifested in how our landscapes are perceived, managed and valued. To this end, however, it is worth briefly considering some of the issues that have been encountered in the changing ways in which landscapes are experienced and perceived over the ten years or so since Gordon wrote this significant series of papers.

Neolithic pasts, Neolithic presents

Most archaeological sites and monuments in Scotland are in private owner- ship, but, beyond the value of ownership, they have a greater set of values to broader society as part of our shared heritage. Thus, the ways in which we care for our archaeological assets in part informs the nature of the relation- ships that broader society can have with them. Until recently, archaeological monuments have been treated in the spatial planning system as relatively small islands of 'pastness' set within the contemporary landscape. Thus, our processes of cultural resource management have often involved focus- ing on the designation and protection of individual monuments to safeguard them against the pressures for change which would have adverse impacts on them. While this approach, as made manifest, for example, by the schedul- ing of ancient monuments, has undoubtedly protected many archaeological sites and monuments from destruction, it can be argued that there have been unintended consequences arising from the creation of such 'red-line boundaries' around monuments. 'Point' systems of heritage protection not only reinforced approaches that managed individual assets in isolated terms, but also perpetuated a perception that such monuments were entities that did not fundamentally relate to the landscape in which they were set in any meaningful way.

However, a number of other concepts have emerged in the past two decades that have had significant ramifications on how such archaeological assets can now be understood and managed. The first was the emergence of 'setting' as a concept; and the second, related, development concerned the definition and adoption of the concept of 'Historic Environment'. Setting is a concept that was introduced in Scotland through National Planning Policy Guidance 5 (1994), in which safeguarding the integrity of the setting of monuments and the need for appropriate settings to be preserved were introduced as material issues in the planning control system. It was not, however, until the early 2000s that setting increasingly became an issue for many more heritage professionals (and other stakeholders) in the spatial planning system with the increasing awareness of the potential for development to cause deleterious indirect effects on archaeological monuments, in particular in the case of wind farms. This prompted further debate in the sector about the definition of setting (e.g., Black 2005), which culminated in Historic Scotland's published guidance on this topic (Historic Scotland 2010). This states that:

> 2.1 Setting should be thought of as the way in which the surroundings of a historic asset or place contribute to how it is experienced, understood and appreciated.
> 2.2 Monuments, buildings, gardens and settlements were not constructed in isolation. They were often deliberately positioned with reference to the surrounding topography, resources, landscape and other monuments or buildings. These relationships will often have changed through the life of a historic asset or place.
> 2.3 Setting often extends beyond the immediate property boundary of a historic structure into the broader landscape. (Historic Scotland 2010: 3)

The emergence of setting as an issue has been important in conceptually extending the scope of archaeology from solely 'bounded' sites and monuments to places that articulate with the wider landscape. This is especially relevant in the case of Neolithic monuments, many of which, as we shall see, can be regarded as having been entangled with the landscapes within which they were built. In some respects this notion can also be seen to be reflected in the emergence of the concept of Historic Environment. This concept is now expressed in Scottish Historic Environment Policy (SHEP) 2011, which offers the following definition:

> Our whole environment, whether rural or urban, on land or under water, has a historic dimension that contributes to its quality and character. It has been shaped by human and natural processes over thousands of years. This is most obvious in our built heritage: ancient monuments; archaeological sites

and landscapes; historic buildings; townscapes; parks; gardens and designed landscapes; and our marine heritage, for example in the form of historic ship-wrecks or underwater landscapes once dry land.

We can see it in the patterns in our landscape – the layout of fields and roads, and the remains of a wide range of past human activities ...

The context or setting in which specific historic features sit and the patterns of past use are part of our historic environment. The historical, artistic, literary, linguistic and scenic associations of places and landscapes are some of the less tangible elements of the historic environment. These elements make a fundamental contribution to our sense of place and cultural identity. (Historic Scotland 2011: 5)

As a consequence of this explicit view from government, there has been a growing appreciation that the archaeological assets we manage cannot be treated simply as bounded physical entities or dots on maps. Indeed, the other dimension of Historic Environment policy that is of importance in this regard is to agendas of sustainable development in the recognition that archaeological sites can contribute social, cultural and economic value to society. As such, archaeological assets are situated in a landscape context where, through different uses of them, the values of a wide range of actors and agencies articulate and compete with each other. Ultimately, we can postulate that, as archaeological monuments having settings and represent important components of the Historic Environment, this means that these past dimensions of our landscapes as represented by such physical remains have become significant in the nexus of policies relating to the future management of our landscapes.

In this respect, perhaps the most influential new factor in terms of our thinking on landscape in recent years was the development and ratification in 2000 of the European Landscape Convention (ELC) (Council of Europe 2000). This has been important for a number of reasons, not least in terms of its definition of landscape as 'an area, as perceived by people, whose character is the result of the action and interaction of natural and/or human factors' (*ibid.*: 9). The ELC foregrounded the role of human action and perception in the context of the dynamic nature of landscapes. This has ramifications for how we understand the landscapes of earlier peoples, but also our relationship to the remains of those past peoples' landscapes. The ELC is, furthermore, important as it has provided a manifesto to underpin measures designed, with public participation, to protect, manage and plan all landscapes (i.e., not simply scenic or high value landscapes, but also degraded landscapes). The national implementation of the ELC requires mechanisms to define a series of objectives in terms of future landscape quality. Thus, from the perspective of the ELC, landscape is the nexus of the living relationships between people and other agents which are inherited from the past, yet at the same time the convention provides the basis for maintaining and improving the future character of landscapes.

Thus, the ways in which we understand and manage past components of landscapes not only have ramifications for these archaeological or heritage assets, but also for people who act on or interact with them. This context in which landscape may now be a concern for everybody means that the historic environment components of landscape are entangled in broader socio-political dynamics, not just in their physical settings.

In the Scottish context, people's relationships with landscapes have been undergoing significant changes in the past few years, some tangible while others arguably more intangible (at this stage). These changes potentially affect people's perception of landscapes and consequently the possible future character of landscapes. Tangible modifications include the right to roam, which was introduced as part of the Land Reform (Scotland) Act 2003. This has arguably altered people's ability to experience much more of Scotland's landscape and, through responsible access to all portions of it, promotes a perception of a common resource, to a wide variety of users, as representing more than simply land to be used exclusively by a landowner. At the same time as the 'right to roam' has been exercised, there has also been major expansion in renewable energy development, particularly in rural upland contexts. This process has stimulated studies about the capacity of our landscapes to carry certain types of development and has provoked extensive debate about the character of Scotland's landscapes in the face of pressures for change. This has in turn articulated with a wider debate, developing over the past decade or so, about the future character of Scotland's landscapes in the context of wilderness, wildland, rewilding and wildness issues (e.g., Scottish Natural Heritage 2002; Ralston 2004; MVA Consultancy Ltd 2012). In short, our relationships with, and perceptions of, Scotland's landscapes are dynamic; and they articulate with a more extensive set of values relating both to heritage and visions for the future.

Have relationships with, and perceptions of, the Neolithic components of Scotland's landscapes changed in light of the factors just discussed? In the vast majority of cases, Neolithic sites are still managed and perceived as isolated assets. However, there are a few landscapes in Scotland where there is a sufficient density of archaeological sites and monuments dating to the period *c.* 4000–2400 BC that some archaeologists consider that they represent, in whole or in part, 'Neolithic Landscapes' and/or 'Prehistoric Landscapes'. Perhaps best known of these is the Heart of Neolithic Orkney World Heritage Site (hereafter HONO WHS), and I want briefly to examine this to establish if perceptions of landscape have been modified by the issues considered in outline in the preceding paragraphs.

It is somewhat ironic, then, in a volume on the Neolithic of Mainland Scotland and in light of the thrust of Gordon's paper 'Between Orkney and Wessex', that I should choose Orkney as a case study. However, it is important to consider the changing perceptions and practices in Orkney, as the experience of managing and researching Neolithic sites and monuments in a landscape context has arguably advanced further here, owing to the clear intersections between research, policy development, spatial planning and heritage interpretation, arguably to an extent that has not as yet occurred on this scale elsewhere in Scotland. As these advances have in part been driven by the HONO WHS designation, the role of different designations, and their relative geographical extents and levels of importance, is brought to the fore in terms of the perception and management of both heritage assets and their associated landscapes. As such, this case study potentially provides insights and lessons to apply elsewhere in Scotland; it also reveals a series of inter-relationships dating from the fourth to the second millennium BC between Orkney, Caithness and the mainland beyond. The HONO WHS therefore cannot be ignored because of either book title or Pentland Firth. Furthermore, such a case study is particularly appropriate in the context of applied policy that Gordon did so much to advance, not least through his recognition of the fact that there were significant inter-relationships between researching and managing archaeological resources (Barclay 1997).

The best-known areas of landscape in Scotland that have a marked inheritance from the Neolithic can be found in Mainland, Orkney Isles. This has been recognised at the international level, as expressed through inscription by UNESCO as the HONO WHS, to encompass the areas of landscape between and around the group of monuments that includes the Skara Brae settlement, the Maeshowe chambered cairn and the Barnhouse Stone; the Stones of Stenness henge and stone circle and the Watch Stone; and the Ring of Brodgar henge and stone circle, and their associated monuments. The UNESCO inscription recognises this zone as having cultural significance at the landscape scale, expressed in the Nomination Document as a monument group that 'constitutes a major relict cultural landscape graphically depicting life in this remote archipelago north of the coast of Scotland five thousand years ago' (UNESCO 1999: 112).

Additionally, the Justification by the State Party in the nomination process stated that, 'The wealth of unexcavated contemporary burial and occupation sites in the buffer zone constitute an exceptional relict cultural landscape' (UNESCO 1999: 112). Problems with the degree of preservation of the 'Neolithic landscape' were however recognised (*ibid*.: 112; added emphasis):

> During the preparation of the revised nomination which is the subject of the present evaluation, consideration was given by the State Party to the possibility of nominating a large area of the island of Mainland as a *cultural landscape*. It was felt, however, that the *Neolithic landscape* had been obliterated to such an extent by post-medieval land allocation and use that Mainland could no longer be considered as a relict landscape of World Heritage quality. ICOMOS concurs in this decision, but applauds the decision of the State Party to include Skara Brae in the nominated property.

There are issues of definition of landscape in this technical instrument, which are clarified by UNESCO's broader set of definitions of cultural landscapes and its delineation of three categories of World Heritage cultural landscapes (e.g., Mitchell *et al.* 2009). It is notable, however, that the only other significant consideration of landscape definition in the inscription process for the Heart of Neolithic Orkney is in terms of this landscape being designated as a National Scenic Area (NSA) (UNESCO 1999: 8). Inevitably, therefore, at this time the definition of this landscape and the delineation of which areas of landscape were deemed significant or sensitive were in part determined by pre-existing designations. However, the NSA designation (in this case the Hoy and West Mainland NSA, Orkney) was made over twenty years earlier on the narrow criteria of visual scenic value (Countryside Commission for Scotland 1978). Decisions made in terms of managing change in the NSA, defined in narrow scenic terms, may also have ramifications for the HONO WHS. As such, it is perhaps therefore the degrees to which the definitions in these instruments evolve and subsequently inform management and interpretation that are of interest.

Following inscription by UNESCO in 1999, a management plan for the HONO WHS was developed by 2001 (Historic Scotland 2001). This management plan covered the period 2001–6, and again there was an emphasis on the landscape scale of the designation. In the foreword it is noted that Orkney provided 'the retention of a well-contexted Neolithic landscape worthy of the accolade of World Heritage Site' (*ibid.*, unpaginated). The management plan also exactly reiterated the UNESCO 'remote archipelago' phrasing cited previously in the inscription.

However, not only are there issues in terms of the HONO WHS regarding the use of terminology (e.g., 'Neolithic Landscape', 'Cultural Landscape'), but also issues as to how the setting of the monuments and the WHS should be defined in terms of its extent. The first definition of the WHS setting, in terms of a series of buffers around the core area of landscape within which are the main Neolithic monument groups, was produced jointly by Scottish Natural Heritage and Historic Scotland (Tyldesley 2001) for its future management in the spatial planning system. This study of landscape capacity (understood as the degree to which change can be accommodated without adversely compromising character or values) used Historic Landscape Assessment and Landscape Character Assessment datasets (i.e., comprising both cultural and natural heritage values) in combination with Zones of Visual Influence (how far can potentially be seen from a particular location) to define the setting of the WHS; and this was taken into account in the management plan which in part seeks to maintain the Universal Values and authenticity of the WHS (but see also Foster and Linge 2002). Additionally, the wider topographic context of the monument groups forming the WHS site has long been recognised as important with regard to how they may have been understood in the Neolithic (cf. Richards 1996), as has the sense that the character of the Orkney landscapes has traditionally been treeless and open (ScARF 2012: 62). As such, management of change through the spatial planning system of other elements impacting on the landscape (e.g., building, forestry plantation, artificial lighting, sound levels of modern activities) in the setting of the WHS may have an impact on the experience and authenticity of the WHS prehistoric monuments.

It is clear that since the HONO WHS was originally established, as it consists of archaeological sites owned and managed by Historic Scotland, who have particular responsibilities for the archaeological and historic environment components of the landscape, and as the Royal Society for Protection of Birds, Orkney Islands Council and Scottish Natural Heritage also have significant stakes (variously in terms of ownership and statutory responsibilities) that there were different perceptions about the nature of the HONO WHS landscape between the cultural and natural sectors. For example, in the 2002 HONO WHS interpretation plan the terms 'Natural Landscape' and 'Cultural Landscape' were both used (pp. 9 and 12, respectively), yet it was recognised that the HONO WHS landscape comprises both natural and cultural components conjoined (*ibid.*: 18, fn. 9).

A HONO research strategy (Downes *et al.* 2005) was also produced which aimed to inform the delivery of the aforementioned management plan. One of its key research themes was 'The Formation and Utilisation of the Landscape', and to this end the evidence base for the long-term changing nature of the HONO WHS landscape was reviewed, with a sensitivity to the experiential nature of dwelling amongst the monuments. Importantly, it was recognised that 'The WHS is best managed in a holistic sense that embraces the wider cultural and natural landscape' (*ibid.*: 33). The need for better integration of the natural and cultural dimensions of HONO WHS landscape was again recognised in a subsequent publication (Card *et al.* 2007: 432), suggesting a growing awareness of the problems of some of the earlier perceptual and definitional differences.

Further study of the boundaries for the settings of the monuments and, beyond them, of the WHS buffers was undertaken in a more recent technical report (Atkins 2008). This contribution was striking in that it deployed phenomenological techniques in its methodologies, drawing on the experiential qualities of the monuments forming the HONO WHS and their settings. In the following management plan (for the period 2008–13), it was noted that: 'These connections all contribute to the feeling that these monuments are situated at the centre of a highly significant *cultural landscape*' (Historic Scotland 2008: 16; added emphasis). This Atkins study, however, starts to take a subtly different approach by considering not simply definitions of landscape, but also the social, natural and landscape values of the HONO WHS site through its deployment of phrases such as 'special character and significance of the historical, cultural and natural landscape of the WHS' (*ibid.*: 43). The HONO WHS was also redefined in terms of its buffer zones in light of the Atkins report (2008), and the redefined buffer zones then formed the basis for the Supplementary Planning Guidance in the Orkney Island Council Local Development Plan (Orkney Islands Council 2010). Also of significance in the context of landscape designations has been the redefinition of NSAs in terms of Special Qualities (Tyldesley 2007; Scottish Natural Heritage 2010). In the case of Hoy and West Mainland National Scenic Area, for example, of the eleven Special Qualities defined, five of them foreground archaeological remains as an element contributing to the Special Quality:

• a palimpsest of geology, topography, archaeology and land use;
• an archaeological landscape of World Heritage Status;
• sandstone and flagstone as an essence of Orkney;
• a long-settled and productive land and sea;
• and a landscape of contrasting curves and lines.

We can therefore begin to see the emergence of a more integrated under-standing and management of this Orcadian landscape in which archaeo-logical and cultural heritage assets, and their associated values, are more explicitly emphasised than previously.

A new management plan for HONO WHS has been agreed for 2014–19 (Historic Scotland 2014), and it is interesting that in the main body of the document landscape is referred to in very limited technical terms. Yet in the appendices to the 2014 document, the 'Brief Synthesis of the Statement of Outstanding Universal Value' still has the phrase: 'The group constitutes a major relict cultural landscape depicting graphically life five thousand years ago in this remote archipelago' (*ibid*.: 64). It is striking in this document that 'biodiversity' appears amongst the terms defined in the glossary of terms, but 'cultural landscape' does not, because this implies that 'cultural land-scape' has either become an accepted and unproblematic term, or is slipping from favour in such official documentation.

There are still examples of how terminology lazily used in the heritage sector could potentially cause confusion about the status of the HONO WHS landscape. For example, the Scottish Ten project[1] describes the Neolithic monuments within the HONO WHS in these terms: 'Together these form one of the richest *surviving Neolithic landscapes* in Western Europe' (cf. Historic Scotland 2013: 13; added emphasis). A key fact about the monu-ments forming the HONO WHS stated in another recent HS publication is that 'Collectively, they represent one of the richest *surviving Neolithic landscapes* in Western Europe' (Historic Scotland 2014: 2; added emphasis). Perhaps the use of such phrases, with their implications that the monu-ments themselves somehow constitute landscape and/or that there are more undiscovered Neolithic archaeological sites in the landscape, is due in part to the fact that there is 'no current Interpretation Plan or Access Strategy for HONO WHS' (Historic Scotland 2014: 32), with the unfortunate consequence that terminology and messages have not been adequately refreshed and aligned. Or perhaps it demonstrates that there are still some fundamentally different perceptions amongst the Archaeological and Historic Environment sector as to the character of the landscapes of the HONO WHS in particular; and more generally about the relative significance of archaeological evidence, particularly upstanding monuments, in contemporary landscapes. What is clear is that, despite some remaining definitional underpinnings directly derived from the HONO WHS Inscription (UNESCO 1999) being evoked in some current phraseology, there has been a shift to a more integrated landscape approach. It can be suggested that, on the one hand, this stems from the partnership working by different stakeholders in delivering to shared visions, but, on the other hand, the ways in which research strategies and management plans have iteratively informed each other.

It is also clear that the processes of cultural resource management have transformed the character of the 'heritagescape' that the HONO WHS represents, and as such have changed the quality of the visitor experience, for example, by more control of the movement of people, the introduction of more parking and fencing, and increased signage (Garden 2006). However, in the case of communication, there is a danger of not expressing clearly and consistently certain things, one of which is the type and status of the landscapes within which monuments created in the Neolithic now reside. The continuing process of management, with multiple competing issues that require balancing, and interpretation, with multiple perspectives and narratives of the Neolithic sites, inevitably reflects the realities of the contested and dynamic nature of landscapes (McClanahan 2013).

In this chapter I have focused on HONO WHS not least because the Neolithic monuments forming it have been subject to a great deal of thought as to how they relate to their landscape context. Perhaps the most significant outcome is how present understandings of the prehistoric components of the HONO WHS now underpin the definition of the special qualities that characterise the Hoy and West Mainland NSA. As well as resulting from the recognition of the concentration and quality of archaeological sites and monuments, this change in NSA definition must in part derive from the results of long-term archaeological research. This research has been taking place in conjunction with new approaches to integrated management and interpretation through partnership working that has arguably emerged largely due to the HONO WHS designation.

Similar issues in terms of definitions and terminology can be found, to lesser degrees, in relation to the treatment of other concentrations of Neolithic monuments in Scotland. Kilmartin, Argyll and Bute, where the excellent Kilmartin House Museum presents Kilmartin Glen as 'Scotland's Richest Prehistoric Landscape' provides an example (Butter 2001). In this case, despite over a decade of research and education in relation to the cultural dimensions of Kilmartin's landscapes, for example, through the work of Kilmartin House Museum, the human dimensions of Moine Moire, the great lowland expanse of bog that occupies a significant portion of the valley and forms part of the broader historical narrative of Kilmartin Glen, were significantly underplayed in its interpretation put forward by Scottish Natural Heritage (Syse 2010). Further research would be useful to establish if the changing inter-relationships between people and their landscape are fairly represented in interpretations in relation to the Neolithic components of other landscapes such as at Calanais, Western Isles, and the concentrations of Neolithic monuments and field systems on Shetland. A rapid assessment of other NSAs that may have marked concentrations of Neolithic and Bronze Age monuments in terms of the definitions of their special qualities shows a marked contrast to the ways in which archaeological sites inform the expression of special qualities in Hoy and West Mainland NSA. In these other cases, archaeological evidence is much more rarely deployed, although there are examples.

In the case of the Assynt-Coigach NSA, Sutherland, there is a marked concentration of Neolithic and later prehistoric monuments. Indeed, the definition of its Special Qualities tries to balance the low levels of contemporary settlement and land use with associated perceptions of wildness through the explicit recognition that 'the lack of human activity is apparent rather than real' (Scottish Natural Heritage 2010: 142). However, developing a proper understanding of the nature of earlier monuments in Assynt-Coigach NSA is made more difficult by a relative lack of research, and by the fact that these prehistoric sites relate to a concentration of monuments to the south along Loch Borralan and into Glen Oykel, and mean that synthesising a proper understanding of the contribution of prehistoric remains to the current landscape character of this NSA is problematic. Indeed, this topic is rendered even more problematic as the eastern boundary of the Assynt-Coigach NSA was 'an arbitrary limit' (Countryside Commission for Scotland 1978: 27) which neither relates to landform nor to scenic value: nor, indeed, to other aesthetic values relating to landscape perception. If archaeological considerations had been given more weight in the process of definition in the case of this NSA (as can now be seen in Hoy and West Mainland NSA), the opportunity to extend the eastern boundary of Assynt-Coigach to include a larger number of Neolithic monuments that are currently excluded may have produced a different perception of its special qualities, and in due course may have influenced more integrated approaches to their management.

Indeed, we can see a similar pattern in other NSAs where concentrations of monuments (or, indeed, individual monuments) dating to the Neolithic are alluded to as significant to the special qualities of the NSA, but the boundary of the NSA itself does not respect significant concentrations of such monuments. This is particularly notable in the case of North Arran NSA, North Ayrshire, with major concentrations of monuments occurring in South Arran; Knapdale NSA, Argyll and Bute, where Kilmartin Glen is not fully incorporated into the NSA; and South Lewis, Harris and North Uist NSA, where major concentrations of monuments in North Uist fall to the south of the NSA, yet the Neolithic remains at Loch Olabhat are highlighted.

However, it is not simply an issue of quantitative evidence. It is also about how Special Qualities are defined or narrated in relation to prehistoric remains (in many cases not stressed at all); yet in some cases individual monuments are drawn out for consideration almost arbitrarily. In the case of the Cuillin Hills NSA, Isle of Skye, this is apparent in relation to the definition of the Special Quality entitled: 'The surrounding wild landscape, a fitting foil for the mountains' (Scottish Natural Heritage 2010: 156). This provides one of the few other explicit references to the Neolithic in the description of an NSA:

> These areas all show minimal signs of human activity, whether buildings, agriculture or forestry, giving a strong appearance of wildness. The area is an SNH Search Area for Wild Land. However, in contrast to the generally minimal human influence inland, there is ample evident of previous use along the fringes of the mountains, particularly in the form of prehistoric hut circles and later shielings. One location, Rudha an Dunain, has exceptionally good evidence of settlement and field systems from the Neolithic period onwards, including a canal, reputed to be of Viking date. (*ibid.*)

Contrastingly, in the case of Kyle of Tongue NSA, Highland, the statement 'The presence of chambered cairns and brochs illustrates that people have occupied this land for many centuries' (*ibid.*: 199) is underpinned by only two recorded chambered cairns.

This coarse analysis would benefit from further detailed work. It nonetheless suggests that, in the absence of coherent research and interpretation programmes and/or designations extending beyond individual archaeological sites in other parts of Scotland, but which like Orkney also have significant concentrations of archaeological remains, the perception of the nature and value of prehistoric sites, in particular landscapes, is not fully appreciated. It can also be argued that this perception has not significantly changed since the 1990s. Furthermore, it points to a potential need to redefine the physical extent of some NSAs more coherently to take into account the distributions of archaeological sites and monuments which can be properly understood only in relation to each other. It also makes clear that the fuller understanding of these archaeological sites and monuments will modify not only our narratives of historical change, but also people's broader perceptions of landscape character and qualities.

In this perspective, the relationship between the existence of significant concentrations of chambered cairns in Caithness and the absence of an

NSA there would be worth exploring further. There could be a potential direct link between the absence within Caithness of an NSA designation, a classification largely based on narrow scenic visual value for the last forty years, and the impact this has had on the management and perception of that county's landscapes. If NSAs are now defined by drawing on a broader series of Special Qualities comprising both natural and cultural components and their complex interplay, it can be argued that some of the landscapes in Caithness (and other parts of Scotland) that have marked concentrations of prehistoric remains could, and should, be managed in more integrated ways, ones that could benefit from reflecting on the lessons learnt from the Orcadian case.

Neolithic futures?

The study of Neolithic archaeology, and references to landscapes of the Neolithic, are often (implicitly at least) undertaken in terms of fundamental knowledge production: in essence, we are interested in the study of the past for its own interest and value. It is clear from the examples above, however, that our knowledge of the Neolithic past and how we narrate it has broader ramifications not least in the continued confusion between landscapes then and now, and the uncertainties as to what extent the landscapes we see around us today reflect those of the Neolithic. Perhaps ironically, it has been pressure for change, in the form of economic development, that has produced the greatest dividend from the planning system in terms of insights into Neolithic sites and landscapes (e.g., Phillips and Bradley 2004). The desire for sustainable economic growth that underpins present-day policies will therefore continue to produce more information about the Neolithic than perhaps any other driver (see also Brophy 2006). Our current model of practice, however, may not provide full value for the loss to society that such infrastructural and other developments entail (Lelong and MacGregor 2014). Furthermore, there is an emerging context in which the understanding of the dynamic pathways through landscapes which archaeological analysis can reveal may be an important contribution, allowing significant challenges faced by society in the future to be addressed (ESF-COST 2010).

Given the changing character of 'human–nature' interactions during the millennium and a half from c. 4000 BC, there are potentially many diverse forms of Neolithic landscape to be identified. In short, there were a series of dynamic inter-relationships over this period which were chronologically specific. However, the truth of the matter is that we have inherited only fragments of these historically successive inter-relationships, although in some cases there are concentrations of archaeological sites and monuments dating from c. 4000–2400 BC which today still form significant components of our historic environment. In some cases, these concentrations of archaeological sites are described (although not always by archaeologists) as Neolithic landscapes.

Many of the issues relating to the at times competing and contradictory definition, perception and management of Neolithic monuments in their landscape, relate to the fact that heritage sector documents (some of which have been alluded to above) are variously used to disseminate information, to educate the public and to communicate with wide audiences, and in so doing interpret Neolithic monuments through an increasingly wide range of media. There are multiple messages to be conveyed, and the 'facts of the matter' can often be overlooked or simplified. Yet this in itself is not necessarily a problem, and could provide an opportunity for increasing awareness and appreciation of Neolithic monuments, in that multiple dialogues about the status and character of these Neolithic sites and the landscapes that surround them give them a resonance in wider debates about the future and character of such contemporary landscapes.

There is debate taking place in society about the character of future landscapes. In the face of pressures for change (e.g., climate change, population growth and migration), there is a process of foresight and scenario modelling of likely future impacts on landscapes increasingly taking place. Rarely, if ever, will the Neolithic evidence and potential contribution be considered. However, as discussed above, archaeology can certainly contribute to integrated landscape research (ESF-COST 2010), and through extending the example of HONO WHS can contribute to more integrated forms of landscape management. Furthermore, there are aspects of the Neolithic (such as themes of mobility, of changing landscape character and quality, of the introduction/adoption of new animals, plants and practices) that, when viewed in the inter-related scales of Scotland, Britain and Europe, are potentially key in understanding dynamic pathways (e.g., Guttman-Bond 2010; Van de Noort 2011) from the past to the future.

There are examples of other perspectives that actively champion a vision for environment and/or nature in Scotland's landscapes, including the John Muir Trust's vision for Wild Lands (e.g., John Muir Trust 2012) and RSPB Futurescapes (e.g., Royal Society for Protection of Birds 2014). There are no equivalent long-term visions articulated for the future of Scotland's past within our historic environment, which is such a key element of all Scotland's landscapes. With issues of integrated landscape research (ESF-COST 2010) to be considered perhaps our remit as archaeologists extends beyond the mapping, interpretation and conservation of archaeological assets. Can integrated landscape research also be applied to, for example, landscapes that have significant concentrations of Neolithic remains? Will archaeologists contribute meaningfully to debates on the future of our landscapes by reimagining and revitalising the meanings of the evidence they contain for the past (Fairclough 2012; Roe 2014)? What is going to be the future of the 'Neolithic' in our landscapes?

In light of these observations, are there any possible Neolithic futures we can imagine?

(1) Vibrant monuments: are there any Neolithic monuments or monument groups that would benefit from altering their setting, either to something more authentic or to something that is more resilient? Could we more actively use monuments, deploying innovative interpretation and enhanced visitor experiences, yet simultaneously understanding and managing them more effectively?

(2) Neolithic regions: is there something fundamental about the regionality of the Neolithic in Scotland that we need to learn more effectively from? Would this help to address the impacts of major pressures for change in the lowlands? Would it help us to ensure that we make better informed management decisions about our rural uplands? Would a better understanding and appreciation of Neolithic regionality foster stronger, more confident communities in different parts of Scotland?

(3) Neolithic landscapes: with the vast size of Scotland's landscape, surely a small portion, still 'landscape' in scale, could be set aside to reconfigure the 'Neolithic landscape' to allow present-day inhabitants to experience what it may have been like to dwell here at different times between 4000 and 2400 BC. Could we monitor such developing new landscape creations over the long term to inform our understanding of past interconnectivity and dynamic pathways to ensure we find more integrated solutions for other more degraded areas of landscape?

(4) Post-Neolithic: in a sense we are still Neolithic. Practices which emerged 6,000 years ago began to change the character of soils, species and habitats. Thus, in a way we are still in part living in Neolithic landscapes, since a wholly post-Neolithic society would arguably be devoid of modes of production that relate to agro-pastoral systems embedded in landscapes, and rely, for example, only on vast hydroponic glasshouses and meat protein grown in vats for all food production. In this sense then we are still 'Neolithic'.

In Conclusion

In this chapter, I have taken an important aspect of Gordon Barclay's work as a point of departure to reflect on the nature of our practices in the arena of the academic study and cultural resource management of Neolithic sites. Gordon's work clearly demonstrates the socio-political nature of narrating the Neolithic to audiences today, and he was clearly well aware of the potential ramifications that these narratives may have in terms of contemporary perceptions of landscapes, regions and nations.

And in the spirit of Gordon's later career work on such issues, I have in this chapter attempted to contextualise Neolithic sites and landscapes within current socio-political debates and to offer a critique of some well-worn tropes. For instance, despite the prolific (and usually unhelpful) use of terms such as 'Neolithic Landscapes', 'Bronze Age Landscapes' and 'Prehistoric

Landscapes', there are clearly no such things. In some locations there are well-preserved upstanding archaeological features that are of a broadly coherent date, and that represent a broad range of components, but these features are often no longer functioning as part of living landscapes. But this does not mean that archaeological features should be described in terms of being of the past, entirely behind us; as Barclay demonstrates, the ways in which we categorise and narrate our Neolithic monuments can create conditions that legitimise ideological positions that have more contemporary resonances.

As we have explored, Neolithic monuments, with their settings and as parts of the Historic Environment, can no longer be treated simply as bounded isolated entities; rather, they are parts of landscapes. Thus, in a sense Neolithic monuments are actively incorporated into stances and dialogues that may affect the future character and quality of our landscapes. Through the example of the HONO WHS and the inter-relationships between concentrations of Neolithic monuments and NSA designation, I have worked through the ways in which this story continues to unfold, entangled as it is with fundamental and applied research and now articulating with the spatial planning system. Several issues are perhaps now converging: the concept of the historic environment; the policy context for archaeological and heritage assets; and the current challenges from development, economic and other, in a landscape context.

Perhaps we should now be engaging with some of our Neolithic inheritances in more active ways? What can we really learn from them in applied ways? How can we re-use or revitalise components of them? Are there options for their management that may be more relevant now than ever before in terms of producing sustainable social, cultural and economic value through more active engagement and use?

Note

1. Available at: www.scottishten.org/property3.

Bibliography

Atkins Report (2008), *The Heart of Neolithic Orkney World Heritage Site Setting Project*, Edinburgh: Historic Scotland.

Barclay, G. J. (1997), *State Funded 'Rescue', Archaeology in Scotland: Past, Present and Future*, Edinburgh: Historic Scotland.

Barclay, G. J. (2000), 'Between Orkney and Wessex: the search for the regional Neolithics of Britain', in A. Ritchie (ed.), *Neolithic Orkney in its European Context*, Cambridge: McDonald Institute, 275–85.

Barclay, G. J. (2001), ' "Metropolitan" and "parochial"/"core" and "periphery": a historiography of the Neolithic of Scotland', *Proceedings of the Prehistoric Society*, 67: 1–18.

Barclay, G. J. (2004), '"Four Nations Prehistory": cores and archetypes in the writ-
    ing of prehistory', in H. Brocklehurst and R. Phillips (eds), *History, Nationhood
    and the Question of Britain*, London: Palgrave Macmillan, 151–9.
Black, M. (2005), 'The protection of the settings of archaeological sites
    in Scotland', in ICOMOS, *Monuments and Sites in their Setting – Conserving
    Cultural Heritage in Changing Townscapes and Landscapes, 17–21 Oct 2005,
    Xi'an, China*, 15th ICOMOS General Assembly and International Symposium,
    available at: http://www.international.icomos.org/xian2005/papers.htm, last
    accessed 21 June 2015.
Brophy, K. (2006), 'Rethinking Scotland's Neolithic: combining circumstance with
    context', *Proceedings of the Society of Antiquaries of Scotland*, 126: 7–46.
Brophy, K. and Barclay, G. J. (eds) (2009), *Defining a Regional Neolithic: The
    Evidence from Britain and Ireland*, Oxford: Oxbow Books.
Butter, R. (2001), *Kilmartin: Scotland's Richest Prehistoric Landscape – An Introduction
    and Guide*, Kilmartin: Kilmartin House Trust.
Card, N., Downes, J., Gibson, J. and Ovenden, S. (2007), 'Bringing a landscape
    to life? Researching and managing the The Heart of Neolithic Orkney World
    Heritage Site', *World Archaeology*, 39: 417–35.
Carver, S. and Wrightham, M. (2003), *Assessment of Historic Trends in the Extent of
    Wild Land in Scotland: A Pilot Study*, Scottish Natural Heritage Commissioned
    Report No. 012 (ROAME No. FO2NC11A), Edinburgh.
Council of Europe (2000), *European Landscape Convention*, CETS No. 176,
    Strasbourg: Council of Europe.
Countryside Commission for Scotland (1978), *Scotland's Scenic Heritage*, Perth:
    Countryside Commission for Scotland.
Downes, J., Foster, S. M. and Wickham-Jones, C. R. (eds) (2005), *The Heart of
    Neolithic Orkney World Heritage Site Research Agenda*, Edinburgh: Historic
    Scotland.
ESF-COST (2010), 'Landscape in a Changing World: Bridging Divides, Integrating
    Disciplines, Serving Society', ESF-COST Science Policy Briefing 41, avail-
    able at: http://www.esf.org/publications/science-policy-briefings.html, last
    accessed 6 October 2015.
Foster, S. and Linge, L. (2002), 'World Heritage Site buffer zones: statements of fact
    or aspiration?', *Conservation and Management of Archaeological Sites*, 5: 141–50.
Fairclough, G. (2012), 'A prospect of time: interactions between landscape archi-
    tecture and archaeology', in S. Bell, I. S. Herlin and R. Stiles (eds), *Exploring the
    Boundaries of Landscape Architecture*, Abingdon: Routledge, 83–114.
Fox, C. (1932), *The Personality of Britain*, Cardiff: National Museums of Wales.
Garden, M.-C. (2006), 'The heritagescape: looking at landscapes of the past',
    International Journal of Heritage Studies, 12: 394–418.
Guttman-Bond, E. (2010), 'Sustainability out of the past: how archaeology can save
    the planet', *World Archaeology*, 42: 355–66.
Historic Scotland (1999), *Nomination of the Heart of Neolithic Orkney for Inclusion on
    the World Heritage List* (reprinted 2000), Edinburgh: Historic Scotland.

Historic Scotland (2001), *Heart of Neolithic Orkney World Heritage Site Management Plan*, Edinburgh: Historic Scotland.

Historic Scotland (2002), *The Heart of Neolithic Orkney World Heritage Site Interpretation Plan*, Edinburgh: Historic Scotland.

Historic Scotland (2005), *Heart of Neolithic Orkney World Heritage Site Research Agenda 2005*, Edinburgh: Historic Scotland.

Historic Scotland (2008), *Heart of Neolithic Orkney World Heritage Site Management Plan 2008–13*, Edinburgh: Historic Scotland.

Historic Scotland (2010), *Setting: Managing Change in the Historic Environment*, Edinburgh: Historic Scotland.

Historic Scotland (2011), *Scotland's Historic Environment Policy*, Edinburgh: Historic Scotland.

Historic Scotland (2013), *Heart of Neolithic Orkney World Heritage Site Research Strategy 2013–18*. Edinburgh: Historic Scotland.

Historic Scotland (2014), *Heart of Neolithic Orkney: A Short Guide*, Edinburgh: Historic Scotland.

Howkins, A. (1986), 'The discovery of rural England', in R. Colls and P. Dodd (eds), *Englishness: Politics and Culture*, London: Croom Helm, 62–8.

John Muir Trust (2012), *Wild Land: The Call for Statutory Protection*, Pitlochry: John Muir Trust.

Lelong, O. and MacGregor, G. (2012), 'Weaving strands: integrating excavations, landscapes and the human past along the A1 major road in East Lothian, Scotland', in J. Bofinger and D. Krausse, D (eds), *Large-scale Excavations in Europe: Field-work Strategies and Scientific Outcome*, EAC Occasional Paper, Archaeolingua, 23–34.

Lelong, O. and MacGregor, G. (2014), 'Archaeological assets or shared resources? Considering the true value of heritage values', *The Archaeologist*, 91: 26–9.

McClanahan, A. (2013), 'Curating "northernness" in Neolithic Orkney: a contemporary monumental biography', *Visual Studies*, 28: 262–70.

McMorran, R., Price, M. F. and McVittie, A. (2006), *A Review of the Benefits and Opportunities Attributed to Scotland's Landscapes of Wild Character*, Scottish Natural Heritage Commissioned Report No. 194 (ROAME No F04NC18), Edinburgh.

Mitchell, N., Rössler, M. and Tricaud, P-M. (2009), *World Heritage Cultural Landscapes: A Handbook for Conservation and Management*, Paris: UNESCO.

MVA Consultancy Ltd (2012), *Public Perceptions Survey of Wildness in Scotland*, survey commissioned by Loch Lomond and The Trossachs National Park Authority, Glasgow, available at: http://www.lochlomond-trossachs.org/look ing-after/public-perception-survey-of-wildness-in-scotland-2012/menu-id-414.html, last accessed 21 June 2015.

National Planning and Policy Guidance 5 (1994), *Archaeology and Planning*, Edinburgh: HMSO.

Orkney Islands Council (2010), *The Heart of Neolithic Orkney World Heritage Site Supplementary Planning Guidance*, Kirkwall: Orkney Islands Council.

Phillips, T. and Bradley, R. (2004), 'Developer-funded fieldwork in Scotland, 1990–2003: an overview of the prehistoric evidence', *Proceedings of the Society of Antiquaries of Scotland*, 134: 17–51.

Piggott, S. (1954), *The Neolithic Cultures of the British Isles*, Cambridge: Cambridge University Press.

Ralston, I. (2004), 'Archaeologists and the possibility of wilderness creation in Scotland', in E. Carver and O. Lelong (eds), *Modern Views – Ancient Lands: New Work and Thought on Cultural Landscapes*, Oxford: British Archaeological Reports, 81–6.

Richards, C. (1996), 'Monuments as landscape: creating the centre of the world in Late Neolithic Orkney', *World Archaeology*, 28: 190–208.

Roe, M. (2014), 'Exploring future cultural landscapes', in M. Roe and K. Taylor (eds), *New Cultural Landscapes*, Abington: Routledge, 224–41.

Royal Society for Protection of Birds (2014), *UK Futurescapes: Summary Guide*, available at: https://www.rspb.org.uk/whatwedo/futurescapes, last accessed 21 June 2015.

ScARF (2012), 'South-east Scotland and north-east England', in A. Sheridan and K. Brophy (eds), *Neolithic Panel Report*, Scottish Archaeological Research Framework: Society of Antiquaries of Scotland, 61–73, available at: http://tinyurl.com/d73xkvn, last accessed 16 June 2015.

Sharples, N. (1996), 'Nationalism or internationalism: the problematic Scottish experience', in J. A. Atkinson, I. Banks and J. O. O'Sullivan (eds), *Nationalism and Archaeology*, Glasgow: Cruithne Press, 77–88.

Sharples, N. and Sheridan, A. (eds) (1992), *Vessels for the Ancestors*, Edinburgh: Edinburgh University Press.

Scottish Natural Heritage (2002), *Wildness in Scotland's Countryside*. Edinburgh: SNH.

Scottish Natural Heritage (2010), *The Special Qualities of the National Scenic Areas*, Edinburgh: SNH Commissioned Report No. 374.

Stevenson, J. B. (1975), 'Survival and discovery', in J. G. Evans, S. Limbrey and H. Cleere (eds), *The Effect of Man on the Landscape: The Highland Zone*, London: Council for British Archaeology, 104–8.

Syse, K. V. L. (2010), 'Expert systems, local knowledge and power in Argyll', *Landscape Research*, 35: 469–84.

Tyldesley, D. (2001), *Landscape Capacity Study of the Heart of Neolithic Orkney WHS*, Scottish Natural Heritage Commissioned Report, Edinburgh.

Tyldesley, D. (2007), *Identifying the Special Qualities of Scotland's National Scenic Areas*, Scottish Natural Heritage Commissioned Report No. 255 (ROAME No. F05NC701), Edinburgh.

UNESCO (1999), *Neolithic Orkney (United Kingdom)* No. 514 rev., Advisory Body Evaluation, UNESCO.

Van de Noort, R. (2011), 'Conceptualising climate change archaeology', *Antiquity*, 85: 1039–48.

CHAPTER 3

'Very real shared traditions'? Thinking about Similarity and Difference in the Construction and Use of Clyde Cairns in the Western Scottish Neolithic

Vicki Cummings

Introduction

In 2009, Gordon Barclay wrote 'We must be careful not to replace "national" prehistories with micro-regional approaches that underplay the *very real shared traditions*, and complex relationships between regions ...' (Barclay 2009: 3; added emphasis). My chapter takes this idea as its starting point: how do we, as archaeologists interested in both regional differences and contextual archaeologies, understand similarity and difference in our evidence? Since most contemporary archaeologists have moved away from a culture–historical narrative, with its emphasis on broad-scale comparative work, I suggest that we do not have a problem understanding difference, but that archaeologists are currently struggling with how to deal with similarities in the archaeological record. Therefore, I shall explore traditions of monumentality and investigate how archaeologists might deal with similarities across broad areas, while still writing regional and contextually specific archaeologies. The Clyde cairns of western Scotland are used as a case study through which to explore these issues.

Introducing western Scotland

Western Scotland from the Solway Firth north to the southern Hebrides is a diverse area, incorporating both lowland and upland zones with a mosaic of agricultural land, peaty moorland and, further north, mountains. One of the key characteristics of its western seaboard is the presence of a range of islands, including those in the Clyde estuary and others, such as Islay and Jura, on the Atlantic façade. While this volume is focused on mainland Scotland, to only consider that land mass in the west would be meaningless: the maritime nature of this part of Scotland is one of its defining characteristics. It seems highly likely that the seaways that traverse this area were key routes in the Neolithic (Garrow and Sturt 2011), connecting communities living along its coasts from the Solway Firth to Jura (Cummings 2009).

Indeed, the Clyde estuary and adjacent lands were originally considered one of the key areas for Neolithic colonisation (e.g., Piggott 1954; Sheridan 2010 offers the latest version of this argument). Therefore in this chapter attention will be paid to both the islands and the mainland of western Scotland.

In terms of Early Neolithic archaeology, narratives on western Scotland have been dominated by discussions of chambered cairns in the Clyde tradition of monument construction (Scott 1969, 1973; Henshall 1972; Noble 2005; Cummings 2009), although other monumental traditions present extend to timber-and-earthwork types (Thomas 2007; forthcoming). The chambered cairns, notably the Clyde series, are certainly the most numerous and luminous form of Neolithic sites to survive in the record, and there has been only limited investigation of direct evidence for settlement (Chapter 10, this volume) in this part of Scotland as a whole, including Argyll (Ritchie 1997).

The Clyde series of monuments consists of a chamber set into one terminal of a long or trapezoidal cairn. The chamber area is typically divided into compartments, and it seems likely that originally access to these chambers was through the roof, and was achieved by removing the roofing slabs. At one terminal of the cairn there is usually a forecourt, frequently, although not exclusively, created by a stone-built façade. In many cases, Clyde cairns also have one or more lateral chambers (Figure 3.1). Fifty-five Clyde cairns are recorded in the main distribution area of

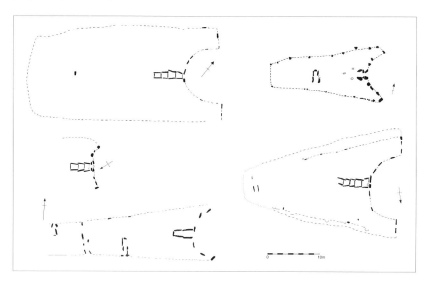

Figure 3.1 Plans of Clyde cairns: top left, Carn Baan, Arran; top right, Blasthill, Kintyre; middle left Monamore, Arran; bottom left Gort na h'ulaidhe, Kintyre; bottom right East Bennan, Arran (image prepared by the author).

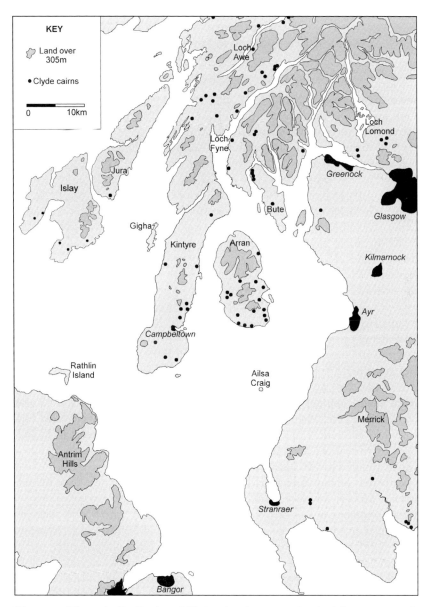

Figure 3.2 The main distribution of Clyde cairns in western Scotland (image prepared by the author).

western Scotland, which lies between the Solway Firth in the south, mid-Argyll to the north and Islay to the west (Figure 3.2). A few outlying Clyde cairns occur far beyond this core distribution, as in North Uist in the Outer Hebrides (Henshall 1972).

Similarity and difference:
from culture–history to contextual archaeology

The culture–historical approaches of the 1930s, 1940s and 1950s advocated the idea that material culture sets such as pots, burial rites and monuments were the material expressions of cultural groups (Childe 1929: vi). Both Gordon Childe (1935) and Stuart Piggott (1954) suggested that the Clyde cairns were the cultural signature of incoming Neolithic groups from out-with Scotland and ultimately from the continent. Childe and Piggott con-sidered western Scotland to share so many similarities with eastern Ireland in the Early Neolithic that they named the particular cultural group that displayed these traits the 'Clyde–Carlingford' culture, after two bodies of water which have substantial distributions of relevant chambered cairns along their shores (Childe 1935: 25–32; Piggott 1954: 152). Thereafter, from the 1960s onwards, there was an increasing shift towards national archaeologies in UK archaeology, and regional sequences that differentiated Irish from Scottish evidence were highlighted. The court cairns of Ireland, for example, were excised from the Clyde–Carlingford culture (Corcoran 1960; de Valera 1960); and the Clyde cairns were considered as a separate wholly Scottish entity within the wider north British Neolithic context of chambered cairn architecture (Scott 1969; Henshall 1972). It can be argued that this differentiation was part of a broader move throughout Britain and Ireland which created distinctive national prehistories at this time.

A quarter of a century later, within the broader post-processual para-digm which dominated in the discipline from the 1980s onwards, it became obvious that generalising about national sequences did not successfully cap-ture key differences and variations in the archaeological record (Kinnes 1985). Thus, there was increasing emphasis on regionally specific studies, which coincided with a growing emphasis on areas of the country without chambered tomb architecture, where aerial photography and, from the fol-lowing decade, developer-funded archaeology revealed a whole range of hitherto unknown sites of a variety of types (Brophy 2006). This focus on a regional approach can be seen in subsequent publications (e.g., Sharples and Sheridan 1992; Cummings and Pannett 2005), and it represented useful inroads into considerations of localised phenomena and sequences. With the emphasis on the consideration of regions *within* Scotland, as opposed to studies of Scotland as a whole, some areas became or remained more fully studied than others. Orkney, notably, saw considerable emphasis (cf. Barclay 2001), while western Scotland was rarely considered in any detail during this period.

Chambered tomb studies: a changing paradigm

The last ten years have seen another key development affecting chambered tomb studies: a move towards more detailed contextual archaeologies, in which individual site biographies have been highlighted and explored (e.g., Benson and Whittle 2007; Whittle *et al.* 2007a). This approach initially occurred primarily with the Cotswold–Severn group of monuments in southern Britain, although it is increasingly being pursued within the context of particular Scottish chambered tombs (e.g., Cummings and Robinson 2015; Harris *et al.* 2010). The Cotswold–Severn work has been highly influential, not just in terms of regional studies in southern England, but also in enhancing the ways in which we understand monuments more generally. This progress in their interpretation has been possible because the Cotswold–Severn sites have been thoroughly investigated and explored over the years, and excellent preservation of materials within them has also helped. While I do not wish to import wholesale results and ideas from southern Britain, the modern studies of these key monuments are significant at a broader theoretical level.

At Ascott-under-Wychwood, Oxfordshire, for example, a detailed discussion of the complex building sequence at the site, illustrates how the monument was built over a fairly short timescale, and on top of earlier occupation activity (Whittle *et al.* 2007b). It appears that during construction its architecture underwent many alterations and additions; a considerable variety of materials was used to construct the covering barrow (McFadyen *et al.* 2007). This monument was thus not a simple, straightforward build, but one which involved the careful orchestration of people, the recurrent selection of different structural materials, and modification to the monument's design over a period of perhaps one or two human generations (Benson and Whittle 2007). This and other detailed contextual studies have also contributed to our knowledge of chambered tombs more generally through the presentation of new sets of radiocarbon dates which have undergone Bayesian modelling (Whittle *et al.* 2007a). This dating programme has shown that these Cotswold–Severn monuments were all built fairly quickly, with deposits of human bone also rapidly succeeding the constructional phases. In the case of West Kennet long barrow in the Marlborough Downs, for instance, the monument was completed, and the primary burial deposits added, over just one to two generations (Bayliss *et al.* 2007). It is also of considerable interest that the dates for the investigated sites indicate that they were not built simultaneously, but rather at different times over roughly four centuries from 3800 to 3400 cal. BC. This theme – the duration over which particular series of monuments were constructed – will be tackled further below.

As a product of this very detailed contextual study of individual Cotswold–Severn monuments, there has been discussion around the idea that these monuments were not planned and then executed with their builders' aim from the outset being to create a pre-determined final, finished form. Instead, there is a suggestion that the significance of these monuments was found more in the construction process itself (Bradley 1993; Barrett 1994; Richards 2004, 2013; McFadyen 2006), where the importance of erecting them lay in the coming together of people and the assembling of materials; these activities in themselves created new memories and arenas for social interactions. As such, those participating in the making of the monument were not striving towards the creation of a finished architectural form, like a cathedral, which, once constructed, could be used for the original purpose for which it had been designed (which in the case of chambered cairns would have been burial). Instead, chambered cairns were essentially ongoing construction sites (cf. McFadyen 2006). This is an attractive idea for a number of reasons. First, it helps us to understand the diversity in their monumental form and why each individual monument is slightly different from the next. Second, at such enduring construction sites, the performance of people, the engagement with place and the manipulation of materials would all have been prioritised, and these processes would all have been powerful in the creation of memories and socialities in the Neolithic. Third, the suggestion that these monuments were primarily erected as places for the burial of the dead can be challenged by proposing that this was just one of their many uses. Such a perspective also leads to the idea that such chambered cairns, *contra* the views prevalent in much of the literature, were not actually built to last. Indeed, it is possible to argue that the permanence of these monuments is actually an *unintended outcome* of the performance of their construction (Whittle *et al.* 2007). At the very least, since people would have noticed that early constructions did in fact endure, we may suggest that a lasting physical presence was not something intended by the first builders of these megalithic constructions. These were places that were designed to be built, experienced, engaged with, and potentially also returned to and reworked. However, it is possible that the initial builders never conceived that these constructions would endure on the ground, and that their focus was instead directed at thinking how these monuments could help shape and reshape their community's worlds.

If individual chambered cairns were essentially unique construction sites, we are nevertheless left with a series of monuments that share many key characteristics. Against this background, how do we start to understand similarities in their forms across broad regions such as western Scotland, without returning to old-fashioned culture–historical interpretations?

Exploring similarity

Individually, each Clyde cairn can be understood on its own terms and within its own immediate context. This understanding can be explored through a detailed biography of place within the surrounding landscape,

although unfortunately few Clyde cairns have been fully excavated and published so, as yet, we cannot examine some of the issues investigated at sites
like Ascott-under-Wychwood. The question is how we understand broader
similarities, and to start with, this will be discussed in relation to architectural form. Plans of Clyde cairns as well as the encounter of these sites on
the ground reveal structural similarities across a broad area (Figure 3.1,
above). These similarities include the layout of the chambers, the presence
of a forecourt and the size and shape of the cairn. While the builders of
each site were clearly not following an exact blueprint, there are manifest
similarities. This issue has been discussed by Gordon Barclay in relation
to Scottish Early Neolithic timber halls (see Barclay *et al.* 2002), but how
should we understand these shared characteristics in relation to chambered
tomb architecture?

Our first problem is that individual Clyde cairns were not constructed in
a single phase. These were monuments that were altered over time, and some
show evidence of multiple phases (Henshall 1972; Noble 2005). Henshall
(1972), for example, suggests that all Clyde cairns with lateral chambers
may well be multi-phase monuments. Some sites seem to have started life as
simple box-like chambers, set within sub-circular cairns: this can clearly be
seen at Mid Gleniron I and II, in western Dumfries and Galloway (Corcoran
1969) (Figure 3.3), Blasthill, Kintyre, Argyll and Bute (Cummings and
Robinson 2015), and has also been convincingly suggested for Cairnholy I
and II in the Stewartry of Kirkcudbright, Dumfries and Galloway (Noble
2005). At a later stage, these simple box-like chambers were either converted
into the characteristic series-of-boxes chambers or further chambers were
added elsewhere within the monument. It seems likely that the addition of
the façade and cairn also happened at this point, although these could have
been added later. The construction of multiple compartmented chambers,
the façade and the cairn seem to make up the main phase of construction,
and at some sites, this may even represent the primary phase. Many monuments then seem to have had minor re-workings: the addition of more chambers; the erection of extra stones in the façade; the extension of the cairn; the
blocking of the forecourt and so on.

Yet, even though many of these sites were potentially remodelled on a
number of occasions over time, there are still some striking similarities in
their final (if not finished) form: the series of small box-like compartments
that make up the terminal chamber, the presence of a concave forecourt and
the trapezoidal cairn are all features found throughout the Clyde cairn sites.
Indeed, it was these features that originally enabled scholars to classify them
as part of the Clyde culture (Scott 1969; Henshall 1972). Similarities in the
principal construction phases are found throughout the main distribution of
Clyde cairns and there are also notable similarities in the later use of these
monuments. Many sites show clear evidence for the forecourt being infilled
so that there was no longer access to either the chambers through the façade

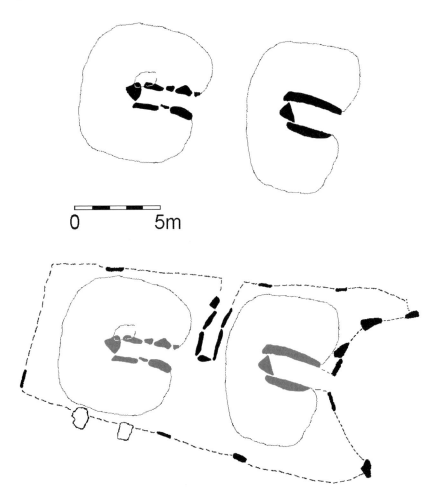

Figure 3.3 The two main phases at Mid Gleniron I, Dumfries and Galloway (after Corcoran 1969; image prepared by the author).

or to the forecourt itself. Many Clyde cairns saw re-use of their chambers in the Early Bronze Age, such as at Cairnholy I, and Beacharra and Brackley (Argyll and Bute) (Piggott and Powell 1949; Scott 1954, 1955). Other sites had new architectural components added in the Early Bronze Age, primarily in the form of small cists.

There are broad comparisons that can be made with regard to the form of Clyde cairns in other ways. The contents of the chambers that have been excavated also show surprising similarities throughout the Clyde monuments. Burnt deposits are found ubiquitously in a variety of contexts, including the chamber, forecourt and also underneath the monument. This observation may suggest that fire was crucial in the preparation not only of

Figure 3.4 Achnagoul, Argyll, looking out over mountains and water (photograph: author).

the land surface prior to construction, but also of the deposits destined to be placed in the monuments. Burnt human bone is found in many Clyde chambers, which suggests that cremation was a common funerary practice associated with these monuments, although this might be an issue of preservation since unburnt bone rarely survives in western Scotland. Some monuments also show evidence of fires in the forecourt, as indicated at Cairnholy I (Piggott and Powell 1949). Compared with other types of material culture, pottery, particularly bowl pottery, was also frequently deposited in Clyde chambers. Its presence confirms the impression that events involving fire played an important part in the rituals associated with Clyde cairn construction and use: the firing of pots, the firing of land, the firing of bodies. Fire has dramatic transformative properties, and would have been important in the Neolithic for creating memorable visual spectacles not just at chambered cairns (cf. Noble 2006: ch. 3).

Elsewhere, it has been detailed how monuments around the Irish Sea were located in remarkably similar landscape settings (Cummings 2009). To briefly summarise those arguments, Clyde cairns are located in very specific parts of the landscape. The vast majority are positioned to have views out over both uplands or mountains and over water (Figure 3.4). Many of the Clyde cairns are situated alongside lochs, particularly on the shores of Loch Fyne and Loch Awe, while those on Arran, Kintyre, Islay and Jura avoid inland areas, being positioned instead overlooking the sea. It has been argued for these monuments and for others elsewhere that their setting was not fortuitous, but carefully and deliberately choreographed (Tilley 1994, 2010; Richards 1996; Cummings 2009). The overall conclusion of this work on the landscape setting of chambered cairns is that the views out to the surrounding landscape were as critical an element of each monument as the stones that make up the chamber and cairn.

Understanding similarity

Clearly, Clyde cairns share many key similarities, in form, setting and use. Without returning to a simplistic culture–historical narrative, how should we interpret these similarities? A significant problem is that we know that shared distinctive types of material culture do not indicate cultural groupings (Hodder 1982). Thus, the fact that groups of people built and used similar monuments throughout this area does not necessarily mean that they were part of a broader community. Invoking traditions of practice highlights the same problem: shared traditions of doing things may underlie real differences in social identity. Thus, apparently similar traditions may be underpinned by radically different agendas, mind-sets and social groupings.

Exploring similarities in Clyde monuments can inform us of some key issues: it shows that people had knowledge of how things *should* be done. '*Form mattered* in building; it both imposed limitations to the construction process and opened possibilities' (McFadyen and Whittle 2007: 356; added emphasis). In western Scotland, even if the ongoing emphasis on construction proposed above is accepted, people were not building monuments with no thought to form. Similarity in form, setting and use was obviously important to the people building these monuments or we should expect to see much more diversity. There are chronological issues here, since many of these monuments are probably multi-phase. At some point in the construction of the Clyde series of cairns, however, potentially quite diverse primary arrangements and architectural practices seem to have been standardised. At this point a decision was made to add features which were in due course widely adopted across a broader area: a trapezoidal cairn, a terminal chamber and a forecourt. These later developments, now clearly visible at Clyde cairns, could, of course, mask very diverse earlier phases of development, but nevertheless traits such as those just mentioned, which seem to have been employed during later phases of use of the Clyde cairn series, are geographically more widespread.

In addition to this, it is possible to suggest that similarities in monument form, use and setting relate to deliberate and genuine attempts to express affinities with broader areas and wider communities beyond western Scotland, as here considered. At the very least, then, similarities indicate that people in this area had knowledge of broader practices, and a desire to partake in them. I have argued elsewhere that one of the key elements of 'being Neolithic' was being part of a wider, connected world.

This observation leads us to another point. Are we still imagining that individual communities built individual monuments? Indeed, who precisely are we envisioning building these monuments? It is possible to argue that Renfrew's 'Monuments, mobilisation and social organisation' paper is still highly influential in this regard (Renfrew 1973). This paper focused on understanding social organisation through the Neolithic, but as part of this exercise Renfrew suggested that long barrows were built by family groups. He also suggested that Early Neolithic cairns may have functioned as territorial markers, and he subsequently used the Clyde cairns of Arran to illustrate this point (Renfrew 1976). While very few scholars nowadays would argue that chambered cairns served as markers of territories, there is, at least implicitly, an idea that individual communities built individual monuments. In discussing the recently re-dated Cotswold–Severn monuments, for example, Whittle and his co-authors (2007a, 137) write: 'Monuments would not act as territorial markers, but as some kind of advertisement for the ability of a sub-group within the local community or area to organise and sponsor the construction of a monument.'

This perspective is not unreasonable, and therefore it remains possible to propose that each monument represents the efforts of an individual community. It should be further clarified that this suggestion is implicit, not explicit, in most accounts of monuments of this type, but, nevertheless, it is not an enormous leap to advocate that each monument represents the physical remains of an individual community. Thus, every national distribution map of any kind of Neolithic monument could be interpreted as indicative of whole sets of individual Neolithic communities (cf. Brophy 2009).

What if we take another approach to monuments, however, and suggest that the same community built monuments recurrently, and at different points in the landscape? This suggestion works particularly well with monuments that are located close to each other, as at the Cairnholy I and II and Mid Gleniron I and II cairns, for example. Again, if we follow the detailed contextual work of McFadyen (2006) and Whittle and colleagues (2007a), each monument represents the coming together of people, places and materials. This visceral engagement of bodies and substances is both process and performance, affecting and changing people's social worlds.

In addition, at paired monuments, as with other chambered cairn sites, the construction process itself may have acted as a social interface, a medium through which to resolve problems or issues, perhaps across the scale from inter-personal disputes up to community-wide concerns (Cummings and Harris 2011). Monuments thus fulfilled a role in society: their construction represented the coming together of people and things. If the key role of a chambered cairn was as a social arena while it was actively being built or used, once the monument had been constructed and the deposits made, it may essentially have fulfilled its principal role.

But what if a community needed anew the social arena that the construction of a monument provided? What if building one monument was not enough? Would people not be tempted to do the same thing again? What if sets of monuments were not the result of several individual communities each building a monument, but the same community building multiple monuments over time? This may explain the presence of a number of monuments at the same location. Indeed, as noted above, the recent dating programme on Cotswold–Severn monuments strongly supports the idea that monuments were built and deposits associated with them made over quite a short timescale (Whittle *et al.* 2007a). This dating programme also intimated that the individual monuments were not constructed simultaneously, although it should be noted that these excavations focused primarily on the chambers and not the mounds, which, if excavated, might yet paint a different picture. We should also not assume that the chronological spans of use of Clyde cairns would necessarily mirror the brevity of use-life apparent in Cotswold–Severn monuments.

This idea – that single communities built neighbouring or, indeed, more distant monuments over time – may also affect how we understand the gaps in our distribution maps. Indeed, whether or not each chambered cairn represents a single community, the blanks in the mapped distributions of chambered cairns may be interpreted as simply spaces where different types of Neolithic community, including those that did not build monuments of these series, were living. After all, chambered cairns are not present in considerable tracts of Scotland and indeed Britain, yet we know that people were living there in the Neolithic. This uneven patterning in the surviving evidence of sites and monuments strengthens the idea that there may have been many different types of Neolithic sites and assemblages across different areas of the country, as so many of Gordon Barclay's contributions have helped to make plain; monument construction, in the sense of erecting, using and modifying chambered cairns, was emphatically not an essential part of being Neolithic. Some communities undoubtedly used Neolithic material culture, and consumed domesticated livestock, but not all built chambered cairns.

There is also the issue of what constituted a community. Again, I think present interpretations frequently still rely on discussions as far back as Renfrew (1973), where he describes a community as consisting of between twenty and a hundred persons. Communities are thus larger than nuclear families, but smaller than 'societies'. This chapter is not the place for a detailed consideration of the notion of Neolithic communities, but this is a concept that needs to be problematised in our future discussions. My conception of a community for the purposes of this chapter is as something rather amorphous and fluid, but, crucially, where considerable elements of continuity in group identity over a number of generations would be displayed.

Conclusion

This chapter has considered an issue raised by Gordon Barclay: how can we begin to understand what seem to be 'very real shared traditions' in Clyde cairn construction? Following the detailed contextual work on Cotswold–Severn monuments, it has been suggested that the act of construction was the significant element of each site (McFadyen 2006); I have argued that this perspective is also relevant to how we can understand Clyde cairns. However, similarities in form, setting and use are demonstrable in the Clyde series of sites across western Scotland, and it has been postulated that this indicates that Neolithic people had a desire to conform to particular structural forms, although shared appearances may mask potentially diverse architectural practices. Behind all this, these communities may well have contained a broader knowledge of monumentality. It is suggested here that instead of trying to explore notions of regionality through these monuments, we should instead challenge one of our preconceptions of the archaeological record. This is the idea that individual communities built individual monuments. If monuments are the material remains of social processes, then it is possible that some communities built many monuments over time and across the landscape. Clearly, further work is required to develop these ideas, but this approach offers new ways of thinking about these sites.

Bibliography

Barclay, G. (2001), '"Metropolitan" and "parochial"/"core" and "periphery": a historiography of the Neolithic of Scotland', Proceedings of the Prehistoric Society, 67: 1–18.

Barclay, G. (2009), 'Introduction: a regional agenda?', in Brophy and Barclay (eds), Defining a Regional Neolithic, 1–4.

Barclay, G., Brophy, K. and MacGregor, G. (2002), 'Claish, Stirling: an Early Neolithic structure in its context', Proceedings of the Society of Antiquaries of Scotland, 132: 65–137.

Barrett, J. (1994), Fragments from Antiquity: An Archaeology of Social Life in Britain 2900–1200 BC, Oxford: Blackwell.

Bayliss, A., Whittle, A. and Wysocki, M. (2007), 'Talking about my generation: the date of the West Kennet long barrow', Cambridge Archaeological Journal, 17: 85–101.

Benson, D. and Whittle, A. (eds), Building Memories: The Neolithic Cotswold Long Barrow at Ascott-under-Wychwood, Oxfordshire, Oxford: Oxbow Books.

Bradley, R. (1993), Altering the Earth, Edinburgh: Society of Antiquaries of Scotland.

Brophy, K. (2006), 'Rethinking Scotland's Neolithic: combining circumstance with context', Proceedings of the Society of Antiquaries of Scotland, 126: 7–46.

Brophy, K. (2009), 'The map trap: the depiction of regional geographies of the Neolithic', in Brophy and Barclay (eds), Defining a Regional Neolithic, 5–25.

Brophy, K. and Barclay, G. (eds), (2009), *Defining a Regional Neolithic: The Evidence from Britain and Ireland*, Oxford: Oxbow Books.

Childe, V. G. (1929), *The Danube in Prehistory*, Oxford: Clarendon Press.

Childe, V. G. (1935), *The Prehistory of Scotland*, London: Kegan Paul, Trench, Trubner.

Corcoran, J. X. W. P. (1960), 'The Carlingford culture', *Proceedings of the Prehistoric Society*, 7: 98–148.

Corcoran, J. X. W. P. (1969), 'Excavation of two chambered tombs at Mid Gleniron Farm, Glenluce', *Transactions of the Dumfries and Galloway Natural History and Antiquarian Society*, 46: 29–90.

Cummings, V. (2009), *A View from the West: The Neolithic of the Irish Sea Zone*, Oxford: Oxbow Books.

Cummings, V. and Harris, O. (2011), 'Animals, people and places: the continuity of hunting and gathering practices across the Mesolithic–Neolithic transition in Britain', *European Journal of Archaeology*, 14: 361–82.

Cummings, V. and Pannett, A. (eds), (2005), *Set in Stone: New Approaches to Neolithic Monuments in Scotland*, Oxford: Oxbow Books.

Cummings, V. and Robinson, G. (2015), 'The life and times of a chambered tomb: the results of survey and excavation at Blasthill Clyde tomb, Kintyre, western Scotland', *Archaeological Journal*, 172: 1–29.

de Valera, D. (1960), 'The court cairns of Ireland', *Proceedings of the Royal Irish Academy*, C60: 1–139.

Garrow, D. and Sturt, F. (2011), 'Grey water bright with Neolithic Argonauts? Maritime connections and the Mesolithic–Neolithic transition within the "western seaways" of Britain c. 5000–3500 BC', *Antiquity*, 85: 59–72.

Harris, O., Richardson, P., Cobb, H., Murtagh, P. and Pringle, I. (2010), 'Cladh Aindreis Chambered Cairn, Swordle Bay, Ardnamurchan. Season 5DSR', unpublished Data Structure Report, University of Manchester.

Henshall, A. (1972), *The Chambered Tombs of Scotland*, Edinburgh: Edinburgh University Press, vol. 2.

Hodder, I. (1982), *Symbols in Action: Ethnoarchaeological Studies of Material Culture*, Cambridge: Cambridge University Press.

Kinnes, I. (1985), 'Circumstance not context: the Neolithic of Scotland as seen from outside', *Proceedings of the Society of Antiquaries of Scotland*, 115: 15–57.

McFadyen, L. (2006), 'Building technologies, quick and slow architectures and Early Neolithic long barrow sites in southern Britain', *Archaeological Review from Cambridge*, 21: 70–81.

McFadyen, L. and Whittle, A. (2007), 'Building: issues of form and completion', in Benson and Whittle (eds), *Building Memories*, 351–6.

McFadyen, L., Benson, D. and Whittle, A. (2007), 'The long barrow', in Benson and Whittle (eds), *Building Memories*, 79–136.

Noble, G. (2005), 'Ancestry, farming and the changing architecture of the Clyde cairns of south-west Scotland', in Cummings and Pannett (eds), *Set in Stone*, 25–36.

Noble, G. (2006), *Neolithic Scotland: Timber, Stone, Earth and Fire*, Edinburgh: Edinburgh University Press.

Piggott, S. (1954), *The Neolithic Cultures of the British Isles*, Cambridge: Cambridge University Press.

Piggott, S. and Powell, T. G. E. (1949), 'The excavation of three Neolithic chambered tombs in Galloway', *Proceedings of the Society of Antiquaries of Scotland*, 8: 103–61.

Renfrew, C. (1973), 'Monuments, mobilisation and social organisation in Neolithic Wessex', in C. Renfrew (ed.), *The Explanation of Culture Change*, London: Duckworth, 539–58.

Renfrew, C. (1976), 'Megaliths, territories and populations', in S. de Laet (ed.), *Acculturation and Continuity in Atlantic Europe*, Bruges: De Tempel, 198–229.

Richards, C. (1996), 'Henges and water: towards an elemental understanding of monumentality and landscape in Late Neolithic Britain', *Journal of Material Culture*, 1: 313–36.

Richards, C. (2004), 'Labouring with monuments: constructing the dolmen at Carreg Samson, south-west Wales', in V. Cummings and C. Fowler (eds), *The Neolithic of the Irish Sea: Materiality and Traditions of Practice*, Oxford: Oxbow Books, 72–80.

Richards, C. (2013), *Building the Great Stone Circles of the North*, Oxford: Windgather Press.

Ritchie, G. (1997), 'Early settlement in Argyll', in G. Ritchie (ed.), *The Archaeology of Argyll*, Edinburgh: Edinburgh University Press, 38–66.

Scott, J. G. (1954), 'The chambered cairn at Beacharra, Kintyre, Argyll', *Proceedings of the Prehistoric Society*, 9: 134–58.

Scott, J. G. (1955), 'The excavation of the chambered cairn at Brackley, Kintyre', *Proceedings of the Society of Antiquaries of Scotland*, 89: 22–59.

Scott, J. G. (1969), 'The Clyde cairns of Scotland', in T. G. E. Powell, J. X. W. P. Corcoran, F. Lynch and J. G. Scott (eds), *Megalithic Enquiries in the West of Britain*, Liverpool: Liverpool University Press, 175–222.

Scott, J. G. (1973), 'The Clyde cairns of Scotland', in G. Daniel and P. Kjærum (eds), *Megalithic Graves and Ritual*, Copenhagen: Jutland Archaeological Society, 117–28.

Sharples, N. and Sheridan, A. (eds) (1992), *Vessels for the Ancestors: Essays on the Neolithic of Britain and Ireland in Honour of Audrey Henshall*, Edinburgh: Edinburgh University Press.

Sheridan, A. (2010), 'The Neolithization of Britain and Ireland: the "big picture"', in B. Finlayson and G. Warren (eds), *Landscapes in Transition*, Oxford: Oxbow Press, 89–105.

Thomas, J. S. (2007), *Place and Memory: Excavations at the Pict's Knowe, Holywood and Holm Farm, Dumfries and Galloway, 1994–8*, Oxford: Oxbow Books.

Thomas, J. S. (forthcoming), *Excavations at Dunragit, Dumfries and Galloway, 1999–2002*, Oxford: Oxbow Books.

Tilley, C. (1994), *A Phenomenology of Landscape*, Oxford: Berg.

Tilley, C. (2010), *Interpreting Landscapes: Geologies, Topographies, Identities*, Walnut Creek, CA: Left Coast Press.

Whittle, A., Barclay, A., Bayliss, A., McFadyen, L., Schulting, R. and Wysocki, M. (2007a), 'Building for the dead: events, processes and changing worldviews from the thirty-eighth to the thirty-fourth centuries cal. BC in southern Britain', *Cambridge Archaeological Journal*, 17: 123–47.

Whittle, A., Barclay, A., McFadyen, L., Benson, D. and Galer, D. (2007b), 'Place and time: building and remembrance', in Benson and Whittle (eds), *Building Memories*, 327–64.

Whittle, A., Bayliss, A. and Wysocki, M. (2007), 'Once in a lifetime: the date of the Wayland's Smithy long barrow', *Cambridge Archaeological Journal*, 17: 101–21.

CHAPTER 4

Who Were These People?
A Sideways View and a Non-answer
of Political Proportions

Alex Gibson

Introduction

Gordon Barclay raised this important question – who were these people? – in 2005 when it was demonstrated, thanks to the National Museums of Scotland's dating of cremated human bone project that the central Food Vessel cremations at North Mains, Strathallan, Perth and Kinross, were broadly contemporary with the construction of the henge within which they were found (Barclay 2005: 92). As has always been the case during my friendship with Gordon, the questions he poses, even during casual conversation, are always worth considering. They are also deeper than they may often appear. 'Who were these people' is a question not just relevant to North Mains, but it can be taken further and extended to the whole range of Neolithic and Bronze Age burials not just in Scotland, but in Britain and Ireland as a whole and indeed elsewhere in Neolithic Europe. This study is by no means exhaustive, rather it plays devil's advocate by examining a range of interpretations, many unprovable but by no means ignorable, and hope-fully it may stimulate thoughts (or not) amongst colleagues and challenge some current thinking. These musings are offered to Gordon as a small way of thanking him for the work over the past few decades on which I have been hugely reliant and by which I have been significantly influenced. We have mainly been in agreement: we may not be now. They are also offered in the hope that they may be entertaining, questioning and contentious, but also in the full understanding that they may bore him to tears now that his research has changed to things more modern.

The old division with which Gordon and I grew up of multiple disar-ticulated burials in the Neolithic and crouched inhumation, then cremation, burials in the Bronze Age is now known to be totally inadequate (Gibson 2007, and see Chapter 5, this volume). Thanks to the widespread application of radiocarbon dates from carefully selected samples, crouched inhumations can be seen to span both periods, the rite of cremation is equally long-lived and disarticulated remains persist into the second millennium. Cremations, crouched inhumations and disarticulated inhumations are still all classed as burials, and those that are accompanied by broadly contemporary artefacts are normally classed as 'rich'. Bronze Age burials in particular are often deemed to be those of a 'social elite'. These interpretations are influenced by our modern ideas of what constitutes a burial and by our materialistic environment that equates possessions with wealth: the variables are rarely considered. Unless a body has been left to medical science and/or involved in serious trauma, in our present society a 'burial', whether by inhumation or cremation is a respectful way of disposing of the complete mortal remains of (usually) a loved one. It is most frequently arranged by the family and is a discrete and final act bestowed upon an individual: an act of closure removing the deceased from the realm of the living. Tributes are normally floral and/or charitable and the grave may be tended (but not disturbed) for a considerable time after the event. The word 'burial' therefore, when dealing with human remains, means something quite specific to us. There is, however, absolutely no evidence to suggest that these views were held by Neolithic and Bronze Age populations. Indeed, it is becoming increasingly obvious that the treatment of human remains in the fourth to second millennia BC was totally alien to our own ideas. Evidence for exposure might suggest that the dead stayed amongst the living for a considerable time. Other variables demonstrate that the methods of disposing of the dead were many. Rather than 'burial' we may be better resorting to a more wordy but less prejudicial term, such as 'the structured deposition/discard of human remains'.

Inhumations: single, multiple and partial

First, there is the question of the individual. Multiple remains are clearly known in the Neolithic and this needs no reiteration here. But multiple inhumations are also encountered in the Beaker period and later as most conclusively demonstrated by Petersen in 1972. Petersen recorded multiple inhumations in both Beaker and Food Vessel graves, particularly, but not exclusively, from the Yorkshire Wolds. These reached up to eleven individuals at Rudston 62 and at least fifteen at Aldro 54 (Peterson 1972: 31), where at both sites articulated burials and 'dismembered remains' were found (Mortimer 1905: 64). More recent finds continue to demonstrate the widespread occurrence of these phenomena. Seven individuals were found associated with a Beaker at South Dumpton Down in Kent (Perkins 2004). These were largely contracted, but also included bone bundles (B7) and incomplete remains (B6), and radiocarbon dates suggest that the deposition, if sequential, was rapid.

The deposit of seven individuals with a Beaker in a cist at Bee Low, Derbyshire, resembles more the chamber of a long barrow than it does a cist in terms of the burial deposit (Marsden 1970). A similar pattern of articulated, disarticulated and partial remains of nine or ten individuals was noted in the grave of the Boscombe Bowmen, Wiltshire (Fitzpatrick 2011). At least one adult (represented only by a skull and fragment of femur) and five children were found in a cist at Linlithgow in West Lothian (Cook 2000), and a crouched inhumation associated with the incomplete disarticulated remains of three others was located with approximately one-third of a Beaker at Monkton in Kent (Bennett *et al.* 2008).

The disturbing of a body by a secondary addition is easy to understand; but less easy to explain is the partial removal of remains, assuming that they were actually there in the first place. What was so important about the missing parts that necessitated their removal or indeed retention? Why not displace or remove the whole body? Who were these people who could share the same grave yet be treated so very differently?

This difference in treatment is further illustrated by the finding of cremations and inhumations in the same grave. Petersen (1972) records thirteen instances on the Yorkshire Wolds where the two modes of burial are in physical contact suggesting that if not actually deposited at the same time, they were closely sequential. What were the factors that governed the choices between these two contemporary but very different rites? The graves that Petersen identifies are associated with Food Vessels and this is interesting. Despite the discrepancy in dates, Food Vessels developed from Middle Neolithic Impressed Ware. The similarities in form and decoration are too close to be coincidental (Gibson 2013). The Middle Neolithic was also a time when cremations and inhumations were being deposited simultaneously as evidenced by the later burials at Duggleby Howe, North Yorkshire (Gibson and Bayliss 2010). Is this evidence for the reinvention of tradition? What is (are) the relationship(s) between the inhumed and the cremated? The status of each individual either in life or immediately prior to death must have been very different for them to have warranted such drastically different treatments.

Second, there is the question of discrete deposits. As well as the multiple examples mentioned above, there are partial examples too as already noted at South Dumpton Down and Linlithgow. The Amesbury Archer, Wiltshire, though at first seeming largely complete, was found to lack a rib (Fitzpatrick 2011). At Manston in Kent, a particularly spineless individual lacked vertebrae (David Perkins, pers. comm.). Some incomplete burials may be explained by taphonomic processes, but this is certainly not the case in all (arguably most?) examples, especially where long and other robust bones are missing. A Beaker burial from Bredon Hill, Worcestershire, lacked a finger – until it was discovered *inside* the skull. Other palaeo-environmental data suggested that the corpse had been exposed (Thomas 1965), and must have been at least cadaverous when deposited. Who were *these* people whose corpses could be mutilated or their skeletal remains rendered incomplete? A particularly striking crouched inhumation at Newborough in Northumberland was associated with a bronze dagger. The bone was poorly preserved and lifted in blocks. Laboratory excavation and analysis found that only the lower part of an individual was represented and that the 'head' was in fact the pelvis and that the arms and legs comprised a leg each (Newman and Miket 1973). Initially identified as a female, this burial has now been re-examined and it is thought more likely to be male as befits the dagger association (Gamble and Fowler 2013). In this case, it does not seem to have been the removal of bones that accounts for the situation, but rather the deliberate placing of partial skeletal remains to resemble a complete deposit. Who was *this* person? What on earth is going on here?

Other so-called deviant burials can be documented in antiquarian and more recent literature. At Grendon, in Northamptonshire, within a pit group, an adult was laid over an infant in Pit 9: both were face down. In Pit 6, only a lower leg and foot was found, apparently articulated (Gibson and McCormick 1985). The possible 'head' burials at Dalgety, Fife, are also notable in this context. Though the preservation was poor, it appeared that the teeth had been in their mandibles when deposited and the size of the pits precluded the presence of complete bodies (Watkins 1982: 81–3). From the dental evidence, Pit 2 contained the teeth of a child and three young adults. Pit 3 included the teeth of a child and a young adult, and Pit 6 produced the teeth of one child and the token cremation of another. This practice is reminiscent of a pit at Esh's Barrow, East Yorkshire, that contained three skulls that had been 'placed in contact with each other so as to present the trefoil figure' (Greenwell 1877: 206). Two skulls had been positioned on their crowns and represented mature adults, one being described as 'an aged woman'. The third, that of an adolescent of about 15 years old, was set on its base and was associated with 'some cervical vertebrae and others from amongst the upper bones of the body lying in connection with it and apparently *in situ*' (*ibid.*). Who were *these* people?

Cremations: single, multiple and partial

Fragmentary burial is at its most obvious amongst cremations. Aside from the 'crematoria' underneath some long barrows, now widely believed to be burnt mortuary structures (Vyner 1984, 1986), the rite of cremation escalates in the later Neolithic. Once again, in Bronze Age contexts, more than one individual is frequently identified amongst the cremated bone, with at least four individuals represented by a Collared Urn cremation at Weasenham Lyngs, Norfolk (Petersen and Healy 1986). This multiple deposit is unlikely to be explained as accidental incorporation resulting from the re-use of a pyre site. Though some pyre sites have been identified from areas of burning below round barrows, our idea of pyres is heavily influenced by ethnography and the descriptions of Virgil and Homer (where, incidentally, the sacrificed bodies of twelve Trojan prisoners were placed on the pyre of Patroklos;

Iliad, Book 23). At Carneddau in Powys, there was clear evidence for the burning not of a body, but of body parts, possibly defleshed, in a pit. The pit was too small to have held a complete body, but it had cremated bone and charcoal mixed through its fill; it had been slightly undercut as if the flames had been stoked with a pole, and the edges of the pit were heavily burnt (Gibson 1993: 8). Other cremation-bearing pits with heat-affected sides have been explained as resulting from the deposition of the cremated remains while they were still hot (e.g., Longworth 1984: 47). This, however, is clearly not the case as it would take considerable and sustained heat to completely oxidise the pit sides, and it is more likely that they also provide evidence for *in situ* cremation or at least pyro-ritual activity. From this it is evident that not all cremations need to have been pyre cremations and once again there is evidence for selection of body parts (and probably individuals). It is well known that some cremation deposits are little more than token amounts of human bone. Complete cremations are rare even when allowing for the greater combustion combustibility of some bones (McKinley 1989, 2013). The infant ear bones from Collared Urn burials in north Wales clearly indicate selection, even allowing for their comparative density and therefore their greater chance of surviving cremation (Lynch 1991). Who were *these* people?

Around 3000 BC at Balbirnie in Fife, deposits of cremated bone were being placed in holes in the ground at the same time as stones were being inserted into them (Ritchie 1974; Gibson 2010a). With the exception of cremation IV (adult, ?female), the deposits are far less than one might expect for the cremated remains of an individual (McKinley 2013). They are token deposits and, where the sex can be determined, they appear to be female. Who were *these* women that small amounts of their remains could be placed in a pit prior to it receiving a stone? Surely they were special. Specialness, however, does not imply rank or social status. Surely the importance of these deposits results from their treatment and their context. Their importance in death and the act of deposition need not reflect their status in life. They may have been propitiatory, dedicatory, sacrifices in the broadest sense. They may even have been unknown – bones taken from a mass repository. The apparent uniformity of gender, however, may argue against this. Similar careful selection, and mixing, of human remains appears to be evident at the Middle Neolithic cremation cemetery at Forteviot, Perth and Kinross, where nine discrete cremation burials were found pre-dating the henge within which they were found. At least some of these deposits indicate the mixing of cremated bones of adults and children (Noble and Brophy 2011, 2015).

Grave goods

The social status of the deceased in the Neolithic and Bronze Age is, to say the least, ambiguous. Floral and food (animal bone) tributes can be documented, although in only one instance, the Early Bronze Age Forteviot dagger burial, Perth and Kinross, have flowers been recovered from such a grave, in this case copious quantities of meadowsweet (Noble and Brophy 2011). Tipping's analysis of the pollen recovered from Bronze Age graves concluded that the dominance of single pollen types suggested that the pollen was 'the product of anthropogenic deposition' (Tipping 1994: 137). The lime (Tilia) pollen at Ashgrove, Fife, coming from the Beaker, may also have represented honey (Henshall 1964). Cattle and sheep bones were recovered from the grave of the Boscombe Bowmen (Fitzpatrick 2011), whilst pig bones were associated with the primary and secondary cremations at Sarn-y-bryn-caled in Powys. Usually interpreted as food remains, this may again be over-simplistic given that the pig bone from the secondary cremation at Sarn-y-bryn-caled produced a radiocarbon date much older than that obtained from the cremated human bone (Gibson 2010b).

Nevertheless, the majority of tributes that survive in the archaeological record comprise a suite of artefacts many of which had their origin in the Middle Neolithic (Gibson, forthcoming). These artefacts have been considered as representative of the deceased in life (Case 1977: 81; Woodward 2000: 37). Thus, arrowheads in a grave represent an archer; leather-working tools represent former artisans; dagger and gold-associated skeletons represent high-status individuals – the social elite. Indeed, the very fact that some of these people are being given formal burial may itself be a sign of their elevated status. But this too may be over-simplistic and heavily biased by our own experience. Before the hypothesis is blandly accepted, it must be questioned.

For example, it is being shown that many of the artefacts that accompany Early Bronze Age skeletons were already old when deposited (Woodward 2002). Indeed, some were broken. Some cups from Early Bronze Age cremations in Scotland have been identified as firing wasters (Gibson 2004) and are incomplete. Ongoing research on the English corpus is also identifying a comparatively large number of wasters. At Fan in south Wales, the firing spall had been retained with the cup, and the Collared Urns from the same barrow were also firing wasters, the fabrics having sintered and bloated (Gibson, in Schlee 2014). These may well have been fired on the pyre and may have been made specifically for the funerary ritual. Many urns and Food Vessels that accompany skeletal material are also far from complete. The Food Vessel from Doune, Stirling, is but a sherd (McLaren 2004). From North Mains, Strathallan, also Perth and Kinross, the Food Vessel with Burial E comprised six sherds and the Beaker with Burial F was 'substantially complete wanting only parts of the lower body' – in other words *not* complete (Cowie, in Barclay 1983: 157). The desire to illustrate archaeological ceramics at their best and the restoration of many specimens in museum collections makes the actual extent of survival difficult to assess from published literature alone. While in some cases plough damage can be invoked to account for the incomplete pots, in others, such as cists or contexts protected below cairns and barrows, it is clear that the pot could not have been complete at the time of deposition (unless, like body parts, some artefacts suffered later disturbance and partial removal). Fragments of rim missing from inverted Collared Urns (Gibson 1993: 17) and use-wear traces on vessels attesting earlier episodes in their biographies (MacGregor 1998) both illustrate that many pots associated with skeletal material were less than pristine.

Some of the items that comprise this old and damaged material have been described as 'curated' or as 'heirlooms' (Woodward 2002: *passim*). The latter term in particular should be avoided as it is loaded with a significance that may not have been intended by the depositors of the material. Interpreting these artefacts as heirlooms assumes that they belonged to the individual (or his/her kin-group) with whom they were associated. This may have been the case, but it is by no means certain. In examples of modern 'sacrifice', such as the donation of objects to charities, old items are often donated, heirlooms seldom are. The artefacts that we find associated with Neolithic and Bronze Age skeletal remains must have been deposited by the living and therefore they may equally have belonged to those attending the rites rather than to the subject of them. Some were not just old, but broken, no longer fit for purpose: disposable.

These grave goods may therefore have been votive, symbolic, saying more about the living than the dead. Within recent memory, the makeshift shrines that followed the death of Diana, Princess of Wales, comprised not just extensive floral tributes but also symbolic 'votive gifts' from mourners: teddy bears, children's toys including dolls and Lego, football colours and other personal items were all deposited. Many (probably most, but this cannot be evaluated) had been used. They may have held significance, even value, to the depositors, but they were *not* heirlooms. This public outpouring of grief and the need to leave mementoes attests how Diana was regarded by the public rather than what she actually represented in life: there were none of the expensive trappings that one associates with aristocracy and royalty. That came later, in the funeral ceremony and ritual, and those rites have left little archaeological trace. If, in some future documentary, a panel is tasked with naming three things that represented Diana, it is highly unlikely that teddy bears, Barbie dolls or Manchester United scarves would rate highly. Landmines (and the awareness she brought to their dangers and brutality) may more readily come to mind.

When considering who these people were, 'the Diana principle' must be kept in mind. Arrowheads do not necessarily imply an archer, an observation

unequivocally made at Stonehenge (Evans 1984) where the arrowhead
trauma in the individual is unlikely to have been self-inflicted! Artefacts
that we deem to have high status do not *necessarily* reflect the individual's
position in life. Even if wearing items (necklaces, wristguards), this does
not prove that those items originally *belonged* to the individual. The ritual
practice of depositing old items in pits is well attested in the Neolithic and
Bronze Age (Harding 2006; Garrow 2007), and at the writer's own site of
Upper Ninepence in Powys, the flint artefacts and ceramics had all come
from the domestic sphere. The flints showed evidence of trampling and it
was suggested that it was midden material that was being votively buried
(Gibson 1999). Rather than formal discrete burials, it may be possible to
regard some graves as elaborate pit deposits involving not just the deposition
of artefacts, but also the structured deposition of human remains, perhaps
complete, perhaps multiple, perhaps incomplete, perhaps burnt. The skeletal remains therefore may not represent a burial in the modern sense, but
rather a component of artefact deposition: the ultimate in structured deposition, a sacrifice in the broadest sense. Who were *these* people?

Burial context

The associated burial furniture is therefore ambiguous in the extreme and
cannot be treated at face value. The richness of an artefact need not be
directly transferable to the human remains with which it was associated.
The human remains may have formed part of this rich deposition. In order
to address the question of who these people were, context rather than artefactual association may be a more profitable route. The burials within the
henge at North Mains may be a case in point, assuming that they are directly
connected to the construction of the monument rather than just broadly
contemporary. Parallels may be drawn with the central Beaker burial at
Balfarg, Fife (Mercer 1981); perhaps the dagger burial at Forteviot, Perth
and Kinross (Noble and Brophy 2011); the Beaker associated monumental
cist burials at Cairnpapple, West Lothian (Piggott 1948); and the infant with
the cleft skull at Woodhenge, Wiltshire (Cunnington 1929). Once again several scenarios present themselves.

The henge monuments may have been reconstructed around the burials out of respect to their occupants' former rank in life. This is difficult to
prove as our chronologies are rarely so precise as to be specific about the
sequence in absolute terms. However, if the burials are later than the construction of the earthwork, for example, at Cairnpapple Hill (Piggott 1948)
and the Forteviot dagger burial (Noble and Brophy 2011; Kenneth Brophy,
pers. comm.), then the same conclusion could be drawn: the status of the
individual warranted burial in such a prestigious position. As argued above,
associations may not necessarily denote status, therefore the artefactual pov-
erty of the graves need not counter this hypothesis. The cleaving of the skull

of the Woodhenge child, however, does not overtly suggest a prestigious individual except in the manner of his or her death and the context of his or her deposition. That said, this particular act may also be ambiguous and the manner of execution a result of the child's status: the end of a dynasty, for example, or the captured child of a rival and hostile chief. This is admittedly subjective and unprovable, but without written records to flesh the bones it is offered as an example of another possible scenario.

The internal ditches of henges, it has been claimed, may have been designed to keep dark internal forces contained within their realms (Warner 2000). Warner was referring to later prehistoric Irish sites, but his hypothesis has proved attractive to Neolithic studies in Britain (e.g., Barclay 2005; Bradley 2011; Brophy and Noble 2012). If this hypothesis is accepted, then perhaps those buried within henge enclosures were perceived as having powers that needed containing. The large cist covers at Forteviot and Balfarg might support this conjecture. The lack of any monumental grave construction at North Mains and Woodhenge might not. The burials at Cairnpapple were contained by the massive stones of the dismantled stone circle seemingly associated with the building of one monument (the henge) and the dismantling of another (the stone circle) (Piggott 1948; Barclay 1999; Bradley 2011). But it is often forgotten that as well as a flint cairn over the grave at Woodhenge, the internal area may also have been sealed by a mound as the monument was originally named 'The Dough Cover' from its low mounded interior (Cunnington 1929: 3). So, too, may the Balfarg henge have had an internal mound accounting for the paucity of plough marks in the interior (Gibson 2010a), and a similar argument has been made for Forteviot henges 1 and 2 (Brophy and Noble 2012). The mound at Cairnpapple is clear.

A more prosaic explanation for the internal ditches of henges has been proposed elsewhere, namely, that they provide a means of delineating and closing a site that has already had a ritual biography (Gibson 2010c). The dumping of the spoil on the *outside* does not compromise the internal space. The ditch is the important enclosing feature with banks (if any existed – there was none, for example, at Llandegai B (Lynch and Musson 2004)) often having an unfinished appearance (Avebury, Arbor Low), though admittedly they may still have formed a screen. If this is the case, then it may be that people buried within these monuments, rather than representing an elite, were in fact propitiatory as has been suggested above and that their interment formed part of the closing ritual.

This perspective may be supported by the fact that recent research is demonstrating that henges such as Gordon Barclay's own site at North Mains (Barclay 1983) were constructed on sites that already possessed ritual significance and, often, a previous monumental history (Gibson 2010a; Bradley 2011; papers in Gibson 2012; Chapter 7, this volume). In enclosing this ritual space and confining the otherworld forces, did these forces also have to be pacified? Was the deposition of human remains the means of this pacification? Admittedly, this is conjecture and as archaeologists we should shun the speculative, but it is not at all sensationalist as human sacrifice or ritual killings can be well-supported in later prehistory (e.g., Lindow Man), the Classical literature, ethnographically and historically; and it is commonly agreed from historical and ethnographic parallels that people in the Neolithic must have had deep superstitions, complex mythologies and powerful belief systems that doubtless required proper ritual responses. Whilst there may be no direct evidence for this hypothesis, there is equally no evidence against it. It may be unprovable, but it is logical and the suggestion should not be ignored. These 'henged' burials were the original subjects of Gordon Barclay's question.

Violence and outsiders

There is also a considerable quantity of data for the violent deaths of individuals in prehistory generally, but increasingly so in the fourth to second millennia (Schulting and Wysocki 2005). As well as cranial trauma, arrowhead burials where the projectile point is actually within the skeleton are also known; and the body from the Stonehenge ditch has already been mentioned. Doubtless more examples will be found as detailed palaeo-osteology becomes more routinely applied and more advanced. Death by soft tissue damage must also have occurred, yet will leave no skeletal traces identifiable by current methods. Recent work on the burial sequence at Duggleby Howe has also identified not just trauma, but other questions relating to those interred (Gibson and Ogden 2008; Gibson and Bayliss 2010). Burial K, for example, at the base of the 2.75 m deep pit and within a wooden coffin, showed no sign of trauma amongst the surviving bones, but his mandible showed signs of weathering. He had been exposed, buried when skeletal, yet arranged in a contracted position according to Mortimer's (1905) description. Above him, Burial I has signs of possible perimortem cranial trauma, though it is obscured by Mortimer's reconstructive materials. The accompanying Skull J, however, had major blunt force trauma to both parietals and the symmetry of the damage suggests that he or she (either female or a gracile male; Gibson and Ogden 2008) may have been executed by means of a blow from above whilst the head was resting on an anvil stone. Traces of a cut to the forehead and a healed nasal fracture further demonstrate that this individual had a less than cosseted life. Who were *these* people?

    Isotope analysis has shown that, whoever they were, they were not local to the chalk (Montgomery *et al.* 2007). With isotope analysis it is often easy to say where people did *not* originate, but tracing their origins is somewhat more problematic. Given this, it is possible that the individual in Duggleby Howe Burial K came from as far away as north-western Scotland or Cornwall. The places of origin of the others may have been closer to Duggleby, but they were not from the chalk. On current evidence, the inhumation burial sequence at Duggleby Howe lasted for just over half a millennium, yet no chalk-dwellers seem to have featured in this sequence. Were they brought to the area for burial? Were they vanquished enemies or slaves? The brutally executed Skull J may be important here. If foreigners were being buried, where does this leave our notions of the importance of ancestry in the Neolithic? Perhaps ancestors or any social elite that may have existed were buried differently; not for them being dumped in a hole in the ground.

A similar scenario has been demonstrated in a multiple pit burial of a woman and three children at Monkton Up Wimborne, Dorset (Green 2000). DNA analysis shows that the group comprised a mother and her young daughter and a brother and sister unrelated to the other two. The youngest child suffered from malnutrition and the others were iron deficient. Isotope analysis suggests that, like Duggleby, these people were foreign to Cranborne Chase possibly coming from the lead-rich area of Mendip (Green 2000: 78–9). There is nothing in the stratigraphy of the grave to suggest sequential burial here and the question as to why four foreigners of different ages were buried simultaneously remains unanswered. Who were *these* people?

In the early third millennium, aside from six child inhumations, the preferred rite changed to cremation at Duggleby. Instead of in the ground, these remains were deposited above it, in the primary mound itself constructed around the twenty-ninth century cal. BC (Gibson and Bayliss 2010). There was clearly a change in context as well as in rite. Who were *these* people? The cremated remains from Duggleby can no longer be located so any patterns of age and gender must, unfortunately, remain unknown.

Some 'burials' also appear to have been sealed rather more securely than necessary. The monumental cists at Cairnpapple Hill have already been mentioned as has the huge cist cover at Balfarg (Mercer 1981). At Forteviot, the cist capping stone weighed several tonnes (Noble and Brophy 2011) and a large cist cover was also found at Cist 1 at Dalgety (Watkins 1982, fig. 3). Could this have been to keep in hostile spirits or, more prosaically, to keep out grave robbers? Certainly, the conspicuous effort involved in the procuring, moving and placing of these large stones sets these cists above the norm. It is, however, generally assumed that the large cist covers and cairns or barrows sealed the graves of the dead, but what if their occupants were not dead at the time of deposition? Human sacrifice or ritual killing has been discussed above at Stonehenge, Woodhenge and Duggleby Howe. It was also suggested at Sarn-y-bryn-caled (Gibson 1994). It has been mentioned above that perimortem trauma is seen on some skeletons, but equally fatal soft-tissue injury must remain undetected. At the circular ditched enclosure (*Kreisgrabenanlage*) at Ippesheim, Bavaria, a skeleton was found inverted in a pit at the centre of the enclosure. The sex of the skeleton could not be determined, but careful excavation allowed a reconstruction to be made and it could be seen that the left hand had been held downwards towards the pit base in order to break a fall, whilst the right hand covered the mouth to protect against inevitable suffocation (Schier 2005). The late *Linearbandkeramik* (LBK) enclosure at Ippesheim cannot be directly compared in either time or space with the henges of the British Neolithic, but that is not the point of this example. Rather, it illustrates that live burial was practiced in Neolithic Europe, but that detecting it must rely on exceptional circumstances. Whether this explains the monumental cist covers or not, the perimortem trauma that survives on some human remains, and the arrowhead injuries in others suggest that some bodies were treated very differently in death and subsequent deposition; not all was cornfields and pan-pipes amongst our early farming communities.

The Bronze Age pit graves such as Aldro 54 (Mortimer 1905: 64–6) may be another way of ensuring containment of the bodies. This was over 3 m deep and the treatment of the bones within it diverse. The basal deposit was of an adult and child and 'some of the adult leg bones seemed to have been split lengthways in the manner in which animal bones are frequently found' (Mortimer 1905: 66). The second burial, associated with a Beaker, comprised a 'large heap' of human bone and the 'calvarium of an adult was the receptacle for a collection of tarsal and metatarsal bones, vertebrae, the joint end of a large leg bone and portions of a skull' (Mortimer 1905: 66). Mortimer observed that the skull had been deliberately packed. There were also child bones and six jaws representing four children under ten and two adults. At Garton Slack, C41, at the base of a pit almost 2 m deep was the inhumation of a man, with pig bones and over his hips was an articulated human fore-arm and hand from another individual (Mortimer 1905: 259). In the middle fill of the pit was a burial with a handled Food Vessel and a cup. The pit grave (*c.* 2 m deep) at Garton Slack 75 was also associated with a Food Vessel, and the primary burial of a mature male seems to have been in a slightly odd position with one hand under the chin and the other down by his knees. These pit graves recall Duggleby Howe almost two millennia earlier. Once again are we seeing the return to pre-Beaker ways? Do the depths of the pits ensure containment of these individuals in an area devoid of large stones which elsewhere could have achieved the same result?

Mortimer's descriptions of many of the interments he recorded do not seem to conform to the accepted 'crouched inhumation' norm. Bodies may be in unusual positions as mentioned above; and at Garton Slack 81, the body of a female who appears to have had part of her foot amputated, was placed with her head forced back, one hand by her chest and the other by her thighs (Mortimer 1905: fig. 602). She seems to have been dumped rather than placed, and this can be seen elsewhere in Mortimer's descriptions. Who were *these* people?

Conclusion

One of the fundamental problems with any approach to the archaeology of human remains in the Neolithic and Bronze Ages are the words 'burial' and 'funerary'. They are loaded with modern interpretations and influenced by current practices and values. No matter how we try to detach ourselves, the idea of burying an individual and the funeral rites that are performed come from our current cultural backgrounds and mind frames. The use of the term 'deviant' for burials that do not conform to our norms illustrates this perfectly. Indeed, in the fourth to second millennia BC, it may have been the complete discrete burial that was considered 'deviant'. Our twenty-first-century minds must be opened and it must be recognised that the hugely diverse treatments of human remains in the Neolithic and Bronze Age probably requires equally diverse explanations and interpretations.

Gordon's original question was specifically asked of the people buried with Food Vessels at the time that the North Mains henge was constructed, but, as Gordon doubtless knew at the time, the question is much deeper. 'Who were these people?' is a fundamental question that all archaeologists must strive to answer, but answers must, at least for the time being, remain elusive. We have no historical records. The data that we use to reconstruct Neolithic and Bronze Age society are not only ambiguous but also incomplete. Material remains represent but a small part of what must have been complex and deep-rooted belief systems and rituals. The deposition of bone must have played a part in those rituals, but not necessarily or always an important part.

It is also clear that not all (possibly the minority) of the population were receiving burial; for instance, the multiple burials at some long barrows seem to have happened over a very short time interval in relation to the duration of the Early Neolithic (Whittle *et al.* 2011). What was happening to the majority of the population? From the treatment of some of the remains noted above, it appears unlikely that it was only the elite that were being buried. Rather, it seems that particular people/bodies/bones were being selected for burial. Who were these people and who were the selectors? The answer to the specific question is, at present, known only by those specific people who treated the remains of their contemporaries in such a rich variety of different ways and over a considerable space of time and place.

Bibliography

Barclay, G. J. (1983), 'Sites of the third millennium BC to the first millennium AD at North Mains, Strathallan, Perthshire', *Proceedings of the Society of Antiquaries of Scotland*, 113: 122–281.

Barclay, G. J. (1999), 'Cairnpapple revisited: 1948–1998', *Proceedings of the Prehistoric Society*, 65: 17–46.

Barclay, G. J. (2005), 'The henge and hengiform in Scotland', in V. Cummings and A. Pannett (eds), *Set in Stone: New Approaches to Neolithic Monumentality in Scotland*, Oxford: Oxbow Books, 81–93.

Bennett, P., Clark, P., Hicks, A., Rady, J. and Riddler, I. (2008), *At the Great Crossroads. Prehistoric, Roman and Medieval Discoveries on the Isle of Thanet, 1994–95*, Canterbury: Canterbury Archaeological Trust.

Bradley, R. (2011), *Stages and Screens: An Investigation into Henge Monuments in Northern and North-eastern Scotland*, Edinburgh: Society of Antiquaries of Scotland.

Brophy, K. and Noble, G. (2012), 'Henging, mounding and blocking: the Forteviot henge group', in A. Gibson (ed.), *Enclosing the Neolithic. Recent Studies in Britain and Europe*, Oxford: British Archaeological Reports, 21–35.

Case, H. J. (1977), 'The Beaker cultures in Britain and Ireland', in R. Mercer (ed.), *Beakers in Britain and Europe: Four Studies*, Oxford: British Archaeological Reports, 71–101.

Cook, M. (2000), 'An Early Bronze Age multiple burial cist from Mill Road Industrial Estate, Linlithgow, West Lothian', *Proceedings of the Society of Antiquaries of Scotland*, 130: 77–91.

Cunnington, M. E. (1929), *Woodhenge: A Description of the Site as Revealed by Excavations Carried out there by Mr & Mrs B. H. Cunnington, 1926–7–8*, Devizes: George Simpson.

Evans, J. G. (1984), 'Stonehenge: the environment in the Late Neolithic and Early Bronze Age and a Beaker Age burial', *Wiltshire Archaeological and Natural History Magazine*, 78: 7–30.

Fitzpatrick, A. P. (2011), *The Amesbury Archer and the Boscombe Bowmen. Bell Beaker Burials at Boscombe Down, Amesbury, Wiltshire*, Salisbury: Wessex Archaeology.

Gamble, M. and Fowler, C. (2013), 'A re-assessment of Early Bronze Age human remains in Tyne and Wear Museums: results and implications for interpreting Early Bronze Age burials from north-east England and beyond', *Archaeologia Aeliana*, 5th ser., 42: 47–80.

Garrow, D. (2007), 'Placing pits: occupation and depositional practice during the Neolithic in East Anglia', *Proceedings of the Prehistoric Society*, 73: 1–24.

Gibson, A. M. (1993), 'The excavation of two cairns and associated features at Carneddau, Carno, Powys, 1989–90', *Archaeological Journal*, 150: 1–45.

Gibson, A. M. (1994), 'Excavations at the Sarn-y-bryn-caled cursus complex, Welshpool, Powys and the timber circles of Great Britain and Ireland', *Proceedings of the Prehistoric Society*, 60: 143–223.

Gibson, A. M. (1999), *The Walton Basin Project: Excavation and Survey in a Prehistoric Landscape*, York: Council for British Archaeology and Cadw.

Gibson, A. M. (2004), 'Small but perfectly formed? Some observations on the Bronze Age cups of Scotland', in A. Gibson and A. Sheridan (eds), *From Sickles to Circles*, 270–88.

Gibson, A. M. (2007), 'A Beaker veneer? Some evidence from the burial record', in M. Larsson and M. Parker Pearson (eds), *From Stonehenge to the Baltic*, 47–64.

Gibson, A. M. (2010a), 'Dating Balbirnie: recent radiocarbon dates from the stone circle and cairn at Balbirnie, Fife, and a review of its place in the overall Balfarg/ Balbirnie site sequence', *Proceedings of the Society of Antiquaries of Scotland*, 140: 51–78.

Gibson, A. M. (2010b), 'New dates for Sarn-y-bryn-caled, Powys, Wales', *Proceedings of the Prehistoric Society*, 76: 351–56.

Gibson, A. M. (2010c), 'Excavation and survey at Dyffryn Lane Henge complex, Powys and a reconsideration of the dating of henges', *Proceedings of the Prehistoric Society*, 76: 213–48.

Gibson, A. M. (ed.) (2012), *Enclosing the Neolithic. Recent Studies in Britain and Europe*, Oxford: British Archaeological Reports.

Gibson, A. M. (2013), 'Neolithic ceramic sequence in the Milfield Basin: holy grails and missing points. Some comments on Millson *et al.* 2011', *Archaeologia Aeliana*, 5th ser., 42: 35–46.

Gibson, A. M (forthcoming), 'Beaker burials in the context of the Neolithic and Bronze Age', in M. Parker Pearson (ed.), *The Beaker People Project*.

Gibson, A. and Bayliss, A. (2010), 'Recent research at Duggleby Howe, North Yorkshire', *Archaeological Journal*, 166: 39–78.

Gibson, A. M. and McCormick, A. (1985), 'Archaeology at Grendon Quarry, Northamptonshire, Part 1: Neolithic and Bronze Age sites excavated 1974–75', *Northamptonshire Archaeology*, 20: 23–66.

Gibson, A. and Ogden, A. (2008), 'Duggleby Howe, Burial J and the Eastern Yorkshire Club scene', *Yorkshire Archaeological Journal*, 80: 1–13.

Gibson, A. and Sheridan, A. (eds) (2004), *From Sickles to Circles: Britain and Ireland at the Time of Stonehenge*, Stroud: Tempus.

Green, M. (2000), *A Landscape Revealed: 10,000 Years on a Chalkland Farm*, Stroud: Tempus.

Greenwell, W. (1877), *British Barrows*, Oxford: Clarendon Press.

Harding, J. (2006), 'Pit-digging, occupation and structured deposition on Rudston Wold, Eastern Yorkshire', *Oxford Journal of Archaeology*, 25: 109–26.

Henshall, A. S. (1964), 'A dagger-grave and other cist burials at Ashgrove, Methilhill, Fife', *Proceedings of the Society of Antiquaries of Scotland*, 97: 166–79.

Larsson, M. and Parker Pearson, M. (eds) (2007), *From Stonehenge to the Baltic. Living with Cultural Diversity in the Third Millennium BC*, Oxford: British Archaeological Reports.

Longworth, I. H. (1984), *Collared Urns of the Bronze Age in Great Britain and Ireland*, Cambridge: Cambridge University Press.

Lynch, F. (1991), *Prehistoric Anglesey*, 2nd edn, Llangefni: Anglesey Antiquarian Society.

Lynch, F. M. and Musson, C. R. (2004), 'A prehistoric and early medieval complex at Llandegai, near Bangor, North Wales', *Archaeologia Cambrensis*, 150: 17–142.

MacGregor, G. (1998), 'The excavation of a Cordoned Urn at Benderloch, Argyll', *Proceedings of the Society of Antiquaries of Scotland*, 128: 143–59.

Marsden, B. M. (1970), 'The excavation of the Bee Low Round Cairn, Youlgreave, Derbyshire', *Antiquaries Journal*, 50: 186–215.

McKinley, J. (1989), 'Cremations: expectations, methodologies and realities', in C. A. Roberts, F. Lee and J. Bintliff (eds), *Burial Archaeology. Current Research, Methods and Developments*, Oxford: British Archaeological Reports, 65–76.

McKinley, J. (2013), 'Cremation: excavation, analysis and interpretation of material from cremation related-contexts', in S. Tarlow and L. Nilsson Stutz (eds), *The Oxford Handbook of the Archaeology of Death and Burial*, Oxford: Oxford University Press, 147–72.

McLaren, D. (2004), 'An important child's burial from Doune, Perth and Kinross', in Gibson and Sheridan (eds), *From Sickles to Circles*, 289–303.

Mercer, R. J. (1981), 'The excavation of a Late Neolithic henge-type enclosure at Balfarg, Markinch, Fife, Scotland', *Proceedings of the Society of Antiquaries of Scotland*, 111: 63–171.

Montgomery, J., Cooper, R. E. and Evans, J. A. (2007), 'Foragers, farmers or foreigners? An assessment of dietary strontium isotope variation in Early and Middle Neolithic East Yorkshire', in Larsson and Parker Pearson (eds), *From Stonehenge to the Baltic*, 65–75.

Mortimer, J. R. (1905), *Forty Years' Researches in British and Saxon Burial Mounds of East Yorkshire*, London: A. Brown & Sons.

Newman, T. G. and Miket, R. F. (1973), 'A Dagger grave at Allerwash, Newborough, Northumberland', *Archaeologia Aeliana*, 5th ser., 1: 87–95.

Noble, G. and Brophy, K. (2011), 'Ritual to remembrance at a prehistoric ceremonial complex in central Scotland: excavations at Forteviot, Perth and Kinross', *Antiquity*, 85: 787–804.

Noble, G. and Brophy, K. (2015) 'Transforming place and architecture through cremation: cremation traditions at the third millennium BC monument complex at Forteviot, Central Scotland', in L. Larsson (ed.), *What's New in the Neolithic?* Lund: Lund University Press, 164–72.

Perkins, D. (2004), 'Oval barrows in Thanet', in J. Cotton and D. Field (eds), *Towards a New Stone Age. Aspects of the Neolithic in South-East England*, York: Council for British Archaeology, 76–81.

Petersen, F. (1972), 'Traditions of multiple burial in later Neolithic and early Bronze Age Britain', *Archaeological Journal*, 129, 22–55.

Petersen, F. and Healy, F. (1986), 'The excavation of two round barrows and a ditched enclosure on Weasenham Lyngs, 1972', *Barrow Excavations in Norfolk, 1950–82, East Anglian Archaeology*, 29: 70–103.

Piggott, S. (1948), 'The excavations at Cairnpapple Hill, West Lothian, 1947–48', *Proceedings of the Society of Antiquaries of Scotland*, 10: 68–123.

Ritchie, J. N. G. (1974), 'Excavation of the stone circle and cairn at Balbirnie, Fife', *Archaeological Journal*, 131: 1–32.

Schier, W. (2005), 'Kopfüber ins Jenseits – Ein Menschenopfer in der Kreisgrabenanlage von Ippesheim?', in F. Daim and W. Neubauer (eds), *Zeitreise*

Heldenberg Geheimnisvolle Kreisgräben: Niederösterreichische Landesausstellung 2005, Horn-Wien: Berger, 234–8.

Schulting, R. J. and Wysocki, M. (2005), ' "In this chambered tumulus were found cleft skulls …": an assessment of the evidence for cranial trauma in the British Neolithic', *Proceedings of the Prehistoric Society*, 71: 107–38.

Schlee, D. (2014), 'The excavation of Fan round barrow, near Talsarn, Ceredigion, 2010–11', *Archaeologia Cambrensis*, 162: 67–104.

Tipping, R. (1994), ' "Ritual" floral tributes in the Scottish Bronze Age: the palynological evidence', *Journal of Archaeological Science*, 21: 133–9.

Thomas, N. (1965), 'A double Beaker burial on Bredon Hill, Worcestershire', *Birmingham Archaeological Society Transactions and Proceedings*, 82: 58–76.

Vyner, B. E. (1984), 'The excavation of a Neolithic cairn at Street House, Loftus, Cleveland', *Proceedings of the Prehistoric Society*, 50: 151–96.

Vyner, B. E. (1986), 'Evidence for mortuary practices in the Neolithic and burial mounds and cairns of northern Britain', *Scottish Archaeological Review*, 4: 11–16.

Warner, R. (2000), 'Keeping out the otherworld. The internal ditch at Navan and other Iron Age "hengiform enclosures" ', *Emania*, 18: 39–44.

Watkins, T. (1982), 'The excavation of an Early Bronze Age cemetery at Barns Farm, Dalgety, Fife', *Proceedings of the Society of Antiquaries of Scotland*, 112: 48–141.

Whittle, A. W. R., Healy, F. and Bayliss, A. (2011), *Gathering Time: Dating the Early Neolithic Enclosures of Southern Britain and Ireland*, Oxford: Oxbow Books.

Woodward, A. (2000), *British Barrows. A Matter of Life and Death*, Stroud: Tempus.

Woodward, A. (2002), 'Beads and beakers: heirlooms and relics in the British Early Bronze Age', *Antiquity*, 76: 1040–7.

CHAPTER 5

Pathways to Ancestral Worlds: Mortuary Practice in the Irish Neolithic

Gabriel Cooney

Introduction: bodies of evidence

In an important contribution to Neolithic studies in Scotland, Gordon Barclay (2003: 132) argued that our understanding of Neolithic society is based on interpretations of burial and ceremonial structures and the changes in practices associated with them. While we have to temper this view with the stunning increase and diversity of settlement-related information arising from recent development-led excavation (e.g., Smyth 2014; Whitehouse *et al.* 2014), it is still largely the case in relation to our understanding of Neolithic people and the treatment of the dead by the living. I wish to address this key issue in the context of the Irish Neolithic. In recent discussion, cremation has been seen as the main mortuary rite during this period (e.g., Malone 2001: 138–40, 163; Jones 2008: 190). By contrast, a number of recent contributions have emphasised the role of inhumation both within particular monumental traditions, such as court tombs and in particular areas, for example, the limestone uplands of the Burren, Co. Clare (Beckett 2011; Schulting *et al.* 2012). The most striking addition to this strand of the literature has been the publication of the Early Neolithic portal tomb of Poulnabrone, also on the Burren, where the unburnt remains of at least thirty-five individuals were recovered (Lynch 2014). It seems an appropriate time then to consider the character of mortuary practice during the Neolithic (3800–2500 cal. BC) in Ireland and to contribute to the discussion about the relationship between the practices of cremation and inhumation (see Schulting *et al.* 2012: 36–9). A related paper focuses particularly on the role of cremation (Cooney 2014); for a focus on inhumation and cremation practice in Britain, see Chapter 4, this volume.

Exploring the 'cremation-dominant' view of mortuary practice during the Irish Neolithic in more detail also indicates the way in which cremation and inhumation have been seen as opposed practices. Bradley (2007a: 60–1, 2007b), in presenting an interpretation of the wider social significance of earlier Neolithic (3800–3600 cal. BC) mortuary practice, contrasted the dominance of cremation as the rite in burial monuments in Ireland and western Scotland with southern Britain, where the human remains indicated that inhumation was the primary mortuary rite in comparable mortuary monuments. Bradley sees this contrast as having a wider interpretive value, showing links between the worlds of the living and the dead. Hence, the burning of contemporary Early Neolithic rectangular houses in Ireland (see Smyth 2014) matches the treatment of human corpses in cremation, while in southern Britain the use of multi-stage inhumation facilitates the circulation of unburnt bone in a context of greater mobility of settlement. These regional contrasts could be seen as continuing into the Middle Neolithic. The mortuary rite in Irish developed passage tombs of the later fourth millennium cal. BC is described as communal cremation (Herity 1974; Eogan 1986; Bergh 1995). The broadly contemporary Maes Howe or Quanterness–Quoyness group of passage tombs in Orkney have many points of similarity with developed Irish passage tombs (Sheridan 1986, 2004). However, in Orkney the burial deposits predominantly consist of inhumed human remains, the result of the successive reduction of corpses to disarticulated bone and re-arrangement within the tombs (Laurence 2006; Schulting *et al.* 2010: 5–11, 25–30).

So what are we to make of this broad characterisation of regional contrasts and the view of cremation and inhumation as opposed mortuary rites? Discussion has demonstrated the contemporary and complementary use of cremation and inhumation in different societies in the past (e.g., Larsson 2003; Larsson and Nilsson Stutz 2014; Williams 2014), and suggests that cremation and inhumation should not be viewed as incompatible. Instead, they are often complementary elements of a coherent set of mortuary practices for handling the remains of the dead and making sense of death (Larsson and Nilsson Stutz 2014: 49). In the context of the Irish Neolithic, Whittle and colleagues (2011: 875) expressed caution about the scenario put forward by Bradley for the earlier Neolithic in light of the short chronology of rectangular houses and the variation of mortuary practice within Ireland. On this latter point, Davidsson (2003: 326) pointed out that different mortuary rites were deployed by people using the same type of megalithic tomb. Kuijt and Quinn (2013: 176), focusing on the character of the commingled human remains in one of the cists at the Mound of the Hostages, Tara passage tomb, Co. Meath (O'Sullivan 2005), commented that in Irish passage tombs mortuary practice included cremation, the inclusion of unburned skeletal parts, complete inhumations or the inclusion of individual unburned bones. Contrasting this potential and proven complexity of practice to the widespread, implicit assumption in the literature that cremation and inhumation were alternative, opposed practices for the post-mortem treatment of the dead in the Irish Neolithic, the extent of the evidence for the contemporaneous and complementary use of the practices of inhumation and cremation clearly needs to be explored.

Perhaps not surprisingly with over 1,500 examples known (Cody 2002), megalithic tombs have tended to dominate discussion of mortuary practice (e.g., Jones 2007). There are four main types of megalithic tomb in Ireland (de Valera and Ó Nualláin 1961). Court, portal and passage tombs all date to the fourth millennium cal. BC, with the most numerous type, wedge tombs, dating to the period 2450–2050 cal. BC (O'Brien 1999; Schulting *et al.* 2008) in the Final Neolithic/Early Bronze Age. Carlin (2011) has demonstrated that wedge tombs represent a notable re-invention of the megalithic tradition at the end of the Neolithic, a period of notable diversity in mortuary practice (Schulting *et al.* 2008: 10–13). But this point about diversity in mortuary practice can be applied more widely to the Irish Neolithic itself and an overview is presented below, focusing on mortuary rites in the Early and Middle Neolithic.

The Early Neolithic (3800–3600 cal. BC): placing the dead in monuments

The evidence from this period is dominated by the results of excavations at megalithic tombs. The portal tomb of Poulnabrone, Co. Clare (Figure 5.1) has produced the earliest, most important and best-dated mortuary assemblage from a tomb of this type (Lynch 2014). Here the disarticulated remains of a minimum of thirty-five individuals (eighteen adults and seventeen sub-adults) were placed on the chamber floor and in grykes in the limestone pavement which formed the floor of chamber over the period from before 3800 cal. BC to 3200 cal. BC (Schulting 2014). There have been changing interpretations of the character of the mortuary deposits at Poulnabrone (Lynch and O'Donnabháin 1994; Cooney 2000; Beckett and Robb 2006). Re-analysis for publication indicates a complex multi-stage mortuary rite which involved the placement of corpses in the tomb, subsequent re-arrangement of, and possible circulation of, disarticulated bone. A small number of bones appear to have been scorched or burnt after the flesh had gone (Beckett 2014; O'Donnabháin and Tesorieri 2014). Commenting on the few dates from other portal tombs in Ireland and south-western Britain, Kytmannow (2008: 110) suggested that cremation generally postdates inhumations in portal tombs, but in reality there is relatively little data from other sites.

Schulting *et al.* (2012) have demonstrated that the range 3700–3570 cal. BC is currently the most probable timeframe for the first use of court tombs with initial construction slightly earlier. This is similar to the date for the rectangular house horizon in Ireland (Smyth 2014: 41–50), and brings us back to the link that has been seen between house burning and cremation as the rite in earlier Neolithic monuments in Ireland and western Scotland, but the evidence is much more complex. Notable links can be seen in the earlier Neolithic between the Clyde Cairns of western and southern Scotland

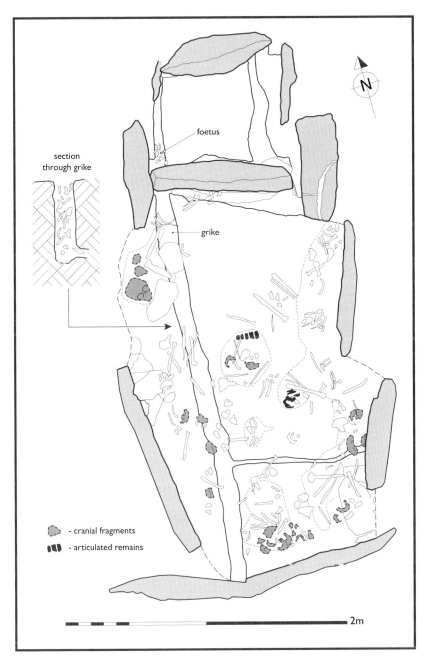

Figure 5.1 The portal tomb at Poulnabrone. Distribution of larger skeletal elements within chamber and portico (after Lynch 2014: fig. 3.6).

(Noble 2006: 104–13) and Irish court tombs, with the concept of shared traditions captured in the term Clyde–Carlingford culture (e.g., Piggott 1954: 152–92). While inhumation actually appears to have been the main rite in Clyde Cairns (Henshall 1972: 82), mortuary practice in court tombs involved the use of both inhumation and cremation (Herity 1987; Schulting *et al.* 2012). Back in Ireland, the best-dated and most comprehensively analysed assemblage is from the tomb at Parknabinnia, Co. Clare, on the limestone upland of the Burren (Jones 2004, 2007; Beckett 2011; Schulting *et al.* 2012). The two chambers contained the remains of a minimum of twenty individuals, 75 per cent of whom were adults, the majority young adults with some older individuals. The character of the material and the depositional patterns suggest that these represent primary inhumations disturbed in the course of successive interments. There was also evidence suggesting the presence of cremated and scorched bone (Beckett 2011: 405).

By contrast, in other court tombs such as Tully, Co. Fermanagh (Waterman 1978) cremation is the only documented mortuary rite (Figure 5.2). Here the front of two chambers contained fragments of cremated bone from two children as part of a floor deposit of burnt soil, charcoal and pottery. In the back chamber a deposit of clay contained the cremated bone of a young adult and in a small cist built against the outer side of the gallery

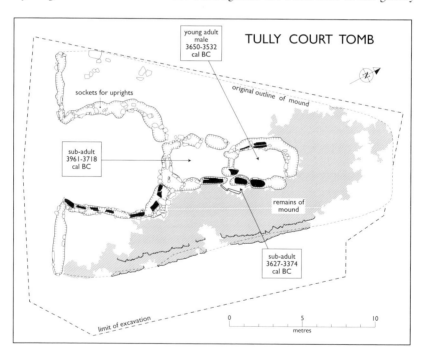

Figure 5.2 Plan of Tully court tomb (based on Waterman 1978) with details of cremation deposit.

there were the fragmentary cremated remains of a child sealed by small stone slabs. Dooey's Cairn, Ballymacaldrack, Co. Antrim (Evans 1938; Collins 1976) provides important evidence of the link between court tomb/Clyde Cairns and non-megalithic funerary traditions in Early Neolithic Ireland and south-west Scotland (Cooney 2000: 99–103; Sheridan 2006), and brings us back to the link with the burning of houses. The burning of a wooden or composite structure containing human remains may have been the process that resulted in the cremated bone deposits representing at least five adults found at Dooey's Cairn. At Pencraig Hill, East Lothian, a similar timber structure of early to mid-fourth millennium cal. BC date in its final phase appears to have been a pyre where disarticulated human remains were cremated (Duffy and MacGregor 2008; see also Chapter 8, this volume).

The Middle Neolithic (3600–3000 cal. BC): a wider place for the dead

Recent discussion framed in the context of a 'boom' after the establishment of farming in Ireland followed by a 'bust' in the Middle Neolithic has suggested that sites belonging to the passage tomb tradition are the most important aspect of the archaeological evidence from this period (Whitehouse *et al.* 2014). In reality, the remains of the dead are found in a wide range of contexts and were treated in diverse ways in the second half of the fourth millennium cal. BC.

Smyth (2014: 116–17) has commented that while the number of pits known from the Middle (and Late) Neolithic is significantly fewer than for the Early Neolithic, the complexity and arrangement of material in them is greater. This includes the deposition of human remains. For example, at Caltragh, Co. Sligo, a small oval pit dating to 3490–3040 cal. BC was dug beside a boulder into the mound of a possible megalithic structure. The first deposit in the pit was a hoard of fifteen flint flakes (all knapped from the same core) and one chert flake. The upper fill consisted of a token deposit of pyre material: charcoal, cremated bone and soil (Danaher 2007: 63). This could be related to a wider and consistent appearance of burnt material in pits, suggesting, first, that fire and burning had an important role in depositional activity (Smyth 2014), and, second, that some pits were used as graves. At Lough Gur, Co. Limerick, a fire appeared to have been lit in a pit prior to the deposition of the flexed body of a child dating to between 3650–3370 cal. BC along with a fragment from a polished stone axehead placed in the mouth cavity (Cleary 1995). Earlier excavations at Site C in this settlement complex revealed the crouched inhumation of an adolescent accompanied by a decorated bipartite bowl upslope for the settlement area (Ó Ríordáin 1954: 371–2). At Martinstown, Co. Meath, the skeleton of an adult was found with a decorated bipartite bowl and a fragment of lignite. This burial has been dated to 3640–3370 cal. BC (Hartnett 1951; Brindley and Lanting 1990).

Decorated bipartite bowls occur with burials in a range of Middle Neolithic contexts (Sheridan 1995), and their contexts suggest that there were shared traditions of practice that focused on the formal placement of a pottery vessel (and in some cases other artefacts) with an individual as part of the post-mortem treatment of particular people, and in other cases the deposition of a pot in the chambers of portal and court tombs and the court features of the latter (Cooney 2000: 185). The best known element of this range of contexts are the Linkardstown burials, which are characterised by the placement of one or more inhumed individuals (either articulated or disarticulated) in a central cist under a cairn covered by a mound and accompanied by a highly decorated round-based ceramic bowl. They are focused in a specific region in the central southern part of the island and have been interpreted as communal memorials to leading individuals (*ibid.*: 97). The individuals mostly date to 3600 to 3300 cal. BC (see Cooney *et al.* 2011: 637). While the focus appears to be on specific individuals, they are sometimes accompanied by the deposition of the bones of a child, as at Ashley Park, Co. Tipperary (Figure 5.3) (Manning 1985). Inhumation and multi-stage mortuary treatment is dominant, as at Poulawack, Co. Clare on the Burren, where it appears that the disarticulated bones of three adults (with the bones of an infant in the deposit) had come from well-preserved skeletons (Beckett 2011). Alongside inhumation, cremation was used on occasion; one of two burials in the cist at Jerpoint West, Co. Kilkenny, was the articulated skeleton of a young adult male, the other was a cremation (Ryan 1973).

Fourteen caves, all in areas of limestone geology, have produced human bone from the Neolithic period, with a marked concentration of dates in the period 3600–3400 cal. BC (Dowd 2008). The bone mostly occurs as isolated, unburnt bones, but complete inhumation burials, at Annagh, Co.

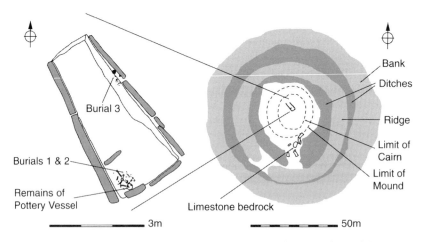

Figure 5.3 Plan of Ashley Park, Linkardstown burial (based on Manning 1985).

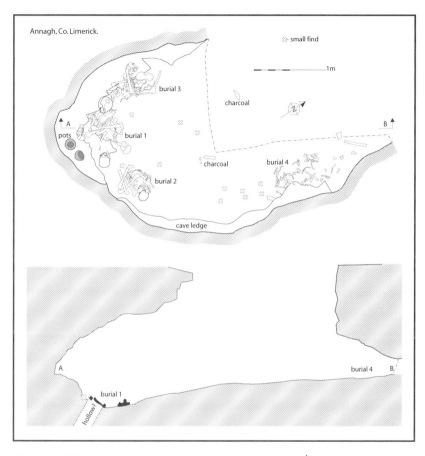

Figure 5.4 The burial deposit in the cave at Annagh (based on Ó Floinn 2011).

Limerick (Ó Floinn 2011) and Kilgreany, Co. Waterford (Dowd 2002) are known. Dowd (2008: 309–10) suggests that the repeated occurrence of small numbers of human bone in caves is reflective of two practices; excarnation, where temporary burial in the cave is followed by removal from that context, and token deposition. The Annagh burials (and the associated ceramics) in particular suggest a link with the commemoration of particular individuals seen in the Linkardstown tradition. Here at least five adults were buried (Figure 5.4), all mature males, two of whom would have been old adults who died in their sixth decade (O'Donnabháin, in Ó Floinn 2011). These date to between 3760–3120 cal. BC. O'Donnabháin (2011) commented that the distribution of arthritic features in the non-vertebral joints suggests that these men led vigorous, physically active lives. Two of the burials had head wounds, which could have been caused by small projectiles such as a (sling) stone, and one had suffered a broken nose and the other a fractured rib. All of these seem likely to be the result of interpersonal violence. The similarity of morphological traits suggests that there was a considerable degree of consanguinity (descent from the same ancestor) among them. O'Donnabháin (*ibid.*) concluded that this was an important locus in the treatment of the dead, perhaps for a community's heroes or a place reserved for old, venerable men.

Having explored the range of Middle Neolithic mortuary practice, it is appropriate to end consideration of this phase of the Neolithic by commenting on mortuary practice in passage tombs. As we saw above, the passage tomb tradition has been highlighted as a key element of the Middle Neolithic. There is debate about the date of the beginning of the passage tomb tradition (Whittle *et al.* 2011: 848–53; Sheridan 2010; Bergh and Hensey 2013), but it is clear that more elaborate forms of passage tomb date to the second half of the fourth millennium cal. BC (Brindley *et al.* 2005; Cooney *et al.* 2011; Bayliss and O'Sullivan 2013; Schulting *et al.* forthcoming). As mentioned in the introduction, the practice of cremation constituted the major treatment of the body after death in this tradition, but the deposits frequently include inhumed remains. Discussing the human remains from the Mound of the Hostages passage tomb at Tara, O'Sullivan (2005: 119–23) drew attention to the fact, first, that every significant collection of cremated bone in the tomb included a small amount of unburnt infant bone, and, second, that radiocarbon dating demonstrates that unburnt skulls were an important element of the assemblage. The number of people represented within tombs varies, with exceptions such as the Mound of the Hostages, Tara (O'Sullivan 2005) producing a large assemblage. The mortuary rite in passage tombs is a focus of discussion in Cooney (2014), and an interpretive account of the deposits at Tomb 1 B East, Knowth (Cooney forthcoming) discusses the complexity of the formation processes responsible for the deposits at this site, one of the two tombs under the main mound at Knowth, which is the subject of a forthcoming volume (Eogan forthcoming).

Here attention is drawn to the wider implications of an important discussion by Kuijt and Quinn (2013) of Cist II at the Mound of the Hostages. The remains in the cist, one of three cists set against the external faces of the tomb orthostats and covered by the cairn of the tomb (O'Sullivan 2005: 65–6), probably represent an intact collection of material from a single depositional event during the intense period of use of the passage tomb between 3350–2970 cal. BC (Bayliss and O'Sullivan 2013: 43). The cremated remains of at least thirty-four individuals were present, along with unburned human skulls, unburned bones of children/infants, and the fragmentary remains of beads and pins (Figure 5.5). Kuijt and Quinn (2013) discuss the complexity of the multi-stage mortuary practices represented by the deposit in Cist II and suggest that this can be seen as representative of the character of deposits in passage tombs more widely. Thinking in terms of the post-mortem pathways that the dead represented in passage tombs would have been taken

Figure 5.5 Part of the burial deposit, including two skulls, eastern end of Cist II, Mound of the Hostages passage tomb (from O'Sullivan 2005: fig. 70).

along by the living (see Figure 5.6), Kuijt and Quinn argued that we need to consider the probability that this included the cremation of corpses, the cremation of dry (disarticulated) bone, and the retention and deposition of unburnt bones (*ibid.*).

The 'communal' deposits in passage tombs indicates then the mingling together of the remains of different individuals. The frequent occurrence of unburnt bone in these deposits suggest that there was a primary stage in the post-mortem treatment of some bodies where the soft tissue was allowed to decompose or facilitated in its decomposition, as, for example, at Millin Bay, Co. Down (see Collins and Waterman 1955; Murphy 2003), and that at some point before cremation selected bones were used for other purposes. The combined use of the rites of cremation (bodies and bones) and inhumation is backed up by the broader dating evidence from the Mound of the Hostages, Tara (Brindley *et al.* 2005; Bayliss and O'Sullivan 2013);

the subterranean passage tomb-related chamber found at Ballynahatty, Co. Down (MacAdam 1855; Schulting *et al.* 2012); and the Knowth passage tomb complex (Schulting *et al.* forthcoming) for the same pattern. This implies that in the passage tomb tradition the two rites were used in parallel and combined at the stage of *deposition*, or that, as in Balinese Hindu practice today (Hobart *et al.* 1996: 122; Downes 1999: 24), the *rites* were combined in a complex, multi-stage mortuary rite, with cremation possibly taking place immediately after death in some cases, in others at a length of time after death.

Smith and Brickley (2009: 41) have commented that an underlying theme in the treatment of human remains in the earlier Neolithic in southern Britain was a wish to transform the remains of the deceased by breaking bodies down into multiple, smaller fragments; to produce remains that are both skeletonised and disarticulated. In developed passage tombs of the later fourth millennium BC in Ireland the presence of unburnt skulls (and other bones) indicates that excarnation, which could have been practiced in a number of ways, was carried out as part of the treatment of dead bodies and that, at least in some cases, it was only after this process had taken place that bone was cremated. This suggests that the cremation process itself and the associated spectacle and rituals as human remains were transformed by fire was an integral part of the ancestral past that was created by the deposition of human remains in tombs.

Cremation and inhumation: linked practices in the Irish Neolithic

Across the range of Neolithic mortuary practice explored here, it is clear that in the Early and Middle Neolithic the deposited human remains, inhumed or cremated, have to be seen as representing only a small proportion of the contemporary, living society at any time (see Smith and Brickley 2009: 87–8; Whittle *et al.* 2011: 871–5, for relevant discussion). Allowing for biasing factors, such as poor preservation of inhumed bone in the acidic soils that are common in northern and western Ireland, a contrast can be drawn, for example, between the number of people who would have been required to construct monuments, the long, if punctuated, history of use of some tombs and the restricted remains in monuments illustrated above. Even bearing in mind the high number of individuals represented at a site like the Mound of the Hostages (over 200) (O'Sullivan 2005: 122–3), if this number is spread over the six or seven human generations that would have lived during the intense period of the construction and use of the tomb in the centuries before 3000 BC, it seems likely that the remains of particular people were selected for deposition in the tomb after death. In terms of thinking about the basis for this selection in different contexts, and despite Whitley's (2001) reservations, it is useful to think in terms of ancestors. Helms (1998: 43–54) talks about ancestors as the 'distinguished dead', which can refer to either beings from a remote past who were involved in social origins or to specific, named people who are remembered as having lived a socially successful life. It is the latter who appear to be commemorated in particular contexts such as the Middle Neolithic Linkardstown burials. This complements Kuijt's (2008) approach in looking at secondary mortuary rites in Early Neolithic villages in the Near East. As he points out, over time in these villages the remembrance of particular people shifted from being a direct, experienced memory to a more open, socially referenced one that would have facilitated the forgetting of specific dead people (Kuijt 2008: 172). Hence, the recently deceased may have a relatively short after-life as ancestral beings and/or over time they become remembered collectively as anonymous, creator ancestors. The key role of the remains of such people is that they represented the physical link between the living and previous generations. This seems to be a useful approach to interpreting the remains placed over several generations in monuments like Poulnabrone.

The role of human skulls, particularly seen in passage tomb contexts, is important in thinking about this relationship between personal and collective identity. The skulls in passage tomb contexts are clearly the result of the particular post-mortem treatment of specific individuals, but the pattern of their deposition (e.g., at the Mound of the Hostages) suggests that by the time of their deposition they had lost the link with specific individuals. Rather, they seem to be deposited to reinforce the concept of a collective, reference set of human/ancestral remains (e.g., Talalay 2004; Kuijt 2008). This could be seen as paralleling the practice in Neolithic Orkney, where it appears that the selection, placement and excarnation of corpses in tombs was followed by re-arrangement and the concentration of skulls in particular locations (Henshall 2004; Laurence 2006).

So who were the 'distinguished dead'? Human remains are dominated by adults (70–75 per cent), with non-adults present in general at a figure of 25–30 per cent (Cooney and Grogan 1994) and in some instances at a higher level. Lewis (2007: 22) suggests that the figure of 30 per cent presence of non-adults should be the standard by which under-representation is measured. This suggests that there may have been a deliberate choice to include non-adolescents in deposits, a pattern replicated in collective burials in Atlantic Europe (Waterman and Thomas 2011). This is particularly evident in the developed passage tomb tradition, where specific inclusion of the bones of infants and young children (mostly un-burnt) can be contrasted to the exclusion of young children noted by Waterman and Thomas (*ibid.*) in a case study of Late Neolithic tombs in the Portuguese Estremadura. That communities and people made active choices about both who was to be represented in the 'distinguished dead' and the type of monument in which they were placed is seen in the contemporary use of three different monument types: Parknabinnia (court tomb); Poulnabrone (portal tomb);

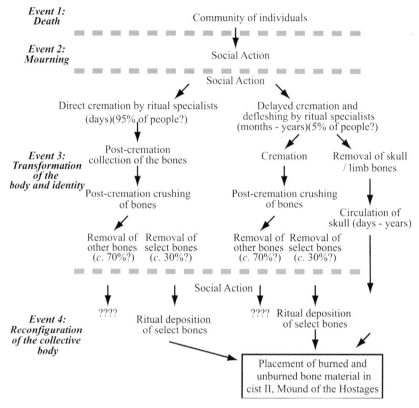

Event 1: Death — Community of individuals

Event 2: Mourning — Social Action

Social Action

Direct cremation by ritual specialists (days)(95% of people?)

Delayed cremation and defleshing by ritual specialists (months - years)(5% of people?)

Event 3: Transformation of the body and identity

Post-cremation collection of the bones

Post-cremation crushing of bones

Removal of other bones (c. 70%?) — Removal of select bones (c. 30%?)

Cremation

Removal of skull / limb bones

Post-cremation crushing of bones

Circulation of skull (days - years)

Removal of other bones (c. 70%?) — Removal of select bones (c. 30%?)

Social Action

Event 4: Reconfiguration of the collective body

???? — Ritual deposition of select bones

???? Ritual deposition of select bones

Placement of burned and unburned bone material in cist II, Mound of the Hostages

Figure 5.6 Conjectural pathways of the adult Neolithic dead, Cist II, Mound of the Hostages (from Kuijt and Quinn 2013: fig. 3).

and Poulawack (Linkardstown burial) during the later part of the fourth millennium cal. BC within a radius of 3 km of each other on the limestone escarpment of the Burren in the south-west (Lynch 2014: 183).

Interestingly, the isotopic analysis of individuals from Poulnabrone suggests that they lived locally. So another way of thinking about the distinguished dead might be in terms of individuals who had local social significance, in contrast to others who might have been representative of a large social polity. In this context, the clustered distribution of passage tombs, allied to the large size and labour requirement of central tombs in passage tomb clusters, has been seen as reflecting a more differentiated, larger-scale society (Bergh 1995; Cooney 2000) compared with locally based, smaller-scale social groupings of the Early and Middle Neolithic. In this context, the particular character of the mortuary deposits in developed passage tombs may well have facilitated a specific view of an ancestral past and the emergence of a particular way of life and death, a tradition in Robb's (2008) terms.

In an important recent discussion, Schulting and colleagues (2012: 36–9) have considered the question of the contemporanity of cremation and inhumation, particularly in the context of court tombs and passage tombs and passage tomb-related sites. There is a focus in their discussion on examining the contemporanity of these practices at specific sites. As we have seen above, mortuary rites at passage tombs clearly revolve around the contemporary, often combined deposition of cremated and unburnt bone. In relation to court tombs, the question of the contemporaneous use of the two rites at specific sites remains open (Schulting *et al.* 2012: 36). In drawing together the strands of the argument presented above and going back to the issues raised in the introduction, the first key point to emphasise is that we need to move away from seeing inhumation and cremation as opposed mortuary rites. As mentioned above, even in the examples of classic anthropological case studies such as Bali which archaeologists look to understand cremation rites, in reality cremation forms part of a complex set of choices in the post-mortem treatment of the dead (Figure 5.7). Williams (2011, 2014) has pointed out in relation to the early Anglo-Saxon period in England that rather than seeing them as contrasting treatments of the dead, inhumation and cremation could be much more usefully regarded as related mortuary technologies employed in strategies of distinction, within and between communities and groups. More generally, as Williams puts it, we should

Figure 5.7 Preparations to place wrapped disarticulated bones with other human remains in hollow animal effigy for cremation, eastern Bali, 2011 (photograph: author).

not be worried about whether or why cremation and inhumation were used together and instead start from a premise of accepting that multiple disposal methods were (and are) the norm in most societies. In this context, the interesting question becomes how cremation and inhumation were employed in relation to one other (Williams 2014: 102). When used in combination, as, for example, in passage tombs, these rites are unlikely to have had a single meaning or message. The unburnt adult skulls and infants' bones in deposits of human remains in all likelihood will have had a different but related frame of symbolic meaning to the cremated remains (and may have come from different individuals). If cremation or inhumation was used preferentially, then there is choice and decision involved. The use of particular rites may have been governed by tradition, but tradition also incorporates the agency of individuals or communities actively working with structuring principles of ritual practice.

What the evidence clearly indicates is that inhumation was a more important rite in the Early and Middle Neolithic in Ireland across a range of burial and depositional contexts than has previously been recognised. This is despite the problem of the survival of inhumed bone in the acidic soil conditions that are typical of many regions of western and northern Ireland. Smith and Brickley (2009: 57–60) have made a similar comment in relation to cremation in the earlier Neolithic of southern Britain, which was practiced alongside the more dominant rite of inhumation. In Scotland, cremation seems to have become a significant form of practice from the Middle Neolithic onwards (Noble and Brophy 2015), and here too bone preservation is a significant issue at least on the mainland. Hence, we do need to be cautious in drawing regional contrasts that rely on seeing cremation and inhumation as opposed rites (and see Chapter 4, this volume). Both rites were used within particular cultural traditions. In court tombs, this might have been exhibited as a preference for one or other rite by particular communities, but cremated bone was deposited with the inhumation-dominant deposits at Parknabinnia. A particular deployment of cremation by communities who focused on inhumation as the favoured treatment of distinguished dead individuals (mostly adult males) can also be seen in the Linkardstown burials at Jerpoint West. It is also apparent that multi-stage mortuary rites, which could have involved different locations at different stages, were in widespread use and that there was a focus on selected individuals, particularly adults.

Some aspects of this picture also apply to the passage tomb tradition, but in other ways mortuary practice in developed passage tombs, as with many other aspects of this tradition, seems quite different to what had gone before in the Early and Middle Neolithic. The combined use of inhumation and cremation to signal distinctions is much more apparent. At individual sites this is activated in particular ways by the location and character of the mortuary deposits and their association with the monument. Mortuary practice creating the material embodiment of ancestor spirits (Jones 2008: 194) had a focal role and the distinction of the dead from the living is architecturally echoed in the passage of the tomb. Multi-stage post-mortem treatment of particular people is seen in other traditions, but mortuary pathways in passage tombs now include retention of skulls for circulation and commemoration and probably the cremation of disarticulated bones as central elements. Cremated and unburnt bones were deliberately and frequently deposited together. At sites such as the Mound of the Hostages (O'Sullivan 2005) and Millin Bay (Collins and Waterman 1955), specific depositional events or episodes involving a small number of individuals can be recognised and distinguished from the larger-scale deposits that we have tended to see as characterising mortuary and memory practice in this tradition (Cooney 1992; Cooney and Rice 2013).

In illustrating the range and diversity of mortuary practice in the Early and Middle Neolithic, it is important to remember just what an important source of information it is for understanding the inter-connection between Neolithic ways of life and death. Rather than the dominance of any one mortuary rite, what is suggested is that during the Neolithic in Ireland the living deliberately chose, and sometimes combined, the use of cremation or inhumation to treat particular individuals after their death so that they would continue to have an active role as the 'distinguished dead'. As Kathleen Jamie (2012: 71) put it in her essay relating her experience working on the excavation directed by Gordon (Barclay 1983) at North Mains, Strathallan, Perth and Kinross, 'you are placed in landscape, you are placed in time. But, with that, there's a bit of room for manoeuvre'.

Bibliography

Barclay, G. J. (1983), 'Sites of the third millennium BC to the first millennium AD at North Mains, Strathallan, Perthshire', *Proceedings of the Society of Antiquaries of Scotland*, 113: 122–281.

Barclay, G. J. (2003), 'The Neolithic', in K. J. Edwards and I. B. M. Ralston (eds), *Scotland: Environment and Archaeology 8000 BC–AD 1000*, Chichester: Wiley, 127–49.

Bayliss, A. and O'Sullivan, M. (2013), 'Interpreting chronologies for the Mound of the Hostages, Tara and its contemporary contexts in Neolithic and Bronze Age Ireland', in O'Sullivan, Scarre and Doyle (eds), *Tara*, 26–104.

Beckett, J. (2011), 'Interactions with the dead: a taphonomic analysis of burial practices in three Megalithic tombs in County Clare, Ireland', *European Journal of Archaeology*, 14: 394–418.

Beckett, J. (2014), 'A taphonomic assessment of the human bone assemblage', in Lynch (ed.), *Poulnabrone*, 56–61.

Beckett, J. and Robb, J. (2006), 'Neolithic burial taphonomy, ritual, and interpretation in Britain and Ireland: a review', in R. Gowland and C. Knüsel (eds), *The Social Archaeology of Funerary Remains*, Oxford: Oxbow Books, 57–80.

Bergh, S. (1995), *Landscape of the Monuments. A Study of the Passage Tombs in the Cúil Irra Region, Co. Sligo, Ireland*, Stockholm: Riksantikvarieämbetet Arkeologiska Undersöknigar.

Bergh, S. and Hensey, R. (2013), 'Unpicking the chronology of Carrowmore', *Oxford Journal of Archaeology*, 32: 343–66.

Bradley, R. (2007a), *The Prehistory of Britain and Ireland*, Cambridge: Cambridge University Press.

Bradley, R. (2007b), 'Houses, bodies and tombs', *Proceedings of the British Academy*, 144: 347–55.

Brindley, A. L. and Lanting, J. N. (1990), 'Radiocarbon dates for single burials', *Journal of Irish Archaeology*, 5: 1–7.

Brindley, A. L., Lanting, J. N. and van der Plicht, J. (2005), 'Radiocarbon-dated samples from the Mound of the Hostages', in M. O'Sullivan (ed.), *Duma na nGiall. The Mound of the Hostages, Tara*, Dublin: Wordwell, 281–96.

Buckley, L., Power, C., O'Sullivan, R. and Thakore, H. (forthcoming), 'The human remains', in Eogan (ed.), *Excavations at Knowth 6* (forthcoming).

Cahill, M. and Sikora, M. (2011), *Breaking Ground, Finding Graves: Reports on the Excavations of Burials by the National Museum of Ireland 1927–2006*, Dublin: Wordwell/National Museum of Ireland.

Carlin, N. (2011), 'A Proper Place for Everything: The Character and Context of Beaker Depositional Practice in Ireland', unpublished PhD thesis, University College Dublin.

Cleary, R. M. (1995), 'Later Bronze Age settlement and prehistoric burials, Lough Gur, Co. Limerick', *Proceedings of the Royal Irish Academy*, 95C: 1–92.

Cody, E. (2002), *Survey of the Megalithic Tombs of Ireland, vol. VI: County Donegal*, Dublin: Stationery Office.

Collins, A. E. P. (1976), 'Dooey's Cairn, Ballymacaldrick, Co. Antrim', *Ulster Journal of Archaeology*, 39: 1–7.

Collins, A. E. P. and Waterman, D. M. (1955), *Millin Bay, a Late Neolithic Cairn in Co. Down*, Belfast: HMSO.

Cooney, G. (1992), 'Body politics and grave messages: Irish Neolithic mortuary practices', in N. M. Sharples and A. Sheridan (eds), *Vessels for the Ancestors: Essays on the Neolithic of Britain and Ireland in Honour of Audrey Henshall*, Edinburgh: Edinburgh University Press, 128–42.

Cooney, G. (2000), *Landscapes of Neolithic Ireland*, London: Routledge.

Cooney, G. (2014), 'The role of cremation in mortuary practice in the Irish Neolithic', in Kuijt, Quinn and Cooney (eds), *Transformation by Fire*, 189–206.

Cooney, G. (forthcoming), 'Interpretation of mortuary practices', in Eogan (ed.), *Excavations at Knowth 6* (forthcoming).

Cooney, G. and Grogan, E. (1994), *Irish Prehistory: A Social Perspective*, Dublin: Wordwell.

Cooney, G. and Rice, K. (2013), 'The use of stone in the Mound of the Hostages', in O'Sullivan, Scarre and Doyle (eds), *Tara*, 147–69.

Cooney, G., Bayliss, A., Healy, F., Whittle, A., Danaher, E., Cagney, C., Mallory, J., Smyth, J., Kador, T. and O'Sullivan, M. (2011), 'Ireland', in A. Whittle, F. Healy and A. Bayliss (eds), *Gathering Time: Dating the Early Neolithic Enclosures of Southern Britain and Ireland*, Oxford: Oxbow, 562–669.

Danaher, E. (2007), *Monumental Beginnings: The Archaeology of the N4 Sligo Inner Relief Road*, Dublin: National Roads Authority.

Davidsson, M. (2003), 'On the anatomy of Megaliths: the interrelation between physical interment and morphology in Irish megalithic tombs', in G. Burenhult and S. Westergaard (eds), *Stones and Bones: Formal Disposal of the Dead in Atlantic Europe during the Mesolithic–Neolithic Interface 6000–3000 BC*, Oxford: British Archaeological Reports, 235–41.

de Valera, R. and Ó Nualláin, S. (1961), *Survey of the Megalithic Tombs of Ireland, vol. I: County Clare*, Dublin: Stationery Office.

Dowd, M. (2002), 'Kilgreany, Co. Waterford: biography of a cave', *Journal of Irish Archaeology*, 11: 77–97.

Dowd, M. (2008), 'The use of caves for funerary and ritual practices in Neolithic Ireland', *Antiquity*, 82: 305–17.

Downes, J. (1999), 'Cremation: a spectacle and a journey', in J. Downes and T. Pollard (eds), *The Loved Body's Corruption*, Glasgow: Cruithne Press, 19–29.

Duffy, P. R. J. and MacGregor, G. (2008), 'Cremations, conjecture and contextual taphonomies: material strategies during the 4th to the 2nd millennia in Scotland', in F. Fahlander and T. Oestigaard (eds), *The Materiality of Death: Bodies, Burials, Beliefs*, Oxford: British Archaeological Reports, 71–7.

Eogan, G. (1986), *Knowth and the Passage Tombs of Ireland*, London: Thames & Hudson.

Eogan, G. (ed.) (forthcoming), *Excavations at Knowth 6: The Archaeology of the Large Passage Tomb at Knowth, Co. Meath*, Dublin: Royal Irish Academy.

Evans, E. E. (1938), 'Doey's Cairn, Dunloy, County Antrim', *Ulster Journal of Archaeology*, 1: 59–78.

Hartnett, P. J. (1951), 'A Neolithic burial from Martinstown, Kiltale, Co. Meath', *Journal of the Royal Society of Antiquaries of Ireland*, 81: 19–23.

Helms, M. (1998), *Access to Origins: Affines, Ancestors and Aristocrats*, Austin, TX: University of Texas Press.

Henshall, A. S. (1972), *The Chambered Tombs of Scotland*, Edinburgh: Edinburgh University Press, vol. 2.

Henshall, A. S. (2004), 'Scottish passage-graves: some confusions and conclusions', in A. Gibson and A. Sheridan (eds), *From Sickles to Circles: Britain and Ireland at the Time of Stonehenge*, Stroud: Tempus, 78–91.

Herity, M. (1974), *Irish Passage Graves*, Dublin: Irish University Press.

Herity, M. (1987), 'The finds from Irish court tombs', *Proceedings of the Royal Irish Academy*, 87C: 103–281.

Hobart, A., Ramseyer, U. and Leemann, A. (1996), *The People of Bali*, Oxford: Blackwell.

Jamie, K. (2012), *Sightlines*, London: Sort of Books.

Jones, A. (2008), 'How the dead live: mortuary practices, memory and the ancestors in Neolithic and Early Bronze Age Britain and Europe', in J. Pollard (ed.), *Prehistoric Britain*, Oxford: Blackwell, 177–201.

Jones, C. (2004), *The Burren and the Aran Islands: Exploring the Archaeology*, Cork: Collins Press.

Jones, C. (2007), *Temples of Stone: Exploring the Megalithic Tombs of Ireland*, Cork: Collins Press.

Kuijt, I. (2008), 'The regeneration of life: Neolithic structures of symbolic remembering and forgetting', *Current Anthropology*, 49: 171–97.

Kuijt, I. and Quinn, C. P. (2013), 'Biography of the Neolithic body: tracing pathways to cist II, Mound of the Hostages, Tara', in O'Sullivan, Scarre and Doyle (eds), *Tara*, 170–83.

Kuijt, I., Quinn, C. P. and Cooney, G. (eds) (2014), *Transformation by Fire: The Archaeology of Cremation in Cultural Context*, Tucson, AZ: University of Arizona Press.

Kytmannow, T. (2008), *Portal Tombs in the Landscape. The Chronology, Morphology and Landscape Setting of the Portal Tombs of Ireland, Wales and Cornwall*, Oxford: British Archaeological Reports.

Larsson, A. M. (2003), 'Secondary burial practices in the Middle Neolithic: causes and consequences', *Current Swedish Archaeology*, 11: 153–70.

Larsson, A. M. and Nilsson Stutz, L. (2014), 'Reconcilable differences: cremation, fragmentation and inhumation in Mesolithic and Neolithic Sweden', in Kuijt, Quinn and Cooney (eds), *Transformation by Fire*, 47–66.

Laurence, D. (2006), 'Neolithic mortuary practice in Orkney', *Proceedings of the Society of Antiquaries of Scotland*, 136: 47–59.

Lewis, M. (2007), *The Bioarchaeology of Children*, Cambridge: Cambridge University Press.

Lynch, A. (ed.) (2014), *Poulnabrone: An Early Neolithic Portal Tomb in Ireland*, Dublin: Stationery Office.

Lynch, A. and O'Donnabháin, B. (1994), 'Poulnabrone, Co. Clare', *The Other Clare*, 18: 5–7.

MacAdam, J. (1855), 'Discovery of an ancient sepulchral chamber', *Ulster Journal of Archaeology*, 3: 358–65.

Malone, C. (2001), *Neolithic Britain and Ireland*, Stroud: Tempus.

Manning, M. (1985), 'A Neolithic burial mound at Ashley Park, Co. Tipperary', *Proceedings of the Royal Irish Academy*, 85C: 61–100.

Murphy, E. (2003), 'Funerary processing of the dead in prehistoric Ireland', *Archaeology Ireland*, 17: 13–15.

Noble, G. (2006), *Neolithic Scotland: Timber, Stone, Earth and Fire*, Edinburgh: Edinburgh University Press.

Noble, G. and Brophy, K. (2015), 'Transforming place and architecture through cremation: cremation traditions at the third millennium BC monument complex at Forteviot, central Scotland', in L. Larsson (ed.), *What's New in the Neolithic?* Lund: Lund University Press, 164–72.

O'Brien, W. (1999), *Sacred Ground: Megalithic Tombs in Coastal South-west Ireland*, Galway: Galway University Press.

O'Donnabháin, B. (2011), 'Human remains (Annagh, Co. Limerick)', in Cahill and Sikora (eds), *Breaking Ground, Finding Graves*, 34–47.

O'Donnabháin, B. and Tesorieri, M. (2014), 'Bioarchaeology', in Lynch (ed.), *Poulnabrone*, 61–86.

Ó Floinn, R. (2011), 'Annagh, Co. Limerick', in Cahill and Sikora (eds), *Breaking Ground, Finding Graves*, 17–47.

Ó Ríordáin, S. P. (1954), 'Lough Gur excavations: Neolithic and Bronze Age houses on Knockadoon', *Proceedings of the Royal Irish Academy*, 54C: 297–459.

O'Sullivan, M. (2005), *Duma na nGiall. The Mound of the Hostages*, Tara, Dublin: Wordwell.

O'Sullivan, M. Scarre, C. and Doyle, M. (eds) (2013), *Tara: From the Past to the Future*, Dublin: Wordwell/University College Dublin School of Archaeology.

Piggott, S. (1954), *Neolithic Cultures of the British Isles*, Cambridge: Cambridge University Press.

Robb, J. (2008), 'Tradition and agency: human body representations in later prehistoric Europe', *World Archaeology*, 40: 332–53.

Ryan, M. (1973), 'The excavation of a Neolithic burial mound at Jerpoint West, Co. Kilkenny', *Proceedings of the Royal Irish Academy*, 73C: 107–27.

Schulting, R. (2014), 'The dating of Poulnabrone', in Lynch (ed.), *Poulnabrone*, 93–113.

Schulting, R. J., Bronk Ramsey, C., Reimer, P. J., Eogan, G., Cleary, K., Cooney, G. and Sheridan, A. (forthcoming), 'Dating the human remains from Knowth', in Eogan (ed.), *Excavations at Knowth 6* (forthcoming).

Schulting, R. J., Murphy, E., Jones, C. and Warren, G. (2012), 'New dates from the north and a proposed chronology for Irish court tombs', *Proceedings of the Royal Irish Academy*, 112C: 1–60.

Schulting, R. J., Sheridan, A., Clarke, S. R. and Bronk Ramsey, C. (2008), 'Largantea and the dating of Irish wedge tombs', *Journal of Irish Archaeology*, 17: 1–17.

Schulting, R. J., Sheridan, A., Crozier, R. and Murphy, E. (2010), 'Revisiting Quanterness: new AMS dates and staple isotope data from an Orcadian chamber tomb', *Proceedings of the Society of Antiquaries of Scotland*, 140: 1–50.

Sheridan, A. (1986), 'Megaliths and megalomania: an account, and interpretation, of the development of passage tombs in Ireland', *Journal of Irish Archaeology*, 3: 17–30.

Sheridan, A. (1995), 'Irish Neolithic pottery: the story in 1995', in I. A. Kinnes and G. Varndell (eds), *Unbaked Urns of Rudely Shape*, Oxford: Oxbow Books, 3–22.

Sheridan, A. (2004), 'Going round in circles? Understanding the Irish Grooved Ware complex in its wider context', in H. Roche, E. Grogan, J. Bradley, J. Coles and B. Raftery (eds), *From Megaliths to Metals: Essays in Honour of George Eogan*, Oxford: Oxbow Books, 26–37.

Sheridan, A. (2006), 'A non-megalithic funerary tradition in Early Neolithic Ireland', in M. Meek (ed.), *The Modern Traveller to Our Past*, Newtownards: DPK Publishing, 24–31.

Sheridan, A. (2010), 'The Neolithization of Britain and Ireland: the "big picture"', in B. Finlayson and G. Warren (eds), *Landscapes in Transition*, Oxford/London: Oxbow Books/Council for British Research in the Levant, 89–105.

Smith, M. and Brickley, M. (2009), *People of the Long Barrows: Life, Death and Burial in the Earlier Neolithic*, Stroud: The History Press.

Smyth, J. (2014), *Settlement in the Irish Neolithic: New Discoveries at the Edge of Europe*, Oxford: Oxbow Books/Prehistoric Society/The Heritage Council.

Talalay, L. E. (2004), 'Heady business: skulls, heads and decapitation in Neolithic Anatolia and Greece', *Journal of Mediterranean Archaeology*, 17: 139–63.

Waterman, A. J. and Thomas, J. T. (2011), 'When the bough breaks: childhood mortality and burial practice in Late Neolithic Atlantic Europe', *Oxford Journal of Archaeology*, 30: 165–83.

Waterman, D. M. (1978), 'The excavation of a court cairn at Tully, Co. Fermanagh', *Ulster Journal of Archaeology*, 41: 3–14.

Whitehouse, N. J., Schulting, R. J., McClatchie, M., Barratt, P., McLaughlin, T. R., Bogaard, A., Colledge, S., Marchant, R., Gaffrey, J. and Bunting, M. J. (2014), 'Neolithic agriculture on the European western frontier: the boom and bust of early farming in Ireland', *Journal of Archaeological Science*, 51: 181–205.

Whitley, J. (2001), 'Too many ancestors', *Antiquity*, 76: 119–26.

Whittle, A., Bayliss, A. and Healy, F. (2011), 'Gathering time: the social dynamics of change', in A. Whittle, F. Healy and A. Bayliss (eds), *Gathering Time: Dating the Early Neolithic Enclosures of Southern Britain and Ireland*, Oxford: Oxbow Books, 848–914.

Williams, H. (2011), 'Mortuary practices in early Anglo-Saxon England', in H. Hamerow, D. Hinton and S. Crawford (eds), *The Oxford Handbook of Anglo-Saxon Archaeology*, Oxford: Oxford University Press, 238–59.

Williams, H. (2014), 'A well-urned rest: cremation and inhumation in early Anglo-Saxon England', in Kuijt, Quinn and Cooney (eds), *Transformation by Fire*, 93–118.

PART II

Non-megalithic Monuments

CHAPTER 6

Hiatus or Hidden?
The Problem of the Missing
Scottish Upland Cursus Monuments

Roy Loveday

In 1978, Gordon Maxwell drew attention to the fact that a number of pit alignments in Scotland appeared to form enclosures and that these found their closest parallels in the ditched cursus monuments of England. Today at least thirty-five cursus monuments of timber and earthwork varieties have been recorded in Scotland along with perhaps half as many smaller sites of comparable morphology (Brophy 2015) prompted by Maxwell's interpretive leap. Nobody has done more to elucidate these enigmatic monuments and contemporary sites through fieldwork than Gordon Barclay. His meticulous excavations (see Chapter 1, this volume) have furnished a record of fourth millennium BC development that is the envy of those south of the Border. In heightening perception of cursus monuments and related sites in Scotland his contribution to the remarkable populating of Strathmore, Strathearn and the lower Nith valley, as well as, progressively, other areas such as Stirling, Fife and Argyll, has been central. However, as cursus sites have been added to distribution maps (Figure 6.1) a problem has emerged – why are they effectively absent from the uplands, here defined for simplicity as land between approximately 100 m and 400 m OD (i.e., hill land not highland)? South of the Border, it was on the uplands that cursuses were first identified (notably the Greater and the Lesser Stonehenge Cursuses and the Dorset Cursus: Stukeley 1740; Atkinson 1955) and Scotland hardly lacks hills!

An obvious answer lies in the soil's potential for cropmark production. Light gravel soils in the drier east of the country readily reflect the critical moisture differential that is central to cropmark production, whereas those on neighbouring uplands are heavier and so are far less responsive (Barclay 1992; Millican 2007: 23). The latter are additionally much more likely to be under pasture that masks the evidence totally. Nevertheless, above the limits of agricultural destruction (recorded as about 122 m OD in south-east Perth) surveys have consistently failed to identify characteristic earthworks (RCAHMS 1994; 1997).

This is by no means a problem exclusive to Scotland. In North Yorkshire cursus monuments are found where the Swale and Ure enter the flatlands

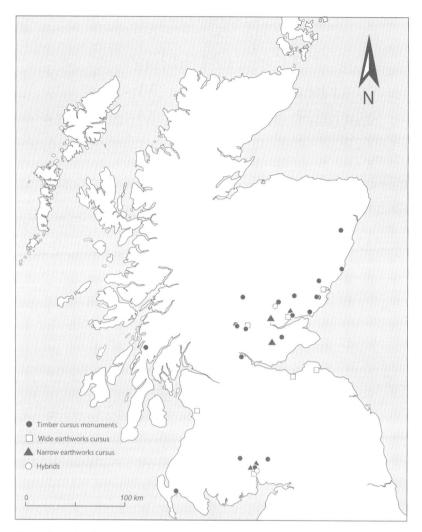

Figure 6.1 Distribution of various forms of cursus monument in Scotland (from Brophy 2015; drawing prepared by Lorraine McEwan).

(at Scorton and Thornborough, respectively), not higher up the valleys, and this pattern is repeated through the East Midlands (Harding and Healy 2007: 277), the Upper Thames valley (Holgate 1988: 371) and as far south as Devon (Griffith 1989). By contrast, earlier causewayed enclosures and later henges were sited across a variety of terrains (Griffith 1985; Holgate 1988: 343, 375; Harding and Healy 2007: 277). So consistent is the pattern that we might conclude that flatland was a prerequisite of cursus construction were it not for the chalkland sites. As Gordon Barclay has robustly questioned the use of Wessex models for the interpretation of Neolithic activity in distant and quite distinct regions (2001, 2009), should we view the cursus monuments in Wessex as simply another example of a peculiar – and here irrelevant – southern practice? The fact that cursus monuments also run from hillside to hillside across the Gypsey Race valley at Rudston, East Yorkshire (Stoertz 1997), across the Walton Basin in Radnorshire (Britnell and Jones 2012) and along the gently sloping, raised top at Hasting Hill, Co. Durham (Newman 1976), suggests that is not the case. The Rudston complex is some 80 km closer to the Southern Uplands than it is to Wessex, and the Hasting Hill cursus is some 280 km closer. That must lead us to expect similar sitings to have been chosen in Scotland.

Since the pattern of pasturing that ensured survival of the Wessex and Yorkshire Wolds sites recalls Scottish use of upland landscapes, we must it seems look beyond historical patterns of landscape exploitation for an explanation for the 'missing' Scottish sites. Might an answer instead lie in the Neolithic itself? A simple explanation might be sought in progressive landscape clearance: the presence of henges and stone circles on upland terrain reflecting their common third millennium BC dates in contrast to the fourth millennium range of cursus monuments (Barclay 2005: 90–1; Ashmore 2007: 248–51). Yet broadly contemporary chambered cairns and earthen long barrows occur across upland landscapes (e.g., Balnacraig and Blue Cairn in the Grampians; Dour Hill, Devil's Lapful, Langknowe and the Currick in the Cheviots). At 43–112 m in length they would, of course, have made far fewer demands in terms of clearance than even a minor cursus (180–800 m in length; Loveday 2006a: 26), but their clustering in certain areas implies considerable aggregate opening of the canopy contemporary with, or just prior to, the period of cursus construction. Three upland areas possessing long and/or chambered cairns therefore deserve particular scrutiny: Upper Strathtay and Strathearn, both Perth and Kinross; Nithsdale, Dumfries and Galloway; and the Biggar region, South Lanarkshire.

Upper Strathearn and Strathtay

These valleys represent narrow salients of lowland stretching beyond the Greenock–Stonehaven Highland Boundary Fault. Their sides rise increasingly steeply along their length to rocky moorland hills above. This significantly reduces the extent of available upland (100–400 m OD) and the placing of Neolithic cairns seems to reflect that fact (Henshall 1972: 468–78): from gently sloping or undulating land on the valley sides in lower reaches (Cultoquhey and Derculich), to level ridges or platforms further along the valley (Rottenreoch), and finally to floor locations near valley heads (Fortingall and Kindrochat), where restricted space may have rendered home-base cereal cultivation non-viable. Alternatively, rather than reflecting a practice of peripheral cairn placement, this pattern could be a product of later agricultural destruction (cf. south-east Perth: RCAHMS 1994: 8–9). In the absence of ditches, long cairns formerly set on the valley floor would have left no traces in the long-cultivated lower reaches of the valleys. Survival – perhaps by chance – of the Neolithic round mound of Pitnacree close to the River Tay some 7 km downstream from Aberfeldy confirms monumental construction on the valley floor (Coles and Simpson 1965). In similar locations cursus monuments have been recorded as cropmarks: at Castle Menzies near Aberfeldy in Strathtay near Pitnacree (Halliday 2002), and Craggish and Tullichettle in upper Strathearn near Comrie, with examples at Broich and Bennybeg at Crieff where the River Earn leaves the uplands (Brophy 1998, 2015; Brophy and Millican 2015). The fact that the Neolithic cairns are fairly evenly spaced between these known cursus monuments suggests the integration of valley floor ceremonial and home-base activity (assuming long mounds were placed within a close orbit of settlements).

Those cursus sites lying in the upper reaches of the Tay and Earn could be claimed as upland cursuses were it not for the fact that they lie solely where valley floors widen sufficiently to accommodate them. They are in essence, then, river valley cursuses in the uplands, not upland cursuses in the Rudston (cross-valley) or Hasting Hill (level-top) mode. The presence of a regionally unusual ditched cursus of major size (c. 900 m × 80–100 m) (Brophy 1998: 101) where the River Earn leaves the uplands at Broich recalls the placing of the Scorton and Thornborough sites just beyond the eastern extremity of the Pennines; Cleaven Dyke is not dissimilarly placed along the Tay (Barclay and Maxwell 1998).

The long cairns of Clach na Tiompan above the River Almond and the former Cairn Wochel set between the Machany Water and the Knaik were placed in positions more characteristic of upland cursuses in the South (Henshall 1972: 468–72, 478), but no neighbouring earthworks have been recorded. This could, of course, relate to the characteristic slightness of cursus ditches and to subsequent peat growth or to a lack of closely directed survey. Definition of their outline by posts as in the valleys must be doubted on account of the bedrock and such sites, had they existed, would be almost impossible to find.

With the springhead locations and cross-valley characteristics of the Rudston and Dorset cursuses in mind, the upper reaches of Glen Dochart and Strathfillan in the shadow of Ben More also perhaps deserve scrutiny, particularly as this mountain is the focus for routes along Strathtay, Strathearn and Loch Lomond. Elsewhere the topography furnishes little or no opportunity to construct an upland-top site of Hasting Hill-type, the low watershed dome between the Knaik/Allan Water and the Machany Water/ Earn around Muthill and Braco being a possible exception.

Nithsdale

Unlike the previous region, the uplands that flank the lower reaches of Nithsdale where the Holywood, Holm, Gallaberry and Curriestanes cursus monuments are located, are gentle and of modest proportions (Brophy 2007a; Millican 2012). Frequent rounded, ridge-like edges to the valleys bear a closer resemblance to those upland locations selected for cursus siting south of the Border. The long cairns of Fleuchlarg and Capenoch Moor, set at 122 m OD and 168 m OD respectively on the Keir Hills to the west, lie within 12 km of the Holywood–Gallaberry complex sited on the valley floor, and just 5 km from the similarly placed timber cursus site at Kirkland Station on the Cairn Water tributary. The Stiddrig long cairn (c. 200 m OD), on the lower slopes of the Lowther Hills edging Annandale to the east, lies a comparable distance from the Lochbrow cursus and post circle. All the long cairns stand on moorland or rough grazing just above the limits of enclosed land (Henshall 1972: 117–20, 159). As in Strathtay and Strathearn, this could indicate destruction of evidence at lower levels. Close to the Fleuchlarg and Capenoch mounds, at Bardennoch, the cropmarks of the flanking ditches of a long barrow set on a terrace overlooking the Nith provide confirmation of the destructive potential of the plough (Cowley and Brophy 2001: 51).

By contrast, the Holywood–Gallaberry–Curriestanes cursus monuments lie on extensive flat or gently undulating land rising only some 20–25 m OD (Cowley and Brophy 2001: 54–6; Thomas 2007). That is also the case with the timber cursus monument partially recorded at Kirkland Station in the steep-sided valley of the Cairn Water (Brophy 2007a; Millican 2012). As in Strathearn and Strathtay, the latter has been set to run along the flat valley floor where arable farming revealed it; both here and at Lochbrow, the sites appear to have been specifically tailored to the immediate topography of the terrace edge (Millican 2012). Opportunities for both cross-valley and level-top cursus layouts are relatively few in the valley of the Cairn Water, but seem likely to have presented themselves in the main valley of the Nith. Recognition of a bank barrow (known as Eskdalemuir) apparently laid out to cross the White Esk in upland cursus fashion 45 km to the east supports this idea (RCAHMS 1997: 107–9), as may a possible cursus running uphill on the lower slopes of Criffel at Cavens, although the aerial photographic evidence for this site is tenuous (Brophy 2007a: 162 and pers. comm.). Despite a modern field survey of the east of this region (RCAHMS 1997) no earthworks have been recognised as possible elements of cursus monuments. The headwaters of the Nith between Wanlockhead and Cumnock perhaps deserve particular directed attention in this regard.

The Biggar area

This area differs markedly from the previous two. Whereas they represent valley-based monument distributions, the area around Biggar is essentially a watershed concentration. To the west, drainage is to the Clyde, to the east to the Tweed, and in between runs a glacial breach that forms a flat hollow 11 km in length known as the Biggar Gap. Despite lying at some 200 m OD, its fall is sufficiently slight as to have created three wetland areas. Either side of this Gap lie the Pentland and Culter Hills, while just beyond, across the Clyde, lie the Tinto Hills. Around this nodal upland area a major concentration of sites and monuments occurs.

The long cairns of Burngrange, Greensmoor and Dunsyre cluster around the south-western end of the Pentland Hills on moorland and rough grazing, the latter two within a kilometre of each other (Henshall 1972: 457–60; Ordnance Survey Archaeological Division 1972, 51), while the long cairn on Biggar Common stands adjacent to a cemetery of round cairns (Johnston 1997). All lie between 250 and 300 m OD and, as in the previous regions, agricultural destruction at lower levels is a possibility. Field work by the Biggar Archaeology Group has recorded an extensive earlier Neolithic domestic presence that was preceded by Mesolithic activity (Noble 2006: 213). Excavations at Brownsbank by Glasgow University in 2005–6 revealed a possible Neolithic rectangular timber structure, situated within a hengiform enclosure; both sites survive only as cropmarks and were almost wholly destroyed by the time of their excavation (Brophy and Noble 2006). At nearby West Lindsaylands, at the western end of the Gap adjacent to the River Clyde, cropmarks have revealed one of the best contenders for a causewayed enclosure in Scotland (Oswald *et al.* 2001: 83) and immediately adjacent, a pit-defined long enclosure (Brophy and Millican 2015). At 50 m × 15 m, this site lacks the size for it to be claimed as a cursus, but it clearly belongs in the same tradition. It invites comparison with long enclosures found adjacent to causewayed enclosures at Roughton in Norfolk and Abingdon and Buckland in the Upper Thames valley (Oswald *et al.* 2001), and with the cursus and possible causewayed enclosure at Hasting Hill, Co. Durham (Newman 1976) (Figure 6.2). Albeit that it lies on a terrace of the Clyde, in standing at approximately 200 m OD it is positioned at a not too dissimilar level to the long cairns and henges of the area: 250–300 m OD. There would thus appear to be a real possibility of an upland cursus being discovered here, perhaps most plausibly on the relatively level ridges of Lindsaylands and Biggar Common.

The presence of a classic Seamer axe made of Yorkshire coast flint accompanying a burial in a pit cut into the Biggar Common long mound confirms contact with the region that boasts the largest cursus complex in northern Britain (Sheridan 1992: 206–7; Finlayson 1997), while some of the densest concentrations of worked Arran pitchstone in Scotland additionally point to a western connection (Ballin 2009). It may be significant that at the western end

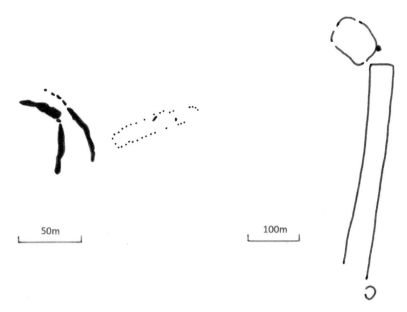

50m

100m

Figure 6.2 The Hasting Hill cursus and enclosure (right), and the West Lindsaylands 'causewayed enclosure' and possible timber long enclosure (left) (West Lindsaylands was drawn by Kirsty Millican).

of the topographically straightforward River Irvine–Avon Water and River Ayr–Douglas Water routes westward from the Middle Clyde (today followed by the A71 and A70) lies the isolated lowland cursus at Drybridge, overlooking the Firth of Clyde and Arran. The nodality of the Biggar area, coupled with the presence there of the largest grouping of probable henges in southern Scotland (Barclay 2005, fig. 8.4; Noble 2006: 150 and fig. 6.11) and an embanked enclosure of comparable size and probable date to Avebury at Blackshouse Burn (Lelong and Pollard 1998), led Gordon Noble to suggest it as a long-lived interaction zone resulting from upland pasturing by communities moving up the Tweed and Clyde valleys (2006: 188–190). Pollen analysis of peat columns from the Blackshouse Burn bog, adjacent to the embanked enclosure, points to a decline of woodland cover after 7500 BP, perhaps assisted by anthropogenic firing to encourage game. There is no evidence of subsequent regeneration. Ramsay suggests on the basis of the bog edge diagram that grassland became dominant in the region, probably being maintained by grazing animals (1998: 37–40). This has resonance for cursus placement elsewhere (see below), but palaeo-environmental evidence from the Biggar long cairn is less clear-cut, suggesting rough pasture and mixed woodland associated with soils that have a history of deep disturbance, perhaps from tillage (Johnston 1997: 239). Whatever the case, extensive clearance seems to have been a feature of this upland landscape, yet to date no cursus has been reported from it.

Hidden monuments?

In the three areas of upland Scotland examined Neolithic cairn patterning varies somewhat, but the restriction of cursus monuments (or in the case of West Lindsaylands, a cursus-related site) to valley bottoms appears consistent. The site at Upper Largie in Argyll, similarly surrounded by significant hills, confirms this. Terrain may largely have determined the pattern but level ridges and gentle-sided valleys are present in Upper Nithsdale and around Biggar. The inescapable conclusion is that destruction at lower levels has provided us with cropmarks, but that preservation at higher ones, although delivering us long barrows, has failed to furnish cursus earthworks.

Might the problem be one of recognition? Major long mounds and the wider, deeper ditches of henges, with their commensurately more substantial banks, undoubtedly more readily arrest attention than minimally monumental cursuses (Loveday 2006a: 36); as classic features of aerial photography these are firmly associated in fieldworkers' minds with permeable river valley soils. Nationally, upland cursus sites are a rarity. Only in the Stonehenge landscape were they identified purely from their physical remains and that in the eighteenth century. Elsewhere recognition of the real import of rare upstanding sections of bank and ditch has been dependent upon levelled sections of the monuments producing linking cropmarks (Atkinson 1955; Dymond 1966), a mechanism unavailable on heavier Scottish upland soils. Sections of slight ditch or upcast bank are unlikely therefore to be readily entertained as potential elements of cursus monuments.

The possibility of different precinct definition in upland landscapes must also be considered. The employment of spaced stones rather than posts, or simply banks rather than ditches and banks, would have had the attraction of minimising the need to break potentially intractable bedrock. It would also mean that any sites of this kind and period so defined are likely to have been differently classified in the archaeological record – as avenues or field banks, for instance.

Alignments of spaced stones are certainly familiar ceremonial features. They are, however, conspicuous by their absence across the upland areas of southern and eastern Scotland. While pairs of stones are recorded in some numbers in Tayside (Burl 1993: 182) along with a few three-stone rows (*ibid.*: 149), double and multiple rows are restricted to Caithness and Sutherland and the all-important detached and tangential avenues are absent entirely (*ibid.*: 76, 79, 118). The stone avenues at Broomend of Crichie and Callanish, like the ditched avenue across the border at Milfield in Northumberland, are features associated with henges and stone circles (Bradley 2011), as apparently was the avenue at Shap in Cumbria (Clare 1978; Burl 1993: 47–8). The reported pre-destruction complexities of the latter recall on a vastly greater scale the tangled alignments of Holm, sited 2 km east of the Holywood cursus complex (Thomas 2007), but a more definite avenue of moderately

Figure 6.3 The Shap avenue, drawn by Lady Lowther in 1775 (Source: *Transactions of the Cumberland and Westmoreland Antiquarian and Archaeological Society*, 15 (Old Series), 1898–9, plate II).

sized stones was recorded running south from the town of Shap. It stretched for 1.2 km to the stone circle of Kemp Howe. It was drawn by Lady Lowther in 1775 (Figure 6.3), and in 1800 was remarked upon by Colt Hoare (cited by Burl 1993: 48), who recorded 'a long avenue of large stones, placed at different intervals and extending for nearly two miles ... the avenue closes with a row of stones placed in a semi-circular form'. The latter, Aubrey Burl notes (1993: 48), was probably the already wrecked circle of Kemp Howe, but the reported close similarity of avenue width (*c.* 20 m) and circle diameter (24.4 m) – confirmed by Lady Lowther's drawing (Figure 6.3) – would be unique amongst these ancillary structures. Two possibilities suggest themselves: that this was a cursus with a convex end defined by stones rather than posts, or that the relationship mirrored that of post-defined cursus and superimposed post-circle revealed at Upper Largie, Argyll (Cook *et al.* 2010). The fact that the Shap site lies some 100 km south of the Curriestanes–Holywood complex and some 100 km north of that at Thornborough, Yorkshire, may be significant since both of these complexes possessed convex-ended cursuses (Vatcher 1960; Cowley and Brophy 2001: 54–6; Loveday 2006a: fig. 56). There is, however, no escaping its isolation and apparent uniqueness. Elsewhere in the North, the only suggestion that upland cursus monuments resembled stone avenues or double rows comes from the highly unusual (but undated) U-shaped sites of Achavanich (Figure 6.4) and Broubster in distant Caithness that closely echo long enclosures in both plan and dimension (Burl 1993: 117).

The other possible structural form – stone or earthen banks – which might have delineated such sites is hinted at by a number of instances of much later field boundaries incorporating the slight boundary earthworks of cursus enclosures. This is most clearly detailed at Drayton in Oxfordshire where a field ditch running from a second century AD Roman enclosed

Figure 6.4 The U-shaped stone setting (*c*. 70 m × 30 m) at Achavanich, Caithness (photograph: author).

settlement met and was then re-aligned to run exactly alongside a cursus ditch for 150 m. Since excavation had established that the latter had been reduced to a mere depression 0.20 m deep three to four centuries earlier when it had begun to fill with alluvium (Barclay *et al.* 2003: 104–17), it could not have been an obvious landscape feature. But something that fossilised its alignment was clearly being respected. That was almost certainly a relict hedge line, originating perhaps from vegetation colonisation of stake fencing once set on the monument's banks or along its ditch edge. This pattern of respect is repeated less dramatically elsewhere (Loveday 2006a: 40–3). The possibility that turf walling was used in the construction of early timber hall prototypes for cursus monuments adds a further potential structural medium that would leave no trace in arable landscapes (Loveday 2006b).

Might upland cursus monuments then have resembled field boundaries and might their banks have been incorporated into, and masked by, later field systems? The answer to the first of these questions could be yes; like field ditches and unlike henge ditches, those that define cursuses do not increase in scale in tandem with site dimensions (Loveday 2006a: 35–6). Their banks are likely to have been of moderate size therefore, whether derived from a ditch or from scrapes or surface stone gathering. The answer to the second question must depend on the size, shape and layout of later fields. Long cultivation terraces are a relatively widespread phenomenon in the Border counties (Topping 1989: 171–5), but in running overwhelmingly along the contours to create staircases rising up–slope they are quite distinct from known upland cursus monuments; only the northern 2 km of the almost 10 km long Dorset cursus follows the contours (RCHME 1975: 25). This observation does not, of course, preclude the possibility that quite different topographic alignment could have been selected in other areas, but the balance of probability, based on current evidence, is against it. Field systems possessing large rectangular components that might even more effectively mask a cursus than cultivation terraces (e.g., Ellershie Hill, Lanarkshire (RCAHMS 1978: 110) and Tamshiel Rig in former Roxburghshire (RCAHMS 1956: 427)) are unusual in the south of Scotland, and the few known examples are distanced from henges and ritual enclosures. The fact that unenclosed settlements lacking any relationship to defined fields are the norm in this region (RCAHMS 1956) suggests pastoralism was the common strategy during the first millennia BC–AD, particularly on land over 300 m OD. Areas of cord rig argue that this did not preclude some arable cultivation, but the size of the ridges is insufficient to hide earlier field walls or, in our case, potential cursus banks (Topping 1989: pl. 30a and fig. 4). Therefore, it seems unlikely that the remnants of such agricultural activity can be used to explain the apparent absence of cursuses from the Cheviots and Southern Uplands where earlier and later Neolithic monuments register an obvious presence.

Cursus monuments in the landscape

If Scottish cursus monuments are neither masquerading as stone avenues nor seemingly hidden beneath field banks, how are we to explain their apparent exclusion from all but valley bottoms? In approaching an answer we need to remind ourselves that cursus distribution is markedly uneven across all landscapes. Despite regular surveys, clusters of sites such as that around Dumfries still contrast with areas of complete absence, as in the Tweed valley, or relative dearth, such as the Lothian Plain. The fact that East Lothian exhibits the highest incidence of cropmark enclosures of other types in any part of Scotland confirms the uneven pattern as more than a simple product of drift geology (RCAHMS 1997: 115). In Strathmore loose clusterings of sites are separated by equally receptive but blank areas (Brophy 1998; RCAHMS 1994). Thus, upland hiatuses in the distribution of cursus monuments are not alone. A very few closely grouped or major upland monuments might it seems be expected at most. Predicting likely locations is therefore hazardous, but regularities noted south of the Border may furnish clues.

Recent work there has demonstrated that chalkland and valley-bottom cursus sites are united by their environmental settings: all appear to have been constructed in open or semi-open grassland. Buried land surfaces preserved under the banks of the Dorset and Greater Stonehenge cursus monuments point to close-cropped sward (Allen and Gardiner 2009; French 2009), and environmental evidence from the Maxey/Etton complex in the Welland valley, Eynesbury in the Great Ouse, both Cambridgeshire, and Raunds in the Nene, Northamptonshire, point to the floodplains and first terraces being less densely vegetated than higher terraces – carrying grass with scrubby woodland at most (Brown 2000; Allen 2004: 91–3; French and Pryor 2005; Campbell and Robinson 2007). Snail shells unusually preserved in the primary silts of the long enclosure of precisely rectangular, cursus-like plan on the floodplain at Yarnton in Oxfordshire also indicate open conditions at the time of construction (Robinson 2009). This evidence has supported Barclay's and Hey's (1999) argument that the large clearances implied by cursus monument construction vastly exceeded the demands of local, small-scale arable agriculture and must therefore have been associated with widespread communal grazing of cattle.

In Scotland, the comparatively early dates returned by cursus monuments (from *c.* 3700 cal. BC based on short-life samples: Ashmore 2007; Whittle *et al.* 2011: 830; Brophy 2015) appear to present too short a time-scale for the prior creation of extensive upland clearings, but note needs to be taken of the potential Mesolithic contribution to the associated open landscapes in southern Britain (Bush and Flenley 1987; Bush 1988; Allen and Gardiner 2009; French 2009). Naturally open or lightly wooded locales may have had a long history of use for gatherings. In the Southern Uplands, the Biggar area with its significant record of Mesolithic and later activity stands out in this regard (see above), but that could in part reflect the intensity of fieldwork carried out there. Valley-head, and nodal, locations best fit a model of Neolithic upland collective pasturing succeeding Mesolithic summer assembly.

If cursus monuments arose from the enclosure of communal halls by fencing as I have previously argued (Loveday 2006a: 78–84, 2006b: 81–4), and if this fencing developed as a symbolic form in its own right (Barclay *et al.* 2002; Brophy 2007b), the size of a monument may simply have reflected the size of the group constructing it. Summer pastures suitable for transhumant exploitation by groups drawn from a widespread area would have had the greatest potential. But even at these locales the extent of unified monument construction – most plausibly perhaps to ensure the continued presence of the collective 'others' (ancestors and deities) on the pasturelands during the winter absence of the living – would necessarily have reflected the degree of social cohesion that seasonal assembly engendered. In the English Midlands and East Anglia, construction at some locales seems never to have developed beyond a general clustering of disparate monuments (e.g., Raunds, Northamptonshire: Harding and Healy 2007), while at others monuments of enlarged long enclosure-type (minor cursus monument) point to limited extra-local coalescence (Loveday 1989). The presence of three timber cursus or cursus-related sites around Friockheim, north of Arbroath, recalls the latter and uniquely appears to record the process of unit duplication and/or enlargement (Barclay 1995; Brophy 1998: 95–7; Brophy 2015). Their broad grouping over some 3 km implies at least a semi-open landscape; absence of banks and ditches denies us a source of environmental data, but potential palaeo-channels of the nearby Lunan Water hold out possibilities for investigation in the future.

It seems likely that cursus concentrations around Crieff, Comrie, Dundee and Dumfries also indicate extensive open landscapes. If each resulted from extra-local seasonal pasturing, those with the additional advantage of nodality could be predicted to attract the largest and most far-flung population groupings. It may be significant then that two of the largest cursus monuments in Scotland – the earthwork sites at Broich and Curriestanes – are to be found in the Crieff and Dumfries complexes, respectively. Both locations are the focus of corridors at topographic interfaces that have historically been key drovers' markets. Curriestanes, along with the outlying Holywood–Gallaberry sites, resembles the cluster of similarly orientated smaller sites around the major Dorchester-upon-Thames cursus in Oxfordshire (Loveday 1999, 2006a: 138–42), while the placing of cursus enclosures on opposing river banks of the Earn at Crieff (Broich and Bennybeg, the latter a timber variant) recalls complexes at Lechlade–Buscot in the Upper Thames valley (Barclay *et al.* 2003: 190–213) and Maxey/Etton in the lower Welland (Pryor *et al.* 1985; French and Pryor 2005). The common alignment of

Broich and Bennybeg additionally hints at a cross-valley layout of the type encountered in the English chalklands.

There is no reason to believe that the social and environmental dynamics that produced cursus monuments on both uplands and lowlands south of the Border differed significantly from those in the north of Britain. The artefacts that accompanied the Middle Neolithic burial at Biggar, and the discovery of a further Seamer axe in the same parish (Sheridan 1992: 207), confirm familiarity on the part of the local population with practice arising in eastern Yorkshire in the shadow of the great cross-valley Rudston cursus complex (Manby 1988; Loveday 2009). Open landscapes appear to have been key, so it may be that future palaeo-environmental investigation will highlight potential areas for focused fieldwork. Meanwhile, the nodal area around the Biggar Gap with its long record of activity (Johnston 1997; Noble 2006: 148–54) undoubtedly best fits the expectations generated in the South, although Upper Nithsdale and the Strathfillan/Glen Dochart area should not be overlooked. Comparatively recent identification of the albeit more substantial bank barrows at Auchenlaich, near Callendar, Stirling and Eskdalemuir, Scottish Borders, encourages hope (Foster and Stevenson 2002; RCAMHS 1997: 107–9) particularly as the site at Scorton, North Yorkshire confirms that such mounds may, in some instances, have lain within a cursus (Topping 1982).

Conclusion

Despite best efforts to the contrary, this chapter seems on re-reading to be tainted by Wessocentricity, a particular *bête noire* of Gordon's. I can only plead that when dealing with upland cursuses this is largely unavoidable. What has also emerged though, I hope, is that the Scottish evidence – as Gordon Barclay has so often and thought-provokingly demonstrated – furnishes major lessons for cursus studies south of the Border. Just as the major cursus at Crieff (Broich) at the opening of Strathearn is not isolated (Tullichettle and Craggish lying further up the valley, and Bennybeg across the Earn), so there must be every reason to suppose that the same is true of Swaledale and Wensleydale, where pasture in the upland valleys hides all. The lack of apparent association between Scottish cursus monuments and long mounds also has major implications in view of their apparent chronological primacy. It confirms that long mound incorporation, as witnessed in Wessex, can no longer furnish a *raison d'être* for the cursus concept. Equally, the use of larger posts for early cursus and long enclosure terminals (e.g., Kendrick 1995; Halliday 2002) casts doubt on the belief that enlarged cursus terminal banks were intended to imitate long mounds (Barrett *et al.* 1991: 51); rather they would appear to have been integral to the cursus concept, presumably replicating the gable ends of houses or halls (Barclay *et al.* 2002; Loveday 2006b; Brophy 2015). And at Upper Largie the observation that this feature would have blocked the view along the glen for people within the monument, while those walking down the outside would have had extensive views, has furnished an invaluable insight into human engagement with these monuments (Cook *et al.* 2010: 194; see also Millican 2012). Rituals comparable to the walking of the fields in the Roman Ambarvalia festival (and perpetuated in Rogationtide 'beating of the bounds': Hutton 1996: 277–87) could be envisaged with groups processing around a symbolically rendered long house of the 'others', most plausibly perhaps on arrival at, and dispersal from, the communal pasture zone. It is noteworthy that ring ditch placement almost invariably leaves an empty zone around the immediate periphery of a cursus.

Gordon Barclay's exceptional, closely directed and thoroughly reported work has hugely facilitated such observations. Without it, excavators' perceptions of cursus monuments would have been much reduced and our knowledge of the unique Scottish contribution to the genesis of these monuments, very much poorer.

Note

Since this chapter was written an earthwork upland cursus has been confirmed by RCAHMS fieldwork north-east of Biggar. The bank and ditch of the south-east terminal had previously been classified as field boundaries. Significantly, it crosses the natural valley routeway, the Biggar Gap. For more information, see at: http://canmore.rcahms.gov.uk/en/site/73422/details/broomy+law+black+mount.

Bibliography

Allen, M. (2004), 'Discussion: the development of a farmed landscape', in C. J. Ellis (ed.), *A Prehistoric Ritual Complex at Eynesbury, Cambridgeshire*, East Anglian Archaeology/Wessex Archaeology, 91–4.

Allen, M. J. and Gardiner, J. (2009), 'If you go down to the woods today; a re-evaluation of the chalkland postglacial woodland; implications for prehistoric communities', in Allen, Sharples and O'Connor (eds), *Land and People*, 49–66.

Allen, M., Sharples, N. and O'Connor, T. (eds) (2009), *Land and People. Papers in Memory of John G. Evans*, Oxford: Oxbow Books (= *Prehistoric Society Research Papers* 2).

Ashmore, P. (2007), 'Radiocarbon dates from the Pict's Knowe, Holywood and Holm', in Thomas (ed.), *Place and Memory*, 248–259.

Atkinson, R. J. C. (1955), 'The Dorset cursus', *Antiquity*, 29: 4–9.

Ballin, T. B. (2009), *Archaeological Pitchstone in Northern Britain*, Oxford: Archaeopress.

Barclay, A. and Harding, J. (eds) (1999), *Pathways and Ceremonies. The Cursus Monuments of Britain and Ireland*, Oxford: Oxbow Books.

Barclay, A. and Hey, G. (1999), 'Cattle, cursus monuments and the river: the development of ritual and domestic landscapes in the Upper Thames Valley', in Barclay and Harding (eds), *Pathways and Ceremonies*, 67–76.

Barclay, A., Lambrick, G., Moore, J. and Robinson, M. (2003), *Lines in the Landscape. Cursus Monuments in the Upper Thames Valley*, Oxford: Oxford Archaeological Unit.

Barclay, G. J. (1992), 'The Scottish gravels: a neglected resource?', in M. Fulford and E. Nichols (eds), *Developing Landscapes of Lowland Britain. The Archaeology of the British Gravels: A Review*, London: Society of Antiquaries of London, 106–24.

Barclay, G. J. (1995), 'Discussion', in Kendrick, *Proceedings of the Society of Antiquaries of Scotland*, 125: 36–9.

Barclay, G. J. (2001), '"Metropolitan" and "parochial"/"core" and "periphery": a historiography of the Neolithic of Scotland', *Proceedings of the Prehistoric Society*, 67: 1–18.

Barclay, G. J. (2005), 'The "henge" and "hengiform" in Scotland', in V. Cummings and A. Pannett (eds), *Set in Stone. New Approaches to Neolithic Monuments in Scotland*, Oxford: Oxbow Books, 81–96.

Barclay, G. J. (2009), 'Introduction: a regional agenda?', in Brophy and Barclay (eds), *Defining a Regional Neolithic*, 1–25.

Barclay, G. J., Brophy, K. and MacGregor, G. (2002), 'Claish, Stirling: an Early Neolithic structure in its context', *Proceedings of the Society of Antiquaries of Scotland*, 132: 65–137.

Barclay, G. J. and Maxwell, G. S. (eds) (1998), *The Cleaven Dyke and Littleour: Monuments in the Neolithic of Tayside*, Edinburgh: Society of Antiquaries Scotland.

Barrett, J., Bradley, R. and Green, M. (1991), *Landscape, Monuments and Society. The Prehistory of Cranborne Chase*, Cambridge: Cambridge University Press.

Bradley, R. (2011), *Stages and Screens. An Investigation of Four Henge Monuments in Northern and North-eastern Scotland*, Edinburgh: Society of Antiquaries of Scotland.

Britnell, W. and Jones N. (2012), 'Once upon a time in the west: Neolithic enclosures in the Walton Basin', in W. Britnell and R. Silvester (eds), *Reflections on the Past. Essays in Honour of Frances Lynch*, Welshpool: Cambrian Archaeological Association, 48–77.

Brophy, K. (1998), 'Cursus monuments and bank barrows of Tayside and Fife', in Barclay and Maxwell (eds), *The Cleaven Dyke and Littleour*, 93–108.

Brophy, K. (2007a), 'The cursus monuments of south-west Scotland', in Thomas (ed.), *Place and Memory*, 158–65.

Brophy, K. (2007b), 'From big houses to cult houses: Early Neolithic timber halls in Scotland', *Proceedings of the Prehistoric Society*, 73: 75–96.

Brophy, K. (2015), *Reading Between the Lines: The Neolithic Cursus Monuments of Scotland*, London: Routledge.

Brophy, K. and Barclay, G. J. (eds), *Defining a Regional Neolithic: The Evidence from Britain and Ireland*, Oxford: Oxbow Books.

Brophy, K. and Millican, K. (2015), 'Wood and fire: Scotland's timber cursus monuments', *Archaeological Journal*, 172: 1–21.

Brophy, K. and Noble, G. (2006), 'Brownsbank, South Lanarkshire (Biggar Parish), excavation', *Discovery and Excavation in Scotland*, N.S., 7: 158.

Brown, A. G. (2000), 'Floodplain vegetation history: clearings as potential ritual spaces', in A. S. Fairburn (ed.), *Plants in Neolithic Britain and Beyond*, Oxford: Oxbow Books, 49–62.

Burl, A. (1993), *From Carnac to Callanish. The Prehistoric Stone Rows and Avenues of Britain, Ireland and Brittany*, London: Yale University Press.

Bush, M. B. (1988), 'Early Mesolithic disturbance: a force in the landscape', *Journal of Archaeological Sciences*, 15: 453–62

Bush, M. B. and Flenley, J. R. (1987), 'The age of the British chalk grassland', *Nature*, 329: 434–6.

Campbell, G. and Robinson, M. (2007), 'Environment and land use in the valley bottom', in Harding and Healy (eds), *The Raunds Area Project*, 18–36.

Clare, T. (1978), 'Recent work on the Shap "Avenue"', *Transactions of the Cumberland and Westmoreland Antiquarian and Archaeological Society*, 78: 5–15.

Coles, J. M. and Simpson, D. D. A. (1965), 'The excavation of a Neolithic round barrow at Pitnacree, Perthshire, Scotland', *Proceedings of the Prehistoric Society*, 31: 34–57.

Cook, M., Ellis, C. and Sheridan, A. (2010), 'Excavations at Upper Largie Quarry, Argyll and Bute, Scotland: new light on the prehistoric ritual landscape of the Kilmartin Glen', *Proceedings of the Prehistoric Society*, 76: 165–212.

Cowley, D. and Brophy, K. (2001), 'The impact of aerial photography across the lowlands of south-west Scotland', *Transactions of the Dumfries and Galloway Natural History and Antiquarian Society*, 75: 47–72.

Dymond, D. P. (1966), 'Ritual monuments at Rudston, East Yorkshire, England', *Proceedings of the Prehistoric Society*, 32: 86–95.

Finlayson, B. (1997), 'Chipped stone: hammerstone and axeheads', *Proceedings of the Society of Antiquaries of Scotland*, 127: 185–253.

Foster, S. M. and Stevenson, J. B. (2002), 'The Auchenlaich long cairn', in Barclay *et al.*, 'Claish, Stirling: an early Neolithic structure in its context' (2002), 114–19.

French, C. (2009), 'A landscape tale of two soil histories in lowland zones of England: the fen-edge of Cambridgeshire and the downland of Cranborne Chase', in Allen, Sharples and O'Connor (eds), *Land and People*, 88–104.

French, C. and Pryor, F. (2005), *Archaeology and Environment of the Etton Landscape*, Peterborough: Fenland Archaeological Trust (= *East Anglian Archaeology* 109).

Griffith, F. M. (1985), 'Some newly-discovered ritual monuments in mid Devon', *Proceedings of the Prehistoric Society*, 51: 310–15.

Griffith, F. M. (1989), 'Aerial reconnaissance in mainland Britain in 1989', *Antiquity*, 64: 14–33.

Halliday, S. (2002), 'Excavations at a Neolithic enclosure at Castle Menzies, Aberfeldy, Perthshire', *Tayside and Fife Archaeological Journal*, 8: 10–18.

Harding, J. and Healy, F. (2007), *The Raunds Area Project. A Neolithic and Bronze Age Landscape in Northamptonshire*, Swindon: English Heritage.

Henshall, A. S. (1972), *The Chambered Tombs of Scotland*, Edinburgh: Edinburgh University Press, vol. 2.

Holgate, R. (1988), *Neolithic Settlement of the Thames Basin*, Oxford: British Archaeological Reports.

Hutton, R. (1996), *The Stations of the Sun. A History of the Ritual Year in Britain*, Oxford: Oxford University Press.

Johnston, D. A. (1997), 'Biggar Common, 1987–93: an early prehistoric funerary and domestic landscape in Clydesdale, South Lanarkshire', *Proceedings of the Society of Antiquaries of Scotland*, 127: 185–253.

Kendrick, J. (1995), 'Excavation of a Neolithic enclosure and an Iron Age settlement at Douglasmuir, Angus', *Proceedings of the Society of Antiquaries of Scotland*, 125: 29–67.

Lelong, O. and Pollard, T. (1998), 'The excavation and survey of prehistoric enclosures at Blackshouse Burn, Lanarkshire', *Proceedings of the Society of Antiquaries of Scotland*, 128: 13–53.

Loveday, R. E. (1989), 'The Barford ritual complex: further excavations (1972) and a regional perspective', in A. M. Gibson (ed.), *Midlands Prehistory*, Oxford: British Archaeological Reports, 27–50.

Loveday, R. E. (1999), 'Dorchester-on-Thames: ritual complex or ritual landscape?', in Barclay and Harding (eds), *Pathways and Ceremonies*, 49–66.

Loveday, R. (2006a), *Inscribed Across the Landscape. The Cursus Enigma*, Stroud: Tempus.

Loveday, R. (2006b), 'Where have all the Neolithic houses gone? Turf: an invisible component', *Scottish Archaeological Journal*, 28: 81–104.

Loveday, R. (2009), 'From ritual to riches: the route to individual power in later Neolithic Eastern Yorkshire?', in Brophy and Barclay (eds), *Defining a Regional Neolithic*, 35–52.

Manby, T. G. (1988), 'The Neolithic in eastern Yorkshire', in T. G. Manby (ed.), *Archaeology in Eastern Yorkshire. Essays in Honour of T. C. M. Brewster*, Sheffield: University of Sheffield, 35–88.

Maxwell, G. (1978), 'Air photography and the work of the Ancient and Historic Monuments Commission of Scotland', *Aerial Archaeology*, 2: 37–44.

Millican, K. (2007), 'Turning in circles: a new assessment of the Neolithic timber circles of Scotland', *Proceedings of the Society of Antiquaries of Scotland*, 137: 5–34.

Millican, K. (2012), 'Timber monuments, landscape and the environment in the Nith Valley, Dumfries and Galloway', *Oxford Journal of Archaeology*, 31: 27–46

Newman, T. G. (1976), 'A crop mark site at Hasting Hill, Tyne and Wear NZ 355541', *Archaeologia Aeliana*, 5th ser., 4: 183–4.

Noble, G. (2006), *Neolithic Scotland. Timber, Stone, Earth and Fire*, Edinburgh: Edinburgh University Press.

Ordnance Survey Archaeological Division (1972), 'Revision and resurvey of antiquities', *Discovery and Excavation in Scotland*, 1972: 47–53.

Oswald, A., Dyer, C. and Barber, M. (2001), *The Creation of Monuments. Neolithic Causewayed Enclosures in the British Isles*, Swindon: English Heritage.

Pryor, F., French, C., Crowther, D., Gurney, D., Simpson, G. and Taylor, M. (1985), *The Fenland Project, vol. 1: Archaeology and Environment in the Lower Welland Valley*, Cambridge: Cambridgeshire Archaeological Committee.

Ramsay, S. (1998), 'Pollen analysis', *Proceedings of the Society of Antiquaries of Scotland*, 128: 37–40.

RCHME (1975), *An Inventory of Historical Monuments in the County of Dorset, vol. 5: East Dorset*, London: HMSO.

RCAHMS (1956), *Inventory of the Ancient and Historical Monuments of Roxburgh*, Edinburgh: HMSO, 2 vols.

RCAHMS (1978), *Lanarkshire: An Inventory of the Prehistoric and Roman Monuments, I*, Edinburgh: HMSO.

RCAHMS (1994), *South East Perthshire: An Archaeological Landscape*, Edinburgh: Royal Commission on the Ancient and Historical Monuments of Scotland.

RCAHMS (1997), *Eastern Dumfriesshire: An Archaeological Landscape*, Edinburgh: Royal Commission on the Ancient and Historical Monuments of Scotland.

Robinson, M. (2009), '*Ena montana* (Drap.) and Neolithic woodland regeneration in southern England', in Allen, Sharples and O'Connor (eds), *Land and People*, 198–200.

Sheridan, A. (1992), 'Scottish stone axeheads; some new work and recent discoveries', in N. Sharples and A. Sheridan (eds), *Vessels for the Ancestors. Essays on the Neolithic of Britain and Ireland in Honour of Audrey Henshall*, Edinburgh: Edinburgh University Press, 194–212.

Stoertz, C. (1997), *Ancient Landscapes of the Yorkshire Wolds. Aerial Photographic Transcription and Analysis*, London: Royal Commission on Historical Monuments.

Stukeley, W. (1740), *Stonehenge. A Temple Restored to the British Druids*, London: Innys & Manby.

Thomas, J. (2006), 'On the origins and development of cursus monuments in Britain', *Proceedings of the Prehistoric Society*, 72: 229–242.

Thomas, J. (ed.) (2007), *Place and Memory. Excavations at the Pict's Knowe, Holywood and Holm Farm, Dumfries and Galloway, 1994–8*, Oxford: Oxbow Books.

Topping, P. (1982), 'Excavation at the cursus at Scorton, North Yorkshire, 1978', *Yorkshire Archaeological Journal*, 54: 7–21.

Topping, P. (1989), 'Early cultivation in Northumberland and the Borders', *Proceedings of the Prehistoric Society*, 55: 161–80.

Vatcher, F. de M. (1960), 'Thornborough Cursus, Yorkshire', *Yorkshire Archaeological Journal*, 38: 425–45.

Whittle, A., Healy, F. and Bayliss, A. (2011), *Gathering Time. Dating the Early Neolithic Enclosures of Southern Britain and Ireland*, Oxford: Oxbow Books, 2 vols.

CHAPTER 7

Making Memories, Making Monuments: Changing Understandings of Henges in Prehistory and the Present

Rebecca K. Younger

Introduction

> The interpretation of every excavated site is to some extent 'frozen' in the published report; there is a sort of inertia as far as any reinterpretation is concerned. (Barclay 1999: 17)

Monuments are often presented as static entities, timeless and unchanging. The emphasis placed on the conservation of sites creates an impression that monuments should be preserved as they are – they become 'fossilised', as Gordon Barclay describes the fate of Cairnpapple, West Lothian, cast in concrete (Barclay 1999: 17) (Figure 7.1). Monuments such as henges, preserved in the landscape and perceived as supposedly unchanging relics of the past do indeed become 'frozen' in our perception. However, this view can now be challenged, and Gordon Barclay has demonstrated the scope we have for reconsidering monuments, through his own important reinterpretation of Cairnpapple Hill (1999), through excavation (Barclay 1983), and by writing reflective, critical overviews of our current understanding of henge monuments (Barclay 2005). One outcome of this has been a growing awareness of the repeated reworking of monuments in prehistory, as it has become apparent that henge sites often have a long and complex life-history (Barclay 2005: 92–3). It seems increasingly inappropriate that sites should be 'frozen' in time and interpretation, or that our narratives should regard other aspects of such sites as less significant than the henge earthwork, since prehistoric understandings of these monuments appear to have been dynamic and changeable over time. Just as our contemporary understandings of monuments change, so the monuments themselves were remade and reinterpreted in the past. Here, it is argued that this process of recreating and reinterpreting monuments can be understood as a form of commemoration, by which the creation of memory need not mean consigning monuments to become fossils in the landscape, but rather envisages them as places which could be actively remade. Given the extent to which Gordon Barclay has changed and

Figure 7.1 The contemporary presentation of the henge site at Cairnpapple Hill, including the modern concrete dome which covers part of the site (photograph: author).

challenged contemporary understandings of henge monuments in Scotland, it seems fitting here to consider the ways in which understandings of these monuments changed throughout prehistory.

Monumental traditions in archaeology

The word 'monument' comes from the Latin *monere*, 'to remind' (Bradley 1993: 2). The memorial aspect of monuments seems often to have been taken for granted in archaeological discourse; it is almost tacitly assumed that monuments stand in the landscape as testament to the past (Bradley 1993; Tilley 1994); that their very existence and durability lends them an intrinsic, if abstract, mnemonic quality, independent of the actions of people. However, such an interpretation is unsatisfactory in many respects. It makes the assumption that during the Neolithic, people had the same understandings of the past and of the meaning of monuments in the landscape that we do; and it also assumes that monuments must have been static entities, unchanging, perhaps even unquestioned or uncontested, representations of the past in the landscape. Such approaches are in line with the use of the concept of 'memory', as Dušan Borić notes, as something of an 'umbrella term' referring to a variety of ways of thinking about the 'past in the past' (Borić 2010a: 3).

Critical approaches to memory have, however, been the focus of much interest in archaeology in recent years (Bradley 2002; Van Dyke and Alcock 2003; Jones 2007; Mills and Walker 2008a), as in other disciplines (e.g., Lowenthal 1985; Connerton 1989; Samuel 1994; Winter 1995, 2006; Ricoeur 2004; Treib 2009; Whitehead 2009). In archaeology, some of this work has focused on memory in specific contexts, for example, in relation to materiality and material culture (Jones 2007; Mills and Walker 2008b), or the enduring importance of place and landscape (Driscoll 1998; Hingley 1998; Bradley 2002; Thomas 2007). Memory has largely been considered in abstract terms, however, and there has been little engagement with how the practical role of memory was actually practiced as part of daily life. Alasdair Whittle (2010: 35) has pointed out the lack of an association between memory and agency in archaeological discourse. Archaeological considerations of memory as an abstract concept rather than the product of a lived experience have sometimes given the impression that memory in the past functioned independently of human action and interpretation (although cf. Gosden and Lock 1998; Bradley 2002).

Furthermore, memory has been largely considered an attribute of monuments only after their construction, even after their use. This downplays the importance of the project of building the monument, perhaps one of the most significant aspects in the life of a monument (Bradley 1993); and again neglects the role of human agency. Some redress has been made by Mark Edmonds, who depicts monument building as involving repeated seasonal gatherings, becoming part of people's life-memories, and including vivid encounters with the past such as finding ancestral remains while digging ditches (Edmonds 1999). This emphasises the creation of memory as participative and rooted in human action, rather than a detached historical response to a static entity in the landscape. How might this kind of approach help to re-evaluate henge monuments? I would suggest that considering henges as commemorative in intent might offer a way to consider how memory and monuments actually worked together in practice.

In developing the concept of 'monumental traditions', I refer not only to the entrenched, default assumption that monuments are memorials, but also to the traditional ways in which archaeologists have conceptualised monuments and written about them in archaeological discourse. These have often revolved around typologies and classification, and although there have been moves to understand monuments in different ways – for example, as 'projects' (Bradley 1993), or through landscape and phenomenological approaches (Tilley 1994; Richards 1996) – the somewhat rigid terminologies still prevail. The problems with such typological approaches have been discussed in greater depth elsewhere (e.g., Tilley 1999; Brophy 2005). Nonetheless, classification and terminology have impacted seriously on the study of henge monuments, and therefore some brief discussion will be offered here.

Henge monuments are generally understood to refer to a type of earth-work monument approximately circular in plan built throughout Britain during the Late Neolithic to Early Bronze Age period, the period spanning the third millennium BC (Harding 2003), comprising an external bank and internal ditch, and interrupted by causeways forming normally one or two entrances. Such a simple, tidy definition, however, bears little relation to reality, and the term 'henge' actually encompasses many variations on these criteria. Henges range in size, for example, from small 'mini-henges' and 'hengiforms' little more than 10 m across, to massive monuments such as Avebury, over 500 m in diameter. The bank may be internal rather than external, as at Stonehenge, Wiltshire; or be lacking altogether as at the Ring of Brodgar, Orkney; or there may be a bank but no ditch, such as at Mayburgh, Cumbria. Indeed, almost since the coining of the term 'henge' by T. D. Kendrick in 1932 (Kendrick and Hawkes 1932: 83–98), recognition of this diversity has encouraged attempts to further classify henges based on their morphology and internal features alone (e.g., Burl 1969; Wainwright 1969; Catherall 1971). The pitfalls of such an approach were demonstrated by Tom Clare, who was able to show that the typological obsession culmi-nated in a vast and unworkable number of categories (Clare 1986, 1987). In response, Barclay (1989) observed that any attempt to organise a varied group of complex monuments into simplistic categories would be problem-atic, and suggested instead that a greater understanding of the sequences and development of individual sites was needed. Despite such warnings, the treatment of henges nonetheless seems to represent a classic example of the archaeological love of classification taken to extremes, even gone awry, leading Aaron Watson to make the accusation that the term has been used uncritically almost to the extent of becoming a 'brand' (Watson 2004: 90).

And therein lies the rub. This overriding concern with classification and the uncritical use of the term 'henge' have in all likelihood inhibited our understanding of such monuments as complex, dynamic places, which were constantly being reworked, and of which the henge earthwork might be only one element – and not necessarily the first, last or most significant (Thomas 2001, 132–3; Barclay 2005: 92–3). The bank and ditch of the henge have been privileged over all other features in the way we conceive these sites, at the expense of understanding often long, complex and interesting life-histories. Our understanding of henges has been blinkered to the extent that we see only an earthwork monument – which, being perceived as such, is automatically assumed to have held some kind of memorial function – and we thus too often overlook other dimensions of these sites and the vast time-depth of their use (cf. Barclay 2005: 92–3). In the light of recent excava-tions, such as those at the multi-phase Forteviot henges, Perth and Kinross (Brophy and Noble 2012), the inadequacies of such an approach are becom-ing increasingly apparent.

While monuments cannot be *assumed* to have been memorial and unchanging, this need not mean that they did not sometimes fulfil a memorial role. Understanding henges as commemorative places can help us to overcome pervasive typological approaches, by viewing these monuments not as timeless and unchanging, but as places that were constantly being reworked. In this chapter, I will explore the possibilities of such an approach by considering the possible commemorative aspects of several henge sites – Forteviot 1, Perth and Kinross (Noble and Brophy 2011; Brophy and Noble 2012); Cairnpapple, West Lothian (Piggott 1948; Barclay 1999); and North Mains, Strathallan, Perth and Kinross (Barclay 1983) – and the ways in which these sites have been reworked over time. First, however, I will define what is meant here by the term 'commemoration'.

Commemoration

The term 'commemoration' is not intended as simply an alternative for memory, but should be regarded as a distinctive practice. Whilst the concept of memory in archaeological discourse has often been somewhat abstract, commemoration may be seen as being more thoroughly rooted in human experience. Commemoration is here understood along the lines explained by philosopher Edward Casey in his phenomenological account of remembering (Casey 1987). First, commemoration is communal, and draws on 'collective engagement' with the past, rather than memories which are based on personal experience (*ibid*.: 216–18, 235–6). Although not based on personal memories, commemoration necessarily refers to the past and is, according to Casey, a way in which it is possible to 'overcome the effects of anonymity and spatio-temporal distance' (*ibid*.: 218) – a means by which the past is made present, even if only 'translucently' (*ibid*.: 219), and even if no one involved actually *remembers* the events being commemorated. Whilst drawing on a potentially unknown past, commemoration nonetheless relies on embodied actions and ritual, which may be linked to particular places (Casey 1987: 218ff.), for example, specific monuments – such as henges.

Commemoration is also distinctive from memory in being contingent upon reference to the future as well as the past, in that it functions to perpetuate a concept of the past (Casey 1987: 256). I would suggest that commemoration therefore represents a convergence of past, present and future, and that the repeated reworking and re-use of monuments throughout prehistory could therefore be understood as one means through which past, present and future are brought together through communal, repeated activity (constituting commemoration) in one location. Monuments might therefore become places where time 'flowed' differently, and perhaps where time was imagined as even malleable because of the way commemoration builds in reference to other timescales, thereby making the monuments at which commemoration occurred particularly potent and significant places in the lives of a community. Indeed, in this sense, commemoration may be an important aspect of how a community understood time and their place in it; a means by which they were situated in their 'temporal landscape', and where acts of commemoration were referenced in relation to understandings of time (Nielsen 2008: 207–8).

The distinctions between memory and commemoration are useful to consider in relation to henges, since henge sites were locales that were used over long periods of centuries or more; the idea of collective engagement therefore opens the possibility of recalling and even reworking distant or 'mythical' pasts through commemoration, and of passing this across many generations. Henge earthworks often occupy locations that were used both before and after their construction (Thomas 2001: 132; Barclay 2005: 92–3), places that continued to be significant sites in the landscape over long periods of time. By returning to and re-using sites where there were still visible traces of earlier monuments, people may have been consciously referring to the past when they built new monuments such as henges there.

Places of commemoration, such as henges, might be seen as focal points, not only physically in space, but also in time. Although monuments might have been focal points, they were not necessarily points fixed in time, however; while 'fixed' in the sense that the location remained constant, the monuments were not unchanging, because they were reworked and interpreted in different ways. Henges as commemorative places that were returned to repeatedly and remade time and again, were places that were simultaneously the same and changing, fixed in space but not in time.

Making monuments at three henge sites

Sites such as Cairnpapple, North Mains, Strathallan and Forteviot 1 (Figure 7.2) were repeatedly and extensively reworked in prehistory. This suggests that there was nothing innate in the interpretation of monuments, but that understandings of these sites changed as they were remade. Yet, when these monuments were remade, the same location was being revisited, implying that references to the past were significant. It is this inter-relationship of change, continuity, memory and making new, that implies that these were commemorative places. In order to understand this nexus of inter-relationships, however, it is necessary to understand the sequence of development at each of these sites over time – just as Barclay (1989) noted over two decades ago.

Cairnpapple

Cairnpapple is situated on a hilltop in West Lothian, with views outward to the Firth of Forth, and the Ochil, Pentland and Moorfoot Hills (Piggott 1948: 69–71). Excavated in 1947–8 by Stuart Piggott, Cairnpapple was the first henge in Scotland to be so examined, excepting some antiquarian

Figure 7.2 Location maps for main sites discussed in the text. Contains OS data. © Crown copyright and database right (2015).

interest in other sites. Piggott (1948) identified five main periods, or phases, at the site: an arc-shaped stone setting, cremation cemetery and 'cove' in the Late Neolithic (*ibid*.: 76, 78); a henge, stone circle and monumental Beaker burials dating to around 1700 BC; a cairn, covering two cist burials, erected in the Middle Bronze Age; then a larger cairn, associated with cremation burials in urns; and finally in the Early Iron Age, a group of four inhumations in long graves (*ibid*.: 76–8). Piggott's interpretation was, however, restricted by certain factors. First, he was working within the constraints of a pre-radiocarbon dating compressed chronology of the Neolithic. Second, the nearest geographical parallels for his discoveries known at that time were located over two hundred miles to the south, at Arbor Low in Derbyshire (Barclay 1999: 19). Subsequent excavations in Scotland, including Barclay's excavations at North Mains, Strathallan, have provided local comparisons for Cairnpapple, allowing its reinterpretation by Barclay (1999); and new radiocarbon dates for the site have also recently become available (Sheridan *et al.* 2009: 214).

Having been consolidated soon after Piggott's excavation, the current physical appearance of Cairnpapple for visitors is still based on the earlier interpretation – indeed, the presentation of the monument has been described as an 'exploded diagram' of Piggott's interpretation (Barclay 1999: 17). Today, some of the burials at Cairnpapple are covered by a concrete dome (see Figure 7.1, above), which, along with the large kerbstones of the cairns and the remnants of the henge earthworks, are probably the most visually impressive features apparent on visiting the site. These also seem to dominate our understanding of the site, although they in fact for the most part represent later elements of the long life-history of Cairnpapple.

According to Barclay's (1999) reinterpretation of the sequence, Cairnpapple began life as a place of deposition during the Early Neolithic (Figure 7.3(a)). Fragments of axeheads, and sherds of plain bowl pottery, were deposited in the area that would later be enclosed by the henge (*ibid.*: 39). A series of six hearths, one later sealed beneath the henge bank, and the rest within the central area, also belong to this earliest phase of activity (*ibid.*: 39–40). A series of cremation burials associated with an arc of pits, possibly post-holes, also probably predate the henge earthworks. A bone or antler pin accompanying one of these burials has recently been dated to 3341–3024 cal. BC (SUERC-25561 (GU-19423)) (Sheridan *et al.* 2009: 214) and this fits with the Early Neolithic deposition and burial already noted.

Cairnpapple was then remade, and the area of deposition enclosed by a setting of twenty-four posts (Figure 7.3(b)) (Barclay 1999: 39). Piggott (1948: 70, 76) had identified the ring of twenty-four holes as a stone circle (from which the stones were subsequently withdrawn), and this is a possibility which cannot be ruled out; but based on comparisons with other henge sites, Barclay's postulated timber circle set in these features is equally convincing. Alex Gibson (1998: 36) has noted that where timber circles and henges are found on the same site, the timber structure usually pre-dates the henge earthworks. This relationship has been confirmed at other sites in Scotland, including North Mains (Gibson 1998: 36; Barclay 2005: 86–8) and more recently at Forteviot 1 (Noble and Brophy 2011). It seems likely therefore that at Cairnpapple, the putative timber circle preceded the construction of the henge earthworks.

After the periods of enclosure by timber circle and then earthworks, including both bank and ditch (Figure 7.3(c)), Cairnpapple again became a focus for burials and deposition, over a period of several centuries. These included a small grave with Beaker pottery (Barclay 1999: 39), and the monumental North Grave, a burial surrounded by an oval stone setting and an impressive monolith (Figure 7.3(d)). Barclay suggests this was covered

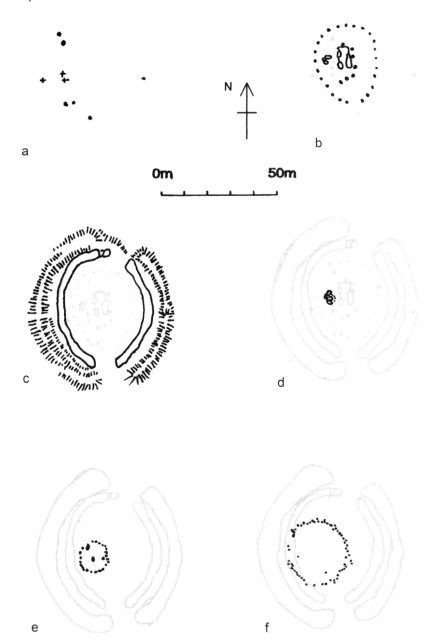

Figure 7.3 Plan of Cairnpapple Hill, showing the development of the site over time, and the spatial relationship to previous monuments: (a) hearths (•) and location of deposition (+); (b) pits, timber/stone circle and arc of post holes with cremation burials; (c) henge bank and ditch; (d) monumental 'North Grave'; (e and f) cairns. (Prepared by the author, based on Barclay 1999: figs 7, 16, 19, 24.)

by a cairn (Figure 7.3(e)), which was also later the focus for several cremation burials (*ibid.*: 39). A second cairn, overlying two cist burials (Figure 7.3(f)), was then constructed on the site. Barclay argues for the construction of a third, larger cairn overlying this; two cremations in urns were inserted into the surface of this third cairn (*ibid.*: 9–41). This series of cairns was constructed within the area enclosed by the earthworks of the henge, but the cairns were offset to the western side of its axis (Piggott 1948: 70, 76, 92; Barclay 1999: 44). Finally, Barclay reinterpreted the long graves as belonging not to the Iron Age, but to the Early Christian period (1999: 41).

North Mains, Strathallan

Like Cairnpapple, the henge site at North Mains also has a long life-history spanning millennia, of which the henge is only one element. On a terrace above the Machany Water, Perth and Kinross, the site was excavated by Gordon Barclay in 1978–9 in advance of the proposed extension of a landing strip across the site (Barclay 1983: 123; Chapter 1, this volume). Excavation revealed a sequence of pit-digging and burial, enclosure by timber circles and henge earthworks, and then the use of the site for burial (Barclay 1983, 2005). Barclay's initial interpretation (summarised from Barclay 1983) considered that activity at the site began in the third millennium BC, and included cultivation of the old land surface, pit-digging and one cremation burial, which could be securely dated to this first phase as it was sealed beneath the bank of the henge (Figure 7.4(a)). This initial activity was followed by the erection of a timber setting or settings (Figure 7.4(b) and (c)), then the construction of the henge earthworks (Figure 7.4(d)), followed by a phase of burning in the early second millennium BC, this last occurring before the timbers which formed the circle had rotted. The site was then used for burial (Figure 7.4(e)) and 'ritual/domestic activity' (Barclay 1983: 126) in the early to mid-second millennium BC, associated with Beaker pottery, Food Vessels and Cinerary Urns. In the late second to early first millennia BC, an area to the north of the henge was used for cremation pyres and interment; and then in the mid- to late first millennium AD, a long grave cemetery was added inside the henge enclosure.

The phasing of the timber circles at North Mains has been reinterpreted by Alex Gibson (1998), leading to some more general reinterpretation of the site by Barclay (2005). As noted above, excavated examples suggest that timber circles usually predate henges (Gibson 1998: 36). At North Mains, Gibson believes this to be the case because the post ramps used in the construction of the timber circle were so close to the henge ditch that the timber circle would have been prohibitively difficult to build if this had been attempted after the digging of the ditch (*ibid.*: 36). Barclay's (2005) reappraisal of the site at North Mains now proposes a sequence where one

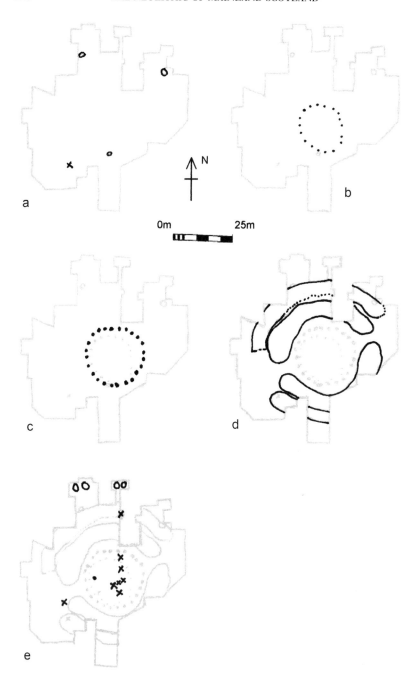

Figure 7.4 Plans of the site at North Mains over time: (a) burial (x) and pits; (b and c) timber circles; (d) henge earthworks – internal ditch and external bank; (e) pits and burials. (Prepared by the author, based on Barclay 1983: fig. 3.)

timber setting was later replaced by a larger timber circle (Figure 7.4(b) and (c)). The henge earthworks were probably constructed much later than the timber settings – and in fact may be more closely related to the use of the site for burial during the Early Bronze Age than with the timber circles (Barclay 2005: 88). The cremation burial sealed by the henge bank has been dated to 2140–1960 cal. BC (GrA-24007), while the range of dates available for the timber settings suggests that they were built 'perhaps up to several centuries earlier' than this (Barclay 2005: 86–8).

Forteviot 1

The site at Forteviot, which shares a number of close parallels with Cairnpapple and North Mains, is part of an extensive complex of prehistoric and early medieval monuments recorded as cropmarks and which includes several hengiform enclosures, both within and outwith a large palisaded enclosure (Noble and Brophy 2011). Revealed by aerial photography during the 1970s (St Joseph 1976, 1978), the cropmark complex is situated on a gravel terrace above the Water of May, a tributary of the River Earn, to the south of the modern village of Forteviot, Perth and Kinross. Excavations at Forteviot as part of the Strathearn Environs and Royal Forteviot (SERF) project have been ongoing since 2007 (Driscoll *et al.* 2010). The 2008–9 seasons of excavation concentrated on the excavation of a henge monument (Forteviot 1) with a cist burial, and an adjacent mini-henge, both enclosed within the earlier massive palisaded enclosure. These excavations have again demonstrated the complexity and longevity of henge sites, and suggest the importance of understanding the commemorative aspects of such places.

As at Cairnpapple and North Mains, the henge was a relative latecomer in the sequence of activities identified at Forteviot 1. Here, there also seems to have been a sequence of deposition of cremations; followed by enclosure by a timber circle; then the making of the henge earthworks; and finally inhumation burial. This sequence, which lasted perhaps a millennium, began with the establishment of a cremation cemetery, set in the area that would later be enclosed on the western side by the henge (Figure 7.5(a)) (Noble and Brophy 2011, 2015). The cremations in the cemetery have been radiocarbon dated to around 3090–2638 cal. BC (Noble and Brophy 2011, 2015), making it, like Cairnpapple, one of only a few known pre-henge cremation cemeteries. This cremation cemetery, which was possibly marked by a standing stone or stone setting and consisted of the burial of at least nine individuals (Noble and Brophy 2015), was later enclosed by the massive palisaded enclosure and, as at Cairnpapple, a timber circle (Figure 7.5(b)). However, unusually, and unlike Cairnpapple and North Mains, the henge earthworks were built *inside* rather than outside the timber circle (Figure 7.5(c)) (Noble and Brophy 2011; Brophy and Noble 2012). Radiocarbon dates of 2850–2488

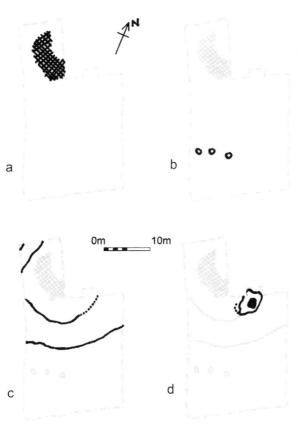

Figure 7.5 Plan of main features at Forteviot henge 1 over time: (a) area of cremation cemetery (hatched) – easternmost extent, possibly truncated by medieval pit; (b) part of the arc of the timber circle; (c) the henge ditch; (d) the cist burial. (Prepared by the author, based on Noble and Brophy 2011: fig. 6.)

cal. BC (SUERC-23237) and 2580–2467 cal. BC (SUERC-23246) have been obtained for the timber circle (Noble and Brophy 2011), which, with regard to its location in relation to the later henge ditch, is likely to have been sealed under the bank of the henge.

It was perhaps not until centuries after the timber circle had been erected that the henge was built at Forteviot. Its earliest ditch fills have been dated to 2468–2236 cal. BC (SUERC-23248) (Noble and Brophy 2011). Given the length of time that passed between the construction of the timber circle and the digging of the henge ditch, it is likely that the timber circle may have been partly decayed by the time the henge was constructed. The henge itself also appears to have had an interesting life-history, its ditch fills representing a sequence spanning possibly hundreds of years, and resulting from a variety of processes, including periods of natural silting and waterlogging, as well as the deliberate deposition of material (Noble and Brophy 2011).

Following these periods of enclosure, Forteviot 1 was used for burial. A cist, placed in a pit that partly cut the back-filled henge ditch (Figure 7.5(d)), was added during the Early Bronze Age, sometime between 2199–1977 cal. BC (SUERC-29196) (Noble and Brophy 2011). It is also possible that this cist, the massive capstone of which had a unique carving on its underside, was at some point covered by a cairn; this is suggested by the presence of a large amount of rubble in the nearby ditch fill, which may have originated from such a cairn (Noble and Brophy 2011; and see Chapter 4, this volume), now totally removed.

In summary, Cairnpapple, North Mains and Forteviot 1 – and other henge sites – did not consist of just a henge monument, but rather were places that were used and developed over a long time period. These sites began as places of deposition and burial, but were returned to and re-imagined repeatedly over the course of the following centuries; they were modified first by the construction of timber settings, and later by enclosure within henge earthworks and then used again as places of burial. Yet the longevity of the use of sites like Cairnpapple, North Mains and Forteviot 1 has in the past been somewhat neglected in archaeological discourse, which has tended to focus on these monuments as singular and unchanging, as has already been noted. Even when monument re-use has been considered, this has usually been from the perspective of much later activity at complete and perhaps already disused monuments. If we are to understand the significance of monumental sites, and the reasons why monuments were constructed, perhaps we would do better to consider the biographies of how such sites were used over the long term. Thinking about the processes of monument construction, and the repeated rebuilding of different monuments at the same location, in terms of commemorative practices, may be one way in which we can begin to unravel why certain locations remained important over time, and why people in the past repeatedly revisited, reconstructed and modified sites such as the henges discussed above.

Making memories: henge sites as commemorative places

If we are to understand henges as commemorative places, an obvious question is, what do they commemorate? At North Mains, Cairnpapple and Forteviot 1, the henges were not the first activity that happened at each location; they were not even the first monuments on their sites, and so we might suggest that henge earthworks commemorate the earlier monuments and previous activities that occurred at these places. At each of these three sites the first archaeologically visible activity is burial and/or the deposition of objects. In each case, it seems that depositional activity preceded the construction of the henge monument by a significant margin, perhaps centuries or more. Nonetheless, when these places were enclosed by timber circles and then by earthworks, it was the area that had been used for deposition and burial that was enclosed. In this sense, the construction of the later timber and earthwork monuments manifestly referred to the past as they were built with reference to the location of earlier activity at each site. Furthermore, this may have been one way in which aspects of the past could have been more permanently remembered. The burial and deposition activities may have left only ephemeral traces, particularly after many years had elapsed; although it is possible that an understanding of such places as being special may have endured for centuries, through oral traditions or aided by other physical markers (Barclay 1999: 39).

The use of these sites for burial is another aspect of their use which may be commemorated by the later monuments. Casey (1987) has noted that commemoration, being a powerful act undertaken by a community, allows people to gain a shared identity by remembering the past together. Perhaps this feeling would be enhanced if there was an understanding that previous generations were being remembered as people gathered together to build a monument. Commemoration need not, according to Casey, be predicated upon a precise knowledge or experience of the past; and so people could still commemorate the dead, even if they had no precise knowledge of who they were or their exact relationship to them, just as in a contemporary context we may commemorate the First World War, although we do not have any direct experience or memories of it (*ibid*.: 218). The knowledge that places such as the sites at Cairnpapple, North Mains and Forteviot 1 had already been used for burial may have been one compelling reason why they were chosen as places for commemoration and subsequently the construction of henge monuments.

However, henge sites were not only used as places of deposition and burial; Cairnpapple, Forteviot 1 and North Mains were also at one time defined by timber circles. Can we understand these henges as also commemorating the timber circles that once stood at them? Although at North Mains and Forteviot 1 the radiocarbon dates suggest that centuries may have passed between the construction of the timber circles and the henge, the henges may still have commemorated these earlier monuments. Certainly, the earthworks seem to be constructed with direct reference to these earlier monuments: the henge ditches at all three examples were built concentrically to the timber circles. It is also possible that the timber circles may have still been at least partly visible at the time the henges were constructed, despite the long passage of time since their construction. At North Mains, the manner in which the post-holes had silted was interpreted by Barclay as suggesting that the timbers were left *in situ* to rot (Barclay 1983: 127, 133); and that the resulting hollows formed by the decay of the posts may have survived for 'many years' (*ibid*.: 134). The posts at North Mains would probably have been substantial, seasoned oak timbers, half a metre or more in diameter (Barclay 1983: 182), and therefore very durable, meaning that the monument was likely to have stood for a century or more. The timber uprights at Forteviot 1 were probably also oak posts of a similar diameter to those at North Mains (Noble and Brophy 2011), and the lack of disturbance to their post-holes implies that the posts were also left to decay in their original positions, rather than being removed, perhaps with the henge bank being constructed around them (Brophy and Noble 2012). It is possible therefore that the timber circles were still visible by the time the henge enclosures were constructed around them at Cairnpapple and North Mains, and within the circle at Forteviot 1.

Although probably still visible, it also seems likely that the timber circles would have appeared noticeably old when the henges were built. If the wooden posts had not almost entirely decayed by this time, they would have been weathered, their colour changed by exposure to the elements and sunlight, perhaps obscured by lichen or moss, and their texture clearly unlike that of freshly hewn timbers. Furthermore, it is possible that the timbers might have become unstable and their positions may have shifted a little over the long time periods they are envisaged to have stood. At North Mains, these post-holes were packed with re-deposited gravel rather than more substantial stones (Barclay 1983: 133); perhaps the posts may thus have shifted slightly in their sockets as they began to decay and the gravel settled? Forteviot 1 is also built on similar gravel subsoil, and here there is the suggestion that at least one of the upright timbers may have slumped, perhaps as the timber circle decayed and was abandoned (Noble and Brophy 2011). If the posts of the timber circles were no longer vertical and the process of decay had already begun when the henge earthworks were constructed, this would have added to an impression that each site was already an 'old' place, somewhere where significant things had happened long previously. To construct a new monument that made explicit reference to an existing monument in terms of its shape and position seems to make a deliberate statement of reference to the past, and to the work of previous generations of monument builders. Even had the meaning and purpose of the timber circles been lost in the intervening years, the construction of the henge earthworks might still be seen as commemorative, in the sense discussed by Casey (1987: 216–18). The henge might therefore be seen as commemorating, if not the timber circle itself, then an idea of the past, as represented by an already ancient monument or ruin at the same location.

Indeed, not only timber circles, but perhaps also henge earthworks would begin to look noticeably old quite soon after their construction. As well as commemorating and referencing the past, henges themselves seem to have been allowed to become part of the past as their banks eroded and ditches silted, becoming ruins in the landscape as their earthworks slumped. At North Mains, Cairnpapple and Forteviot 1, no effort appears to have been made to maintain the henges in their newly made state, and the ditches were allowed to fill naturally with silt (Barclay 1983: 182; Noble and Brophy 2011). North Mains appears 'to have been allowed to fall gradually into disrepair' (Barclay 1983: 182). This may have been another way in which these henges were seen as referring to and commemorating the past. Kenneth Brophy has discussed the ways in which timber mortuary structures may have been made to intentionally look ancient and ruined, in an effort to mimic the earlier Neolithic timber halls which their form resembles (Brophy 2007: 90–1). Perhaps henges can be understood in a similar way: once they had been made, they were intentionally allowed to erode and decay, so that they would no longer look new. The effects of time would be visible in physical changes to the material form and appearance of monuments, for example, through the silting up of ditches, the growth of weeds on earthworks, and the scouring of material from banks. Henges would thus not only have represented the past, but would also be a visible manifestation of the effects of the passage of time.

Cairnpapple, North Mains and Forteviot 1 were still returned to and reworked after the henge at each site had been left to decay naturally. At Cairnpapple, the Bronze Age burials, although located off-centre within the timber circle and henge, nonetheless still take a cue from the earlier monuments. The burials at Cairnpapple are all within the area enclosed by the henge bank, although the cairns that covered them overlay the top of the ditch (Piggott 1948; Barclay 1999). This was interpreted by Piggott (1948) as representing a slighting of the earlier monument; whatever the reason, the cairn overspill served to create a knowing and deliberate reference between the new monument and the old. At Forteviot 1, the cist burial is also off-centre in relation to the timber circle and henge, which were concentric, being located opposite the entrance of the henge; here, too, the cist overlays the ditch of the earlier monument, which would have been partly silted by this time (Noble and Brophy 2011). Perhaps these sites can be understood as still having been in some way commemorative places even after the henge was constructed, as the insertion of the later burials make reference to the past as represented by these earlier monuments. Indeed, perhaps it is better to understand locations such as Cairnpapple, North Mains and Forteviot 1 not as commemorative *monuments* or as henge sites, but as commemorative *places*.

However, these places are not only about commemorating the past: commemoration is also rooted in the time at which the commemoration occurred – the present (Casey 1987). The actual activity of constructing a henge, in the same place where earlier monuments had been built, may have been reminiscent of earlier episodes of monument building; and therefore the practice of building a monument is in itself a form of commemoration. Building a henge and digging ditches, as commemorative acts, might be seen as ways of negotiating between the past and the present, ways of mediating between past actions and present ones, by undertaking similar activities to those deployed in earlier cycles of building at the same location. Indeed, aspects of practice and participation are central to commemoration: therefore, being involved in physically building a monument which refers to the past might be understood as participating in a commemorative act. Richard Bradley (1993) has suggested that the project of building a monument may indeed have been more significant than the monument itself. Perhaps this was also the case where commemoration was concerned. If we are to escape the notion of memory as an abstract quality of monuments, then we must give greater consideration to the processes of making it as an important aspect in the life of a monument. If monuments were left to fall into disrepair, this does not mean they were forgotten and were no longer memorials. More crucially, it is through the practice of constructing monuments that they became commemorative. Although monuments refer to the past, and are memorials in that sense, memories need to be made by people, and do not simply exist because a monument exists. If we consider the emphasis to be on the actual practice of constructing the monument, then memories can be made literally in the minds of those participating in the activity as the monument itself is made. To make a monument is to make memories; it is not the monument itself that is commemorative from the outset, but rather the acts of making monuments, and the memories such construction events engender, which can be sustained through time and thus allow later commemorations at the monument itself.

At henge sites such as Cairnpapple, North Mains and Forteviot 1, the number of times these places were returned to and reworked, and new monuments made there, does indeed suggest that projects of monument building were significant aspects of how these places were used and understood. While each monument built at these places referred to the past, they were in another sense entirely new, different from what went before. These places changed over time; indeed, while these reformulations occurred spatially in the same location, henge sites seem to have been modified almost beyond recognition as they were rebuilt over time. Cairnpapple, North Mains and Forteviot 1, as has been remarked above, varied from being places of burial and deposition; to being enclosed, first by timber and then by earthworks; to being used anew for burial of a very different kind. They changed from being places where pits and graves would leave only slight traces on the surface; to locations where views and movements are controlled by large vertical posts, deep ditches and banks; to being places of impressive burials and monumental cairns. They changed from unenclosed sites to being defined by enclosures, which emphasised circularity and concentricity; only for this emphasis subsequently to transform into often-monumental burial again avoiding the central area of the old enclosures and subverting the symmetry of these places. To discuss such remaking of these sites in terms of 'phases' or 're-use' perhaps underplays the significance of change at these places, by reducing each new monumental incarnation to a passing stage in the life of the site, when in fact the construction of new monuments on an existing site might represent a radical reinterpretation and re-imagining of that place. The tendency to reduce monuments to a history of successive phases of re-use continues despite numerous considerations of the re-use of monuments (e.g., Driscoll 1998; Gosden and Lock 1998; Holtorf 1998; Bradley 2002). The same locations at Cairnpapple, North Mains and Forteviot 1 were completely re-made over time, not just re-used.

It is by considering the commemorative aspects of these sites that we can understand the apparent paradox of such places as these, which change yet stay the same, since commemoration is predicated upon not only reference to the past, but also recurrent practices of building new monuments, and of further changing these over time. Cairnpapple Hill, North Mains and Forteviot 1 were places where the old and the new, the past and the present, coincided and even co-existed, as new monuments were made with explicit reference to the old. These were also places of change, however, and the new monuments were strikingly different from those that preceded them – perhaps because enacting commemoration necessitated grand monumental projects to reinterpret and reclaim the past, rather than simply subtle alterations to old places. At these henge sites, innovation was also commemoration. The new monuments were innovative as much as they were imitations or recollections of the past; they were linked to and directly drew on the past, but were also the product of new styles of monumentality. Therefore, the monuments at these locations continued to commemorate the past, through explicitly up-to-date actions, rooted in time as they evolved (Casey 1987). By way of comparison, Oliver Harris has explored the relationship between place, materials, memory and emotion through a study of Early Neolithic pit-digging. Harris considers that it was through participation in such activities that social relations were worked out, and that Neolithic understanding of certain places would have been intrinsically linked to the memory, emotion and social consequences of the practices undertaken at these locations (Harris 2009: 115–16). The act of doing something, physically, in a certain location and with other people – which applies to monument building as much as pit-digging – is a way in which memories are made (Casey 1987), and an understanding of the significance of a particular place formed.

At henge sites, practices associated with the building of monuments were repeated each time something new was made. Each and every time a monumental project was undertaken at these sites represented an opportunity for the making of memories and for commemoration. It is therefore crucial that we understand monuments as more than timeless entities of memory, as more than just 'fossils', and focus on the project of building monuments (Bradley 1993). It was this which was repeated so many times at North Mains, Cairnpapple and Forteviot 1 as the sites were remade and new monuments constructed.

Conclusion: changing understandings

Henge monuments such as Cairnpapple, North Mains and Forteviot 1 were, far from being timeless mnemonics, dynamic places of change, places where memories were actively made as monuments were built. We should be more open to considering understandings of these monuments as being more than just the bank and ditch of a henge. Henges are only one part in the greater life-history of these places: they were places that literally changed, being used for different activities at different times, and being remade in different forms and materials. The extent of the changes at each site implies that over time understandings of what it was appropriate to do at these places changed. Each reworking of the site may represent a reinterpretation of that place. At Cairnpapple, Forteviot 1 and North Mains, the emphasis changes over time with each new monument: from deposition and burial, to concentric enclosures, to different kinds of burial. Yet despite the changing understandings of place this suggests, there is also explicit reference to the past, and the same site is repeatedly returned to. This effort to maintain a link with the past and to commemorate that past by engaging in projects to build new monuments suggests that the significance of these places may lie in their age: they were places where the past is made visible and present (Casey 1987: 219). The ability to rework these places and to literally reshape this past through commemoration by building new monuments may have been a particularly potent act.

Commemoration allows different timescales to be brought together in one place; not only by contemporary reworkings of the past, but also by reference to the future (Casey 1987: 256). To physically reshape the representations of the past at such a place through commemorative action that would be remembered long into the future, is perhaps also to rework understandings of the past, the present and the future. These were places where different temporalities converged; memories of the past could perhaps be reinvented through commemoration and by reworking the physical traces of the past represented by earlier monuments; and future potentials could be redefined. Making monuments such as henges might be seen as a means of negotiating between the past, present and future, and of reinterpreting the past, the present and the future. The past was commemorated, not as a known fact, but as a malleable story. Making monuments and making memories are inextricably linked and changing places physically may be an integral part of changing understandings of place and time, and a community's place within it. The meanings of these monuments were neither fixed nor inherent. In the light of this, Gordon Barclay's (1989) exhortation to concentrate more on the development of sites over time seems most pertinent, given the longevity and variety of henge sites over time that is now apparent; his own contributions towards understanding this have been invaluable. It is through understanding the sequence of events at these places that we can understand the inter-relationship of time and place, continuity and change, commemoration and reinterpretation played out at these sites. Just as interpretations of these places were evidently not static in the past, so our own contemporary understandings of monuments are also changing as new sites are excavated and old interpretations revisited.

Bibliography

Barclay, G. J. (1983), 'Sites of the third millennium BC to the first millennium AD at North Mains, Strathallan, Perthshire', *Proceedings of the Society of Antiquaries of Scotland*, 113: 122–281.

Barclay, G. J. (1989), 'Henge monuments: reappraisal or reductionism?', *Proceedings of the Prehistoric Society*, 55: 260–2.

Barclay, G. J. (1999), 'Cairnpapple revisited: 1948–1998', *Proceedings of the Prehistoric Society*, 65: 17–46.

Barclay, G. J. (2005), 'The "henge" and "hengiform" in Scotland', in Cummings and Pannett (eds), *Set in Stone*, 81–94.

Borić, D. (2010a), 'Introduction: memory, archaeology and the historical condition', in Borić (ed.), *Archaeology and Memory*, 1–34.

Borić, D. (ed.) (2010b), *Archaeology and Memory*, Oxford: Oxbow Books.

Bradley, R. (1993), *Altering the Earth. The Origins of Monuments in Britain and Continental Europe*, Edinburgh: Society of Antiquaries of Scotland.

Bradley, R. (2002), *The Past in Prehistoric Societies*, London: Routledge.

Brophy, K. (2005), 'Not my type: discourses in monumentality', in Cummings and Pannett (eds), *Set in Stone*, 1–13.

Brophy, K. (2007), 'From big houses to cult houses: Early Neolithic timber halls in Scotland', *Proceedings of the Prehistoric Society*, 73: 75–96.

Brophy, K. and Noble, G. (2012), 'Henging, mounding and blocking: the Forteviot henge group', in A. Gibson (ed.), *Enclosing the Neolithic. Recent Studies in Britain and Europe*, Oxford: British Archaeological Reports, 21–35.

Burl, A. (1969), 'Henges: internal features and regional groups', *Archaeological Journal*, 126: 1–28.

Casey, E. (1987), *Remembering: A Phenomenological Study*, Bloomington, IN: Indiana University Press.

Catherall, P. D. (1971), 'Henges in perspective', *Archaeological Journal*, 128: 147–53.

Clare, T. (1986), 'Towards a reappraisal of henge monuments', *Proceedings of the Prehistoric Society*, 52: 281–316.

Clare, T. (1987), 'Towards a reappraisal of henge monuments: origins, evolution and hierarchies', *Proceedings of the Prehistoric Society*, 53: 457–77.

Connerton, P. (1989), *How Societies Remember*, Cambridge: Cambridge University Press.

Cummings, V. and Pannett, A. (eds) (2005), *Set in Stone: New Approaches to Neolithic Monuments in Scotland*, Oxford: Oxbow Books.

Driscoll, S. T. (1998), 'Picts and prehistory: cultural resource management in early medieval Scotland', *World Archaeology*, 30: 142–58.

Driscoll, S., Brophy, K. and Noble, G. (2010), 'The Strathearn Environs and Royal Forteviot project (SERF)', *Antiquity*, 84: 323.

Edmonds, M. (1999), *Ancestral Geographies of the Neolithic: Landscapes, Monuments and Memory*, London: Routledge.

Gibson, A. (1998), *Stonehenge and Timber Circles*, Stroud: Tempus.

Gosden, C. and Lock, G. (1998), 'Prehistoric histories', *World Archaeology*, 30: 2–12.

Harding, J. (2003), *Henge Monuments of the British Isles*, Stroud: Tempus.

Harris, O. (2009), 'Making places matter in Early Neolithic Dorset', *Oxford Journal of Archaeology*, 28: 111–23.

Hingley, R. (1998), 'Ancestors and identity in the later prehistory of Atlantic Scotland: the reuse and reinvention of Neolithic monuments and material culture', *World Archaeology*, 30: 231–43.

Holtorf, C. (1998), 'The life-histories of megaliths in Mecklenburg-Vorpommern (Germany)', *World Archaeology*, 30: 23–38.

Jones, A. (2007), *Memory and Material Culture*, Cambridge: Cambridge University Press.

Kendrick, T. D. and Hawkes, C. F. C. (1932), *Archaeology in England and Wales 1914–1931*, London: Methuen.

Lowenthal, D. (1985), *The Past is a Foreign Country*, Cambridge: Cambridge University Press.

Mills, B. J. and Walker, W. H. (2008a), 'Introduction: memory, materiality and depositional practice', in Mills and Walker (eds), *Memory Work*, 3–23.

Mills, B. J. and Walker W. H. (eds) (2008b), *Memory Work: Archaeologies of Material Practices*, Santa Fe, NM: School for Advanced Research Press.

Nielsen, A. E. (2008), 'The materiality of ancestors. *Chullpas* and social memory in the late prehispanic history of the south Andes', in Mills and Walker (eds), *Memory Work*, 207–31.

Noble, G. and Brophy, K. (2011), 'Ritual and remembrance at a prehistoric ceremonial complex in central Scotland: excavations at Forteviot, Perth and Kinross', *Antiquity*, 85: 787–804.

Noble, G. and Brophy, K. (2015), 'Transforming place and architecture through cremation: cremation traditions at the third millennium BC monument complex at Forteviot, Central Scotland', in L. Larsson (ed.), *What's New in the Neolithic?* Lund: Lund University Press, 164–72.

Piggott, S. (1948), 'The excavations at Cairnpapple Hill, West Lothian', *Proceedings of the Society of Antiquaries of Scotland*, 82: 68–123.

Richards, C. (1996), 'Henges and water. Towards an elemental understanding of monumentality and landscape in Late Neolithic Britain', *Journal of Material Culture*, 1: 313–33.

Ricoeur, P. (2004), *Memory, History, Forgetting*, trans. K. Blamey and D. Pellauer, Chicago, IL: University of Chicago Press.

St Joseph, J. K. (1976), 'Air reconnaissance: recent results, 40', *Antiquity*, 50: 55–7.

St Joseph, J. K. (1978), 'Air reconnaissance: recent results, 44', *Antiquity*, 52: 47–50.

Samuel, R. (1994), *Theatres of Memory: Past and Present in Contemporary Culture*, London: Verso.

Sheridan, A., Bradley, R. and Schulting, R. (2009), 'Radiocarbon dates arranged through National Museums Scotland Archaeology Department during 2008/9', *Discovery and Excavation Scotland*, n.s., 10: 212–14.

Thomas, J. (2001), 'Neolithic enclosures: reflections on excavations in Wales and Scotland', in T. Darvill and J. Thomas (eds), *Neolithic Enclosures in Atlantic Northwest Europe*, Oxford: Oxbow Books, 132–43.

Thomas, J. (2007), *Place and Memory: Excavations at the Pict's Knowe, Holywood and Holm Farm, Dumfries and Galloway, 1994–8*, Oxford: Oxbow Books.

Tilley, C. (1994), *A Phenomenology of Landscape: Places, Paths and Monuments*, Oxford: Berg.

Tilley, C. (1999), *Metaphor and Material Culture*, Oxford: Berg.

Treib, M. (2009), *Spatial Recall: Memory in Architecture and Landscape*, London: Routledge.

Van Dyke, R. M. and Alcock, S. E. (eds) (2003), *Archaeologies of Memory*, Oxford: Blackwell.

Wainwright, G. J. (1969), 'A review of henge monuments in the light of recent research', *Proceedings of the Prehistoric Society*, 35: 112–33.

Watson, A. (2004), 'Monuments that made the world: performing the henge', in R. Cleal and J. Pollard (eds), *Monuments and Material Culture. Papers in Honour of an Avebury Archaeologist: Isobel Smith*, Salisbury: Hobnob Press, 83–97.

Whitehead, A. (2009), *Memory*, London: Routledge.

Whittle, A. (2010), 'The diversity and duration of memory', in Borić (ed.), *Archaeology and Memory*, 35–47.

Winter, J. (1995), *Sites of Memory, Sites of Mourning. The Great War in European Cultural History*, Cambridge: Cambridge University Press.

Winter, J. (2006), *Remembering War: The Great War between Memory and History in the Twentieth Century*, New Haven, CT and London: Yale University Press.

CHAPTER 8

Seeing the Wood in the Trees: The Timber Monuments of Neolithic Scotland

Kirsty Millican

Introduction

Monuments of stone, earth and wood form an integral part of the way in which the Neolithic period in Scotland is understood. Yet while much has been written in Neolithic studies about earthen and megalithic monuments, those constructed of timber have tended to be afforded a much lesser role, if they are considered at all (e.g., Thomas 1999; Malone 2001). This was rebalanced considerably by Gordon Barclay's research into, and excavations of, a series of timber structures in eastern lowland Scotland (North Mains, Balfarg Riding School, Claish, Carsie Mains and Littleour) from the 1980s to the 2000s, while the excavations of others (e.g., Kendrick 1995; Rideout 1997; Thomas 2007; Noble and Brophy 2011) further raised the profile of timber monuments within the Neolithic monumental repertoire. Studies of Neolithic monumentality none the less continue to remain weighted towards stone and earthen sites.

I would argue that not fully considering timber monumentality leaves us with only a partial account of Neolithic life, particularly considering the wooded nature of the landscape at that time (Tipping 1994; Edmonds 1999; Noble 2006a). This chapter is an attempt to remedy this imbalance and shall focus upon the results of my own research (cf. Millican 2009), which aimed to identify and characterise Neolithic timber monuments across Scotland. The vast majority were initially recorded as cropmarks on aerial photographs and are located in mainland lowland contexts. In considering this range of monuments and evidence that is often overlooked, it is hoped that the picture that emerges will add to traditional considerations of monument building, enriching narratives not just for Scotland, but the Neolithic of Britain as a whole.

Defining timber monuments

Neolithic timber monuments can be characterised as structures built of substantial wooden posts, usually of oak, almost all of which defined enclosures that were unroofed or unroofable (the exceptions being timber halls, discussed below), with non-domestic functions as far we can define these (in other words, I have not included the small group of light timber buildings that may have been houses (see Chapter 10, this volume)). As such, they encompass a wide variety of structures, of very different forms, dimensions and date. By considering them together it is not intended to imply that they performed the same functions or were necessarily associated with one another in any way, other than by the material from which they were constructed (though some may well have had connections both with other timber monuments and structures built of other materials). Instead, by drawing together this disparate set of wooden structures, I hope to highlight the range and ubiquity of such monuments built during the Neolithic, and to begin to place them on a more equal footing with the better known monuments built of earth and stone.

Surviving today simply as pits and post-holes dug to take the upright timbers (Figure 8.1), timber monuments are recorded either as cropmarks on aerial photographs or (far less commonly) as chance discoveries during excavation. Therefore, the nature of these monuments and the

Figure 8.1 Post-holes, initially dug to hold timbers, formed the palisaded enclosure boundary at Forteviot. Timber monuments survive today as negative features like these, which in turn sometimes form cropmarks (photograph: K. Brophy).

manner in which they can be recognised means that they have tended to remain relatively invisible in the archaeological record. Although a handful of timber structures of Neolithic date have been known of in Scotland for a considerable period of time (e.g., Coles and Simpson 1965; Piggott 1971–2; Piggott and Simpson 1971; Masters 1973), it was only with the advent of an annual programme of aerial survey by the Royal Commission on the Ancient and Historical Monuments of Scotland (RCAHMS) in 1976 (Maxwell 1978) that they began to be recorded in significant numbers. Even so, without suitable parallels, not all were initially recognised as timber structures of Neolithic date, the most famous example being the Neolithic timber hall at Balbridie, Aberdeenshire, which was recorded during the first summer's flying by RCAHMS and initially interpreted as an early historic hall (Reynolds 1978). Since the excavation of Balbridie, an increasing number of timber monuments has been excavated in Scotland (e.g., Kendrick 1995; Rideout 1997; Thomas 2007; Lelong and MacGregor 2008), with Gordon Barclay directing some of the key excavations (e.g., Barclay 1983; Barclay and Maxwell 1998; Barclay et al. 2002; Brophy and Barclay 2004). Some of the excavated structures have begun to be integrated into wider narratives of this period (e.g., Noble 2006a; Brophy 2006; Bradley 2007). Yet these excavated sites form only a relatively small proportion of the total number of timber monuments recorded in Scotland, the bulk of which are known from the interpretation of their traces on aerial photographs.

Working with this aerial record is not without its difficulties, and only a limited amount of synthetic work has been carried out to date on those sites recorded as cropmarks. As a result, until the research upon which this chapter is based, which undertook a survey of the aerial record across Scotland in order to identify and characterise timber monuments of potentially Neolithic date (Millican 2009), the full nature and extent of such structures in Scotland was poorly understood. Some surveys had been undertaken, though these usually concentrated upon a single monument form (e.g., Tolan 1988; Brophy 1999a, 1999b; Millican 2007). However, this limited work also means that the attribution of some cropmark sites to the Neolithic period or even their definition as structures of timber, rather than as sockets for stone monuments, for example, can be difficult, and some of the interpretations must be accepted as provisional and potentially subject to change. Nevertheless, the excavated sites provide a solid basis from which to interpret the many plough-levelled sites and, while some difficulties of interpretation remain, it is possible to recognise a large number and wide range of different timber monuments built during the Neolithic period in Scotland. These monuments can be divided into several broad classificatory groupings, outlined below. The categories used here are primarily envisaged as an useful shorthand and are not intended necessarily to indicate functional similarity or equivalence. Essentially, classification here is envisaged as a starting point permitting us to begin to understand and discuss a diverse range of sites.

Early Neolithic timber monuments

Radiocarbon dates obtained from excavated timber monuments suggest that there may have been two episodes of timber monument building, with a division occurring towards the end of the third millennium BC. Between *c.* 4000 cal. BC and *c.* 3300 cal. BC, timber monuments of broadly rectilinear form were built, while after the thirty-fourth century cal. BC new forms of timber monument appear in the archaeological record, mostly of curvilinear form. The available dates, though, are variable both in quality and quantity. Although some of the monument types discussed here were considered within the Bayesian statistical analysis of Whittle, Healy and Bayliss (2011), as yet most timber monuments have not been subject to a comprehensive Bayesian review of dates. The dating for many of these timber monuments, therefore, awaits further analysis and refinement. Nevertheless, from the evidence currently available, this broad division between Early and Later Neolithic timber monuments does appear robust.

The group of Early Neolithic monuments will be considered here first. These comprise monuments usually defined as timber cursus monuments (Brophy 1999a; Thomas 2006; Brophy and Millican 2015), timber halls (Brophy 2007) and timber mortuary structures (Barclay and Maxwell 1991; Lelong and MacGregor 2008; Millican 2009); examples of each have been excavated. The majority of those that have been excavated seem to have been wholly or partially burnt down.

Timber cursus monuments

Turning first to timber cursus monuments, these were long rectilinear enclosures defined by timber posts (Brophy 1998: 92). Cursus monuments as a whole (the majority of which are defined by earthworks) have been discussed in varying degrees of detail elsewhere (e.g., Brophy 1998, 1999a, 1999b; Loveday 2006a; Thomas 2006). In Scotland, twenty-nine definite or probable timber cursus monuments can currently be recognised (Brophy and Millican 2015), most of which have been recorded as cropmarks on aerial photographs; so far no timber cursus monuments have been discovered outwith Scotland (Brophy 2015a). Additionally, a handful of what appear to be partially recorded monuments can be identified in the cropmark record (Millican 2009: 72–3) and, while insufficient of each site has been recorded to provide a definite interpretation, they may represent parts of further timber cursus monuments.

Although there is variation in terms of the form and dimensions of timber cursus monuments (Figure 8.2), most measure more than 100 m in length

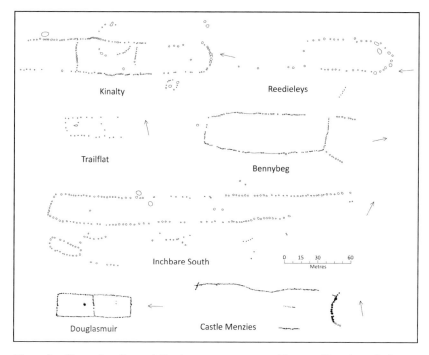

Figure 8.2 Examples of post-defined cursus monuments (Sources: Douglasmuir from Kendrick 1995; Castle Menzies from Halliday 2002; the remainder are transcriptions from cropmarks carried out by the author.)

and vary in width from around 14 m to around 45 m, though width can also vary within an individual cursus. At least one closed terminal has been recorded at most sites, with both terminals known at only a handful. Many sites do not appear to have been recorded to their full extent and the 'missing' terminals may still await discovery, though, considering the large proportion of sites at which only one terminal is known, it is possible that in some cases only one terminal was ever constructed. These terminals tend to be squared or rounded, defined in some cases by cropmark post-pits, which appear to be larger than those defining the enclosure sides, suggesting that the terminals were enhanced by the erection of larger posts (and this phenomenon has been confirmed by excavation, see below). In addition, the cropmark post-pits normally identifiable at cursus monuments do not always appear to be of uniform spacing or size, suggesting these monuments had an irregular form.

Many timber cursus monuments have one or more internal divisions, which are often accompanied by changes in width as the cursus sides curve inwards to meet them (Brophy 2000: 15), while in other cases the cursus changes width either side of the division. Added to this is the fact that the boundaries of some cursus monuments are distinctly uneven and most seem to be 'segmented' in appearance, suggesting different episodes of construction (*ibid.*: 15). Therefore, many of these timber cursus monuments may represent longer-term projects that were reconstructed and added to rather than one-off construction events, and so may have appeared in a number of different forms through their use-life (Brophy and Millican 2015; Brophy 2015a).

A number of post-defined cursus monuments have now been excavated, including those at Douglasmuir in Angus (Kendrick 1995); Bannockburn, Stirling (Rideout 1997); Castle Menzies (Halliday 2002) and Milton of Rattray (Brophy 2000), both in Perth and Kinross; Dunragit, Dumfries and Galloway (Thomas 2004a, 2004b); Upper Largie, Argyll and Bute (Cook *et al.* 2010); and Holywood North and Holm (Thomas 2007), both in Dumfries and Galloway. Most of these cursus monuments were subject to destruction at the end of their lives with episodes of burning and post removal, although in some instances, such as Castle Menzies, all posts were left to rot *in situ*. Oak seems to have been the predominant wood type used for construction. These excavations confirmed many of the observations drawn from the cropmark evidence as outlined above.

Taken together, these excavated sites have provided radiocarbon dates that indicate that the majority of post-defined cursus monuments date to between *c.* 3900 and 3600 cal. BC (Thomas 2006: 233), though not all have accepted the early dating of these monuments (Loveday 2006a). Indeed, recent Bayesian analysis of a suite of radiocarbon dates (Whittle *et al.* 2011: 830ff.) suggests that construction of timber cursus monuments may have begun a century or two later, after *c.* 3700 cal. BC. This was based upon an amalgamation of radiocarbon dates which included the mortuary enclosure at Inchtuthil, Perth and Kinross, as well as timber cursus monuments. Yet in the context of Scotland's Neolithic beginning *c.* 3800 cal. BC, as suggested by Whittle *et al.* (2011), timber cursus monuments would still have been built within the first generations of farmers.

The use and function of these sites have been the subject of a certain amount of debate, with no firm conclusions reached (e.g., Brophy 1998; Harding 1999; Loveday 2006a). The linear nature of cursus monuments in general (regardless of boundary form) has led to suggestions that they may have been processional ways or formalised routes, though other functions suggested include structures aligned on important locations or astronomical events, or linking important areas, barriers between areas of differing significance, symbolic rivers, an area marked off and given over to the gods or ancestors, or for controlling trade or access (Barclay and Maxwell 1998: 114–15; Parker Pearson and Ramilisonina 1998; Loveday 2004, 2006a: 125–6). Others have suggested a connection between cursus monuments and long mortuary enclosures (e.g., Harding 1999; Loveday 2006a), or between post-defined cursus monuments and Early Neolithic timber halls (Loveday

2006a; Noble 2006a: ch. 3; Thomas 2006; Brophy 2007). An individual cursus monument may have encompassed several of these roles, though the wide variation in size and shape evident indicates that no one function is likely to explicate all. Therefore, a single unitary purpose cannot be used to explain these structures. Nevertheless, all are linked by their distinctly linear nature, by the fact that all excavated sites seem to have been constructed of oak and that most of those excavated seem to have been subject to burning.

Timber halls

Timber halls (Figure 8.3) comprise substantial rectilinear timber structures which may have supported a roof (Brophy 2007, and Chapter 10, this volume), measuring between 22 m and 27 m in length and 8–11 m in width. Five such timber halls have so far been excavated: at Balbridie, Aberdeenshire (Fairweather and Ralston 1993); Claish, Stirling (Barclay

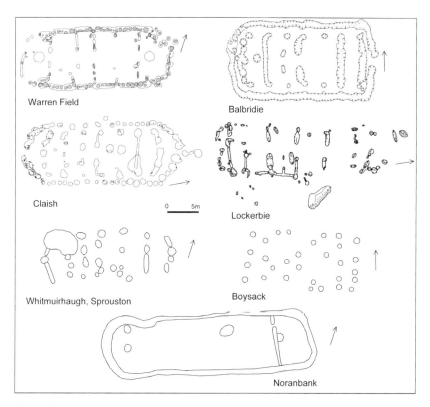

Figure 8.3 Comparative plans of (top) excavated timber halls and (bottom) cropmark sites. (Sources: Warren Field, Murray *et al.* 1999; Balbridie, Fairweather and Ralston 1993; Claish, Barclay *et al.* 2002; Lockerbie, Kirby 2011 and © CFA Archaeology Ltd; the remainder are transcriptions from cropmarks.)

et al., 2002); Doon Hill A, East Lothian (Hope-Taylor 1966, 1980; ScARF 2012); Warren Field, Aberdeenshire (Murray *et al.* 2009); and Lockerbie Academy, Dumfries and Galloway (Kirby 2011). All these sites are remarkably similar in architecture (defined by large wooden posts, with plank or wattle walling between the uprights), morphology and size, appear to date between 3800 and 3600 cal. BC (Brophy 2006: 33; Murray *et al.* 2009: 79; Whittle *et al.* 2011: 832) and were burnt down at the end of their life. Each had a number of internal divisions defined by individual posts or by continuous slots, dividing the interior space up into several distinct compartments (or rooms) and entrance gaps within their short ends. Four unexcavated cropmark sites (Whitmuirhaugh in the Borders, Muircambus in Fife, and Noranbank and Boysack, both in Angus) appear similar enough to these excavated sites to be interpreted as probable roofed timber halls (Brophy 2007; Millican 2009). Additionally, there is a handful of cropmark sites for which it is not possible to provide a definitive interpretation, but that may represent further examples of timber halls. Alternatively, they may be mortuary enclosures or later Neolithic rectangular timber enclosures (both discussed below); general morphological similarities (see Barclay *et al.* 2002, for a detailed discussion) mean it is not always possible to offer a definitive interpretation and only future research can resolve this interpretative quandary.

The timber halls are generally interpreted as roofed structures (Fairweather and Ralston 1993: 315–16; Barclay *et al.* 2002: 98; Murray *et al.* 2009). This is based upon structural elements such as the symmetry of the ground plan and presence of possible roof supports (Murray *et al.* 2009) and the substantial and apparently unitary nature of the structures (Fairweather and Ralston 1993: 316; Barclay *et al.* 2002: 98). Additionally, the intensity of burning at each site indicates that there was more to burn than simply free-standing posts, suggesting roofed and walled structures (Barclay *et al.* 2002: 98), while burnt debris in the upper fills of features at Warren Field may relate to roof collapse after the structure was fired (Murray *et al.* 2009). That these structures definitely were roofed is, however, as yet by no means certain, though the balance of evidence does currently suggest that these buildings were probably roofed.

The functions of these buildings have been the subject of much debate. A purely domestic role could be supported by the cereal grains and pottery uncovered at each excavated site and by recent pollen analysis at Warren Field which indicated that cereals were being grown in a clearance around the hall (Tipping *et al.* 2009). A number of other features, however, suggest a function that goes beyond the purely domestic: an unusually large quantity of cereals at Balbridie (Fairweather and Ralston 1993: 317), pits formed the focus of structured deposits before having fires set within them in the centre of Claish (Barclay *et al.* 2002: 77–8) and pits at both ends of the timber hall at Warren Field which may have held massive free-standing timbers, subsequently removed (Murray *et al.* 2009: 37–40). The relative scarcity of timber halls in the archaeological record, and their large size suggest that they may have played a specialised role within Neolithic life (Brophy 2007). Compared with the smaller and more ephemeral nature of the known domestic architecture (Brophy 2006 and Chapter 10, this volume), timber halls would have truly been monumental structures. Bradley (2005) has equated Balbridie with the concept of 'big houses', that is, massively enlarged versions of domestic structures which would have been important to whole communities rather than just the homes of particular groups of people (*ibid*.: 65). Therefore, these roofed timber halls cannot be considered to be purely domestic structures, but instead may have held significance to whole communities of people, playing an important part in the life of individuals during the early part of the Neolithic period.

Timber mortuary structures

Timber mortuary structures tend to be rectilinear or trapezoidal palisade enclosures of Early Neolithic date. Despite the type name for such monuments, common in the literature, not all sites can definitely be shown to be associated with mortuary deposits (cf. Noble 2006a), and so a mortuary association, for some of these sites at least, is not assured. A small but diverse group of enclosures interpreted as timber mortuary structures have been excavated in Scotland (Figure 8.4): namely, Eweford West and two structures at Pencraig Hill (Lelong and MacGregor 2008), all in East Lothian: Kintore in Aberdeenshire (Cook and Dunbar 2008): Kirkburn, Dumfries and Galloway (Cormack 1962–3): and Inchtuthil, Perth and Kinross (Barclay and Maxwell 1991). All these sites were defined by a continuous timber palisade, were burnt down and, where dates are available, date to the first half of the fourth millennium BC. Only the structure at Kintore seems to have formed a component of a larger monument. Here timbers were erected in recuts of a segmented ditch surrounding an Early Neolithic long mound, probably during the final phase of activity at this complex site. Elements of this palisade may have formed a revetment for the mound (Cook and Dunbar 2008: 46), but the burning and removal of this fence suggests a function other than revetment (these would have removed the very structures that were supposed to maintain the mound's integrity and they were not replaced). Instead, the timber fencing may have acted as a screen, obscuring activities within the enclosure from open view (*ibid*.: 51).

The remainder of the mortuary structures have revealed no evidence of internal mounds and appear to have formed free-standing timber structures enclosing areas of activity. In the case of Eweford West, Kirkburn, and the first structure at Pencraig Hill, this was associated with cremation burning and deposits, while a timber mortuary structure and pyre were uncovered

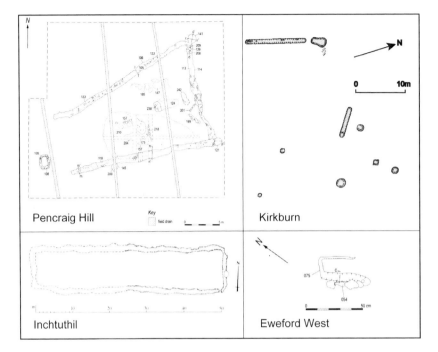

Figure 8.4 Comparative plans of timber mortuary enclosures. (Sources: Cormack 1962–3; Barclay and Maxwell 1991; Lelong and MacGregor 2008.)

within the second, larger structure at Pencraig Hill. These monuments, therefore, appear to have fulfilled mortuary roles. No such evidence, though, was uncovered at Kintore or Inchtuthil. At the latter, excavation revealed two phases of fencing, the second intensely burnt before falling or being pushed over while still on fire (Barclay and Maxwell 1991: 38). The role of this structure remains unclear due to plough truncation. A small number of cropmark enclosures, which are morphologically similar in form to Inchtuthil, have been recorded and may represent additional examples of this form of monument.

Timber settings

The final group of Early Neolithic timber monuments considered here are open-ended trapezoidal or rectangular structures that appear in the crop-mark record as two lines of three or four pits each (Figure 8.5). All are relatively short in length, measuring less than 20 m. Some settings are almost as wide as they are long and widen towards one end, while others are defined by evenly spaced parallel pits. All those known in Scotland (thirteen in total) have been recorded only as cropmarks; none have yet been excavated,

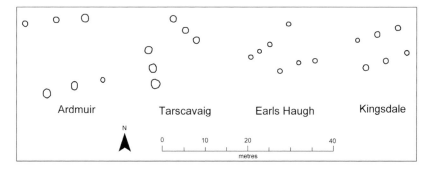

Figure 8.5 Examples of rectangular timber settings, transcribed by the author from cropmark evidence

making dating and interpretation difficult. Therefore, until future excavation provides secure dating, the attribution of these sites to the Neolithic period must remain provisional; even the assumption that these pits held posts has not yet been tested.

Nevertheless, such small rectangular and trapezoidal settings of posts recall structures leading up to the façades of long barrows in England (Kinnes 1992: 92), such as the post structures excavated in the forecourts at Street House (Vyner 1984) in North Yorkshire, Fussell's Lodge in Wiltshire (Ashbee 1966) and Wayland's Smithy in Oxfordshire (Atkinson 1965; Whittle 1991). The trapezoidal group of timber settings in Scotland bears the strongest morphological relationship to these post-settings and so may have had a similar mortuary or ceremonial role. Some may perhaps have abutted undiched turf-built long barrows, which would not necessarily be apparent in the cropmark record. Within Scotland comparisons may also be drawn with the cursus façade at Bennybeg, Perth and Kinross (Brophy 2000; Brophy and Millican 2015); this is a large U-shaped or trapezoidal setting of post-pits abutting the end of the cursus. This little-known group of sites, then, are likely to date to the earlier part of the Neolithic, although definitive dating and interpretation awaits future investigation.

Timber monuments in the Late Neolithic

The construction of these types of Early Neolithic monuments does not appear to have continued into the later part of the Neolithic, and after around 3300 cal. BC new forms of timber monuments were built, including, for the first time, monuments of curvilinear form. As well as new types of timber monument, different forms of practice are also evident in the Late Neolithic: for instance, the majority of the excavated timber structures do not appear to have been burnt down, instead they were left to decay *in situ*. However, not every timber monument of this date represented a break from the past.

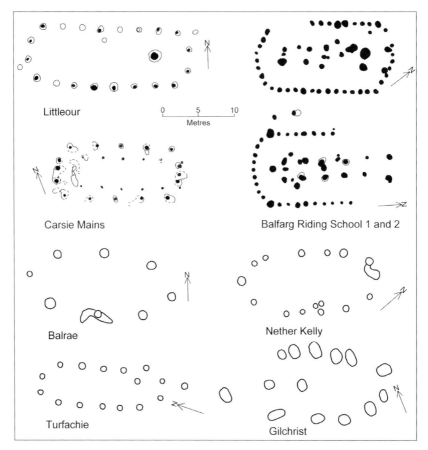

Figure 8.6 Comparative plans of (top) excavated rectilinear timber enclosures and (bottom) cropmark equivalents. (Source: Littleour, Carsie Mains and Balfarg Riding School from Brophy and Barclay 2004; the remainder are transcriptions from cropmarks carried out by the author.)

Rectangular timber enclosures

A group of rectilinear enclosures of apparently free-standing timbers (Figure 8.6), sometimes (unhelpfully) called 'unroofed timber halls' (Brophy 2007, and pers. comm.), were built between 3500 and 2600 cal. BC, and have generally been assigned mortuary or ceremonial roles (*ibid.*). Four such structures have been excavated: at Littleour (Barclay and Maxwell 1998) and Carsie Mains (Brophy and Barclay 2004), both in Perth and Kinross, and two at Balfarg Riding School in Fife (Barclay and Russell-White 1993; and see Chapter 11, this volume). Seventeen unexcavated cropmark sites appear similar enough to belong to the same tradition, and there are several other cropmark sites for which it is not possible to determine if they represent Late Neolithic enclosures, Early Neolithic timber halls or are perhaps not even Neolithic; only future investigation will determine how these more ambiguous sites should be interpreted.

These rectangular enclosures measure between 15 m and 27 m in length and 4–9 m in width. In ground plan, they are very similar to the earlier timber halls, though they do not have such obvious sub-divisions, entrances or internal symmetry. A few of these Late Neolithic structures have one or two axial posts, and some have possible tree throws associated with their boundaries. For instance, a tree throw was enclosed within the east end of the structure at Carsie Mains (Brophy and Barclay 2004: 19), and cropmarks of possible tree throws appear to be associated with the boundary posts at the cropmark examples at Westerton and Balrae, both in Perth and Kinross. None of the sites excavated appear to have burnt down; instead, they seem to have been left to decay.

These sites are usually interpreted as unroofed structures, based upon a number of structural elements that would have made roofing difficult (Hogg, in Barclay and Maxwell 1998: 60–1; Hogg, in Barclay and Russell-White 1993: 169–82; Brophy 2007: 85). The presence of light temporary roofing (Brophy and Barclay 2004) or the use of turf as a structural component (Loveday 2006a, 2006b), making a roofed reconstruction possible, have been suggested for some of these structures. However, the possible incorporation of a tree within the structure at Carsie Mains appears to argue against the possibility of a roof being present, as does the misalignment and spacing of posts at Littleour (Barclay and Maxwell 1998: 60), although the relative chronology of interior features and boundaries at such monuments is rarely clear. Most seem to have been formed by free-standing timbers, though the excavator of Balfarg Riding School interpreted the outer boundary of both of these structures as forming a continuous fence (Barclay and Russell-White 1993).

The broad similarity in plan of these sites to the earlier roofed timber halls is obvious, even down to the inclusion of architectural elements normally associated with roof support, such as axial and 'aisle' posts. It has been suggested (Brophy 2006, 2007) that this indicates the survival of an idea or template across the centuries and the mimicking of earlier architectural features, albeit in a non-functional form. It may reflect some kind of shared 'architectural vocabulary' (Barclay *et al.* 2002: 110) or it may be that, as has been suggested for longhouses and long barrows in central Europe (Bradley 1998, 2002), the survival of the shells of burnt timber halls of the Early Neolithic and a possible association with death and the ancestors resulted in the copying of these architectural forms in reduced or alternative variants (see Brophy 2005, 2006, 2007). Certainly, the architectural similarities between these two types of structure (timber halls and rectangular timber structures) suggest some form of connection despite the

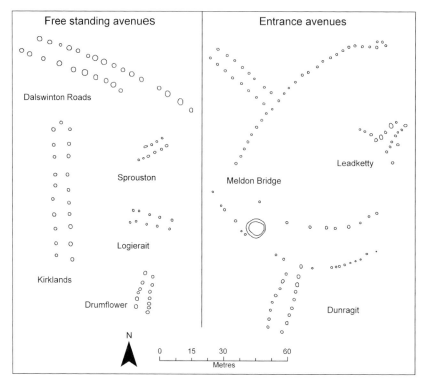

Figure 8.7 Comparison between free-standing avenues and palisaded enclosure entrance avenues, transcribed by the author from cropmark evidence (prepared by the author).

centuries between them. These timber structures have been interpreted as having both ceremonial (e.g., Littleour) and funerary (e.g., Balfarg Riding School) roles.

Avenues

Avenues comprise two roughly parallel lines of posts (sometimes pits) and are characterised by their narrow width relative to length. As cropmarks they are defined by lines of pits which may curve slightly along their length and these avenues are usually open-ended. A number of avenues of varying sizes have been recorded as cropmarks, either free-standing or as part of a larger monument (Figure 8.7). The largest are free-standing avenues measuring more than 60 m in length. Only four of these long avenues have been recorded in Scotland. All but one measure between 6 and 7 m in width and curve slightly along their length. Five shorter avenues, measuring between 14 m and 21 m in length and 5 m or less in width, can also be identified. In terms of dimensions, these shorter avenues are comparable to avenues that form the entrances to palisaded enclosures (see below).

All these sites have been recorded as cropmarks, but only the entrance avenues of the palisaded enclosures at Forteviot and Leadketty, both in Perth and Kinross, have been excavated, though two avenues defined by pits and not posts have been investigated at Holm in Dumfries and Galloway (Thomas 2007) and Upper Largie in Argyll (Cook *et al.* 2010) (interestingly, both in close association with an earlier timber cursus (see Brophy 2015a)). This could suggest that all similar avenues in the cropmark record were also defined by pits, not posts. However, excavation at a number of avenues in the north of England (Harding 1981; Tavener 1996: 184–6; RCAHMS 1997: 117) has demonstrated that these monuments were defined by posts, while the excavation of the entrance avenues at Forteviot (Noble and Brophy 2011) and Leadketty (Noble and Brophy 2014), both Perth and Kinross, showed that these were defined by timber posts. Therefore, it seems reasonable to suggest that at least some of these cropmark avenues may also have been post-defined, though only excavation can determine which of these cropmark sites represent avenues defined by posts and which were defined simply by pits. Earthen banks formed by upcast from post-holes may have formed additional structural elements, though, again, only excavation can determine the presence of such additional components. None of the excavated northern English timber post avenues appears to have been burnt, but instead were left to decay *in situ*.

Dating of avenues is uncertain, but comparison with the entrance avenues at palisaded enclosures suggests that a Late Neolithic date is most likely. In addition, the small number of similar avenues excavated in the north of England provided Late Neolithic or Early Bronze Age dates (Harding 1981: 184–6; Tavener 1996: 117; RCAHMS 1997; Loveday 2006a). Therefore, it is possible to suggest that post-defined avenues may date anywhere between around 3000 and 1800 cal. BC, with further work required to clarify their dating and interpretation. Furthermore, we still have little understanding of what most avenues were leading to, or away from.

The broad similarity of avenues to earlier cursus monuments invites comparison, though avenues are narrower and usually much shorter in length than cursus monuments. While this similarity of form may be coincidental, it could suggest that cursus monuments and avenues fulfilled similar roles, and it is possible that avenues represent a continuation of older concepts and ideas; as noted, two timber cursus monuments may have been replaced by avenues. Certainly, avenues represent a late survival of a linear form of monument, in the same way as the aforementioned rectangular timber structures appear to recall timber halls.

Timber circles

Timber circles are circular or elliptical enclosures defined by posts, and comprise the largest single group of Neolithic timber monuments recorded in Scotland, with over eighty identified (Millican 2007, 2009). Most timber circles are recorded as cropmarks, though a small number were discovered during excavation; thirty have been investigated. Unexcavated cropmark timber circles may not all be Neolithic; interpretation from cropmarks alone is difficult as circles of pits in cereal crops can represent Neolithic timber circles, timber structures erected prior to the construction of barrows or later prehistoric (mostly Iron Age) roundhouses. Nevertheless, there are some distinguishing features which can aid the interpretation of these sites from cropmarks (Millican 2007) and these inform the discussion below, though some difficulties and ambiguities remain, meaning that for a small number of sites it remains difficult to provide a definitive interpretation without excavation.

Taking all the timber circles together (excavated and cropmark), there is considerable variety in terms of dimensions and form (Figure 8.8), with timber circles ranging in diameter from 2.5 m to around 75 m (though the inner circuit of the palisaded enclosure at Dunragit, measuring around 120 m in diameter, could also be considered a timber circle) and varying from truly circular to elliptical in plan (Millican 2007). Most of those excavated were built of large diameter timbers and, where the wood type has been identified, oak was used. Limited material culture has been recovered from these sites, the only exceptions being Balfarg, Fife, (Mercer 1981) and Machrie Moor I on the island of Arran (Haggarty 1991), where structured deposits of stone tools, pottery and animal bone were found within the fill of the post-holes. The presence of carbonised planking at North Mains, Strathallan, Perth and Kinross (Barclay 1983) may suggest the existence of screens or barriers between the uprights in some cases, though other examples may have simply comprised circles of substantial wooden uprights with no obvious fencing or barriers. All but the timber circle excavated at Eweford in East Lothian, which was subject to post burning (Lelong and MacGregor 2008), appear to have been left to decay *in situ*.

Only a small number of timber circles in Scotland has been securely dated. Nevertheless, these dates, along with those from timber circles excavated outwith Scotland (Gibson 2005), indicate that the timber circle was a long-lived monumental form, with origins in the Late Neolithic and construction continuing into the second millennium BC. Some of the earliest dates for timber circles in Britain are associated with sites in Scotland, such as Carsie Mains in Perth and Kinross, which produced a radiocarbon date of 3350–2920 cal. BC (AA-53271) (Brophy and Barclay 2004), while similarly early dates may be suggested for the timber circles pre-dating the henge enclosures they were found within at the aforementioned North Mains and

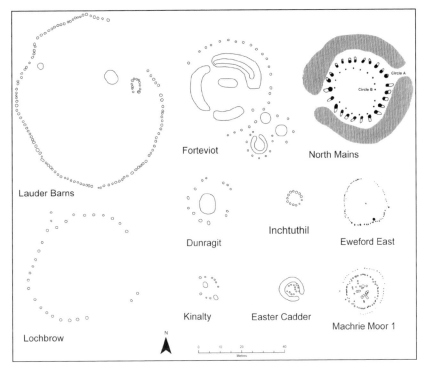

Figure 8.8 Examples of timber circles: North Mains, from Gibson 2005; Eweford East, from Lelong and MacGregor 2008; Machrie Moor, from Haggarty 1991; the remainder are transcriptions from cropmarks carried out by the author.

at Cairnpapple, West Lothian (Barclay 2005). A similarly early radiocarbon date of 3520–3100 cal. BC (GU-11050) has recently been recovered from a timber circle at Ferrybridge in West Yorkshire (Roberts 2005). These dates, therefore, suggest that the emergence of timber circles coincides with the 3300 cal. BC horizon mentioned above.

Construction into the Early Bronze Age is evidenced by the timber circles uncovered at Croft Moraig in Perth and Kinross (Piggott and Simpson 1971; Bradley and Sheridan 2005), Strichen (Phillips *et al.* 2006) and Broomend of Crichie (Bradley 2011), both in Aberdeenshire, and Upper Largie in Argyll and Bute (Cook *et al.* 2010), indicating the longevity of this monument form. Considering the range evident in both date and dimensions, it is highly unlikely that all monuments classified as timber circles served the same purpose. Instead, the structures grouped together in this class of monument likely fulfilled a range of functions and meanings, and are brought together here because of their shared materiality and morphology.

Palisaded enclosures

Palisaded enclosures are massive sub-circular timber enclosures, usually measuring more than 200 m across and dating to the last few centuries of the Neolithic (Gibson 2002a; Noble and Brophy 2011). Five definite and one possible Late Neolithic palisaded enclosures have been recorded in Scotland, all but one as cropmarks (Figure 8.9). Excavations have taken place at the cropmark sites at Meldon Bridge, Scottish Borders (Speak and Burgess 1999); Dunragit, Dumfries and Galloway (Thomas 2004b); and Forteviot and Leadketty, both Perth and Kinross (Noble and Brophy 2011, 2014). The extant embanked enclosure at Blackshouse Burn, South Lanarkshire (Lelong and Pollard 1998), is also considered a palisaded enclosure for the purposes of this discussion. Part of the circuit of what may be an additional palisaded enclosure can be seen as cropmarks at Kinloch in Fife (Millican 2009: 98). Most of these enclosures are defined by individual post-pits with a single entrance in the form of an out-turned avenue, and three have a natural feature (such as a terrace edge or river) as one element of their boundary. There is a clear association with other ritual monuments, such as henges or timber circles, which are often contained within the boundaries of the enclosures themselves or are in close spatial association.

Excavations indicate that these enclosures were constructed between *c.* 2900 and 2500 cal. BC (Lelong and Pollard 1998; Speak and Burgess 1999; Gibson 2002b; Thomas 2004a; Noble and Brophy 2011), though they may have continued in use for a longer period of time, something that is suggested by some of the later dates from Meldon Bridge which extend into the Chalcolithic (Speak and Burgess 1999). All seem to have been constructed using massive oak posts, with smaller posts, which may have supported horizontal planking between the larger boundary posts at Meldon Bridge, Leadketty and the two outer rings at Dunragit, suggesting that at least some of these sites may have presented solid barriers. The fact that most have out-turned entrances further suggests that control and restriction of physical and visual access was a concern (Gibson 2001: 77; 2002b). Some variability is, however, suggested by the fact that no smaller interval posts were found between the main posts of the central ring at Dunragit (Thomas 2004a, 2004b) or as part of the boundary and avenue at Forteviot (Brophy and Noble 2009; Noble and Brophy 2011). These enclosures were probably defined by free-standing timbers, with a low earthwork bank suspected at Forteviot (Noble and Brophy 2011), echoing the stone bank at Blackshouse Burn which incorporated timber posts in the Late Neolithic (Lelong and Pollard 1998).

As only small proportions of these massive palisaded enclosures have yet been excavated, future work may alter the way in which we choose to reconstruct these sites. However we envisage these enclosures, they were massive structures requiring huge investments of time and resources, each needing

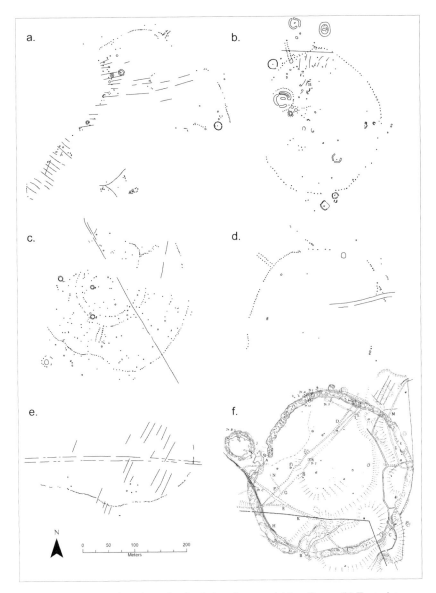

Figure 8.9 Comparative plans of palisaded enclosures: (a) Leadketty; (b) Forteviot; (c) Dunragit; (d) Meldon Bridge; (e) Kinloch; (f) Blackshouse Burn ((f) from Lelong and Pollard 1998, the remainder are transcriptions from cropmarks carried out by the author).

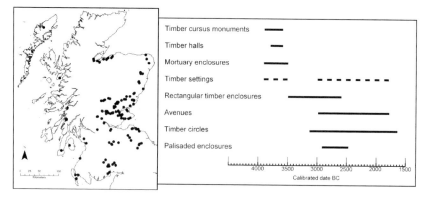

Figure 8.10 The distribution and date ranges of Neolithic timber monuments in Scotland (dashed date ranges where dating uncertain).

hundreds of felled or fallen trees to construct, and their size means that they could easily have accommodated thousands of people, suggesting a role in hosting such large gatherings, presumably for ceremonial purposes. Their sheer scale ensured that they had a long-term impact on the landscape, and became a focus for subsequent monument building and funerary activity. The excavated examples seem to have been left to decay *in situ*, other than the entrance avenue at Forteviot where some posts seem to have been removed, others left to decay and one may even have been burnt.

Timber monuments and Scotland's Neolithic

This brief summary illustrates the variety of different forms of timber monument that were built during the Neolithic period, with around 200 now recognised in Scotland (Millican 2009, and see Figure 8.10). As these structures have been recorded primarily as cropmarks, the distribution must be considered to represent only a partial picture; cropmarks primarily form in the cereal producing and relatively drier east and south of the country, meaning that the known distribution of timber monuments is biased towards those regions (Hanson 2005: 76). The small number of sites that are known in the less intensively flown and non-cropmark producing areas in Western Scotland, Highlands and Islands, hints at a much more widespread distribution than is currently known, and more are likely to be recognised in the future.

The dates obtained for timber monuments indicate that they were built throughout what is traditionally considered the Neolithic period. Indeed, some of these sites may have been amongst the earliest monumental forms constructed in Scotland, and some continued to be built into the Early Bronze Age. Timber monuments, therefore, clearly formed an important part of the Neolithic monumental repertoire and played a more significant and prominent role than has often been recognised in the literature.

Identifying the existence of these monuments and the forms that they took is important and demonstrates that Neolithic communities employed a variety of materials to construct their monuments, of which timber seems to have been an important and often primary element.

Considering the number of monuments now identified and the indication of a widespread distribution, we cannot consider such structures to have merely been improvisation in areas where stone was not available for monument building, as has been argued in the past, nor were they just precursors to stone-built structures (though in some cases stone monuments were built over the locations of timber monuments at a later date). Instead, they formed important monuments in their own right, covering a larger part of the Neolithic landscape than has often been acknowledged, and having an impact on that landscape through tree removal. In terms of numbers, it is possible to speculate that there may have been as many timber monuments as those of other materials. Whether or not this was the case, the numbers now recognised mean that timber monuments should be considered on an equal footing with monuments built of other materials.

Yet the nature of monument building and the practices taking place at these structures does not appear to have remained unchanged throughout the Neolithic period. The current chronology clearly suggests that there were two episodes of timber monument building with a division around 3300 cal. BC (Figure 8.10), though as only a relatively small proportion of sites have been reliably dated, this observation must remain provisional. Nevertheless, this division is given further support by distinct differences between monuments built during the earlier and later Neolithic, suggesting that this is indeed a real pattern. First, all of the earlier structures are primarily linear or rectilinear in form, while the later monuments also include circular and curvilinear forms. Second, the way in which these two groups of sites were treated at the end of their lives also differs. While most monuments built during the earlier part of the Neolithic were burnt down, or at least elements of these structures were burnt, the majority of the monuments of later date show no evidence of burning and instead were left to decay *in situ*.

These factors may indicate distinctly different beliefs, practices and ideas behind the construction, use and destruction of monuments in the earlier and later Neolithic, perhaps suggesting a distinct change in the way in which such monuments were conceptualised and used, and may also reflect wider social changes taking place among Neolithic communities during the important transitional centuries in the middle of the Neolithic (Noble 2006a; Bradley 2007). Indeed, the construction of circular or curvilinear timber monuments after around 3300 cal. BC closely follows the pattern seen in monuments built of other materials as well as domestic structures (Bradley 1998: ch. 7; Chapter 10, this volume). The changes in timber monument architecture, therefore, likely reflect just one element of wider social change, but also remind us that wooden structures cannot be separated from those built of other materials or wider social processes.

Yet within this pattern of change, there are suggestions of continuity; rectilinear timber enclosures may reflect Early Neolithic timber halls and avenues, timber cursus monuments. Within the context of a wider change to curvilinear forms it is interesting that the rectilinear persists within timber monument building. Perhaps this shows a continuation of older ideas, beliefs and concepts, but, considering the distinct differences in specific form and treatment, likely also reflects the transformation of those ideas and concepts, transformations that perhaps culminate in circular and curvilinear monuments. If this is case, it may be possible to see timber enclosures and avenues as some form of transitional monuments, reflecting the old, while transforming it and pointing to the new. The replacement of the rectilinear timber enclosures at Balfarg Riding School with a circular henge may be a reflection of this.

That communities were building monuments of timber should perhaps come as no surprise as, during the Neolithic period, Scotland would have been predominantly forested (Tipping 1994, 2003). The building of monuments from these trees could, then, just reflect the use of the material easiest to hand. However, there are some factors that suggest that the use of timber to build monuments may have had more than just a practical consideration. Where there is surviving evidence from excavations, oak seems to have been preferentially selected, though other wood types were also used, often for minor architectural elements (such as at the Warren Field timber hall and Carsie Mains rectangular enclosure). While the use of decay-resistant oak could indicate nothing more than practical considerations, in the mixed forests of Scotland it did not necessarily predominate (Tipping 1994; Noble 2006a), meaning that the consistent use of this wood type entailed its deliberate selection and more effort being expended to source timbers of suitable girth and height. Additionally, the fact that most of the monuments of Early Neolithic date appear to have been burnt down at the end of their use life indicates that the longevity of these structures was not a prime concern, at least during the earlier part of the Neolithic.

Societies draw meaning from the natural world that surrounds them, with world views and understandings of the world created through practical engagements with their surroundings (Gow 1995: 47; Rival 1998a: 1; Evans et al. 1999; Ingold 2000). In a tree-filled world (as the Neolithic in mainland Scotland would have been), woodland would have formed a major element of the way in which the world was understood by Neolithic communities, and is likely to have been drawn into aspects of the Neolithic world view, of beliefs, values and myths (Rival 1998b; Evans et al. 1999; Noble 2006a: 97). Creating structures from timber cut from the forest, then, is unlikely to have been entirely devoid of meaning and instead would have incorporated and transformed any meanings wood had for its users. As such, timber monuments were built, not just from the building material alone, but from its meanings and associations as well. Here we can draw upon a rich anthropological literature (e.g., Rival 1993, 1998b; Gow 1995; Jones and Cloke 2002) indicating some of the different ways in which the trees, forest and timber may have been conceived. Although not offering direct analogy, these studies demonstrate the widespread nature of tree symbolism and indicate that trees, woodland and structures constructed from the forest are likely to have been intimately connected with Neolithic communities and their beliefs, and embodied with specific meanings and associations. As a result, the predominant use of oak may reflect wider considerations than just the practical nature of the wood itself, drawing on aspects of beliefs and meanings associated with this type of tree.

However, these monuments did not incorporate timber entirely unchanged. Instead, monuments re-ordered the material into new relationships with their surroundings and created new engagements with this material. That the Neolithic was the period when woodland was first cleared and managed on a large scale (Edwards and Whittington 2003; Noble 2006a: 94) may be significant as such clearance required new relationships to be forged between the forest and its human inhabitants (Noble 2006b: 60; Brophy 2015a). Building monuments in timber could have been one way in which these new relationships were expressed and negotiated (Noble 2006b; Brophy and Millican 2015), with some monuments closely associated with the practice of clearance. The building of timber monuments required a certain level of forest clearance, both to provide the material to build the structures and also to open up a space large enough in the forest to construct them (Tipping *et al.* 2009). Therefore, the changing architecture and treatment of timber monuments from the Early Neolithic into the later part of this period may reflect the changing relationship people had with the landscape (Noble 2006a) and changes in the landscape itself. Of course, this is not to suggest that all timber monuments necessarily shared the same meanings. Indeed, the range of forms and dates clearly indicate that this was not the case, but at a broad level the materiality of these monuments appears to have reflected meanings and beliefs associated with the forest, the cutting down of trees and their subsequent placing in pits, thus transforming the life and meanings of the woodland.

Conclusion

The fact that so many timber monuments can now be recognised within the archaeological record clearly has implications for the way in which we can understand the Neolithic period in Scotland. Monumentality cannot be understood as predominantly a phenomenon of stone or earth. Instead, Neolithic communities across mainland Scotland were building monuments of timber along with those of other materials. Such structures were

not derivative from or secondary to those of stone or earth, but an important aspect of the expression of monumentality, and their form, materiality
and treatment can inform us about some of the concerns, values and relationships of Neolithic communities. In particular, they suggest a distinct
change in the middle centuries of the Neolithic, around 3300 cal. BC, in the
way in which communities conceptualised their monuments, the practices
that gave rise to such structures and perhaps also the relationships people
had with the forest. Such a shift coincided with other changes around
this time, the emergence of what Thomas (2010) has called the Grooved
Ware complex, which included the appearance of Grooved Ware (Thomas
1999; Noble 2006a: 19), the construction of other broadly circular monuments, such as henges (Bradley 1998; Noble 2006a) and the development of
round/oval house architecture (Bradley 2007; Brophy 2015b and Chapter
10, this volume). Therefore, the changes obvious in timber monuments
seem to reflect wider social changes occurring around this time (Thomas
2010).

Of course, this is a very broad-brush perspective and there are many
questions and ambiguities remaining. A closer look at individual monuments and their locations (Millican 2009, 2012) suggests subtleties and differences not obvious at the regional scale, while additional work is required
to clarify the nature and date of some of the cropmark sites. Additionally,
those in Scotland form only one part of wider traditions of timber monument building in north-western Europe in the Neolithic (e.g., Gibson 2002a,
2005; Larsson 2008; Noble and Brophy 2011). Therefore, understanding
timber monuments constructed in Scotland, along with reflections upon
their materiality, form and other factors, clearly have much to add to our
comprehension of the Neolithic period and the communities that built these
monuments not just in Scotland, but also more widely.

Bibliography

Ashbee, P. (1966), 'The Fussell's Lodge long barrow excavations, 1957', *Archaeologia*,
    100: 1–80.
Atkinson, R. J. C. (1965), 'Wayland's Smithy', *Antiquity*, 39: 126–33.
Barclay, A. and Harding, J. (eds) (1999), *Pathways and Ceremonies: The Cursus
    Monuments of Britain and Ireland*, Oxford: Oxbow Books,
Barclay, G. J. (1983), 'Sites of the third millennium BC to the first millennium AD at
    North Mains, Strathallan, Perthshire', *Proceedings of the Society of Antiquaries of
    Scotland*, 113: 122–281.
Barclay, G. J. (1995), 'What's new in Scottish prehistory?', *Scottish Archaeological
    Review*, 9: 3–14.
Barclay, G. J. (2001), 'Neolithic enclosures in Scotland', in T, Darvill and J. Thomas
    (eds), *Neolithic Enclosures in Atlantic Northwest Europe*, Oxford: Oxbow Books,
    144–54.

Barclay, G. J. (2005), 'The "henge" and "hengiform" in Scotland', in Cummings and Pannett (eds), *Set in Stone*, 81–94.

Barclay, G. J., Brophy, K. and MacGregor, G. (2002), 'Claish, Stirling: an Early Neolithic structure in its context', *Proceedings of the Society of Antiquaries of Scotland*, 132: 65–137.

Barclay, G. J. and Maxwell, G. S. (1991), 'Excavation of a Neolithic long mortuary enclosure within the Roman legionary fortress at Inchtuthil, Perthshire', *Proceedings of the Society of Antiquaries of Scotland*, 121: 27–44.

Barclay, G. J. and Maxwell, G. S. (1998), *The Cleaven Dyke and Littleour: Monuments in the Neolithic of Tayside*, Edinburgh: Society of Antiquaries of Scotland.

Barclay, G. J. and Russell-White, C. J. (1993), 'Excavations in the ceremonial complex of the fourth to second millennium BC at Balfarg/Balbirnie, Glenrothes, Fife', *Proceedings of the Society of Antiquaries of Scotland*, 123: 43–210.

Bradley, R. (1998), *The Significance of Monuments*, London: Routledge.

Bradley, R. (2002), *The Past in Prehistoric Societies*, London: Routledge.

Bradley, R. (2005), *Ritual and Domestic Life in Prehistoric Europe*, London: Routledge.

Bradley, R. (2007), *The Prehistory of Britain and Ireland*, Cambridge: Cambridge University Press.

Bradley, R. (2011), *Stages and Screens: An Investigation of Four Henge Monuments in Northern and North-eastern Scotland*, Edinburgh: Society of Antiquaries of Scotland.

Bradley, R. and Sheridan, A. (2005), 'Croft Moraig and the chronology of stone circles', *Proceedings of the Prehistoric Society*, 71, 269–81.

Brophy, K. (1998), 'Cursus monuments and bank barrows of Tayside and Fife', in G. J. Barclay and G. S. Maxwell (eds), *The Cleaven Dyke and Littleour*, 92–108.

Brophy, K. (1999a), 'The Cursus Monuments of Scotland', unpublished PhD thesis, University of Glasgow.

Brophy, K. (1999b), 'The cursus monuments of Scotland', in Barclay and Harding (eds), *Pathways and Ceremonies*, 119–29.

Brophy, K. (2000), 'Excavations at a cropmark site at Milton of Rattray, Blairgowrie, with a discussion of the pit-defined cursus monuments of Tayside', *Tayside and Fife Archaeological Journal*, 6: 8–17.

Brophy, K. (2005), 'Not my type: discourses in monumentality', in Cummings and Pannett (eds), *Set in Stone*, 1–13.

Brophy, K. (2006), 'Rethinking Scotland's Neolithic: combining circumstance with context', *Proceedings of the Society of Antiquaries of Scotland*, 136: 7–46.

Brophy, K. (2007), 'From big houses to cult houses: Early Neolithic timber halls in Scotland', *Proceedings of the Prehistoric Society*, 73: 75–96.

Brophy, K (2015a), *Reading Between the Lines: The Neolithic Cursus Monuments of Scotland*, London: Routledge.

Brophy, K. (2015b), Houses, halls and occupation in Britain and Ireland, in C. Fowler, J. Harding and D. Hoffman (eds), *The Oxford Handbook of Neolithic Europe*, Oxford: Oxford University Press, 327–44.

Brophy, K. and Barclay, G. J. (2004), 'A rectilinear timber structure and post-ring at Carsie Mains, Meikleour, Perthshire', *Tayside and Fife Archaeological Journal*, 10: 1–22.

Brophy, K and Millican, K. (2015), 'Wood and fire: Scotland's timber cursus monuments', *Archaeological Journal*, 172: 297–324.

Brophy, K. and Noble, G. (2009), 'Excavations within the Palisaded Enclosure at Forteviot: 2008 Interim Report', unpublished report, University of Glasgow, Department of Archaeology.

Coles, J. M. and Simpson, D. D. A. (1965), The excavation of a Neolithic round barrow at Pitnacree, Perthshire, Scotland, *Proceedings of the Prehistoric Society*, 31: 34–57.

Cook, M. and Dunbar, L. (2008), *Rituals, Roundhouses and Romans. Excavations at Kintore, Aberdeenshire 2000–2006, vol. 1: Forest Road*, Edinburgh: Scottish Trust for Archaeological Research.

Cook, M., Ellis, C. and Sheridan, A. (2010), 'Excavations at Upper Largie, Argyll and Bute, Scotland: new light on the prehistoric ritual landscape of the Kilmartin Glen', *Proceedings of the Prehistoric Society*, 76: 165–212.

Cormack, W. F. (1962–3), 'Burial site at Kirkburn, Lockerbie', *Proceedings of the Society of Antiquaries of Scotland*, 96: 107–35.

Cummings, V. and Pannett, A. (eds), *Set in Stone: New Approaches to Neolithic Monuments in Scotland*, Oxford: Oxbow Books.

Edmonds, M. (1999), *Ancestral Geographies of the Neolithic: Landscapes, Monuments and Memory*, London: Routledge.

Edwards, K. J. and Whittington, G. (2003), 'Vegetation change', in K. J. Edwards and I. B. M. Ralston (eds), *Scotland After the Ice Age: Environment, Archaeology and History 8000BC–AD 1000*, Edinburgh: Edinburgh University Press, 63–84.

Evans, C. and Hodder, I. (2006), *A Woodland Archaeology: Neolithic Sites at Haddenham*, Cambridge, McDonald Institute for Archaeological Research.

Evans, C., Pollard, J. and Knight, M. (1999), 'Life in woods: tree-throws, "settlement" and forest cognition', *Oxford Journal of Archaeology*, 18: 241–54.

Fairweather, A. and Ralston, I. B. M. (1993), 'The Neolithic timber hall at Balbridie, Grampian Region, Scotland: the building, the date, the plant macrofossils', *Antiquity*, 67: 313–23.

Gibson, A. (2001), 'Hindwell and the Neolithic palisaded sites of Britain and Ireland', in A. Gibson and D. Simpson (eds), *Prehistoric Ritual and Religion*, Stroud: Sutton, 68–79.

Gibson, A. (ed.) (2002a), *Behind Wooden Walls: Neolithic Palisaded Enclosures in Europe*, Oxford: British Archaeological Reports.

Gibson, A. (2002b), 'The later Neolithic palisaded enclosures of the United Kingdom', in A. Gibson (ed.), *Behind Wooden Walls*, 5–23.

Gibson, A. (2005), *Stonehenge and Timber Circles*, Stroud: Tempus.

Gow, P. (1995), 'Land, people and paper in Western Amazonia', in E. Hirsch and M. O'Hanlon (eds), *The Anthropology of Landscape: Perspectives on Space and Place*, Oxford: Oxford University Press, 43–62.

Haggarty, A. (1991), 'Machrie Moor, Arran: recent excavations at two stone circles', *Proceedings of the Society of Antiquaries of Scotland*, 121: 51–94.

Halliday, S. (2002), 'Excavations at a Neolithic enclosure at Castle Menzies, Aberfeldy, Perthshire', *Tayside and Fife Archaeological Journal*, 8: 11–18.

Hanson, W. S. (2005), 'Sun, sand and see: creating bias in the archaeological record', in K. Brophy and D. Cowley (eds), *From the Air: Understanding Aerial Archaeology*, Stroud: Tempus, 73–85.

Hanson, W. S. and Macinnes, L. (1991), 'The archaeology of the Scottish Lowlands: problems and potential', in W. S. Hanson and E. A. Slater (eds), *Scottish Archaeology: New Perceptions*, Aberdeen: Aberdeen University Press, 153–66.

Harding, A. F. (1981), 'Excavations in the prehistoric ritual complex near Milfield, Northumberland', *Proceedings of the Prehistoric Society*, 47: 87–135.

Harding, J. (1999), 'Pathways to new realms: cursus monuments and symbolic territories', in Barclay and Harding (eds), *Pathways and Ceremonies*, 30–8.

Hope-Taylor, B. (1966), 'Interim report on Doon Hill', *Medieval Archaeology*, 10: 175–6.

Hope-Taylor, B. (1980), 'Balbridie ... and Doon Hill', *Current Archaeology*, 72: 18–19.

Ingold, T. (2000), *The Perception of the Environment: Essays on Livelihood, Dwelling and Skill*, London: Routledge.

Jones, O. and Cloke, P. (2002), *Tree Cultures: The Place of Trees and Trees in their Place*, Oxford: Berg.

Kendrick, J. (1995), 'Excavation of a Neolithic enclosure and an Iron Age settlement at Douglasmuir, Angus', *Proceedings of the Society of Antiquaries of Scotland*, 125: 29–67.

Kinnes, I. (1992), *Non-megalithic Long Barrows and Allied Structures in the British Neolithic*, London: British Museum.

Kirby, M. (2011), 'Lockerbie Academy: Neolithic and Early Historic timber halls, a Bronze Age cemetery, an undated enclosure and a post-medieval corn-drying kiln in south-west Scotland', *Scottish Archaeological Internet Report* (= *SAIR*), 46: dx.doi.org/10.5284/1017938.

Larsson, L. (2008), 'Ritual structures in south Scandinavian prehistory', *Proceedings of the Prehistoric Society*, 74: 193–214.

Lelong, O. and MacGregor, G. (2008), *The Lands of Ancient Lothian: Interpreting the Archaeology of the A1*, Edinburgh: Society of Antiquaries of Scotland.

Lelong, O. and Pollard, T. (1998), 'The excavation and survey of prehistoric enclosures at Blackshouse Burn, Lanarkshire', *Proceedings of the Society of Antiquaries of Scotland*, 128: 12–53.

Loveday, R. (2004), 'Contextualising monuments: the exceptional potential of the middle Trent Valley', *Derbyshire Archaeological Journal*, 124: 1–12.

Loveday, R. (2006a), *Inscribed Across the Landscape: The Cursus Enigma*, Stroud: Tempus.

Loveday, R. (2006b), 'Where have all the Neolithic houses gone? Turf : an invisible component', *Scottish Archaeological Journal*, 28: 81–104.

Malone, C. (2001), *Neolithic Britain and Ireland*, Stroud: Tempus.

Masters, L. (1973), 'The Lochhill long cairn', *Antiquity*, 47: 96–100.

Masters, L. (1983), 'Chambered tombs and non-megalithic barrows in Britain, in C. Renfrew (ed.), *The Megalithic Monuments of Western Europe*, London: Thames & Hudson, 97–112.

Maxwell, G. S. (1978), 'Air photography and the work of the Royal Commission for the Ancient and Historical Monuments of Scotland', *Aerial Archaeology*, 2: 37–45.

Mercer, R. J. (1981), 'The excavation of a Late Neolithic henge-type enclosure at Balfarg, Markinch, Fife, Scotland, 1977–78', *Proceedings of the Society of Antiquaries of Scotland*, 111: 63–171.

Millican, K. (2007), 'Turning in circles: a new assessment of the Neolithic timber circles of Scotland', *Proceedings of the Society of Antiquaries of Scotland*, 137: 5–34.

Millican, K. M. (2009), 'Contextualising the Cropmark Record: The Timber Monuments of the Neolithic of Scotland', unpublished PhD thesis, University of Glasgow.

Millican, K. (2012), 'Timber monuments, landscape and environment in the Nith Valley, Dumfries and Galloway', *Oxford Journal of Archaeology*, 31: 27–46.

Murray, H. K., Murray, J. C. and Fraser, S. M. (2009), *A Tale of the Unknown Unknowns: A Mesolithic Pit-alignment and a Neolithic Timber Hall at Warren Field, Crathes, Aberdeenshire*, Oxford: Oxbow Books.

Noble, G. (2006a), *Neolithic Scotland: Timber, Stone, Earth and Fire*, Edinburgh: Edinburgh University Press.

Noble, G. (2006b), 'Tree architecture: building monuments from the forest', *Journal of Iberian Archaeology*, 8: 53–72.

Noble, G. and K. Brophy (2011), 'Big enclosures: the later Neolithic palisaded enclosures of Scotland in their Northwestern European context', *European Journal of Archaeology*, 14: 60–87.

Noble G. and K. Brophy, K. (2014), 'Construction, process, environment: altering the landscape in Neolithic lowland Scotland', in M. Furholt, D. Mischka, G. Noble and D. Olausson (eds), *Landscapes, Histories and Societies in the Northern European Neolithic*, Berlin: German Research Foundation, 65–77.

Parker Pearson, M. and Ramilisonina (1998), 'Stonehenge for the ancestors: the stones pass on the message', *Antiquity*, 72: 308–26.

Phillips, T., Hampshire-Monk, I. and Abramson, P. (2006), 'The excavation and reconstruction of the recumbent stone circle at Strichen, Aberdeenshire, 1979–82', *Proceedings of the Society of Antiquaries of Scotland*, 136: 111–34.

Piggott, S. (1971–2), 'Excavation of the Dalladies long barrow, Fettercairn, Kincardineshire', *Proceedings of the Society of Antiquaries of Scotland*, 104: 23–47.

Piggott, S. (1973), 'The Dalladies long barrow: NE Scotland', *Antiquity*, 47: 32–6.

Piggott, S. and Simpson, D. D. A. (1971), 'Excavation of a stone circle at Croft Moraig, Perthshire, Scotland', *Proceedings of the Prehistoric Society*, 37: 1–15.

RCAHMS (1997), *Eastern Dumfriesshire: An Archaeological Landscape*, Edinburgh: RCAHMS.

Reynolds, N. (1978), 'Dark Age timber halls and the background to excavation at Balbridie', *Scottish Archaeological Forum*, 10: 41–60.

Rideout, J. (1997), 'Excavation of Neolithic enclosures at Cowie Road, Bannockburn, Stirling, 1984–5', *Proceedings of the Society of Antiquaries of Scotland*, 127: 29–68.

Rival, L. (1993), 'The growth of family trees: understanding Huaorani perceptions of the forest', *Man*, 28: 635–52.

Rival, L. (1998a), 'Trees, from symbols of life and regeneration to political artefacts', in Rival, L. (ed.), *The Social Life of Trees*, 1–36.

Rival, L. (ed.) (1998b), *The Social Life of Trees: Anthropological Perspectives on Tree Symbolism*, Oxford: Berg.

Roberts, I. (2005), *Ferrybridge Henge: The Ritual Landscape*, Leeds: West Yorkshire Archaeological Service.

ScARF (2012), 'South-east Scotland and north-east England', in A. Sheridan and K. Brophy (eds), *Neolithic Panel Report*, Scottish Archaeological Research Framework: Society of Antiquaries of Scotland, 61–73, available at: http://tinyurl.com/d73xkvn, last accessed 16 June 2015.

Scott, J. G. (1992), 'Mortuary structures and megaliths', in N. Sharples and A. Sheridan (eds), *Vessels for the Ancestors*, Edinburgh: Edinburgh University Press, 104–19.

Speak, S. and Burgess, C. (1999), 'Meldon Bridge: a centre of the third millennium BC in Peebleshire', *Proceedings of the Society of Antiquaries of Scotland*, 129: 1–118.

Tavener, N. (1996), 'Evidence of Neolithic activity near Marton-le-Moor, North Yorkshire', in P. Frodsham (ed.), *Neolithic Studies in No-man's Land: Papers on the Neolithic of Northern England from the Trent to the Tweed*, Northumberland Archaeological Group: Newcastle upon Tyne, 183–8.

Thomas, J. (1999), *Understanding the Neolithic*, London: Routledge.

Thomas, J. (2004a), 'Materiality and traditions of practice in Neolithic south-west Scotland', in V. Cummings and C. Fowler (eds), *The Neolithic of the Irish Sea*, Oxford: Oxbow Books, 174–84.

Thomas, J. (2004b), 'The later Neolithic architectural repertoire: the case of the Dunragit complex', in R. Cleal and J. Pollard (eds), *Monuments and Material Culture: Papers in Honour of an Avebury Archaeologist: Isobel Smith*, Salisbury: Hobnob Press, 98–108.

Thomas, J. (2006), 'On the origins and development of cursus monuments in Britain', *Proceedings of the Prehistoric Society*, 72: 229–41.

Thomas, J. (2007), *Place and Memory: Excavations at the Pict's Knowe, Holywood and Holm Farm, Dumfries and Galloway, 1994–8*, Oxford: Oxbow Books.

Thomas, J. (2010), 'The return of the Rinyo–Clacton folk? The cultural significance of the Grooved Ware complex in Later Neolithic Britain', *Cambridge Archaeological Journal*, 20: 1–15.

Tipping, R. (1994), 'The form and fate of Scotland's woodlands', *Proceedings of the Society of Antiquaries of Scotland*, 124: 1–54.

Tipping, R. (2003), 'Living in the past: woods and people in prehistory to 1000

BC', in T. C. Smout (ed.), *People and Woods in Scotland: A History*, Edinburgh: Edinburgh University Press, 14–39.

Tipping, R., Bunting, M. J., Davies, A. L., Murray, H., Fraser, S. and McCulloch, R. (2009), 'Modelling landuse around an Early Neolithic timber "hall" in north-east Scotland from high spatial resolution pollen analyses', *Journal of Archaeological Science*, 36: 140–9.

Tolan, M. (1988), 'Pit Circles in Scotland: Some Possible Interpretations', unpublished BA dissertation, University of Newcastle upon Tyne.

Vyner, B. E. (1984), 'The excavation of a Neolithic cairn at Street House, Loftus, Cleveland', *Proceedings of the Prehistoric Society*, 50: 151–95.

Whittle, A. (1991), 'Wayland's Smithy, Oxfordshire. Excavations at the Neolithic tomb in 1962–63 by R. J. C. Atkinson and S. Piggott', *Proceedings of the Prehistoric Society*, 57: 61–101.

Whittle, A., Healy, F. and Bayliss, A. (2011), *Gathering Time. Dating the Early Neolithic Enclosures of Southern Britain and Ireland*, Oxford: Oxbow Books, 2 vols.

PART III

Pits, Pots and Practice

CHAPTER 9

Life is the Pits! Ritual, Refuse and Mesolithic–Neolithic Settlement Traditions in North-east Scotland

Gordon Noble, Claire Christie and Emma Philip

Introduction

Pit digging is increasingly recognised as a ubiquitous phenomenon of the Neolithic (and now perhaps the Mesolithic) of Britain and Ireland (Anderson-Whymark and Thomas 2012). Pit digging has much to tell us about settlement strategies, the nature of ritualised action and, more generally, the ways in which people 'altered the earth' in early prehistory (Bradley 1993). Nevertheless, there are many interpretive issues that remain to be addressed in relation to pits. It increasingly seems that pits can no longer be characterised as 'domestic' or 'ritual'; rather, many pits and sites more generally display characteristics that fall on a spectrum between these two opposing interpretations (Brophy and Noble 2012).

Pits have proved difficult and controversial to interpret from their identification in the nineteenth century onwards. The interpretation of pits has become dominated by two theoretical trajectories: pits as settlement evidence and pits as ritualised structured depositions. Pits have been interpreted as dwellings in their own right (e.g., Stone 1934), or as an ancillary to settlement (Clark *et al.* 1960) or seen to perform particular domestic functions, such as grain stores or rubbish pits (Field *et al.* 1964; McInnes 1971; Thomas 2012). Pits as settlement evidence are an attractive proposition for many periods given the lack of settlement data for much of prehistory. The interpretation of pits gained complexity in the 1990s as the concept of 'structured deposition', developed under post-processualism, was specifically applied to pits by Julian Thomas. Thomas argued that the material within the pits was deliberately selected and arranged (1991, 1999). This paved the way for increasingly complex interpretations exploring spectacular depositions (Thomas 1999: 72), multi-sensual qualities (Pollard 2001: 327), the treatment of the artefacts (Pollard 2001: 327; Pannett 2012: 142) and the role of pits in ritualised events (Richards and Thomas 1984; Thomas 2012: 6). However, whilst these interpretations have been readily applied to the later Neolithic, Bronze Age and Iron Age,

discussions of earlier pits are often restricted to considerations of subsistence and settlement evidence. Whilst the concept of structured deposition
has drawn attention to pits, pits which do not fit the typical description,
contain few artefacts or are considered 'empty' are often ill explored and
rarely dated.

In Scotland, the pace of discovery and recognition of pit sites has been
slower than in England owing to the smaller number of development-led
excavations and in Mesolithic contexts perhaps due to a lack of routine
radiocarbon dating of apparently 'empty' pits (Phillips and Bradley 2004;
Brophy 2006; Murray *et al.* 2009). However, since 1990 the impact of development-led excavation has begun to be felt and the publication of these
excavations has led to an increasing number of pit sites being recognised in
Scotland (Phillips and Bradley 2004: 24–7; Brophy 2006; Brophy and Noble
2012). In Aberdeenshire in north-east Scotland, our knowledge of pit digging in the Mesolithic and Neolithic has increased substantially (Figure 9.1),
particularly in the past ten years with the completion of a number of larger
infrastructure and development-led projects (e.g., Alexander 2000; Cook

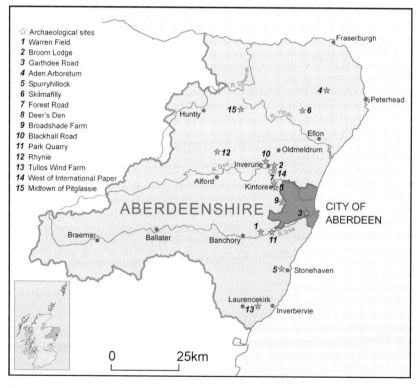

Figure 9.1 Map showing Mesolithic and Early Neolithic pit sites in Aberdeenshire
discussed in the text and in Table 9.1.

and Dunbar 2008). Research excavation has also had some role to play (e.g., Murray *et al.* 2009).

Detailed regional studies are now increasingly possible for pit traditions across Scotland and Britain more generally (Anderson-Whymark and Thomas 2012; Carver 2012; Garrow 2012). Indeed, key to understanding pits in their many forms will be to examine the regional traditions of pit digging in order to understand more fully the variety of functions that pits played in Mesolithic and Neolithic lifestyles in different regional contexts. The true significance of pits can also be better discerned through adopting a long-term perspective that does not seek to artificially separate Mesolithic from Neolithic, but attempts to study these periods on an equal footing with the variations in pit digging the focus, not the chronological label we attach to this phenomena.

Pits in the Mesolithic of Aberdeenshire

In recent years the identification of pit digging in the Mesolithic of Aberdeenshire has increased through the more regular use of radiocarbon dating in combination with larger-scale excavation as part of development-led archaeology. There are now a small but growing number of Mesolithic sites in Aberdeenshire that have associated pit digging or other structural remains. This marks a distinct change in the material evidence for the Mesolithic, which has traditionally been dominated by approaches grounded in lithic analysis. The discovery of pits and other possible structural remains will allow us in the future to adopt a more nuanced landscape approach that can consider in more detail the built and natural environment of the Mesolithic (see also McFadyen 2007).

Recent finds of Mesolithic pits in Aberdeenshire include Garthdee Road, where a pit (between 0.86 and 1.4 m in diameter and 0.39 m deep) containing a basal fill of charcoal was dated to the Late Mesolithic (Murray and Murray forthcoming) (Table 9.1; note all laboratory codes not given below are contained in this table). This pit was covered with tightly packed interlocking stones and was discovered sealed beneath the remains of an Early Neolithic oval structure. A small lithic assemblage typically diagnostic of the later Mesolithic, including a scalene triangle microlith and two microlith fragments, was recovered in association with the pit (Murray and Murray forthcoming). The lack of silting or erosion in the pit appears to indicate that it was filled with charcoal and covered within a short space of time. The structured nature of the deposits, the careful positioning of the interlocking angular stones and the fact that stones of this shape differ from the rounded pebbles found in the vicinity, points to the deliberate sealing of the pit, suggestive of a ritualised end to a phase of activity, rather than the expedient in-filling of a fire or rubbish pit (Murray and Murray forthcoming).

Many of the Mesolithic sites in Aberdeenshire are simply lithic scatters

Table 9.1 Radiocarbon dated sites mentioned in text (in chronological order by earliest date for site, calibrated BC (95 per cent) unless otherwise stated)

Site Name	NGR	Site Type	Description	Years BP	Lab Code	Calibrated 2 Sigma	Reference
Warren Field	NO 737 966	Pit Alignment	Pit 6: Salix sp./ Corylus avellana	8850±40 BP	SUERC-12266	8210-7790 cal BC	Marshall 2009
			Pit 18: Corylus avellana	8765±40 BP	SUERC-10077	7970-7610 cal BC	
			Pit 19: Alnus sp. / Corylus avellana	8755±40 BP	SUERC-10075	7960-7610 cal BC	
			Pit 22: Corylus avellana	8710±40 BP	SUERC-10076	7940-7590 cal BC	
			Pit 22: Wheat	4975±45 BP	SUERC-10074	3940-3650 cal BC	
			Pit 16: Alnus sp./ Corylus avellana	8530±40 BP	SUERC-10078	7600-7520 cal BC	
			Pit 16: Corylus avellana	8460±40 BP	SUERC-10082	7590-7480 cal BC	
			Pit 5: Alnus sp.	8100±40 BP	SUERC-12257	7300-6840 cal BC	
			Pit 5: Betula / Corylus avellana	8080±35 BP	SUERC-12262	7180-6840 cal BC	
			Pit 5: Betula	8040±40 BP	SUERC-12259	7090-6810 cal BC	
			Pit 5: Salix sp.	8040±40 BP	SUERC-12260	7090-6810 cal BC	
			Pit 5: Alnus sp.	7945±40 BP	SUERC-12256	7040-6690 cal BC	
			Pit 5: Quercus sp.	6635±35 BP	SUERC-12258	5630-5510 cal BC	
			Pit 5: Quercus sp.	5200±35 BP	SUERC-12251	4220-3950 cal BC	
			Pit 5: Quercus sp.	5170±35 BP	SUERC-12261	4050-3810 cal BC	
			Pit 5: Quercus sp.	5025±35 BP	SUERC-4031	3950-3710 cal BC	
Broom Lodge	NJ 7782 1954	Pit	Pit 11: Corylus avellana	7905±40 BP	SUERC-15879	7030-6640 cal BC	Murray and Murray 2007
				5905±40 BP	SUERC-15880	4900-4690 cal BC	
Garthdee Road	NJ 923 032	Pit	Pit 56: Alnus sp./ Corylus avellana	6620±35 BP	SUERC-8615	5630-5490 cal BC	Murray 2005; Murray and Murray Forthcoming.
			Pit 56: Corylus avellana	6690±35 BP	SUERC-8614	5670-5540 cal BC	

Site	Grid ref	Feature	Sample	BP	Lab code	Cal BC	Reference
Aden Arboretum	NJ 9790 4758	Pit		5930±40 BP	GU-19161	4931-4716 cal BC	Aberdeenshire SMR (NJ94NE0098)
Spurryhillock	NO 852 862	Pits	Pit 619: Quercus sp	5860±70 BP	Beta-73552	4910-4540 cal BC	Alexander 1997
				5700±70 BP	Beta-73553	4710-4370 cal BC	
Rhynie	NJ 499 268	Pit	Pit 544: Salix sp.	5415±27 BP	SUERC-52927	4336-4237 cal BC	Gondek et al 2013
Skilmafilly	NJ 909 398	Pit	Pit 036: Corylus avellana	5300±40 BP	Poz-7690	4260-3990 cal BC	Johnson and Cameron 2012
			Pit 036: Corylus avellana	5260±40 BP	Poz-7699	4230-3970 cal BC	
			Pit 036: Quercus sp.	5510±40 BP	Poz-7700	4460-4260 cal BC	
			Pit 036: Quercus sp.	5380±40 BP	Poz-7701	4340-4060 cal BC	
			Pit 036: Betula	5600±40 BP	Poz-7702	4510-4350 cal BC	
			Pit 036: Quercus sp.	5500±40 BP	Poz-7703	4450-4260 cal BC	
Forest Road	NJ 7875 1600	Pits (Field A)	Pit 35: Alnus sp.	4965±40 BP	SUERC-1376	3930-3650 cal BC	Cook and Dunbar 2008
			Pit 25: Betula	4895±45 BP	SUERC-1374	3780-3640 cal BC	
			Pit 12: Corylus avellana	4865±50 BP	SUERC-1325	3770-3620 cal BC	
			Pit 21: Alnus sp.	4835±40 BP	SUERC-1375	3710-3620 cal BC	
			Pit 38: Charred Hazelnut Shell	4755±35 BP	SUERC-2654	3640-3380 cal BC	
			Pit 31: Charred Wheat Grain	4740±35 BP	SUERC-2646	3640-3370cal BC	
		Pit (Field B)	Pit 50: Betula	4970±40 BP	SUERC-1384	3930-3650 cal BC	
		Bell-shaped pit with 'windbreak'	ST14: Quercus sp	4855±40 BP	SUERC-1323	3720-3620 cal BC	
			ST14: Corylus avellana	4785±50 BP	SUERC-1324	3660-3379 cal BC	
Tullos Wind Farm	NO 7550 7175	Pits	Pit 009: Corylus avellana	4720±35 BP	SUERC-28768	3640-3370 cal BC	Kirby 2010
			Pit 009: Betula	4690±35 BP	SUERC-28769	3630-3360 cal BC	
			Pit 013: Corylus avellana	4680±35 BP	SUERC-28770	3630-3360 cal BC	
			Pit 013: Alnus sp.	4685±35 BP	SUERC-28771	3630-3360 cal BC	

Table 9.1 (*cont.*)

Site Name	NGR	Site Type	Description	Years BP	Lab Code	Calibrated 2 Sigma	Reference
Deer's Den	NJ 784 160	Pits	Pit 1028: Hazelnut Shell Pit 1173: Charcoal (roundwood) Pit 1028: Charcoal (roundwood)	4945±40 BP 4940±40 BP 4895±40 BP	OxA-8132 OxA-8131 OxA-8133	3890–3640 cal BC 3820–3640 cal BC 3770–3630 cal BC	Alexander 2000
West of International Paper	NJ 7790 1870	Pit	Charred Hazelnut Shell	4875±29 BP	SUERC-42979	3710–3630 cal BC	Murray and Murray 2013b
Midtown of Pitglassie	NJ 7022 4352	Pit	Cremated bone fragment.	4995±35 BP	GrA-34772	3940–3660 cal BC	Sheridan and Bradley 2007
Broadshade Farm	NJ 81705 07807	Pit	Pit 016: Corylus avellana Pit 016: Corylus avellana	4995±35 BP 4990±35 BP	SUERC-26932 SUERC-26933	3940–3660 cal BC 3940–3660 cal BC	Aberdeenshire SMR (NJ80NW0298)
Blackhall Road	NJ 7529 2218	Pits		4980±35 BP 4955±35 BP 5000±40 BP 5025±35 BP	SUERC-15186 SUERC-15189 SUERC-15193 SUERC-15194	3930–3660 cal BC 3800–3650 cal BC 3950–3690 cal BC 3950–3710 cal BC	Aberdeenshire SMR (NJ72SE0226)

and few have been excavated. One exception is the site at Nethermills, Crathes. The site has often been cited, but remains frustratingly unresolved. Recent post-excavation work led by the University of Aberdeen is beginning to flesh out the evidence for this site. The Nethermills site is located amongst extensive lithic scatters, mainly of Mesolithic date found along the banks of the River Dee (Sabnis *et al.* 2008, 2009). The excavations by James Kenworthy at Nethermills uncovered a range of features in association with a concentrated lithic scatter with over 20,000 pieces represented (Kenworthy 1981). Kenworthy's excavations uncovered possible evidence of a small structure interpreted as a Late Mesolithic roundhouse. Kenworthy (1981) suggested that the site represented a multi-phase, seasonal base camp, but at the time his find of a possible Mesolithic structure was difficult to parallel in the British record. More recently, however, a number of structures similar to the one at Nethermills, dated to the Mesolithic have been excavated at Howick, Northumberland (Waddington *et al.* 2003; Waddington 2007), East Barns, East Lothian (Gooder 2007) and possibly at Silvercrest, Elgin (Suddaby 2007). The site included examples of pits, including one feature, a 0.5 m deep pit sealed by river cobbles, which is reminiscent of the pit at Garthdee, but in this case the pit contained a number of worked flints representing a narrow blade industry, including scalene triangles, rods and 'needle points' (Kenworthy 1980).

Unfortunately, post-excavation work carried out in the last year by the University of Aberdeen has shown that Nethermills is not a straightforward site to interpret, representing a complex palimpsest of activity. The evidence suggests that the pit digging and structural features date from the Mesolithic to the Late Neolithic and Bronze Age casting doubt on the presence of a coherent Mesolithic structure. However, the lithic assemblages from Nethermills has been compared with an assemblage recovered from Castle Street, Inverness dated to 7100–5500 cal. BC (Wordsworth 1985: 95). Whilst the dating of lithic typologies in Scotland is far from straightforward (e.g., Finlay *et al.* 2004: 107; Warren 2005: 29–32), components of the Nethermills site could conceivably date to the later Mesolithic. Thus, the pit at Nethermills with its similarities to Garthdee Road can only offer a glimpse into the possible complexities of Mesolithic pit digging.[1]

The excavations at Warren Field, Crathes, point to the surprises and challenges that larger-scale work, supported by extensive radiocarbon dating, can provide for our traditional narratives regarding the nature of the Mesolithic. The site at Warren Field, approximately 1 km from Nethermills, revealed evidence of a remarkable pit alignment, which unexpectedly produced a range of Mesolithic dates. An alignment of twelve pits stretching for approximately 50 m was uncovered, two of which appear to have held timber posts (Murray and Murray 2009: 5). Dating suggests that the first pits were dug around the first half of the eighth millennium cal. BC, and the excavators suggest that the entire alignment was constructed over the following several hundred years, subsequently reworked on a number of occasions until the mid-sixth millennium BC, with evidence for later recuts dating to the early fourth millennium BC (Murray *et al.* 2009).

The nature of the excavation, conducted under research conditions, has allowed detailed insights into the function and context of the pits at Warren Field. Situated in what appears to have been relatively open woodland, excavation of a number of the pits indicated that during their original construction the earth dug out of the pits was piled up around the edges, accentuating their visibility. Charcoal-rich deposits were found in and around most of the pits; in some instances, the charcoal appears to have been deliberately deposited within the pit, while in others the evidence points to fires burning around the edges, the charcoal subsequently slipping into the pit from the surrounding upcast earth (Murray and Murray 2009: 13). Within the deposits of charcoal found in two of the pits, tiny fragments of burnt (mammalian) bone (*ibid.*: 17) were recovered along with some seeds of grasses and fat hen (an edible plant similar to spinach), as well as a burnt fragment of hazelnut shell from another pit (*ibid.*: 7–9). In addition, chemical analysis revealed traces of crushed minerals, which may have been used to produce coloured pigments perhaps for use as paint or tattoos, within three of the pits (Murray and Fraser 2009: 22). Two of these pits containing mineral deposits possibly held timber stakes, although it is difficult to estimate their size accurately due to the loose gravel packing, but these appear to have been small posts rather than large timbers (Murray *et al.* 2009: 13). A small lithic assemblage was recovered from in and around one of the pits that possibly held a timber post in contexts associated with radiocarbon dates of between 7180 and 6840 cal. BC (SUERC-12262) (Table 9.1). The lithics, including a blade fragment and narrow flakes, are generally consistent with Mesolithic stone working in the region (Warren 2009: 99). The conspicuous nature of the pit alignment at Warren Field located on a natural ridge overlooking the river, the evidence that fires were burning around the pits, the possibility that two pits contained timber posts and the apparent deliberate deposition of a variety of materials led to the pit alignment being interpreted within a ritualised framework (Murray *et al.* 2009).[2] The discovery of such an enigmatic construction dating to the Mesolithic period is unprecedented in Scotland; however, comparisons can perhaps be drawn between this site and an alignment of pits uncovered in the car park near Stonehenge. Also apparently situated in what would have been open woodland, three of these pits at Stonehenge appear to have held large timber (pine) posts and dates of between 8820–7730 cal. BC and 7480–6590 cal. BC were obtained from two of the pits (Allen 1995; Cleal *et al.* 1995: 41–7). As at Warren Field, this monument is interpreted as holding some symbolic significance, perhaps akin to the totem poles of the native peoples of the north-west coast of America and Canada, marking this location as sacred long before the construction of the later Neolithic monument at Stonehenge (Allen and Gardiner 2002).

Clearly, we have much to learn about the variety of acts of altering the earth conducted in the Mesolithic, and the Warren Field pit alignment is a timely reminder of the ways in which new fieldwork conducted in an era when radiocarbon dating is more freely applied can radically alter our notions of the archaeology of a particular time period. More routine dating of 'empty' pits is likely to reveal more Mesolithic pit-digging episodes and add a challenge to the interpretive frameworks that centre on the importance of artefact deposition. At Broom Lodge, Aberdeenshire, for example, a group of seemingly deliberately cut features with charcoal-rich fills has recently been identified, and one of these features produced two sets of Mesolithic dates (Table 9.1) (Murray and Murray 2010: 11). These features are located just to the east of the area that became the focus for the construction of a standing stone avenue, stone circle and henge monument complex at Broomend of Crichie near the River Don in the later Neolithic and Early Bronze Age (Bradley 2011). Excavations at Aden Arboretum (Old Deer Churchyard), near the River Ugie, also identified a small Mesolithic fire pit (Table 9.1) (Lelong 2010).

Dating of a pit with only a single lithic at Spurryhillock, near Stonehaven, has also identified it as a Late Mesolithic example (Table 9.1) (Alexander 1997). The Spurryhillock pit measured 2.3 m by 1.78 m and 1.35 m deep with ten clear layers of alternating sand and charcoal, the lowest of which contained unabraded lumps of charcoal (Figure 9.2(a)) (Alexander 1997: 20). The site at Spurryhillock also contained a smaller Early Neolithic pit measuring 0.7 m wide and 0.15 m deep and five small shallow pits with no datable finds (Alexander 1997: 24). The dating of pits without finds will undoubtedly add to the database of known Mesolithic and Neolithic pits in the study area.

Another large Mesolithic pit has been identified at Skilmafilly, near Maud, measuring some 3.2 m by 2.8 m and had a series of fills extending to 1.4 m in depth (Johnson and Cameron 2012). This pit clearly had a complex history with multiple fills and tip lines evident in the section of the feature (Figure 9.2(b)). The stratigraphy suggests a gradual fill process, with at least two recuts in its upper layers. Charcoal of oak, birch and hazel was identified in the upper and lower fills of the pit, and five radiocarbon dates from the pit suggest that it was utilised repeatedly from 4510–4350 to 4230 3970 cal. BC, an indication of the extraordinary longevity of some of these pits and their use within the landscapes of north-east Scotland (Table 9.1).

Many of the Mesolithic pits discussed here do not contain any artefacts, making radiocarbon dating the only means of identification. This absence of material culture poses challenges for identifying what may be low-level Mesolithic activity in archaeologically rich landscapes where dating programmes focus on artefact-rich features or features that are part of more complex structures. An interesting example of this comes from the site at Rhynie, Aberdeenshire, where a Mesolithic pit was discovered within a later

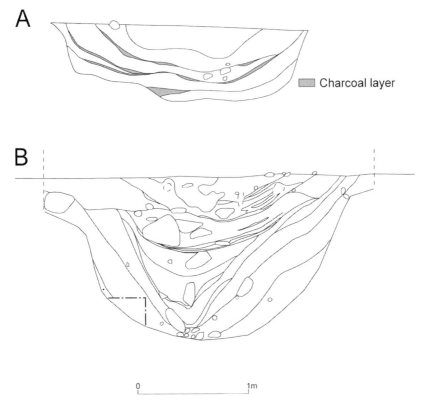

Figure 9.2 (a) The large, possibly monumental, Mesolithic pit at Spurryhillock; (b) a similar pit to Spurryhillock at Skilmafilly (redrawn from Alexander 1997 and Johnson and Cameron 2012).

square enclosure. The large pit, roughly circular in plan, was interpreted as a possible post-hole similar to another pit or post-hole within a second nearby square enclosure (Gondek *et al.* 2013: 16). There were no artefacts within this pit, its only distinguishing feature being a thin upper fill containing significant quantities of charcoal, ash and fire-cracked stone (*ibid.*: 16). A determination of 4336–4237 cal. BC (Table 9.1) subsequently showed this to be a Late Mesolithic pit. It was only through an extensive and intensive dating programme that evidence of Mesolithic activity at this site was revealed.

It is difficult at present fully to interpret the significance of isolated features such as the Mesolithic pits outlined above. What is notable is that some of the most intriguing examples did not contain artefacts (or very few) and were recognised as Mesolithic only through radiocarbon dating. Many of the examples discussed could easily be considered monumental in size, with clear sequences of deposition, but at times consisting of complex charcoal-rich deposits, or different soil layers rather than including large numbers of artefacts. In the cases of Garthdee and Nethermills, there is clear evidence for the closing of the pit through deliberate sealing. The relationship between these pits and their surroundings in later periods is often unclear. At Warren Field there is clear evidence of later recutting and many of the pits occur in locations with a long history of subsequent use. It is clear that much larger investigations are needed and the much more routine dating of pits without diagnostic artefacts will undoubtedly flesh out the picture of Mesolithic settlement and pit-digging traditions.

Pits in the Early Neolithic of Aberdeenshire

In the Early Neolithic of Aberdeenshire pit-digging traditions, as elsewhere in Scotland, extend from the occurrence of isolated examples to much more extensive 'landscapes' of pits (so-called 'pit clusters') and associated activity (Brophy and Noble 2012, and see Chapter 10, this volume). Again, the differing scales of archaeological investigation in different locations bias the picture. An example of an apparently isolated pit is the shallow example discovered at Park Quarry, Durris, containing sherds of Early Neolithic pottery (Sheridan 2007: 481) along with some quartz nodules, flint flakes (all burnt) and a complete Scots Pine cone (Shepherd and Greig 1991). However, more recent identification of a lithic scatter along the riverbank (O'Sullivan 1995) and a smaller scatter and two small pits of an indeterminate date on a sandy terrace nearby (Suddaby 2005), all suggest the presence of more extensive activity in the area of the pit.

Another seemingly isolated pit was discovered during the topsoil stripping and subsequent excavations at Broadshade Farm, on the western edge of Westhill, during the diversion of the Broadshade gas pipeline (Suddaby 2009). This sub-circular pit contained charcoal-rich fills and produced a single sherd of granite-tempered pottery (Suddaby 2009: 7). The pit was dated to the Early Neolithic, 3940–3660 cal. BC (Table 9.1). However, the extent of the excavation again causes difficulties as this 'isolated pit' was discovered at the edge of an area of topsoil stripping only 0.2 m wide along the pipeline (Suddaby 2009: 5). Pit clusters have also been identified within commercial archaeology projects such as at Tullo Wind Farm, Laurencekirk. Here a group of five pits, two of which have been dated to the Early Neolithic, was found on a natural terrace (Kirby 2009: 5) (Table 9.1). As with the isolated pits considered above, the interpretation of this pit group is difficult due to a lack of contextual information.

More extensive area excavations across Aberdeenshire have revealed pit clusters with associated activity. One such site occurred at Blackhall Road, Inverurie, where a group of pits dated to the Early Neolithic (Table 9.1) was found within a rich archaeological landscape (Murray and Murray 2008: 23). One of the larger infrastructure projects in Aberdeenshire in recent years, the A96 Kintore and Blackburn bypass, has also revealed extensive pit-digging episodes (Alexander 2000). Open area excavation at Deer's Den as part of the bypass project uncovered at least twenty pits containing identifiable Neolithic artefacts. Some of these pits were artefact-rich, for example, Pit 1028, dating to the first half of the fourth millennium cal. BC (OxA-8132; 8133) (Table 9.1), produced numerous pottery sherds, including remains of Carinated Bowls, charcoal, burnt hazelnut shells and a large lithic assemblage (Alexander 2000: 15). This assemblage consisted predominantly of flint artefacts, but also a substantial proportion of quartz pieces, an Arran pitchstone flake and one leaf-shaped flint arrowhead (Finlayson 2000: 53). One of the most intriguing aspects of these pits is their spatial layout, which takes the form of a rectangular arrangement reminiscent of Early Neolithic timber halls found elsewhere in Scotland (Figure 9.3). However, the excavator proposed that the distribution, differences in shape and depth, and the variety of material recovered indicated that the pits themselves did not form a single structure (Alexander 2000: 65). The pits may have been located instead within a timber building that left little structural trace, covering an area around 17 m long × 11–12 m wide. Alternatively, it may be that these pits were dug around structures, a suggestion made for similar pit clusters identified at Kilverstone, Norfolk (Garrow *et al.* 2005: 153), or a further possibility is that the scattered remains could represent the remains of a dismantled building or a series of dismantled structures perhaps rebuilt over time.

Until recently, the evidence from Deer's Den represented one of the most extensive pit sites to have been identified in Aberdeenshire. However, the limited evidence for Early Neolithic pit digging in the north-east of Scotland has been boosted following the recent development-led excavations at Forest Road, Kintore, Aberdeenshire (Cook and Dunbar 2008). These extensive excavations revealed multi-period activity, including at least 395 pits; however, only a small number of these are directly dated to the Early Neolithic (between *c.* 3800 and 3500 BC), but undoubtedly some of the many undated pits are likely to fall within the same period (Table 9.1). Many of the pits at Forest Road clustered around an Early Neolithic rectilinear mounded monument, enclosed and divided by ditches, measuring 42 m in length (Cook and Dunbar 2008: 35). This imposing monument was constructed in a number of phases dating from the earliest centuries of the Neolithic, producing dates ranging between 4250 and 3710 cal. BC (Cook and Dunbar 2008: 42). However, four of the seven dates were produced from samples of oak (*Quercus* sp.), introducing the possibility that due to the old wood effect these dates results may be considerably earlier than the structure with which they were associated.

The variety of forms of the Neolithic pits at Kintore has led to substantial confusion as to how to interpret these features. The majority of the Early Neolithic pits are described as 'typical' Neolithic pits in the report (Cook and Dunbar 2008: 54), conforming to the now familiar specifica-

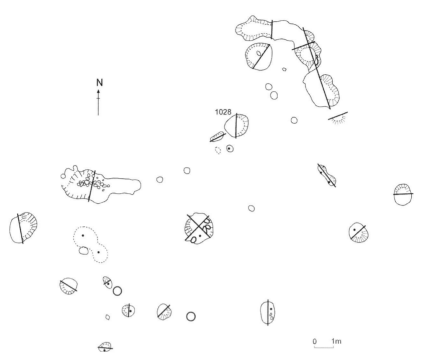

Figure 9.3 Pits at Deer's Den (redrawn from Alexander 2000).

tions, physical dimensions of, and range of material found within Neolithic pits throughout Britain: in sum, relatively shallow features, with few fills, deliberately backfilled, and containing pottery, lithics, burnt bone and charcoal. Also in keeping with patterns of deposition in pits from other regions, the filling of some pits appears more formal, containing distinctive items that could be considered to represent 'structured deposition' (Richards and Thomas 1984; Thomas 1999). Examples included material such as carefully placed or selected pottery sherds, leaf-shaped arrowheads or finely made flint tools and polished stone axes.

Two pits considered to display structured deposits have been dated to the Early Neolithic, with Pit 35 being dated to 3930–3650 cal. BC (SUERC-1376) and Pit 31 as 3640–3370 cal. BC (SUERC-2646) (Table 9.1) (Cook and Dunbar 2008: 65–6). Both pits contained relatively substantial amounts of Neolithic round-based bowl pottery, including Carinated examples in Pit 35 (MacSween 2008; and see Chapter 11, this volume). Some of the pottery sherds from Pit 31 were very abraded and this pit also contained significant amounts of charcoal and charred cereal grain, apparently not burnt *in situ*, suggesting that a selection of material was gathered from an exposed surface deposit, and then placed in the pit (Cook and Dunbar 2008: 65). But, as noted by the excavators, this material could represent the deposition of a selection of waste material from midden deposits rather than the selection of significant items (*ibid.*: 65–6). Pit 35 contained a seemingly deliberate selection of pottery sherds, again possibly derived from a midden, along with charcoal, burnt bone, cereal grains and wild seeds. The pottery in this case was placed in a distinctive manner around the edge of the pit and may have acted as a lining to enable storage or to create the effect of a larger vessel within the pit (*ibid.*: 66). This pit also contained a fragmentary stone axe, thereby significantly providing a date for the occurrence of polished axes, which are rarely recovered from stratified contexts within this region. Another pit within the same field, Pit 12, dated to 3770–3620 cal. BC (SUERC-1325) (Table 9.1), contained only one large pottery sherd and a distal fragment of a finely made bifacial knife of red flint, possibly broken intentionally, this pair of artefacts underlining the variety in pit contents identified in the same locality (Cook and Dunbar 2008: 60).

In addition to differences in contents, the excavations at Kintore suggested that in some cases pits may have been associated with a range of different structures. Within the same field as the aforementioned Early Neolithic rectilinear mounded monument, the remains of a possible structure was uncovered comprising two shallow hollows forming a curvilinear feature measuring 4.5 m across, with a rectangular arrangement of four pits to the north-east (ST07) (Cook and Dunbar 2008: 67–8). This structure is described by the excavators as a natural hollow, surrounded by pits within which Neolithic artefactual material appears to have accumulated (Figure 9.4(a)). These shallow hollows, potentially remnants of the internal floor of a building, contained substantial amounts of round-based bowl pottery (over 100 sherds), including Carinated examples and a number of vessels represented by several large sherds, possibly broken *in situ* (MacSween 2008: 178). These hollows included more pottery than was recovered from any of the other pits at Forest Road (with the exception of one pit associated with cremated remains, see below). In keeping with other pits on site, the pottery was a mixture of fresh and abraded sherds, but most showed signs of use in the form of sooting. Other artefacts recovered included a piece of flint and a fragment of a quern rubbing stone (Engl 2008: 211), and two of the pits contained small quantities of cereal grains. Although not directly dated, this potential pit-defined structure can be compared with a structure investigated at Garthdee Road, Aberdeen, approximately 20 km from Kintore, and overlooking the River Dee. Defined by a series of post-pits, this roughly oval structure measured approximately 12 m in length by 8 m in width, with evidence of hearths and a compacted internal floor; it produced dates ranging between 3850 and 3610 cal. BC (Murray 2005). The presence of the site here within a natural hollow led to the relatively good survival of intact floor deposits, with an obvious resonance for the interpretation of the potential structure and possibly other groupings of pits at Kintore. Another comparable site near Inverurie (West of International Paper) also displayed evidence of pits in association with a structure. Here a pit dated to 3710–3630 cal. BC and containing Carinated Bowl pottery with burnt grain and bone was excavated in close proximity to a hearth and an irregular hollow (Table 9.1) (Murray and Murray 2013a: 12).

One further pit at Kintore, a distinctive bell-shaped example (ST14), also showed evidence of some form of associated structure (Figure 9.4(b)). This pit was surrounded by an arc of stake-holes thought to have formed a windbreak shielding activities connected with the pit (Cook and Dunbar 2008: 54–7). This bell-shaped pit provided radiocarbon dates of 3720–3620 cal. BC (SUERC-1323) and 3660–3379 cal. BC (SUERC-1324), and contained a single rapidly accumulated fill (Table 9.1). This artefact-rich fill included a complete plano-convex knife, pottery, flint, quartz, charcoal, burnt bone, charred hazelnut shells, carbonised cereal grains and a large flat stone placed vertically in the eastern end of the pit (*ibid.*: 54–5). The complete plano-convex knife, of red flint, was finely made and in a fresh

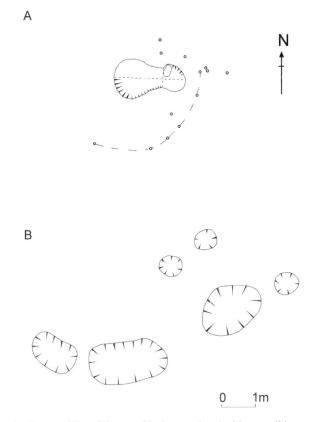

Figure 9.4 (a) Feature ST07, Kintore; (b) pits associated with a possible structure ST14 at Kintore (redrawn from Cook and Dunbar 2008).

condition with little sign of use (Engl 2008: 233). Plano-convex knives of this type and quality of finish have been found elsewhere in ceremonial contexts; however, a knife of this type has also been found at Garthdee Road, under-lining the difficulty in interpreting pits from single finds made within them (Finlayson 1997: 309–11).

One pit at Kintore, above all others, underlines the multiple roles that pits could play in the Neolithic of Aberdeenshire. Pit 25, within the same field as the mounded monument, included direct evidence of funerary activity in the form of a discrete deposit of ash and heat-affected sand with charcoal and small amounts of burnt bone, interpreted as the partial remains of a re-deposited cremation pyre recovered along with contents more familiar in typical Neolithic pits (Cook and Dunbar 2008: 62). It is possible that this pit was connected with the earth and timber monument constructed at Forest Road, since at the eastern end of that monument's mound an area subject to repeated burning was identified and interpreted as the possible residues of fires for cremation pyres (and dated to between 4170–3950 cal. BC and 3960–3710 cal. BC). No human remains were found in this area, but it seems plausible that cremated material was removed and deposited within some of the pits located in the vicinity of the monument. Pit 25, with the cremated bone, was dated to between 3780 and 3640 cal. BC (SUERC-1374) (Table 9.1), and would therefore belong towards the end of the timespan of use of the monument. This pit also contained an artefactual assemblage comparable to that from the bell-shaped pit outlined above – quantities of pottery (deliberately placed with the decoration facing upwards), flint (including formal tools and debitage) and quartz pieces, a hammer stone, a quartz cobble grinding stone and two kite-shaped arrowheads of grey flint, again artefacts with funerary associations elsewhere (Engl 2008: 233). Interestingly, this pit was situated within a tight cluster of Early Neolithic pits, considered as typical examples, and containing the customary although variable collection of pottery, lithics, charcoal, burnt bone, heat-affected stones and relatively small quantities of cereal grain. In most cases, these pits were not dissimilar to some of the pits considered as having structured deposits. While not displaying some of the more distinctive elements of Neolithic pit deposition, the majority of pits around the cremation pit encompassed a degree of structuring, in terms of the selection of material, such as the inclusion of single, or small numbers of, pottery sherds from individual vessels or retouched flint flakes and blades. These forms of deposition are not necessarily expressly associated with ritual or funerary contexts, but at the same time they perhaps reflect something more subtle than casual refuse disposal.

Discussion

Developer-led excavation in Aberdeenshire has led to the identification of an increasing variety of pit-digging traditions of both Mesolithic and Neolithic date. These examples of pit digging extend from single instances to sites with a palimpsest of pit-digging episodes. This variation has led to difficulties in the interpretation of these features, with a desire to 'pigeonhole' particular types of pit to fit particular dominant traditions of interpretation. Increasingly, however, we must accept the diversity of these traditions and look to more nuanced interpretations that account for the variety of contexts, contents and settings for pit digging in the Mesolithic and Neolithic of the county.

The Mesolithic–Neolithic transition was a time of fundamental social, economic and technological changes, yet discussion of it is fraught with methodological and theoretical difficulties. One of the major difficulties in its study has been the lack of sites dating from the fifth millennium cal. BC. More routine dating (almost all of it from developer-funded projects) has significantly fleshed out our chronology of human occupation in north-east Scotland and this includes identifying pits that fall into the chronological black hole between the Late Mesolithic and Early Neolithic that is evident in some regions (Bonsall, Anderson and Macklin 1999: 6; Griffiths 2014).

Pits dated to the fifth millennium cal. BC and the first half of the fourth millennium cal. BC have been collected together in Figure 9.5, which shows that the number of pits dating to the period 4000–3500 cal. BC significantly outnumber those dating to the previous millennium cal. BC. However, nearly all the pits dating to the fifth millennium cal. BC are from recent developer-funded projects, and, as yet, we do not have a consistent research strategy in place to identify such pits in any other way. It can also be observed that the site that shows the greatest overlap between the Mesolithic and Neolithic consisted of a pit that was large in scale (Skilmafilly), but contained no artefacts. In fact, none of the pits dating to the whole of the fifth millennium cal. BC contained any artefacts, with the exception of a single lithic at Spurryhillock. Clearly, developer-funded archaeology has demonstrated that there are features out there in the landscapes of Aberdeenshire that are beginning to populate the problematic chronological zone between the latest Mesolithic and earliest Neolithic phases.

The emerging picture from Aberdeenshire is of longevity in pit-digging traditions at both a general level and at particular locations frequented by both Mesolithic and Neolithic people. This adds complexity to our picture of Mesolithic and Neolithic in north-east Scotland, with important implications for archaeology elsewhere in Britain and Ireland. It points to a much more complex narrative of change across the traditional period divide. Routine radiocarbon dating of seemingly insubstantial features such as pits is essential if we are to understand the ephemeral or at times difficult to characterise evidence for Mesolithic and Early Neolithic lifeways. This crucial transition cannot be meaningfully understood without robust chronologies, for which pits provide a potential source.

As well as important insights into chronology, the Aberdeenshire

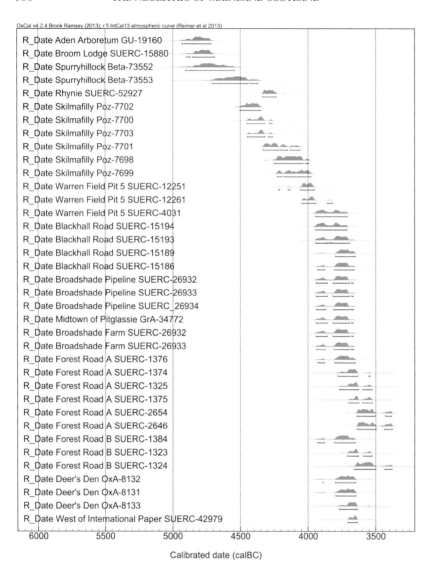

OxCal v4.2.4 Bronk Ramsey (2013); r:5 IntCal13 atmospheric curve (Reimer et al 2013)

R_Date Aden Arboretum GU-19160
R_Date Broom Lodge SUERC-15880
R_Date Spurryhillock Beta-73552
R_Date Spurryhillock Beta-73553
R_Date Rhynie SUERC-52927
R_Date Skilmafilly Poz-7702
R_Date Skilmafilly Poz-7700
R_Date Skilmafilly Poz-7703
R_Date Skilmafilly Poz-7701
R_Date Skilmafilly Poz-7698
R_Date Skilmafilly Poz-7699
R_Date Warren Field Pit 5 SUERC-12251
R_Date Warren Field Pit 5 SUERC-12261
R_Date Warren Field Pit 5 SUERC-4031
R_Date Blackhall Road SUERC-15194
R_Date Blackhall Road SUERC-15193
R_Date Blackhall Road SUERC-15189
R_Date Blackhall Road SUERC-15186
R_Date Broadshade Pipeline SUERC-26932
R_Date Broadshade Pipeline SUERC-26933
R_Date Broadshade Pipeline SUERC_26934
R_Date Midtown of Pitglassie GrA-34772
R_Date Broadshade Farm SUERC-26932
R_Date Broadshade Farm SUERC-26933
R_Date Forest Road A SUERC-1376
R_Date Forest Road A SUERC-1374
R_Date Forest Road A SUERC-1325
R_Date Forest Road A SUERC-1375
R_Date Forest Road A SUERC-2654
R_Date Forest Road A SUERC-2646
R_Date Forest Road B SUERC-1384
R_Date Forest Road B SUERC-1323
R_Date Forest Road B SUERC-1324
R_Date Deer's Den OxA-8132
R_Date Deer's Den OxA-8131
R_Date Deer's Den OxA-8133
R_Date West of International Paper SUERC-42979

6000   5500   5000   4500   4000   3500

Calibrated date (calBC)

Figure 9.5 Oxcal v.4.2.4 plot of radiocarbon dated pits in Aberdeenshire that fall between 5000–3500 cal. BC (see Table 9.1).

evidence also provides an increasingly rich dataset for characterising the form and extent of pit-digging practices in both Mesolithic and Neolithic contexts. In Aberdeenshire, the limited scale of excavation that characterised this county until relatively recently has meant that, like much of Scotland, it has been difficult to categorise pits as isolated or clustered (Brophy and Noble 2012). The isolated examples highlighted above may well simply represent the restricted scale of investigation in the immediate area and limited dating of pits without diagnostic material rather than genuine isolation (see Chapter 10, this volume). Likewise, the study of more clustered pit distributions can also be improved. For instance, the more extensive pit scatters of Scotland, including Aberdeenshire, lack the detailed study that has recently been undertaken for some pit sites in southern England (e.g., Garrow *et al.* 2005). At Kilverstone, in Norfolk, for example, the complete excavation of hundreds of Neolithic pits and in-depth analysis have allowed a number of important conclusions on the nature of Neolithic pit digging in this region to be reached. At Kilverstone, it was concluded that each pit cluster was the result of a single episode of digging as the individual clusters contained refitting artefacts with evidence of rapid backfill (*ibid.*: 156). In conclusion, the excavators argued that there had been 'repeated visits, of one group, or even a small number of groups of people, digging a cluster each visit over what may also have been a relatively long period' (*ibid.*: 154). The pit clusters consequently seem to represent locations to which people returned again and again seasonally or periodically for centuries. The dates from the most extensively excavated cluster of pits at Kintore, in Aberdeenshire, similarly suggest that pits here were dug over an extended period. Likewise the Mesolithic pit alignment at Warren Field may have been the focus of activity for many generations and was perhaps re-used at various points over many millennia. Given the chronological depth to sites such as Kintore and Warren Field, it is unlikely that the significance and purpose of these features were not altered through time. The revisiting of locations such as Kintore and Warren Field point to a more complex negotiation between people and places that stretches our theoretical frameworks for understanding pits.

As well as longevity, many of the Aberdeenshire pit sites also embody diversity. The evidence from Forest Road, Kintore, for example, suggests that episodes of deposition in pits reflect a range of activities carried out during the lifecycle of a group living or visiting a particular location, ranging from the straightforward deposition of material in association with settlement to the more formal deposition of pyre material related to the death of a particular individual or individuals. At Forest Road, as throughout Scotland, a range of activities involving deposition in pits is implied that cannot be neatly attributed to traditional explanations, as either the disposal of domestic refuse or as relating to ritualised behaviour, but rather appears more to reflect a subtle combination of the two (see Brophy and Noble 2012). Therefore, rather than interpreting pits as straightforward evidence for either settlement or ritual, we should instead consider them as a reflection and a product of the lifecycle of communities and groups that involved a variety of events, some routine, others less so; and recognise moreover that these events could take place in the same locales, that is, there was not always clear spatial or temporal separation between differing contexts that involved the placing of materials into the earth. The occurrence of the cremation pit at Forest Road in amongst a cluster of typical pits underlines this point. Similarly, the evidence from Warren Field, difficult as it is to interpret, makes it clear that in the Mesolithic too, there is no easy way for us to differentiate between the functions of particular pits, rather that, in this context too, pit digging characterised a variety of events and activities.

Recognising that pits often represent more than the casual discard of domestic refuse has perhaps led to the disproportionate categorising of deposits as 'structured', implying something outwith the norms of behaviour and drawing distinctions between actions perceived as practical and domestic in opposition to ritual or religious activity, a distinction that may not be appropriate in reality (Brück 1999). As Gordon Barclay (Barclay et al. 2001: 81) commented more than a decade ago, we are in danger of swinging from one extreme to the other in our attempts to understand pits. Simply identifying that deposits are structured does not necessarily equate to their symbolic significance (Barrett and Ko 2009: 290). These interpretative problems are underscored by the fact that, as seen at Forest Road, and whether considered 'typical' or 'structured', the range of material often found in pits is comparable and could be considered as the residue of daily life, while in other cases pits include finely made or specialised artefacts, but are not always directly connected with overtly ritualistic behaviour, occurring, for example, in funerary contexts. It is therefore difficult to identify the subtle differences between the gathering together of deposits potentially connected with a single, formalised ceremonial event, the more informal deposition of certain material that may have been part of everyday practices, and the disposal of a selection of domestic refuse. Furthermore, while recognisable traditions of pit digging can be identified throughout Scotland, acts of deposition do not appear to have been governed by strict rules, suggesting that a degree of improvisation existed within depositional practices, which were designed to suit individual or local circumstances (Thomas 1999: 69). Everyday domestic behaviour is inevitably grounded in cosmological beliefs and social conventions, but is also subject to individual agency and influenced by specific situations, arguably expressed in the comparable, yet variable, selection and deposition of material within individual pits. The seemingly formalised deposition of everyday material in pits reflects the complexity of ritual activity itself; rituals form part of everyday behaviour and in turn the concerns of daily life are reflected in ritual practices (Richards and Thomas 1984; Brück 1999).

What may be important in all these contexts, Mesolithic or Neolithic, is that it was felt necessary to return materials to the ground at all. This may have much to tell us about attitudes to the environment and concepts of purity, cleanliness and the right ways of marking particular lifecycle events in prehistory. What we can say is that in a Neolithic context the contents of pits often achieved a higher degree of formality than in Mesolithic contexts (although here there is likely to be a bias in the kinds of material that survive from both periods), with pits increasingly found in association with monuments and some containing greater evidence for the deliberate orchestration of materials deposited within the pit. Mesolithic pits tend not to be artefact-rich, and in contrast some Neolithic pits can contain many hundreds of artefacts. However, we should not forget that scholarship has tended to concentrate on the more formal pit deposits, ignoring the more ubiquitous (and generally less commonly dated) pits with unremarkable fillings or fills that entirely lack diagnostic artefacts. Nevertheless, deposition and pit digging in the Early Neolithic does occur in a greater variety of contexts than in the Mesolithic.

At Forest Road, Kintore, pit digging appears to have been carried out over a number of centuries in the Early Neolithic in view of an elaborate timber and earth monument. The inauguration of fixed foci in the landscape that more explicitly structured the ways in which landscapes were experienced at the beginning of the fourth millennium cal. BC is one of the major differences from Mesolithic contexts (although the evidence from Warren Field may suggest that there is more to learn on the role of monuments or landscape features in the Mesolithic). However, the character of the pits at Kintore and the possible presence of structures there, make it clear that these monumental locales were not empty ceremonial landscapes, but that again the full spectrum of lifecycle events was carried out in the same landscape with no clear division between ritual and domestic. Several other Early Neolithic monuments in Aberdeenshire have also been found to show evidence for activity in the areas directly around or near monumental mounds. Fieldwalking and test pitting in the area around the site of the now destroyed Hill of Foulzie long barrow, for example, have revealed substantial evidence of lithic production spanning the Mesolithic to Late Neolithic periods, along with small amounts of Early Neolithic Carinated Bowl pottery (Lindsay 2003; Lindsay and Lindsay 2005). It may well be that, as in northern Scotland and on Orkney (e.g., Phillips 2002), the monuments constructed in the Neolithic formed nodes in the landscape that attracted settlement and activity (which may have included pit digging) in their vicinities during and after the construction of these monuments.

If we hypothesise that pit digging was connected to a variety of lifecycle events, then it is clear that, in Aberdeenshire at least, these lifecycle events increasingly included the full spectrum of the lifecycle; in the Early Neolithic pit digging was occasionally linked to the deposition of human remains. The possible cremation pit at Kintore underlines this phenomenon, but the relatively poorly documented barrow monuments of the area may also furnish evidence of the placing of cremated individuals in pits. At Midtown of Pitglassie, for example, pits containing Early Neolithic artefacts, charcoal and cremated human bone were found under the mound of a round barrow. One pit contained cremated bone, while the adjoining pit contained five sherds of Neolithic Carinated Bowl pottery (probably from a single Carinated Bowl; Henshall 1996). A fragment of the cremated bone has been dated to 3940–3660 cal. BC (Table 9.1) (Sheridan and Bradley 2007). Another pit also contained pottery sherds apparently from the same vessel as that recovered from the other pottery-bearing pit, and a leaf-shaped arrowhead of red-brown flint. Further cremated bone, thought to represent a single individual (Powell 1996), was found scattered in the subsoil to the west of these pits. The sequence at Midtown of Pitglassie is complex: it is nonetheless clear that within the first centuries of the Early Neolithic an individual was cremated within a demarcated area and the remains of this cremation and specific artefactual items were then deposited in pits and spread over the ground surface. The construction of the mound, within which quartz pieces were both carefully deposited and randomly scattered (Shepherd 1996), occurred thereafter.

The greater formalisation of pits associated with cremations and other human remains is also apparent in Pit 25 at Kintore. The artefacts within it showed evidence of careful placement, with the pottery sherds in particular having been deliberately positioned with the decoration face up (Cook and Dunbar 2008: 61). This increased formalisation of deposits and other such aesthetic considerations, particularly in association with cremations, can be traced through to the Late Neolithic in Aberdeenshire at sites such as Midmill, Kintore. A pit at Midmill, excavated in association with a cremation complex, contained, for example, a charcoal-rich fill with slightly less than half of a Grooved Ware vessel set within a small circle of stones. The cremated human remains were then spread throughout the, arguably deliberately arranged, surrounding layers of clean, grey and dirty sandy silts (Murray and Murray 2012: 7). The evidence from Midtown of Pitglassie and Kintore may be part of an increased formalisation of digging into the earth and deposition during the Early Neolithic that may have continued into the Late Neolithic and beyond. Indeed, deposition of material is found in a variety of additional contexts, in the voids left by the removed axial post-holes of the timber hall at Warren Field, Crathes, for example, and the inclusion of a greater range of material in Neolithic pits more generally such as pottery, lithics and charred plant material is evident (Murray et al. 2009).

The heightened preoccupation with placing objects in the ground in the Neolithic warrants a fuller consideration of the extent to which this activity was a means of giving back to the environment after particular natural or lifecycle events. With the onset of food production in the Early Neolithic, the need to give back to the environment through votive offering may have been exaggerated due to the greater interventions in the form of a reliance on landscape manipulation and clearance (cf. Bird-David 1999). Thus, environmental evidence should be a major research avenue for future exploration. We could see the interring of select objects, for example, as akin to planting these objects in the ground; and thus, in a Neolithic context at least, an action that may have been redolent of crop growing and the agricultural cycle. It is factors such as these that need to be incorporated into any narrative that attempts to translate the patterns of material deposition and particular traditions of material culture in relation to period specific questions.

Finally, we should also be aware of the potential contrasts that can be drawn out between where pits occur and where they do not. In the Early Neolithic, for example, there is greater evidence for the building of structures that can be interpreted as having fulfilled a role in the settlement traditions of Aberdeenshire. This new built environment perhaps points to major changes in the ways in which landscape was occupied in the early phases of the fourth millennium cal. BC. Buildings include two excavated timber halls at Warren Field and Balbridie and an oval structure at Garthdee Road (Fairweather and Ralston 1993; Murray et al. 2009; Murray and Murray forthcoming). In relation to pit digging, what is notable about these three sites, however, is the rarity of pit digging (other than for the insertion of upright timbers) in direct association with these structures. It may be that pit digging characterised a *particular kind of settlement* that did not involve the construction of structures founded on earthfast timbers set in major post-holes.

However, the evidence from Nethermills may suggest that, in a Mesolithic context, light timber structures were also built in association with pit digging. Only further work will elucidate the full detail surrounding the continuity and/or contrasts in Mesolithic and Neolithic pit digging.

Conclusions

Detailed regional studies of pits for counties such as Aberdeenshire will undoubtedly affect the ways in which we write the grand narratives of the Neolithic and, within this, interpret pit digging in a more holistic sense. Developer-funded archaeology has not only begun to transform our knowledge of pit digging in a quantitative sense, but has also led to unexpected revelations regarding the variety of pit forms, their chronology and other structural remains from both the Neolithic and Mesolithic. It is possible that developing an understanding of the variations in pit-digging activities through time may throw further light on the origins of the practice. In this respect, the wider dating of pits that do not contain diagnostic finds (or indeed finds at all) will undoubtedly continue to challenge our expectations of the kinds of activity that characterised particular forms of landscape inhabitation in the past. Attempts to ascribe particular forms of pit digging to rigid classificatory categories need to be resisted – such conventional groupings do not account for the variety of pit forms, fills, artefact associations and contexts in which pit digging took place. There is a need to recognise the continuum that existed between pits that resulted from the disposal of everyday refuse and those that were associated with funerary and ritual activity. In this respect, pits were associated with the lifecycles of communities and the multitudes of events that characterised Mesolithic and Neolithic lifeways, and at any given site there was not necessarily any clear spatial or temporal separation between pit-digging events that encompassed many aspects of life (and death) in the Mesolithic and Neolithic.

Notes

1. Recent development-led excavations in advance of the Aberdeen Western Peripheral Route have begun to reveal the extent of Mesolithic activity along the River Dee. A few miles down the river from Nethermills, the site of Maryculter Bridge has revealed Mesolithic pits within an area of significant Mesolithic activity, including worked flint scatters (Dingwall 2014: 85).
2. Indeed, a more recent article on the pit alignment has suggested that the structure may have had some role in tracking the movements of the sun and moon, but other interpretations are possible (Gaffney *et al.* 2013).

Bibliography

Alexander, D. (1997), 'Excavation of pits containing decorated Neolithic pottery and early lithic material of possible Mesolithic date at Spurryhillock, Stonehaven, Aberdeenshire', *Proceedings of the Society of Antiquaries of Scotland*, 127: 17–27.

Alexander, D. (2000), 'Excavations of Neolithic pits, later prehistoric structures and a Roman temporary camp along the line of the A96 Kintore and Blackburn bypass, Aberdeenshire', *Proceedings of the Society of Antiquaries of Scotland*, 130: 11–76.

Allen, M. (1995), 'Before Stonehenge', in Cleal, Higgs and Longworth (eds), *Stonehenge in its Landscape*, 41–62.

Allen, M. J. and Gardiner, J. (2002), 'A sense of time: cultural markers in the Mesolithic of southern England?', in B. David and M. Wilson (eds), *Inscribed Landscapes: Marking and Making Place*, Honolulu: University of Hawai'i Press, 139–53.

Anderson-Whymark, H. and Thomas, J. (eds) (2012), *Regional Perspectives on Neolithic Pit Deposition: Beyond the Mundane*, Oxford: Oxbow Books.

Ashmore, P. J. (2004), 'A date list (to October 2002) for early foragers in Scotland', in A. Saville (ed.), *Mesolithic Scotland and its Neighbours*, Edinburgh: Society of Antiquaries of Scotland, 95–158.

Barclay, G. J., Carter, S. P., Dalland, M. M., Hastie, M., Holden, T. G., MacSween, A. and Wickham-Jones, C. R. (2001), 'A possible Neolithic settlement at Kinbeachie, Black Isle, Highland', *Proceedings of the Society of Antiquaries of Scotland*, 131: 57–85.

Barrett, J. and Ko, I. (2009), 'A phenomenology of landscape: a crisis in British archaeology?', *Journal of Social Archaeology*, 9: 275–94.

Bird-David, N. (1999), ' "Animism" revisited: personhood, environment, and relational epistemology', *Current Anthropology*, 40: 67–91.

Bonsall, C., Anderson, D. E. and Macklin, M. G. (2002), 'The Mesolithic–Neolithic transition in western Scotland and its European context', *Documenta praehistorica*, 29: 1–19.

Bradley, R. (1993), *Altering the Earth: The Origins of Monuments in Britain and Continental Europe*, Edinburgh: Society of Antiquaries of Scotland.

Bradley, R. (2011), *Stages and Screens: An Investigation of Four Henge Monuments in Northern and North-eastern Scotland*, Edinburgh: Society of Antiquaries of Scotland.

Brophy, K. (2006), 'Rethinking Scotland's Neolithic: combining circumstance and context', *Proceedings of the Society of Antiquaries of Scotland*, 136: 7–46.

Brophy, K. and Noble, G. (2012), 'Within and beyond pits: deposition in lowland Neolithic Scotland', in Anderson-Whymark and Thomas (eds), *Regional Perspectives on Neolithic Pit Deposition*, 63–76.

Brück, J. (1999), 'Ritual and rationality: some problems of interpretation in European archaeology', *Journal of European Archaeology*, 2: 313–44.

Carver, G. (2012), 'Pits and place-making: Neolithic habitation and depositional practices in East Yorkshire c. 4000–2500 BC', *Proceedings of the Prehistoric Society*, 78: 111–34.

Clark, J. G. D., Higgs, E. and Longworth, I. (1960), 'Excavations at the Neolithic site of Hurst Fen, Mildenhall, Suffolk (1954, 1957 and 1958)', *Proceedings of the Prehistoric Society*, 26: 202–45.

Cleal, R. M. J., Walker, K. E. and Montague, R. (eds) (1995), *Stonehenge in its Landscape: Twentieth-century Excavations*, London: English Heritage.

Cook, M. and Dunbar, L. (eds) (2008), *Rituals, Romans and Roundhouses: Excavations at Kintore, Aberdeenshire 2000–2006, vol. 1: Forest Road*, Edinburgh: Scottish Trust for Archaeological Research.

Dingwall, K. (2014), 'Aberdeen Western Peripheral Route/Balmedie–Tipperty Lot 3 – Southern Leg. Assessment Report on the Results of Trial Trenching and Sample Excavations', unpublished Client Report Submitted to Aberdeenshire Council, Headland Archaeology, Edinburgh.

Engl, R. (2008), 'Chipped stone', in Cook and Dunbar (eds), *Rituals, Romans and Roundhouses*, 226 37.

Fairweather, A. and Ralston, I. B. M. (1993), 'The Neolithic timber hall at Balbridie, Grampian Region, Scotland: the building, the date, the plant macrofossils', *Antiquity*, 67: 313–23

Field, N. H., Matthews, C. L. and Smith, I. F. (1964), 'New Neolithic sites in Dorset and Bedfordshire, with a note on the distribution of Neolithic storage pits in Britain', *Proceedings of the Prehistoric Society*, 30: 352–80.

Finlay, N., Warren, G. and Wickham-Jones, C.R. (2004), 'The Mesolithic in Scotland: east meets west', *Scottish Archaeological Journal*, 24: 101–20.

Finlayson, B. (1997), 'The plano-convex knife', in R. J. Mercer and M. S. Midgley,

'The Early Bronze Age cairn at Sketewan, Balnaguard, Perth & Kinross', *Proceedings of the Society of Antiquaries of Scotland*, 127: 309–11.

Finlayson, B. (2000), 'Chipped Stone', in Alexander, *Proceedings of the Society of Antiquaries of Scotland*, 130: 53–8.

Gaffney, V., Fitch, S., Ramsey, E., Yorston, R., Ch'ng, E., Baldwin, E., Bates, R., Gaffney, C., Ruggles, C., Sparrow, T., McMillan, A., Cowley, D., Fraser, S., Murray, C., Murray, H., Hopla, E. and Howard, A. (2013), 'Time and a place: a luni-solar "time-reckoner" from 8th millennium BC Scotland', *Internet Archaeology*, 34: dx.doi.org/10.11141/ia.34.1.

Garrow, D. (2012), 'Reply to responses', *Archaeological Dialogues*, 19: 133–44.

Garrow, D., Beadsmoore, E. and Knight, M. (2005), 'Pit clusters and the temporality of occupation: an earlier Neolithic site at Kilverstone, Thetford, Norfolk', *Proceedings of the Prehistoric Society*, 71: 139–57.

Gondek, M., Noble, G. and Sveinbjarnarson, O. (2013), 'Excavation of Two Square Enclosures, Square Barrows and other Features at Rhynie, Aberdeenshire', unpublished Data Structure Report, Rhynie Environs Archaeological Project, University of Aberdeen.

Griffiths, S. (2014), 'Points in time: the Mesolithic–Neolithic transition and the chronology of late rod microliths in Britain', *Oxford Journal of Archaeology*, 33: 221–43.

Gooder, J. (2007), 'Excavation of a Mesolithic house at East Barns, East Lothian, Scotland: an interim view', in Waddington and Pedersen (eds), *Mesolithic Studies*, 48–59.

Henshall, A. (1996), 'The pottery', in Shepherd, *Proceedings of the Society of Antiquaries of Scotland*, 126: 29–33.

Johnson, M. and Cameron, K. (2012), 'An Early Bronze Age unenclosed cremation cemetery and Mesolithic pit at Skilmafilly, near Maud, Aberdeenshire', *Scottish Archaeological Internet Report* (= *SAIR*), 53 (updated 2014): dx.doi.org/10.5284/1017938.

Kenworthy, J. B. (1980), 'Banchory, Nethermills Farm, Crathes, Grampian Region. Mesolithic flint scatter', *Proceedings of the Prehistoric Society*, 46: 364.

Kenworthy, J. B. (1981), 'Nethermills Farm, Crathes, Excavations 1978–80', unpublished Interim Report, University of St Andrews.

Kirby, M. (2009), 'Tullo Wind Farm, Laurencekirk, Aberdeenshire, Archaeological Works', unpublished Report 1700, CFA Archaeology Ltd, Musselburgh.

Kirby, M. (2010), 'Tullo Wind Farm, Laurencekirk, Aberdeenshire, Post-Excavation Archive Report', unpublished Report 1787, CFA Archaeology Ltd, Musselburgh.

Lelong, O. (2010), 'The Monastery of Deer Archaeological Project: Desk-based Assessment and Field Evaluation', unpublished report 2712, Glasgow University Archaeological Research Division.

Lindsay, S. and Lindsay, W. J. (2005), 'Hill of Foulzie', *Discovery and Excavation in Scotland*, n.s., 6: 16.

Lindsay, W. J. (2003), 'Hill of Foulzie', *Discovery and Excavation in Scotland*, n.s., 4: 19.

MacSween, A. (2008), 'The prehistoric pottery', in Cook and Dunbar (eds), *Rituals, Romans and Roundhouses*, 173–89.

McFadyen, L. (2007), 'Mobile spaces of Mesolithic Britain', *Home Cultures*, 4: 115–26.

McInnes, I. J. (1971), 'Settlement in later Neolithic Britain', in D. D. A. Simpson (ed.), *Economy and Settlement in Neolithic and Early Bronze Age Britain and Europe*, Leicester: Leicester University Press, 113–30.

Murray, H. K. (2005), 'David Lloyd Leisure Centre, Garthdee Road, Aberdeen', *Discovery and Excavation in Scotland*, n.sr., 6: 8–9.

Murray, H. K. and Fraser, F. (2009), 'Discussion of the pit alignment', in Murray, Murray and Fraser (eds), *A Tale of the Unknown Unknowns*, 20–9.

Murray, H. K. and Murray, J. C. (2008), 'Phase 3, Westgate housing development, Inverurie', *Discovery and Excavation in Scotland*, n.s., 9: 23.

Murray, H. K. and Murray, J. C. (2009), 'The pit alignment', in Murray, Murray and Fraser (eds), *A Tale of the Unknown Unknowns*, 4–14.

Murray, H. K. and Murray, J. C. (2010), 'Broom Lodge, Mill Road, Inverurie, Aberdeenshire; Excavation Report', unpublished report, Murray Archaeological Services.

Murray, H. K. and Murray, J. C. (2012), 'Midmill Industrial Estate Kintore, Aberdeenshire; Archaeological Evaluations and Excavations carried out 2007– 2012', unpublished report, Murray Archaeological Services.

Murray, H. K. and Murray, J. C. (2013a), 'Site West of International Paper, Port Elphinstone, Inverurie, Aberdeenshire, Part 1: Archaeological Excavation Report', unpublished report, Murray Archaeological Services.

Murray, H. K. and Murray, J. C. (2013b), 'Site West of International Paper, Port Elphinstone, Inverurie, Aberdeenshire, Part 2: Tables and Appendices', unpublished report: Murray Archaeological Services.

Murray, H. K. and Murray, J. C. (forthcoming), 'An Early Neolithic building and Mesolithic occupation at Garthdee Road, Aberdeen', *Proceedings of the Society of Antiquaries of Scotland* (forthcoming).

Murray, H. K., Murray, J. C. and Fraser, S. M. (eds) (2009), *A Tale of the Unknown Unknowns: A Mesolithic Pit Alignment and a Neolithic Timber Hall at Warren Field, Crathes, Aberdeenshire*, Oxford: Oxbow Books.

O'Sullivan, J. (1995), 'Park Quarry, Drumoak', *Discovery and Excavation in Scotland*, 1995: 34.

Pannett, A. (2012), 'Pits, pots and plant remains: trends in Neolithic deposition in Carmarthenshire, South Wales', in Anderson-Whymark and Thomas (eds), *Regional Perspectives on Neolithic Pit Deposition*, 126–43.

Phillips, T. (2002), *Landscapes of the Living, Landscapes of the Dead: The Location of the Chambered Cairns of Northern Scotland*, Oxford: British Archaeological Reports.

Phillips, T. and Bradley, R. (2004), 'Developer-funded fieldwork in Scotland, 1990–2003: an overview of the prehistoric evidence', *Proceedings of the Society of Antiquaries of Scotland*, 134: 17–51.

Pollard, J. (2001), 'The aesthetics of depositional practice', *World Archaeology*, 33: 315–33.

Powell, F. V. H. (1996), 'Cremated human remains', in Shepherd, *Proceedings of the Society of Antiquaries of Scotland*, 126: 38.

Richards, C. and Thomas, J. (1984), 'Ritual activity and structured deposition in later Neolithic Wessex', in R. Bradley and J. Gardiner (eds), *Neolithic Studies: A Review of Some Current Research*, Oxford: British Archaeological Reports, 189–218.

Sabnis, H., Kenworthy, J. and Over Fifties Archaeological Research Society (OFARS) (2008), 'Nether Mills Farm, Crathes, Banchory', *Discovery and Excavation in Scotland*, n.s., 9: 16–17.

Sabnis, H., Kenworthy, J. and Over Fifties Archaeological Research Society (OFARS) (2009), 'Nether Mills East', *Discovery and Excavation in Scotland*, n.s., 10: 16.

Shepherd, A. (1996), 'A Neolithic ring-mound at Midtown of Pitglassie, Auchterless, Aberdeenshire', *Proceedings of the Society of Antiquaries of Scotland*, 126: 17–51.

Shepherd, I. and Greig, M. (1991), 'Park Quarry', *Discovery and Excavation in Scotland*, 1991: 35.

Stone, J. F. S. (1934), 'Three "Peterborough" dwelling pits and a doubly stockaded Early Iron Age ditch at Winterbourne Dauntsey', *Wiltshire Archaeological and Natural History Magazine*, 46: 445–53.

Sheridan, A. (2007), 'From Picardie to Pickering and Pencraig Hill? New information on the "Carinated Bowl Neolithic" in northern Britain', in A. Whittle and V. Cummings (eds), *Going Over: The Mesolithic–Neolithic Transition in North-West Europe*, Oxford: Oxford University Press (= *Proceedings of the British Academy*), 144: 441–92.

Sheridan, A. and Bradley, R. (2007), 'Radiocarbon dates arranged through National Museums Scotland during 2006/7', *Discovery and Excavation in Scotland*, n.s., 8: 220.

Suddaby, I. (2005), 'Park Quarry, Drumoak', *Discovery and Excavation in Scotland*, n.s., 6: 15.

Suddaby, I. (2007), 'Downsizing in the Mesolithic? The discovery of two associated post-circles at Silvercrest, Lesmurdie Road, Elgin, Scotland', in Waddington and Pedersen (eds), *Mesolithic Studies*, 60–8.

Suddaby, I. (2009), 'Broadshade Pipeline Diversion, Westhill, Aberdeenshire. Archaeological Watching Brief and Data Structure Report', unpublished Report 1658, CFA Archaeology Ltd, Musselburgh.

Thomas, J. (1991), *Rethinking the Neolithic*, Cambridge: Cambridge University Press.

Thomas, J. (1999), *Understanding the Neolithic*, London: Routledge.

Thomas, J. (2012), 'Introduction: beyond the mundane?' in Anderson-Whymark and Thomas (eds), *Regional Perspectives on Neolithic Pit Deposition*, 1–12.

Waddington, C. (2007), *Mesolithic Settlement in the North Sea Basin: A Case Study from Howick, North-East England*, Oxford: Oxbow Books and English Heritage.

Waddington, C., Bailey, G., Bayliss, A., Milner, N., Pedersen, K., Shiel, R. and Stevenson, T. (2003), 'A Mesolithic settlement site at Howick, Northumberland: a preliminary report', *Archaeologia Aeliana*, 5th ser., 32: 1–12.

Waddington, C. and Pedersen, K. (eds) (2007), *Mesolithic Studies in the North Sea Basin and Beyond*, Oxford: Oxbow Books.

Warren, G. (2005), *Mesolithic Lives in Scotland*, Stroud: Tempus.

Warren, G. (2009), 'Stone tools', in Murray, Murray and Fraser (eds), *A Tale of the Unknown Unknowns*, 97–107.

Wordsworth, J. (1985), 'The excavation of a Mesolithic horizon at 13–24 Castle Street, Inverness', *Proceedings of the Society of Antiquaries of Scotland*, 115: 89–103.

CHAPTER 10

On Ancient Farms:
A Survey of Neolithic Potentially Domestic
Locations in Lowland Scotland

Kenneth Brophy

Preamble

The headline on the BBC website in November 2010[1] was clear and une-
quivocal: 'Ancient farm found at site of new Forth Crossing.' Yet the brief
story contained far less information than one would like to back up its central claim:

> Archaeologists believe they may have unearthed the remains of a Neolithic
> farm on the site where the new Forth road bridge is to be built. Trial trenches
> have been dug in a field on the outskirts of South Queensferry on land
> reserved for the planned Forth Replacement Crossing. Archaeologists plan
> further excavations to confirm what they believe is an early version of a croft
> or small farm.

There are a few assumptions packaged up in this journalistic interpretation
of a press statement: that it is possible to find and identify a 'Neolithic farm';
and that it represented a crofting level of economy. The search for Neolithic
houses, farms, settlements, villages (whichever terms you wish to use) in
Scotland has for over a century been dogged by such assumptions: that such
basic units of life should take on a form recognisable to us from our own
experiences today. After all, what else would we expect of the first farmers,
but that they lived in farmhouses and farmed?

In fact, the excavations that followed the evaluation reported on by
the BBC, at a site called Echline Fields, City of Edinburgh, revealed not
a Neolithic farm, but rather a Mesolithic settlement site (of considerable
significance in itself), although evidence for Neolithic activity was noted.
This evidence does not accord with the 'Neolithic farm' expectations of the
media and public imagination, but does go some way to illustrate the more
typical remains of the everyday activities and materials that we would expect
to find left behind by the early farmers of mainland, lowland Scotland. The
only features dated to the Neolithic period at Echline Fields were three
isolated pits, one of which produced sherds from an Impressed Ware pot

and a hazel nutshell (dated to the final centuries of the fourth millennium cal. BC), and the other two contained sherds of Grooved Ware (Robertson *et al.* 2013: 83). The latter features were identified by the excavators as being indicative of 'domestic deposition' with associated structures perhaps lost; curiously the third pit was regarded as being ritual in nature containing meaningful, structured deposits (*ibid.*: 132–3). Such a clear ritual/domestic division could be regarded as problematic (Brophy and Noble 2012), but regardless, these three pits are sadly rather typical of what lies beneath many of the dots on maps of Neolithic settlement sites in Scotland, such as Figure 10.1.

Another Forth crossing tells a similar story, but on a very different scale. Excavations ahead of the construction of the Clackmannanshire Bridge (which is located near Kincardine, and 20 km upstream from the Forth bridges) in 2005–6 revealed dozens of pits and post-holes scattered over a wide area, many of which contained diagnostically Neolithic material. This site, known as Meadowend Farm, Clackmannanshire, is at yet unpublished, but clearly represents a significant Neolithic 'pit cluster' (one of the largest yet found in Scotland) and the evidence suggests that this was the location of intensive pit digging, deposition and other activities such as post erection (Jones 2006: 46–7). Many pits contained, like Echline Fields, Impressed Ware sherds, and some possible hearths were identified. In other words, this is a location where it seems likely that domestic activity happened, a place that was used again and again, perhaps over many decades or generations. As to where people were actually living, it is tempting to imagine that any earth-fast components of flimsy and light-scale seasonally built and/or occupied tents and timber structures would long since have been scraped away by the plough. And so we are left with negative features, repositories of the detritus of life, barely detectable ghostly shadows of once special places.

But things have moved on in the two decades since Gordon Barclay wrote that the 'search for settlement is hampered by the limits to our understanding of the guises in which it will appear' (Barclay 1996: 75). We are aware now that Neolithic houses, farms and settlements appear in a range of guises and that these might not be what we once expected, nor wholly mundane and domestic in nature. The evidence we have speaks not of crofts and farmhouses, but of very different rhythms of life, frequencies of occupation, semi-mobility and a range of different structures for living in. This means that normative assumptions about where we might find settlement, such as being close to water (Graves 2011), may not always apply. In fact, there is no blueprint for what Neolithic settlement might actually look like or where we might find it, as we shall see.

This chapter offers the most comprehensive review to date of evidence for Neolithic settlement and domestic structures on the mainland of Scotland. The vast majority of the evidence is concentrated in the lowlands, with the identification of upland settlement considerably more challenging, for the reasons outlined by Roy Loveday in this volume (Chapter 6). Furthermore, in stark contrast to decades of work on Orcadian Neolithic houses and villages, the mainland has received relatively little depth of coverage. But on reviewing the evidence, one thing is clear: 'we emerge into the 21st century with a Scottish landscape more densely, and more evenly, distributed with the remains of our Neolithic past' (Barclay 2004: 41–2).

Neolithic house hunting in Scotland

How things have changed. For decades, discussion has raged amongst scholars of the Neolithic of Scotland as to the nature of Neolithic houses, settlement and sedentism (outwith Orkney where such things curiously seem to have been taken for granted). This reflects wider debates across Britain and Ireland where there has been something of a 'house problem' in British (less so Irish) Neolithic studies, the problem being that it was very difficult to find houses, or at least securely to interpret structures and buildings as being domestic spaces (see, e.g., Gibson 2003; Brophy 2015). The mid-twentieth century optimism that was provoked by discoveries of stone houses in the Northern Isles gradually gave way to a mood of pessimism for the rest of Scotland, pessimism that equivalent evidence perhaps might never be found. This mood, cultivated in the 1970s and 1980s (e.g., Kinnes 1985), coincided with the 'interpretive turn' in archaeology where new models of the Neolithic developed that were more in tune with an apparently 'houseless' British lowlands. Rather than rethink what we might interpret as a house, a model of the Neolithic was developed (largely based on evidenced from the south of England) that *did not need houses*. And so Julian Thomas was able to suggest that, 'the majority of the population lived for most of the time in rather flimsy and temporary dwellings' (Thomas 1996: 2). Thus, the so-called 'mobile Neolithic hypothesis' (most clearly articulated by Whittle 1996 and Thomas 1999) became a dominant explanatory model in British Neolithic studies by the late 1990s, and a generation of PhD scholars emerged within this context (myself included).

Yet alternative narratives also emerged at that time, utilising data from different parts of the British Isles. Gordon Barclay (1996, 2003a, 2004) and Gabriel Cooney (1996, 1999) argued that the settlement evidence from mainland Scotland and Ireland, respectively, demanded a much more nuanced reading. Both argued that houses, sedentism and domesticity *were* apparent in the archaeological record. For instance, much against the grain, Gordon Barclay argued that people in Scotland's Early Neolithic:

1. lived in *light timber houses*; …
2. resided in one area, probably based in *permanent settlements*, but possibly with some of the population moving seasonally, to summer grazing or fishing;
3. worked for part of the year in productive hoe- and spade-, if not ard-

cultivated plots, perhaps of considerable extent ... (Barclay 2003b: 148, added emphasis)

This vision of the Early Neolithic (essentially the fourth millennium BC) was very much at odds with the aforementioned theoretical models that were in vogue at the time and Barclay was well aware of this. Yet when he wrote this, to my mind, it also seemed at odds with the evidence available for mainland Scotland, and Gordon and I discussed this difference of opinion frequently. Comprehensive reviews of Scotland's Neolithic (such as Kinnes 1985; Ritchie and Ritchie 1991: chs 2 and 3; Ashmore 1996) agreed that there was little evidence for timber houses or permanent settlement outwith the Northern and Western Isles. Even the supposed 'holy grail' of Neolithic house hunters, the Early Neolithic Balbridie timber hall, Aberdeenshire, found via cropmarks and excavated in the late 1970s (Fairweather and Ralston 1993), was a source of interpretive disagreement (see Barclay *et al.* 2002; Brophy 2007).

To back up his conviction, Barclay set out to collate evidence for domestic activity in mainland Scotland in the many and variable forms in which he argued it took, utilising various untapped datasets. This involved, for instance, drawing on the large and relatively new dataset that had been serendipitously provided by the boom in developer-funded archaeology across Scotland from the late 1980s onwards, and had essentially provided a random sample of the landscape that would not have been possible within a traditional research-driven context (cf. Carter 2002; Phillips and Bradley 2004; Brophy 2006). The much under-utilised cropmark record, and field-walking results, were both also mined to great effect. Barclay presented his results in two synthetic papers (1996, 2003a), but he also actively sought additional evidence through his AHRC-funded 'First Farmers Project' (2001–3), based at Stirling University.[2] This project included the excavation or test-pitting of a number of sites discovered by fieldwalking (and in some cases backed up by aerial survey) that had a potentially domestic, Neolithic character, all in Perth and Kinross. The results were, as perhaps one would expect for such an experimental approach, varied. Two cropmark sites – Upper Gothens and Mains of Duncrub – were not Neolithic (Barclay 2001, 2002a). Three other sites, all lithic scatters, revealed little, with only one, Nethermuir, producing any meaningful results; in this case, cut features one of which provided an Early Neolithic date (Barclay and Wickham-Jones 2002). Other excavations around this time associated with this programme of work were more successful however. A site with a possible domestic element, Claish timber hall, Stirling was investigated (Barclay *et al.* 2002; and see Figure 10.2); while the superficially similar sub-rectangular mid-Neolithic timber structure at Carsie Mains may not have been a roofed building, but revealed fascinating evidence for tree and post relationships (Brophy and Barclay 2004).

Before Gordon finally moved on to new interests, he collated an (unpublished) document in 2002 entitled 'A survey of Neolithic potentially domestic locations in lowland Scotland' (henceforth known as the 'Barclay 2002 list' (Barclay 2002b)). It contains an annotated list of all sites across mainland Scotland that showed evidence for settlement, and Neolithic pits not explicitly associated with a burial or ceremonial monument were also included. Barclay's document forms the starting point for the remainder of this chapter, which offers a review of the evidence he collected updated in light of the decade of discoveries and research that have taken place since its compilation. There are now over one hundred sites in mainland Scotland that could be interpreted as indicative of settlement or domestic activity (with the proviso that these are malleable and ambiguous terms), including structures which were surely houses.

The outcome of Barclay's diligent research was the emergence of a completely new conception of Neolithic settlement patterns in mainland Scotland (Barclay 2004). Barclay's tenacious belief that houses and other domestic traces were out there, waiting to be found (or had been found but not recognised) was prophetic, and over the past decade our understanding of Neolithic settlement in Britain and Ireland has been completely transformed, even in southern England where the 'mobile Neolithic' hypothesis had taken firmest hold (Bradley 2007; Parker Pearson 2012; Brophy 2015). This chapter is, I hope, not only a contribution to this discussion, but also my modest attempt to follow in the footsteps of Gordon Barclay. Before commencing the discussion of the evidence, however, it is worth briefly reflecting on how approaches to finding and defining evidence for domestic life have changed in Scotland and beyond, and how our terminology has evolved.

The search for the domestic – and clarity

There is no doubt in my mind that one of the main stumbling blocks to identifying domestic sites and houses in the Scottish (and indeed British) Neolithic has been the failure to adequately define what we mean by 'domestic' and 'house' in the first place, and the consequent loss of confidence that this caused. If we return to accounts of Neolithic settlement sites from over a century ago, the assignment of a domestic function to pits, hearths, post-holes and (rare) structures was viewed unproblematically. For instance, a series of pits and firespots associated with broken potsherds, found in several locations at Easterton of Roseisle, Moray, in the 1890s, were interpreted as Neolithic settlement evidence at the time by antiquarian Hugh Young (see Walker 1968). In 1902, Ludovic MacLellan Mann claimed to have identified a 'Stone Age village' in south-west Scotland. The site was Mye Plantation, Dumfries and Galloway, uncovered within sand dunes. Here, Mann found a series of pits with wooden stakes at the bottom, associated with Late Neolithic pottery; he called these 'pit-dwell-ings' (Mann 1903). This discovery was rapidly followed by the investiga-tion of a settlement site at Townhead, Bute (included in this discussion as this interpretation is very much representative of its time in relation to such discoveries), where multiple pits and post-holes were found in association with Neolithic pottery, lithics, querns and carbonised material (Marshall 1930). The value of pits as indicative of Neolithic settlement was subse-quently reinforced by Callander (1929) in an overview of the Neolithic pottery held by the National Museum of Antiquities. Five 'domestic sites' were identified as sources of what he called 'domestic dishes', a term we would today baulk at when describing Neolithic ceramics, even if some were indeed used to hold foodstuffs.

Many decades after Callander's synthesis and Mann's tireless efforts such simplistic assumptions became viewed as increasingly problematic, and pits in particular went through many interpretive twists and turns. Piggott (1954: 306) suggested that Mann's Mye Plantation pits were 'pit-fall traps', and in one of the few other references to pits in his review of the British Neolithic he argued that some may have been 'brick-earth pits', that is, sources for clay (*ibid.*: 36). Notions of pits as functional places, receptacles for activities such as storage, cooking and rubbish dis-posal flourished around the middle decades of the century (e.g., Field *et al.* 1964), but the post-processual turn of the 1980s and 1990s saw pits recast as vessels for highly symbolic 'structured deposition', with Thomas (1999: ch. 4) providing the classic account of this interpretive turn. Thus, the contents of pits such as those at Townhead and Easterton of Roseisle became mechanisms by which we could scrutinise and read the rules and structures of society. As noted above, this in part reflected a loss of nerve on the part of archaeologists in the face of earlier expectations about Neolithic settlement not being met, leading to the conclusions that (a) we could never find traces of Neolithic buildings in the plough zone (cf. Gibson 2003), or (b) such structures never existed (Whittle 1996). Gordon Barclay was amongst the loudest voices calling for such pessimism to be overcome, as we have seen.

It should also be noted that our conception today of Neolithic settle-ment sites and domestic activity has benefitted greatly from the theoreti-cal approaches of the past few decades. Critical reflection has enabled our understanding of settlement, house and domesticity to be so much more complex and nuanced than Mann or Callander would have recognised. As was noted in the recent Scottish Archaeological Research Framework (ScARF) Neolithic panel document:

> There is ... a realisation that expecting to find wholly domestic activity may be inappropriate for Neolithic contexts, but also recognition that ritualised aspects of buildings, pit digging and deposition do not preclude their associa-tion with everyday life and daily routine. (Sheridan and Brophy 2012: s. 4.3)

In other words, we can now recognise that 'domestic dishes' were also indicators of social identity, or could play a role in highly structured rituals while
at the same time holding hot meat stew. Later in this chapter I shall stress
how inappropriate it is to draw clear divisions between ritual and mundane
in Neolithic contexts; in part this problematic distinction emerged because
of ongoing problems in defining 'settlement', 'house' and the 'domestic'. I
have taken a broad, and rather basic, view of these terms, namely, to imply
that for each of the sites mentioned here, people may have spent time in
these locations carrying out everyday activities (sleeping, eating, watching
over animals, crop monitoring, making things, talking to one another, looking after children, playing and so on.) This is not to preclude the potential
ritual, or ritualised, nature of the everyday and mundane.

The way that houses and their role within society are viewed within
Neolithic studies has changed dramatically in recent decades from the simplistic assumptions of domestic life that initially characterised the search
for such buildings (Brophy 2015). This is because there has been much
serious reflection on whether concepts such as 'house' and 'home' had any
relevance in the Neolithic period, at least as we understand these terms;
certainly, the 'mobile Neolithic hypotheses' challenged these preconceptions. In this context the use of words such as house and home became,
for a time, problematic (see contributions in Darvill and Thomas 1996).
Less loaded terms such as 'building' and 'structure' were used (e.g., in the
title of the excavation report on the Claish timber hall (Barclay *et al.* 2002),
where even Gordon Barclay preferred a neutral architectural term). Terms
such as 'household' were also the subject of critique (Thomas 1996: 5). At
the same time, however, the term house was commonly used in studies of
the Orcadian and Irish Neolithic (compare the titles of the regional review
chapters in Darvill and Thomas 1996). This discussion was not just about
semantics. For instance, material culture found within buildings – such as
broken pottery – could be interpreted in radically different ways depending
on whether the writer believed the building to be a house or some kind of
ritual or cult structure. Cutting through this debate with a common-sense
observation, Cooney (1999) argued that the terms 'house' and 'household'
are perfectly acceptable in a Neolithic context, given the cross-cultural
nature of these concepts. His argument was that archaeologists shied away
from calling buildings 'houses' in the 1990s because of an overall Neolithic
mobility model that had no place for permanent dwellings, rather than considering each building on its own merits.

Buildings identified as houses across the Neolithic of Britain and Ireland do
not produce evidence that is either explicitly domestic or ritualistic in nature,
and this may be because there was little or no difference between the two in
the Neolithic. Structures that are widely accepted as being domestic, such as
at Skara Brae and Barnhouse villages, both in Orkney, provide evidence for
ritualistic deposition, connections between burial and ceremonial architecture,

and cosmological schemes (Richards 1990, 2005), but they were also places where people lived, ate and slept. Arguments related to the domestic versus ritual nature of pit deposits have also been well rehearsed (e.g., contributions in Anderson-Whymark and Thomas 2012) and have been alluded to above. There is room here for a middle ground. There is nothing inherent in 'structured deposition' that excludes domestic life going on in the same location, and indeed the routines of everyday life are akin to – and may have had the status of – ritual (Whittle 2003; Bradley 2005; Brophy and Noble 2012).

Thus, long-forgotten sites such as Townhead are places that we now, once again, can comfortably call settlement sites, in much the same way as two of the three pits found at Echline Fields and the pit cluster at Meadowend farm have been so characterised. The agonising that has led us to this position has been, in the end, positive, in that words like 'house', 'settlement' and 'domestic' are in use, but used critically; this opens up the genuine potential for helping us to understand everyday life and social structures at one and the same time.

In this spirit, I have taken a fairly broad approach to what we might call settlement evidence in the selection of sites for discussion in this chapter. Some are structures or buildings that we could characterise as 'houses' (i.e., buildings where people lived either seasonally or all year round), although the majority are indicated by pits that contain material that *could* be indicative of domestic everyday activity such as rubbish, hearth sweepings, coarse stone tools and broken pottery. In this sense, I have included all structures that could have been roofed, and do not have any other apparently explicit function such as mortuary structures; my discussion therefore includes the timber halls, which I do not believe were 'normal' house structures, but nonetheless may have had a domestic element (Chapter 8, this volume). A wide range of pits, from isolated features to clusters, have been included; many were found during developer-funded work, for instance in evaluation trenches, with little context for the immediate environs (and see Chapter 9, this volume). Pits found in close association with burial and ceremonial monuments (e.g., at Balfarg, Fife or Holywood, Dumfries and Galloway) have for the most part not been included in this survey, although in some instances these contain deposits of a very similar nature to isolated and clustered pits, and thus a domestic aspect to these cannot be ruled out. Overall this broad-brush, largely inclusive approach will, I hope, offer a dataset from which future research can develop.

A survey of Neolithic potentially domestic locations in lowland Scotland

Let us now return to the aforementioned 'Barclay 2002 list', which would best be described as a working list, one from which synthesis could be drawn (e.g., Barclay 2003a, 2004) and future research stimulated (see e.g., Brophy

2006; Brophy and Noble 2012, and contributions to this book). Barclay's dataset consists of a great variety of sites ranging from timber halls, to isolated pits, to Neolithic potsherds associated with curvilinear ditches, to find-spots with almost nothing known about them. He divided the sites into two categories: those 'possibly representing settlement activity' and 'isolated pits or poorly contexted finds probably not indicative of settlement'. My chapter does not follow this binary division, as most sites lie somewhere on a spectrum of probability between these two descriptions, which is sometimes difficult to assess. In the following discussion therefore I have broken down the sites into broad structural categories: timber halls, rectangular timber buildings, oval/round timber buildings, four-post buildings and pit sites. I am mindful that some sites fall into more than one of these categories, such as Beckton Farm, Dumfries and Galloway, where three of these types of settlement evidence were found (Pollard 1997).

There are sixty-one sites in Barclay's list (Figure 10.1), ten of which are either sites for which nothing or very little is known, or they have no clear contextual information for Neolithic material recovered from them. Of the remainder, only sixteen were characterised as 'sites possibly representing settlement activity', with the vast majority dealt with rather more circumspectly. Since the '2002 list' (Barclay 2002b) was constructed, subsequent excavations at a few sites have revealed additional elements. For instance, at Upper Callernie (Highland Council, but in a lowland location) one pit which contained charcoal and several arrowheads had been found at the time of the compilation of the list (Wordsworth 1991: 41), but further work in the vicinity discovered additional pits and hearths, some of which are of Neolithic date (Farrell 2010: 110). In other cases, Barclay's classification has been overtaken by subsequent research, perhaps the most obvious example being Greenbogs, Aberdeenshire. Barclay classed this site (unpublished at the time) as consisting of a 'possible Neolithic surface' alongside undated structures, that is, within his 'poorly contexted finds probably not indicative of settlement' class. Since then, this site has been reinterpreted as including a Late Neolithic four-poster building with Grooved Ware associations (Noble *et al.* 2012, and see below), something that Gordon could not have predicted. Finally, Barclay's list shows a preponderance of sites in the eastern lowlands of Scotland, with twenty-nine of the sites located in the north-east and Tayside (now Angus, Fife and Perth and Kinross), as this was the area that he had studied most fully.

Since 2002, additional potential settlement sites of Neolithic date in mainland Scotland have been identified, partly from a trawl through *Discovery and Excavation in Scotland* (Brophy 2006). Furthermore, new syntheses of the timber halls (Noble 2006; Thomas 2006; Brophy 2007; Murray *et al.* 2009), pits (Brophy and Noble 2012), cropmark evidence (Millican 2009 and Chapter 8, this volume) and four-post roundhouses (Noble *et al.* 2012) have taken place.

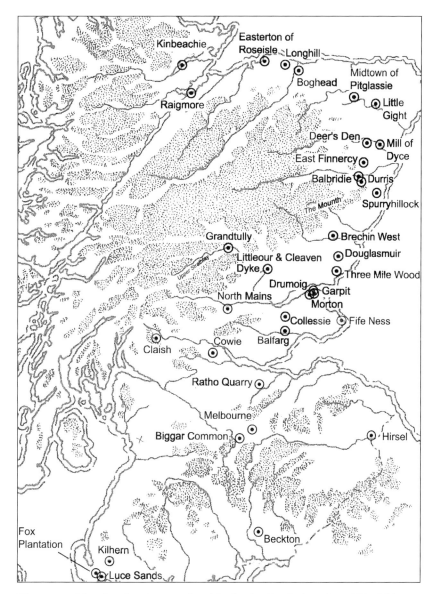

Figure 10.1 Map showing sites mentioned in Gordon Barclay's review of Neolithic settlement evidence for mainland Scotland, published in 2003 (from Barclay 2003: 72, fig. 8.1).

Timber halls

There has been much discussion and dispute about the precise meaning that timber halls had in the lives of early farmers in Scotland, but, despite a lack of consensus, they still play a significant role in the literature of Early Neolithic Scotland's settlement patterns (cf. Thomas 2006; Bradley 2007). (It should be noted that comprehensive discussions of this small group of monumental buildings have already been published (Barclay *et al.* 2002; Brophy 2007; Murray *et al.* 2009; and see Chapter 8, this volume), and so this offering presents a brief summary rather than definitive account.) Barclay's '2002 list' included only two of these structures – Balbridie and Claish – both of which had been excavated by that time, although only the latter published in full (Fairweather and Ralston 1993; Barclay *et al.* 2002). Two other timber halls have since been excavated, at Lockerbie Academy, Dumfries and Galloway (Kirby 2011) and Warren Field, Crathes, across the River Dee from Balbridie (Murray *et al.* 2009). It is from these excavation reports that much of the information here is derived. Recent re-evaluation of Hope-Taylor's 1960's excavations at Doon Hill, East Lothian (Hope-Taylor 1980), suggests that the earlier of the two timber halls discovered there was Neolithic (the latter being Anglian), although we await publication in full (Sheridan and Brophy 2012: s. 3.3.2), and so this site does not inform the discussion here. Further possible examples, four of which are convincing, have been identified in the cropmark record in Angus, East Lothian and the Scottish Borders (Smith 1991; Brophy 2007).

These structures form the majority of what is a very small group of substantial roofed buildings of the Early Neolithic period in the British Isles, with ground plans suggesting structures in the range of 22–27 m in length and 8–11 m in width, each having straight or convex gable ends, and doorways at both ends (see Chapter 8, Figure 8.3, in this volume). These were truly monumental buildings, defined by closely spaced large timber posts (as at Claish; Figure 10.2), or large posts set into bedding trenches (Warren Field) or a combination of the two (Balbridie, Lockerbie), supporting either plank-built walls or wattle-and-daub weatherproofing. All four buildings have very similar internal layouts, divided into compartments by various slots and internal post-settings (from four to seven 'rooms' depending on how these are defined). Such internal partitions, as well as axial posts and other internal features, coupled with the substantial walls and gables, suggest that all four excavated structures could have supported pitched or hipped roofs, perhaps up to 8 m in height at the apex. The finer detail of each site reveals as many differences as similarities. The Warren Field hall appears to have had an open yard at the eastern end, while Lockerbie may have had a detached smaller timber structure at its northern end. Three of the sites show evidence for repair, or secondary post erection (Claish, Lockerbie, Warren Field), while most posts appear to have been oak,

Figure 10.2 Excavations at Claish timber hall in 2001, a companion piece to Barclay's 'First Farmers Project'. Gordon Barclay is planning towards the far end of the trench while co-director Gavin MacGregor gives a context sheet master class near the foreground (photograph: author).

although ash and willow were also used at Warren Field. Internal features varied also and suggest differing forms of practice and activity took place in buildings: pits within Claish, for instance, were lined with broken, burnt sherds of Carinated pottery; possible 'totem' poles may have been included in the Warren Field structure; while large quantities of cereal grains were encountered widely in various structural features within Balbridie. All four buildings were burnt down at the end of their use life, for which a considerable effort would have been required.

The chronology of these buildings increasingly suggests they were a relatively short-lived phenomenon of the earliest Neolithic in eastern and southern Scotland. Initial analysis of radiocarbon dates from Warren Field, Balbridie and Claish suggested they were all built in the thirty-eighth to thirty-seventh centuries cal. BC (Murray *et al.* 2009: 79). More recently, Whittle, Healy and Bayliss (2011: 832–3) have argued, through Bayesian re-analysis of the dates for the same three halls, that they were built in the period 3800–3705 cal. BC and ended their use-life in the period 3705–3630 cal. BC, although not all were built and burnt down at precisely the same time. In other words, they were constructed by the second or third generation of farmers present in Scotland (*ibid.*: 833). As well as being contemporaneous, it seems likely these structures were relatively short-lived, perhaps standing for no more than fifty years, or two generations (estimated to 68 per cent probability; Murray *et al.* 2009: 79–80). This brief flourishing of large timber rectangular buildings was replicated in Ireland at more or less the same time, albeit with more, but smaller, structures (Smyth 2014).

The role and function of the timber halls has been much debated (see Brophy 2007; Murray *et al.* 2009, for comprehensive overviews of the arguments). They have been interpreted as 'communal residences' (Sheridan 2010: 98), cult buildings (Topping 1996), feasting halls (Ashmore 1996), chiefly homes (or big houses) (Bradley 2005) or multi-functional buildings (Brophy 2007), and regarded as either colonial structures (Sheridan 2010) or buildings that arose as a response to new farming lifestyles (Brophy 2007). Their rarity adds weight to the argument that these were not typical domestic places (Noble 2006: 23), although we should be cautious about seeing ceremonial explanations as primary. These are buildings that defy easy explanation in part because of the patchy survival of evidence directly related to how they were used, but we can speculate that they served many roles, both sacred and profane. The innovative pollen analysis that identified Warren Field as having stood in a cleared area some 2 km in diameter (Tipping *et al.* 2009) points us towards acknowledging that these were rare but significant buildings that dominated the landscape of the first farmers. And perhaps they make a little more sense when we consider other evidence for where people were living in the Early Neolithic.

Rectangular timber buildings

Compared with the 'boom' in Irish house discoveries of the 1990s and 2000s (cf. Grogan 2002; Smyth 2014) progress in Scotland has been relatively modest. As Barclay himself identified (2003a: 71), there are a number of reasons for this, not least the fact that major motorway and road improvement programmes took place in Scotland decades earlier than in Ireland under very different archaeological monitoring conditions than we have been used to in recent years. Even then, it also seems that the character of rectangular houses in Scotland is different from those in Ireland; Scotland's timber halls (discussed above) are much larger, despite some parallels being drawn between Scottish and Irish 'halls' (Cross 2003), while the slighter rectangular buildings identified on the Scottish mainland lack the homogeneity in form and date of the Irish sites. Surveys of Neolithic buildings in mainland Scotland (Barclay 1996, 2003a; Brophy 2006: 18–22; Sheridan and Brophy 2012: s. 4.3) suggest rectangular buildings remain very rare in the archaeological record in mainland Scotland. Fewer than a dozen are known (not including the timber halls), and even within such a small group there is considerable variability. For instance, the sites that are known range in size from 4 m to 15 m in length, with most examples tending towards the shorter end of this scale. Furthermore, some structures are little more than architectural possibilities imposed upon scatters of sub-surface features, and it is by no means certain that all of these were roofed, or roofable, or even coherent structures. Add a lack of floor surfaces, no clear indication of function at most sites, and limited dating evidence and local context, and it is clear that there remains a good deal of uncertainty in making sense of what is a problematic and frustratingly small dataset.

For Kinnes in the 1980s, the identification of Neolithic rectangular buildings outwith Orkney and Shetland was also a source of frustration. He noted only two such structures in the whole of mainland Scotland, Raigmore and Auchategan (1985: 27). (The latter is in Argyll and Bute, in a location that could be described as highland in character.) Raigmore, Highland (in a lowland estuarine location), was a structure defined by fifty-two posts uncovered beneath a Clava-type cairn in 1972–3 (Simpson 1996). This structure was built in a location already marked by a cluster of pits dated to the early centuries of the Neolithic; it enclosed a large centrally placed sandstone-lined hearth and was contemporary with pits filled with Grooved Ware dating to 2900–2500 cal. BC. The excavator suggested that this was a roofed building, perhaps with two phases, the larger of which measured up to 14 m in length and 6 m across. Barclay noted that this is a 'fairly convincing settlement site' (2003a: 73). Yet doubts remain whether this structure would have been roofable or not (Ashmore 1996: 67), while the presence of cremated (possibly human) bone in the hearth and in some post-holes left Simpson unsure of a domestic interpretation (1996: 63).

Since Kinnes' review (1985) of Scotland's Neolithic, a few candidates for Neolithic houses have been found across mainland Scotland, some more convincing than others. The small rectangular structure uncovered at Kinbeachie, Highland, was excavated in 1997 after initial fieldwork by the farmer (Barclay et al. 2001). Here a spread of pits and post-holes were uncovered, largely attesting to Neolithic activity. Amongst various features was identified a small and heavily plough-truncated rectangular timber setting, measuring 7 m by 4 m, defined by the bases of post-holes. The collection of wild resources and the farming of cereal crops were indicated. Radiocarbon determinations from these features indicate that they date from the second half of the fourth millennium cal. BC, and sherds from eight Impressed Ware vessels were recovered from the post-holes along with a deposit of burnt barley. The excavators concluded that, 'the site was a small farming settlement comprising one or more small rectangular timber buildings' (ibid.: 75).

At Drumoig, Fife, a sub-rectangular setting of ten rectangular pits defining an area 4.5 m by 2.6 m was found in advance of golf course development (James and Simpson 1997: 35–8) in the mid-1990s. A similar structure was more recently excavated at Kingarth Quarry, Bute (not on the mainland, but included in this discussion as it indicates the serendipitous ways that Neolithic settlement sites are generally discovered). Here, a rectangular

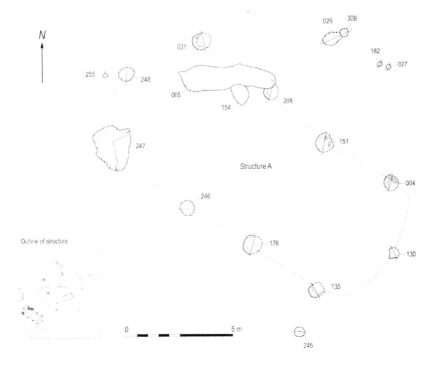

Figure 10.3 Plan of the Laigh Newton house and associated features (from Toolis 2011, after illustration 4, © GUARD Archaeology Ltd).

structure with round ends and defined by a slot/palisade was uncovered in advance of quarrying in 2001. This structure was interpreted by the excavators as a possible Early to Mid-Neolithic house owing to its shape and size (7 m by 3.5 m) and the discovery of a Neolithic lithic assemblage in the vicinity during the excavations (Mudie and Richardson 2006).

The largest rectangular building found to date not characterised as a timber hall was identified at Laigh Newton, East Ayrshire, in 2007, in advance of quarrying (Toolis 2011; and Figure 10.3). Amidst a complex series of prehistoric features was a rectangular setting of post-holes ('structure A'), suggesting a building or structure with an area measuring 12.8 m by 15.1 m (giving a floor space of 193 m²). The internal frame of the building was defined by five pairs of large post-holes, which would have held posts with diameters of approximately 0.3 m, interpreted by the excavator as supports for the roof. This element of the building, measuring 6 m by 12 m, was surrounded by less obvious features, which may have been an outer wall consisting of lighter posts and hazel and willow wattle. This building was probably erected and in use in the latter centuries of the third millennium cal. BC (*ibid.*: 34) and sat amidst a series of other post-holes, some of which may define small structures and also some pits. A far less clearly defined rectangular building was claimed by the excavators during excavations at Biggar Common, South Lanarkshire, in the early 1990s. Here, in a location with evidence for long-term occupation and mortuary activity, a series of post-holes was interpreted by the excavators as a 'sub-rectangular, bow-sided arrangement' (Johnston 1997: 199). Nonetheless, evidence for Neolithic pits, activities and possible structures was found here in a project that stemmed from fieldwalking, very much in the Barclay spirit.

None of the aforementioned structures and arrangements of cut features amount to an unambiguous example of a timber rectangular building: at best we can say that 'some sites have definite or possible rectilinear structures ... ranging from vague suggestions to pronounced features' (Barclay 2003a: 81). The nature of the evidence means that we have a poor understanding of the architecture of these structures (roofed or not), and there is little associated evidence for what these buildings (if buildings they were) might have been used for, or for how long.

Other rectangular structures recovered during excavation on mainland Scotland may be of limited relevance. Larger timber rectangular structures of the Early to Mid-Neolithic such as the pair of rectangular timber settings at Balfarg Riding School, Fife (Barclay and Russell-White 1993) are more substantial than the structures discussed above, but were almost certainly not roofed. Carsie Mains, Perth and Kinross, an aisled timber rectangular structure, was offered as a possible parallel for Laigh Newton (Toolis 2011: 38). But the arrangement of internal features within Carsie Mains means that this structure is unlikely to have been roofed, and a living tree appears to have stood within this enclosure (Brophy and Barclay 2004). Therefore, the few light rectangular roofed structures that have so far been excavated form a relatively small corpus upon which to synthesise Neolithic settlement patterns and lifeways in mainland Scotland in the fourth millennium BC.

Round / oval timber buildings

Two sites – Beckton Farm, Dumfries and Galloway, and Cowie, Stirling – have produced the majority of the evidence in mainland Scotland for circular/oval timber buildings. Once again the architecture and function of the buildings at both of these sites is open to interpretation, but there are associations with domestic deposits such as midden material and quernstones, while most of these buildings have a centrally placed hearth and patches of floor surface have been recorded. Where dated they appear to be, on the whole, Later Neolithic in date, with strong Grooved Ware associations. Very few other such structures have been found to date, probably due to their ephemeral nature, and the difficulty in identifying features associated with them within complex and large scatters of truncated cut features.

One of the best understood Neolithic settlement sites in Scotland is at Cowie, near Stirling (Atkinson 2002). Here, six possible sub-circular to oval structures were found, defined by stakes set into very slight pressure trenches (fence slots); these structures were little more than 2.5–4.5 m across, quite irregular in plan, and some had internal hearths and appear to have been associated with pits containing Early Neolithic pottery. Two larger and later oval buildings (B and H) were defined by double stake-lines, and one of these had a clay floor. These eight structures overlapped and cut one another, indicating that not all stood at the same time, and that this location was used for domestic and other activity on multiple occasions. Pits, also intercutting these buildings, contained an impressive assemblage of smashed pottery and a range of quernstones, anvils, pounders and hammerstones. The smaller structures were tentatively interpreted as tent-like houses of the Early Neolithic surrounded by pits with domestic rubbish and structured deposits; the larger oval buildings can be paralleled with similar Grooved Ware structures found at Beckton Farm (*ibid.*: 184–5). Excavation here revealed remarkably similar evidence to Cowie, albeit the buildings there also comprised four-post structures (Pollard 1997; and see below). Structure 111 was a double stake-walled sub-circular building some 4 m across with a clay floor and an entrance in the south-east quadrant, with internal features that may have helped to support a roof. A Grooved Ware sherd associated with this building was from a vessel that also provided sherds found in a nearby cremation burial pit. A smaller, less convincing, oval structure was found nearby, with hints of a 'trampled floor' layer (*ibid.*: 111). There is no reason why the Cowie, and Beckton Farm, structures cannot be viewed as small houses, perhaps in the form of substantial bender structures.

Recent developer-funded work has revealed an intriguing group of circular and oval structures, often in association with pits with domestic-waste deposits. For instance, an oval free-standing single structure defined by post-holes and measuring 12 m by 8 m was found in 2005 in advance of the construction of the David Lloyd Leisure Centre on the fringes of Aberdeen. This building had a 'thick trodden floor deposit' (Murray 2005: 8) and an internal hearth; evidence for both emmer and bread wheat, and naked barley was recovered; Early Neolithic dates were obtained. And long-term investigation at Charlestown, Inverness, Highland, in advance of housing development, has revealed many prehistoric traces, including, in 2009, a 'small circular structure and a group of pits' (Jones 2009: 105) of Neolithic date as well as sherds of Impressed Ware pottery and midden material (*ibid.*). A series of possible small oval stake-defined structures was identified at Station Brae, Dreghorn, South Ayrshire; these form another tantalising, but as yet unpublished, discovery (Addyman *et al.* 2004). Finally, in advance of the upgrade of the A1 in the early 2000s, a Late Neolithic settlement site including an oval timber building (structure A) measuring 6 m by 5 m with possible adjacent 'yard' was excavated at Overhailes, East Lothian (MacGregor and Stuart 2008: 70ff.). This building was defined by oak stakes, and abutted a larger space also defined by stakes and, possibly, wicker hurdling (Figure

Figure 10.4 Reconstruction drawing of Overhailes structure A and adjacent yard (drawing by David Hogg, from MacGregor and Stuart 2008: 95, reproduced with permission).

10.4); two pits, replete with materials apparently selected for deposition, were found within this enclosure. The small, round house may have been a 'rudimentary structure' offering shelter during short periods of occupation, associated with depositional activities, and possibly animal corralling in the yard (*ibid.*: 96). This sample of recently recovered evidence facilitated by road and suburban development suggests that it is likely more discoveries of this nature will be made in the future; these structures are unlikely to be captured in the cropmark record.

Four-post buildings

One of the most exciting and important recent developments in the study of Neolithic houses in mainland Scotland has been the identification of a series of Late Neolithic timber roundhouses, each with a central four-post setting. Two such structures were identified at Greenbogs, Aberdeenshire, in 1995, but only recently confirmed as Late Neolithic through dating and ceramics (Noble *et al.* 2012). Crucially, this observation prompted a detailed look at other evidence in Scotland by Noble and collaborators (2012), who listed four such buildings in Scotland: the two at Greenbogs and a pair at Beckton Farm (sites tentatively listed by Barclay (2002b, 2003a)). Crucially, further putative examples have also been identified in the cropmark record, no more remarkably than at least eight roundhouse structures at Chapelton, Angus; looking rather like buttons on the aerial views, these structures were assumed to be Iron Age upon their discovery by RCAHMS, but are yet to be tested by excavation. Of the other cropmark possibilities, one – Leadketty, Perth and Kinross – was subsequently excavated in 2012 (Figure 10.5) and

Figure 10.5 The Leadketty four-post structure during excavation in 2012 (© SERF Project, reproduced with permission).

confirmed to have an association with Grooved Ware pottery (Brophy *et al.* 2012). Yet another possible example was excavated in Perth and Kinross, at Pittentian near Crieff (Becket 2014). Late Neolithic potsherds were recovered from the upper fill of one of the central post-holes. This substantial structure was discovered by chance in 2011 in advance of an electricity tower being constructed and is a useful reminder that not all these sites have been, or will be, recorded as cropmarks.

These buildings typically consisted of a central setting of four large posts in a square setting, in the order of 3.5–7 m across (based on cropmark and excavation evidence); this setting in turn sat centrally within a circular 'outer post setting' up to 16 m across, although often smaller (Greenbogs A being 9.5 m across, for instance) (Noble *et al.* 2012: 161) A double post-ring was recorded at Pittentian, the inner 14 m across, the outer 23 m in diameter (Becket 2014). No such outer structure was apparent at either four-poster at Beckton Farm, which led Pollard (1997: 115) to come up with various possible interpretations, and caused Barclay (2002b, 2003a) to discount them as buildings. The Leadketty building fits within this range, having a four-post setting about 3 m square located within a circular post-ring some 14 m across; in this case, the structure also appears to have had a formal entrance or porch on its north-east side. An architectural characteristic of these buildings is that the outer wall is far more ephemeral than the large, sturdy, central posts which would have borne most of the load if these structures were roofed. The reconstructed Greenbogs house at the now defunct Archaeolink

Figure 10.6 Half-scale reconstruction of Pittentian timber circle/four-post building, located in Strathearn Community Campus, Crieff (photograph: author).

prehistory park suggests what such buildings may have looked like (Noble *et al.* 2012: fig. 20). A half-scale reconstruction of the Pittentian timber setting, constructed in 2014, suggests another possibility, however, that these sites may have been complex timber circles (Figure 10.6); as with the timber halls, such structures were roofable, but not necessarily roofed.

The date of the six excavated examples – at Beckton Farm, Greenbogs, Leadketty and Pittentian – seems clear through radiocarbon dating (they are attributable to the first half of the third millennium cal. BC) and/or by ceramic associations. And similar structures found in England and Ireland, for instance, at Wyke Down, Dorset (Green 2000), Durrington Walls, Wiltshire (Parker Pearson 2012) and Knowth, Meath (Eogan and Roche 1997), are more or less of the same age. Thomas (2010: 5) has suggested that such structures could be termed 'Grooved Ware houses', and were an element of a Late Neolithic 'Grooved Ware package' of material culture, monuments and practices. Bradley (2012: 12–13) has noted the significance of the recurring 'square within a circle' motif inherent in such buildings, shared with other structures, including huge ceremonial enclosures, although roofs appear to have been a variable element of this motif. Noble and colleagues (2012: 158–60) have rightly pointed out other four-poster structures that have clearly non-domestic roles and contexts, for instance, in the case of a timber four-poster at Machrie Moor, Arran – while the square standing stone setting at the heart of the Late Neolithic passage grave of Maes Howe also springs to mind. Bradley's suggestion (2012: 13) that such four-poster buildings and their monumental equivalents could be regarded as 'Great Houses' is perhaps the most appropriate way to regard these relatively rare, but substantial structures – not typical houses, but perhaps houses for high status people and activities, not wholly domestic spaces, but monumental buildings. The location of the Leadketty building, apparently the only one of its kind within a vast Late Neolithic timber palisaded enclosure, perhaps further hints at the special nature of this building, although the Chapelton 'village' may be something altogether different again. Perhaps we should tentatively view them as the timber halls of the Late Neolithic.

Pits and pit clusters

As noted earlier in this chapter, our understanding of Neolithic pits and their contents has changed dramatically since the late nineteenth century, with the interpretive pendulum swinging from uncritical domestic explanations, to specialised roles such as storage and rubbish pits, then on to structured deposition. Now, we have a more nuanced view of Neolithic pits (see contributions in Anderson-Whymark and Thomas 2012), viewing them as, in part, a proxy for settlement (Garrow *et al.* 2005) or 'occupation practices' (Carver 2012) such as cooking (Becket and MacGregor 2009), but also as indicative of a range of other Neolithic activities, from toilet pits, to pit-firings for pottery, to repositories for broken, dangerous or taboo items. Regardless of the purpose, pits seem strongly connected to a Neolithic sense of place and place-making (Pollard 1999; Garrow 2006; Harris 2009). Therefore, moving beyond either strictly ritual or domestic explanations allows us to view pits and clusters of pits as possible indicators of Neolithic settlement activity, with the proviso that we are aware pits may mean other things too. In some cases, pits may even have been in locations kept away from where people were living. Pits without associated features are most problematic in terms of settlement evidence, while larger pit clusters seem to offer compelling cases for some form of settlement or at least recurring activity. But there are exceptions to both these statements.

Single pits and groups of pits of Neolithic origin are an increasingly common discovery across mainland Scotland. Yet the identification of such pits was rare until the onset of developer-funded archaeology in Scotland in the late 1980s, which occasioned something of a 'boom'. As noted above, chance discoveries in the nineteenth and early twentieth centuries were generally regarded as being associated with settlement activities, but discoveries such as a large pit in a sand quarry at Brackmont Mill, Fife, in 1960, in advance of sand extraction, began to change this (Longworth *et al.* 1967: 67ff.). This pit contained, among other things, fifty-one potsherds, thirty of them rim sherds, and they represented at least twenty different Impressed

Figure 10.7 Excavations at the Grandtully pit cluster in the mid-1960s (reproduced courtesy of Gordon Barclay).

Ware vessels (Cowie 1993: No. 7). It was suggested that these startling observations implied that these were the specially selected remnants of vessels 'associated with death, as containers of a funerary feast or offerings' (Longworth *et al.* 1967: 74). In other words, this was not ordinary or domestic. A second discovery at more or less the same time offered yet another narrative. In advance of pipeline construction at Grandtully, Perth and Kinross, excavations were carried out at a range of sites in 1966–7 (Simpson and Coles 1990; Figure 10.7). These included a cluster of fifty-two pits, many of which contained, as at the Brackmont Mill 1960 pit, Impressed Ware sherds, with some vessels represented in multiple pits. These pits were only open for a short time, and were thought by the excavators to be remnants of a 'Neolithic occupation site', with at least one feature a 'grain storage pit' (*ibid.*: 35). In other words, here pits are explicitly viewed as a proxy for settlement, with evidence for any buildings and other structures missing, presumed lost. Our interpretation of Neolithic pits underwent increased reflection in the late 1980s and 1990s as the body of evidence grew rapidly, in no small part due to the rise in developer-funded excavations (Phillips and Bradley 2004; Brophy 2006). For instance, between 1985 and 2008, at least seventy sites with one or more Neolithic pits were found and excavated in mainland Scotland (Figure 10.8), consisting of literally hundreds of pits ranging in date from the earliest to latest Neolithic (Brophy and Noble 2012), and many more sites with pits have been identified since.

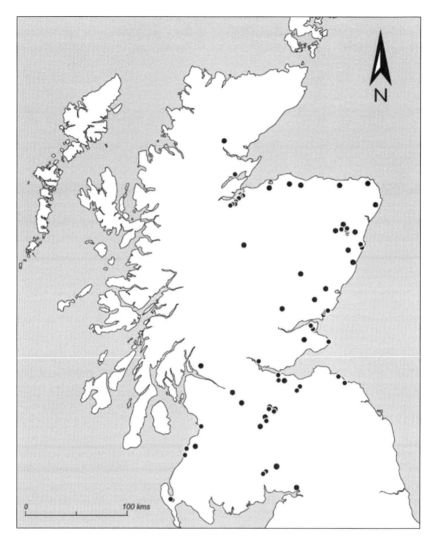

Figure 10.8 Location map showing pits with Neolithic material in them found in
Scotland between 1985 and 2008 (first reproduced in Brophy and Noble 2012, prepared
by Lorraine McEwan).

Single pits have been found containing all sorts of material from the commonplace (carbonised remains such as cereals and nuts, as well as potsherds
and lithics) to the rare: for example, Arran pitchstone and smashed polished
stone axe fragments contained within in a large pit at Carzield, Dumfries
and Galloway (Maynard 1993); a single Scots Pine cone recovered towards
the bottom of a shallow pit from Park Quarry, Aberdeenshire (Shepherd and
Greig 1991); and a jet bead in a pit with Grooved Ware at Craighead Golf

Course, Fife (Dalland 1996). Without further work in their surrounds, such pits must remain only circumstantial indications of domestic life.

Clusters of pits offer more hope, with substantial ceramic, lithic and environmental assemblages recovered from some sites. As noted already, the Meadowend Farm site was extensive and may have consisted of over one hundred Neolithic pits (Jones 2006: 46–7). An even larger cluster of pits was found in advance of construction of William Grant Warehouse 37, Girvan, South Ayrshire, in 2007. Here well over one hundred pits and post-holes were found, with Neolithic material contained in many of them (Francoz 2007). A cluster of pits at nearby Maybole, also South Ayrshire, revealed an incredible range of pit contents. One pit (010), dating to the middle of the fourth millennium cal. BC, contained burnt human bones, goat faecal pellets, worked lithics including pitchstone, potsherds, burnt hazel nutshells and a fragment of an apple core amongst other things (Becket and MacGregor 2009: 107–8). Such sites are invaluable indicators of settlement practices. For instance, a series of giant pits (up to 2.7 m across and 1.8 m deep) at Dubton, Angus, included Early and Late Neolithic ceramics suggesting long-term social memory and repeated depositional practice. These pits were so large excavators had to use ladders to access some of them (Cameron 2002), suggesting that even pits can be monumental in scale. And similarly huge pits at Wellhill, Perth and Kinross (near the Leadketty four-poster), excavated in summer 2014 and associated with Neolithic pottery and lithics, and possibly also ardmarks (Wright 2014; Dene Wright pers. comm.), were so large that they were initially identified as cropmarks (Figure 10.9).

Not all pits occur in the absence of structures. Many of the aforementioned houses and structures had pits in close attendance, some of which may well have been contemporary. This includes, for instance, some of the timber halls (but not Balbridie), Laigh Newton, Beckton and Cowie. The last mentioned is the most intriguing case as the pits there were intercut with some of the oval structures, and Atkinson spent a good deal of his excavation report discussing the nature of the deposits found within these pits, some of which had a 'structured deposit' feel to them (2002: 188), but crucially it was felt that this was not a bar to discussing them in a domestic settlement context. The intriguing phrase 'minor ritual activity' (from Barclay and Russell-White 1993: 167) was evoked and is perhaps an appropriate concept to describe activities at many pit sites. One final note: in some instances possible settlement evidence in the form of pits has been identified at locations that later became burial monuments, such as Raigmore (Simpson 1996), East Finnercy round cairn, Aberdeenshire (Leivers et al. 2000) and Boghead cairn, Moray (Burl 1984). Clearly, these are locations where different emergent trajectories were followed; places with pits developed in a variety of different functional directions. And in some cases pit clusters were located near ceremonial structures. A cluster of depressions, post-holes and pits was found within 100 m of the Douglasmuir timber cursus monument and these

Figure 10.9 Huge Neolithic pit at Wellhill, Perth and Kinross, during excavations in 2014; here, a quarter of a pit has been excavated (© SERF Project, reproduced with permission).

may have been roughly contemporary with the cursus (Kendrick 1995: 35; Brophy and Millican 2015). Noble (2006: 67) has suggested that three other pits found just 5 m away from Douglasmuir cursus may also represent some kind of domestic activity. Pits therefore occur in many different contexts, and domesticity may be evident in the most unusual of places.

The contribution that pit sites can make to our understanding of Neolithic settlement activity depends on a number of factors. First, the way we conceptualise these features is vital. Second, the means of excavation is also significant. Often pits are found during evaluation phases, trial trenches or keyhole investigations, and thus vital contextual information may not have been recovered. Third, many pits remain consigned to grey literature (a more general problem). Finally, the means of excavation and the levels of sampling and analysis of fills remain inconsistent (again, an issue not simply restricted to pits). Despite these cautionary points, there is no doubt that pits and pit clusters are rich repositories of much information about Neolithic life, activities, rituals, social rules and routines – and are by far the most widespread and numerous evidence we have for possible domestic activity in mainland Scotland.

Discussion

This chapter has offered a summary of some of the main evidence that we have for a broad range of possible, probable and certain Neolithic settlements, domestic sites and houses in mainland Scotland. There are at least one hundred such sites, although this is still remarkably low for 1,500 years' worth of activity over an area replete with good farming land that presumably had a population in at least the tens of thousands (Sheridan and Brophy 2012: s. 6.1). Darvill (2010: 124) has suggested that in Britain and Ireland as a whole, it would not be unreasonable to suggests a Neolithic population in the order of 200,000. Compare this quantity of settlement evidence with, for instance, the comparatively small land mass of the Orkneys, islands which have produced evidence for tens of houses and settlements (cf. Barclay 1996: 62–70; Richards 2005) or the putative fifty-odd stone houses identified by Calder (1956) on the Shetlands. This imbalance is in no small part because of the materials and form that Neolithic settlement sites took in mainland Scotland – stone appears not to have been used, with a preference for (mostly) light timber structures, some of which were little more than sturdy tents or benders. Loveday (2006a) reminds us that we may be missing turf houses in the lowlands, while many settlement sites and repositories for domestic refuse are represented now only in the form of pits, hollows, firespots, scoops and stake-holes. The exceptional big houses of the earliest (the timber halls), and latest, Neolithic (four-posters), have been discovered as cropmarks for the most part only due to the exceptional size of posts used in their construction; given the extensive aerial coverage of Scotland that has now taken place, it has to be conceded that we may by now have already found more or less all of these structures in certain regions, although Pittentian offers hope, and there are lowland areas of mainland Scotland (notably in Argyll and the north) that have yet to receive concerted aerial survey. And this, along with chance discoveries such as those found at the two Forth Crossings where this chapter started reminds us that more or less all of these settlement sites are in the plough-zone or in areas that have already been built on or urbanised.

Therefore, it is all the more remarkable that we have such a rich and varied range of sites, even though in some instances the record is still regarded as poor (e.g., Graves 2011). It seems likely that we have discovered at the very least a sample of the different levels and intensities of domestic settlement activity that went on in the lowlands, from the act of tossing a broken potsherd into a shallow pit, to the construction and subsequent conflagration of the massive timber buildings. More unusual discoveries, such as a double concentric circular ditched enclosure some 50 m in diameter at Kinloch Farm, Collessie in Fife, associated with Late Neolithic pottery (Barber 1982), hint at other possible settlement forms. Barclay (2003a: 72) calls this site a 'probably domestic Neolithic enclosure' and it is clear that such rare discoveries deserve more of our attention. But other attempts to identify Neolithic settlement enclosures of this nature, whether Barclay's at Upper Gothens, Perth and Kinross (2001) or my own at Leadketty (Brophy and Wright 2013), have largely failed.

It seems to me that this spectrum of activities – tents, camps, houses, halls – represents not a hierarchy of society with more important people living in bigger houses or digging more pits, but rather a series of places that were used for a variety of purposes, at different levels of sedentism, and with different social capital attached. And the evidence outlined in this chapter suggests that a wide variety of activities were taking place at the sites outlined above, included things such as cooking, eating, sheltering, sleeping and carrying out bodily functions, as well as crafts, caring for animals and crops, preparing for hunting or fishing, ceremonies, negotiations and bartering, storytelling and maybe even hanging around bored or enjoying nice weather. In a much briefer and earlier synthesis of the settlement record for Scotland (Brophy 2006), I argued that the evidence points towards at least some level of mobility within the landscape, mobility that involved different groups moving about for different motivations and durations, in part related to subsistence strategies or perhaps transhumance:

> We could also speculate that [settlement] traces were indicative of a tran-shumance economy, left by small groups travelling (taking with them ideas, expertise and material culture), or by certain social groups spending some time away from the main community (such as adolescents, menstruating women, the ill or dying) … There seem to have been many different strategies and responses to finding shelter and defining communal spaces, but this should not surprise us. (Brophy 2006: 25)

The creation of big houses may have been one of the primary tethering elements of Neolithic life – buildings for forms of domestic life associated with important locations (perhaps places that were established as important before the building was built) or especially significant activities. Or perhaps these big buildings are simply reflections of a social hierarchy after all, 'manors rather than crofts' as Ian Kinnes (1985) might have put it. There would have been other fixed points for early farmers too (aside from monuments, natural features and woodland clearances). Sturdy timber buildings such as Laigh Newton could well have stood for substantial periods of time; and some campsites may have either been in continuous use, or returned to year after year for extended periods over many generations or centuries. Huge pits may have made permanent marks on the landscape even when largely backfilled. The whole picture appears to be one of complexity, dynamism and flexibility – indicative of lifestyles with different rhythms.

One of the most interesting outcomes of recent research into Neolithic settlement sites across Britain and Ireland has been an improved chronological resolution (in some cases to generational levels), which has in turn enabled us to develop narratives of architectural trends and fashions (such as the rapid rise and fall of timber halls), which in turn reflect trends within Neolithic society. The recognition that rectangular houses were largely of the Earlier Neolithic, while circular to oval structures were later developments, is not a new observation (cf. Darvill 1996; Grogan 2002). But more recently Bradley (2007) has argued that this sequence reflects more widely developments in Neolithic monumentality, with a tendency towards the rectangular and linear in the fourth millennium cal. BC (cursus monuments, bank barrows, long barrows, mortuary enclosures, and many chambered and long cairns) and the development of more circular forms in the later Neolithic (from timber circles to henges and palisaded enclosures). This is not a hard and fast rule, and there are chronological overlaps, but nonetheless this astute observation allows houses to be viewed within wider social trends or fashions. In turn, this has allowed various arguments to be made suggesting that houses and monuments fundamentally referenced one another architecturally and perhaps cosmologically through these millennia. This argument has been made for timber halls and timber cursus monuments (Thomas 2006), houses and cursus monuments (Loveday 2006b), timber halls and rectangular enclosures (Barclay *et al.* 2002; Brophy 2007), and Grooved Ware houses and larger timber circles and henges (Noble *et al.* 2012; Bradley 2013). Here, we can perhaps see a mechanism by which timber houses could be viewed as representational of social order and cosmologies as well as being domestic spaces. This should not surprise us; similar observations have been made about the Orcadian stone buildings for decades (e.g., Richards 1990).

The elevation of houses to the status of embodiments of the rules and structure of society both in their form, but also perhaps in how they stage-managed movement and structured activities (Cooney 1996; Brophy 2015) is very much in line with the observations I made earlier about the ambiguous and slippery nature of concepts such as 'ritual', 'mundane', 'routine' and 'everyday'. This change in the way we think about houses suggests that buildings could act as places to sleep in and as a welcome home base, but also could have a spiritual or sacred dimension at the same time; these are not mutually exclusive. The daily rules and routines of life can include the utterly commonplace. And the same too can be said about pits. These commonly found features, which act as repositories from which we can retrieve Neolithic stuff, could have been, at one and the same time, places for the deposition of rubbish and the focus of ritually charged and even dangerous activities. The concept of structured deposition is too one-dimensional in its common interpretation (cf. Thomas 2012) to adequately capture the way that everyday activities can seem casual or functional, but at the same time be rule-bound and important. Pits and their fills represent a whole range of activities and deposits, and we should be cautious about seeing them all as proxies for settlement activity (Thomas 1999), but there is no doubt that larger concentrations of pits such as Grandtully or Grant's Warehouse represent long-term commitments (potentially extending across multiple generations) to a specific place and way of being. The order in which materials find their way into a pit may say as much about society as the position of the hearth in the house, or the type of timbers used to support a roof.

This chapter has made much of the remarkable, but problematic, dataset that represents Neolithic domestic life in the lowlands of Scotland. The poor survival of much of this material should not, however, be a reason for pessimism. We can learn much from the amazing evidence we have from houses in Orkney, Shetland (a largely untapped resource) and the Western Isles, but it seems likely that 'house societies', as they are currently being termed (Thomas 2010; Richards 2013: ch. 3), were not restricted to the islands and fringes of Scotland. Indeed, the increased recognition of Neolithic timber buildings on Orkney at Wideford Hill and Ha'Breck (Richards 2003; Lee and Thomas 2012; Carey 2014), as well as at the Scord of Brouster on Shetland (Whittle *et al.* 1986), seems to suggest that ideas emerging for the study of lowland mainland houses may be useful in helping to make sense of island house development. For instance, an Early Neolithic timber building found at Ha'Breck, on the island of Wyre, Orkney, would not look out of place if found in Aberdeenshire or South Lanarkshire, consisting as it does of a rectangular post-built structure (House 1) measuring 6.5 m by 3.7 m with internal hearth (Thomas 2009). In other words, with continued diligent research and excavation we can make much of relatively little.

Conclusion

In one of his most recent published statements on the subject, Gordon Barclay (2003a: 81) concluded that 'the detailed analysis of the existing evidence has scarcely begun, but we can already see that the apparently diffuse and truncated remains of settlement in the lowlands of Scotland are beginning to provide the outline of a picture'. In this chapter I hope that I have in a modest way contributed to the ongoing painting of the exciting and dynamic picture of where people lived, worked, ate, slept and carried out many other everyday and not so commonplace activities in Scotland's Neolithic. Ever improving chronological resolution, combined with wider awareness and synthesis of the results of developer-funded excavations, research and analysis of cropmark sites and aerial photographs, and ongoing fieldwalking campaigns have together helped to move things on considerably in little more than the decade or so since Gordon wrote those words. The challenge now is for us to develop narratives that account for the broad range of Neolithic activities across mainland Scotland, both typical and atypical. Gordon created a wonderful platform from which to begin this journey.

Notes

1. See: www.bbc.co.uk/news/uk-scotland-edinburgh-east-fife-11846078, last accessed 19 January 2015.
2. See: http://archaeologydataservice.ac.uk/archives/view/barclay_na_2003/overview.cfm#intro

Bibliography

Addyman, T., Donnelly, M. and Wilson, T. (2004), 'Station Brae, Dreghorn', *Discovery and Excavation in Scotland*, n.s., 5: 87–8.

Anderson-Whymark, H. and Thomas, J. (eds) (2012), *Regional Perspectives on Neolithic Pit Deposition: Beyond the Mundane*, Oxford: Oxbow Books.

Armit, I., Murphy, E., Nelis, E. and Simpson, D. D. A. (eds) (2003), *Neolithic Settlement in Ireland and Western Britain*, Oxford: Oxbow Books.

Ashmore, P. (1996), *Neolithic and Bronze Age Scotland*, London: Batsford and Historic Scotland.

Atkinson, J. A. (2002), 'Excavation of a Neolithic occupation site at Chapelfield, Cowie, Stirling', *Proceedings of the Society of Antiquaries of Scotland*, 132: 139–92.

Barber, J. (1982), 'The investigation of some plough-truncated features at Kinloch Farm, Collessie in Fife', *Proceedings of the Society of Antiquaries of Scotland*, 112: 524–33.

Barclay, G. J. (1996), 'Neolithic buildings in Scotland', in Darvill and Thomas (eds), *Neolithic Houses in Northwest Europe and Beyond*, 61–75.

Barclay, G. J. (2001), 'The excavation of an early medieval enclosure at Upper Gothens, Meikleour, Perthshire', *Tayside and Fife Archaeological Journal*, 7: 34–44.

Barclay, G. J. (2002a), 'GIS-mounted digital historical mapping as an aid to aerial photograph interpretation: a case-study in Scotland', *Aerial Archaeology Research Group News*, 25: 8–12.

Barclay, G. J. (2002b), 'A survey of Neolithic potentially domestic locations in lowland Scotland', unpublished manuscript.

Barclay, G. J. (2003a), 'Neolithic settlement in the lowlands of Scotland: a preliminary survey', in Armit *et al.* (eds), *Neolithic Settlement*, 71–83.

Barclay, G. J. (2003b), 'The Neolithic', in K J Edwards and I B M Ralston (eds), *Scotland after the Ice Age: Environment, Archaeology and History 8000 BC–AD 1000*, Edinburgh: Edinburgh University Press, 127–50.

Barclay, G. J. (2004), '"… Scotland cannot have been an inviting country for agricultural settlement": a history of the Neolithic in Scotland', in I. A. G. Shepherd and G. J. Barclay (eds), *Scotland in Ancient Europe*, Edinburgh: Society of Antiquaries of Scotland, 31–44.

Barclay, G. J., Brophy, K. and MacGregor, G. (2002), 'Claish, Stirling: an Early Neolithic structure in its context', *Proceedings of the Society of Antiquaries of Scotland*, 132: 65–137.

Barclay, G. J., Carter, S. P., Dalland, M. M., Hastie, M., Holden, T., MacSween, A. and Wickham-Jones, C. R. (2001), 'A possible Neolithic settlement at Kinbeachie, Black Isle, Highland', *Proceedings of the Society of Antiquaries of Scotland*, 131: 57–85.

Barclay, G. J. and Russell-White, C. (1993), 'Excavations in the ceremonial complex of the fourth to second millennium BC in Balfarg/Balbirnie, Glenrothes, Fife', *Proceedings of the Society of Antiquaries of Scotland*, 123: 43–210.

Barclay, G. J. and Wickham-Jones, C. (2002), 'The investigation of some lithic scatters in Perthshire', *Tayside and Fife Archaeological Journal*, 8: 1–9.

Becket, A. (2014), 'Beauly to Denny 400kV Overhead Transmission Line Access Track 81–Tower TD125. Pittentian, Crieff, Perth and Kinross', unpublished Data Structure Report, Northlight Heritage Report 25, Glasgow.

Becket, A. and MacGregor, G. (2009), 'Forest grazing and seaweed foddering: Early Neolithic occupation at Maybole, South Ayrshire', *Proceedings of the Society of Antiquaries of Scotland*, 139: 105–22.

Bradley, R. (2005), *Ritual and domestic life in Prehistoric Europe*, London: Routledge.

Bradley, R. (2007), *The Prehistory of Britain and Ireland*, Cambridge: Cambridge University Press.

Bradley, R. (2013), 'Houses of commons, houses of lords: domestic dwellings and monumental architecture in Prehistoric Europe', *Proceedings of the Prehistoric Society*, 79: 1–18.

Brophy, K. (2006), 'Rethinking Scotland's Neolithic: combining circumstance with context', *Proceedings of the Society of Antiquaries of Scotland*, 136: 7–46.

Brophy, K. (2007), 'From big houses to cult houses: Early Neolithic timber halls in Scotland', *Proceedings of the Prehistoric Society*, 73: 75–96.

Brophy, K. (2015), 'Houses, halls and occupation in Britain and Ireland', in C. Fowler, J. Harding and D. Hoffman (eds), *The Oxford Handbook of Neolithic Europe*, Oxford: Oxford University Press, 327–44.

Brophy, K. and Barclay, G. J. (2004), 'A rectilinear timber structure and post-ring at Carsie Mains, Meikleour, Perthshire', *Tayside and Fife Archaeological Journal*, 10: 1–22.

Brophy, K. and Millican, K. (2015), 'Wood and fire: the Early Neolithic timber cursus monuments of Scotland', *Archaeological Journal*, 172: 1–28.

Brophy, K. and Noble, G. (2012), 'Within and beyond pits: deposition in lowland Neolithic Scotland', in H. Anderson-Whymark and J. Thomas (eds), *Regional Perspectives on Neolithic Pit Deposition*, 63–76.

Brophy, K., Gould, A., Noble, G., Wright, D. and Younger, R. (2012), 'Leadketty Excavations 2012', unpublished SERF Project interim report, University of Glasgow.

Brophy, K. and Wright, D. (2013), 'Leadketty Excavations 2013', unpublished SERF Project interim report, University of Glasgow.

Calder, C. S. T. (1956), 'Report on the discovery of numerous Stone Age house sites in Shetland', *Proceedings of the Society of Antiquaries of Scotland*, 89: 340–97.

Callander, J. G. (1929), 'Scottish Neolithic pottery', *Proceedings of the Society of Antiquaries of Scotland*, 63: 29–97.

Cameron, K. (2002), 'The excavation of Neolithic pits and Iron Age souterrains at Dubton Farm, Brechin, Angus', *Tayside and Fife Archaeological Journal*, 8: 19–76.

Carey, G. (2014), 'Around the houses. Towards a more robust interpretation and analysis of the Early Neolithic domestic settlement record in Britain – lessons from Orkney', *Assemblage*, 13: 39–62.

Carter, S. (2002), 'Contract archaeology in Scotland', *Antiquity*, 76: 869–73.

Carver, G. (2012), 'Pits and place-making: Neolithic habitation and deposition practices in East Yorkshire c. 4000–2500 BC', *Proceedings of the Prehistoric Society*, 78: 111–34.

Cooney, G. (1996), 'Images of settlement and the landscape in the Neolithic', in Darvill and Thomas (eds), *Neolithic Houses in Northwest Europe and Beyond*, 23–31.

Cooney, G. (1999), *Landscapes of Neolithic Ireland*, London: Routledge.

Cowie, T. G. (1993), 'A survey of the Neolithic pottery of eastern and central Scotland', *Proceedings of the Society of Antiquaries of Scotland*, 123: 13–41.

Cross, S. (2003), 'Irish Neolithic settlement architecture: a reappraisal', in Armit *et al.* (eds), *Neolithic Settlement*, 195–202.

Dalland, M. (1996), 'Craighead Golf Course, Balcomie, Fife Ness (Crail Parish), Mesolithic shelter, Neolithic/Bronze Age pits, Iron Age and Dane's Dyke', *Discovery and Excavation in Scotland*, 1996: 46–7.

Darvill, T. (1996), 'Neolithic buildings in England, Wales and the Isle of Man', in Darvill and Thomas (eds), *Neolithic Houses in Northwest Europe and Beyond*, 77–112.

Darvill, T. (2010), *Prehistoric Britain*, 2nd edn, London: Routledge.

Darvill, T. and Thomas, J. (eds) (1996), *Neolithic Houses in Northwest Europe and Beyond*, Oxford: Oxbow Books.

Eogan, G. and Roche, H. (1997), *Excavations at Knowth 2: Settlement and Ritual Sites of the Fourth and Third Millennium BC*, Dublin: Royal Irish Academy.

Fairweather, A. and Ralston, I. B. M. (1993), 'The Neolithic timber hall at Balbridie, Grampian Region, Scotland: the building, the date, the plant macrofossils', *Antiquity*, 67: 313–23.

Farrell, S, (2010), 'Upper Cullernie, Balloch, Inverness, Highland (Petty Parish), excavation and watching brief', *Discovery and Excavation in Scotland*, n.s., 11: 101.

Field, N. H., Mathews, C. L. and Smith, I. F. (1964), 'New Neolithic sites in Dorset with a note on the distribution of Neolithic storage pits in Britain', *Proceedings of the Prehistoric Society*, 30: 352–81.

Francoz, C. (2007), 'William Grant and Sons Distillers Ltd, Warehouse 37: excavation', *Discovery and Excavation in Scotland*, n.s., 8: 181.

Garrow. D. (2006), *Pits, Settlement and Deposition during the Neolithic and Early Bronze Age in East Anglia*, Oxford: British Archaeological Reports.

Garrow, D., Beadsmoore, E. and Knight, M. (2005), 'Pit clusters and the temporality of occupation: an earlier Neolithic site at Kilverstone, Thetford, Norfolk', *Proceedings of the Prehistoric Society*, 71: 139–57.

Gibson, A. (2003), 'What do we mean by Neolithic settlement? Some approaches, 10 years on', in Armit *et al.* (eds), *Neolithic Settlement*, 136–45.

Graves, D. (2011), 'The use of predictive modelling to target Neolithic settlement and occupation activity in mainland Scotland', *Journal of Archaeological Science*, 38: 633–56.

Green, M. (2000), *A Landscape Revealed: 10,000 Years on a Chalkland Farm*, Stroud: Tempus.

Grogan, E. (2002), 'Neolithic houses in Ireland: a broader perspective', *Antiquity*, 76: 517–25.

Harris, O. (2009), 'Making places matter in Early Neolithic Dorset', *Oxford Journal of Archaeology*, 28: 111–23.

Hope-Taylor, B. (1980), 'Balbridie … and Doon Hill', *Current Archaeology*, 7: 18–19.

James, H. and Simpson, B. (1997), 'Drumoig, Craigie Hill, Fife, DSR Part 1: The Golf Course and Compound', unpublished interim report, GUARD, Glasgow.

Johnston, D. A. (1997), 'Biggar Common, 1987–93: an early prehistoric funerary and domestic landscape in Clydesdale, South Lanarkshire', *Proceedings of the Society of Antiquaries of Scotland*, 127: 185–254.

Jones, E. (2006), 'Upper Forth crossing: excavation', *Discovery and Excavation in Scotland*, n.s., 7: 46–7.

Jones, E. (2009), 'Bellfield, North Kessock, Highland (Knockbain parish), excavation', *Discovery and Excavation in Scotland*, n.s., 10: 105.

Leivers, M., Roberts, J. and Peterson, R. (2000), 'The cairn at East Finnercy, Dunecht, Aberdeenshire', *Proceedings of the Society of Antiquaries of Scotland*, 130: 183–95.

Kendrick, J. (1995), 'Excavation of a Neolithic enclosure and an Iron Age settlement at Douglasmuir, Angus', *Proceedings of the Society of Antiquaries of Scotland*, 125: 29–67.

Kinnes, I. (1985), 'Circumstance, not context: the Neolithic of Scotland as seen from the outside', *Proceedings of the Society of Antiquaries of Scotland*, 115: 115–57.

Kirby, M. (2011), 'Lockerbie Academy: Neolithic and early historic timber halls, a Bronze Age cemetery, an undated enclosure and a post-medieval corn-drying kiln in south-west Scotland', *Scottish Archaeological Internet Report* (= *SAIR*), 46: dx.doi.org/10.5284/1017938.

Lee. D. and Thomas, A (2012), 'Orkney's first farmers: Early Neolithic settlement on Wyre', *Current Archaeology*, 268: 13–19.

Longworth, I., with Candow, R. D. M., Crerar, R. and Henderson, D. (1967), 'Further discoveries at Brackmont Mill, Brackmont Farm and Tentsmuir, Fife', *Proceedings of the Society of Antiquaries of Scotland*, 99: 60–92.

Loveday, R. (2006a), 'Where have all the Neolithic houses gone? Turf: an invisible component', *Scottish Archaeological Journal*, 28: 81–104.

Loveday, R. (2006b), *Inscribed Across the Landscape. The Cursus Enigma*, Stroud: Tempus.

MacGregor, G. and Stuart, E. (2008), 'Everything in its place: excavations at Eweford West, Overhailes, Pencraig Wood and Eweford Cottages (3300–1700 BC)', in O. Lelong and G. MacGregor (eds), *The Lands of Ancient Lothian. Interpreting the Archaeology of the A1*, Edinburgh: Society of Antiquaries of Scotland, 69–98.

Mann, L. M. (1903), 'Report on the excavation of prehistoric pile structures in pits in Wigtownshire', *Proceedings of the Society of Antiquaries of Scotland*, 37: 370–415.

Marshall, J. N. (1930), 'Archaeological notes: Townhead, Kilmichael and Kingarth', *Transactions of the Buteshire Natural History Society*, 10: 50–4.

Maynard, D. (1993), 'Neolithic Pit at Carzield, Kirkton, Dumfriesshire', *Transactions of the Dumfriesshire and Galloway Natural History and Antiquarian Society*, 68, 25–32.

Millican, K. (2009), 'Contextualising the Cropmark Record: The Timber Monuments of the Neolithic of Scotland', unpublished PhD thesis, University of Glasgow.

Mudie, G. and Richardson, P. (2006), 'Excavation of a possible Neolithic structure, lithic finds and later ditch features at Kingarth Quarry, Isle of Bute', *Scottish Archaeological Journal*, 28: 105–24.

Murray, H. K. (2005), 'David Lloyd Leisure Centre, Garthdee Road (Aberdeen parish), Early Neolithic structure', *Discovery and Excavation in Scotland*, n.s., 6: 8.

Murray, H. K., Murray, C. and Fraser, S. M. (2009), *A Tale of the Unknown Unknowns: A Mesolithic Pit Alignment and Neolithic Timber Hall at Warren Field, Crathes, Aberdeenshire*, Oxford: Oxbow Books.

Noble, G. (2006), *Neolithic Scotland. Timber, Stone, Earth and Fire*, Edinburgh: Edinburgh University Press.

Noble, G., Greig, M. and Millican, K. (2012), 'Excavations at a multi-period site at Greenbogs, Aberdeenshire, Scotland and the four-post timber architecture tradition of the Late Neolithic of Britain and Ireland', *Proceedings of the Prehistoric Society*, 78: 135–72.

Parker Pearson, M. (2012), *Stonehenge. Exploring the Greatest Stone Age Mystery*, London: Simon & Schuster.

Piggott, S. (1954), *The Neolithic Cultures of the British Isles*, Cambridge: Cambridge University Press.

Pollard, T. (1997), 'Excavations of a Neolithic settlement and ritual complex at Beckton Farm, Lockerbie, Dumfries and Galloway', *Proceedings of the Society of Antiquaries of Scotland*, 127: 69–121.

Pollard, J. (1999), '"These places have their moments": thoughts on settlement practices in the British Neolithic', in J. Brück and M. Goodman (eds), *Making Places in the Prehistoric World*, London: UCL Press, 76–93.

Phillips, T. and Bradley, R. (2004), 'Developer-funded fieldwork in Scotland,

1990–2003: an overview of the prehistoric evidence', *Proceedings of the Society of Antiquaries of Scotland*, 134: 17–51.

Richards, C. (1990), 'The Late Neolithic house in Orkney', in R. Samson (ed.), *The Social Archaeology of Houses*, Glasgow: Cruithne Press, 111–24.

Richards, C. (2003), 'Excavation of the Early Neolithic Settlement at Wideford Hill, Mainland, Orkney: Structures Report for Historic Scotland', unpublished report, University of Manchester.

Richards, C. (ed.) (2005), *Dwelling Among the Monuments: The Neolithic Village of Barnhouse, Maeshowe Passage Grave and Surrounding Monuments*, Cambridge: Cambridge University Press.

Richards, C. (ed.) (2013), *Building the Great Stone Circles of the North*, Oxford: Windgather Press.

Ritchie, G. and Ritchie, A. (1991), *Scotland. Archaeology and Early History: An Introduction*, 2nd edn, Edinburgh: Edinburgh University Press.

Robertson, A., Lochrie, J. and Timpany, S. (2013), 'Built to last: Mesolithic and Neolithic settlement at two sites beside the Forth Estuary, Scotland, *Proceedings of the Society of Antiquaries of Scotland*, 143: 73–136.

Shepherd, I. and Greig, M. (1991), 'Park Quarry, Durris', *Discovery and Excavation in Scotland* 1991: 35.

Sheridan, A. (2010), 'The Neolithization of Britain and Ireland: the big picture', in B. Finlayson and G. Warren (eds), *Landscapes in Transition*, Oxford: Oxbow Books, 89–105.

Sheridan, A. and Brophy, K. (eds) (2012), *ScARF Neolithic Panel Report*, Scottish Archaeological Research Framework: Society of Antiquaries of Scotland, available at: www.scottishheritagehub.com/content/scarf-neolithic-panel-report.

Simpson, D. D. A. (1996), 'Excavation of a kerbed funerary monument at Stoneyfield, Raigmore, Inverness, Highland, 1972–3', *Proceedings of the Society of Antiquaries of Scotland*, 126: 53–86.

Simpson, D. D. A. and Coles, J. M. (1990), 'Excavations at Grandtully, Perthshire', *Proceedings of the Society of Antiquaries of Scotland*, 120: 33–44.

Smith, I. M. (1991), 'Sprouston, Roxburghshire: an early Anglian centre of the eastern Tweed basin', *Proceedings of the Society of Antiquaries of Scotland*, 121: 261–94.

Smyth, J. (2014), *Settlement in Neolithic Ireland: New Discoveries on the Edge of Europe*, Oxford: Oxbow Books and the Prehistoric Society.

Thomas, A. (2009), 'The Braes of Ha'Breck, Wyre, Orkney (Rousay and Egilsay Parish), excavation', *Discovery and Excavation in Scotland*, n.s., 10: 134–5

Thomas, J. (1996), 'Neolithic houses in mainland Britain and Ireland: a sceptical view', in Darvill and Thomas (eds), *Neolithic Houses in Northwest Europe and Beyond*, 1–12

Thomas, J. (1999), *Understanding the Neolithic*, London: Routledge.

Thomas, J. (2006), 'On the origins and development of cursus monuments in Britain', *Proceedings of the Prehistoric Society*, 72: 229–41.

Thomas, J. (2010), 'The return of the Rinyo-Clacton folk? The cultural significance of the Grooved Ware complex in Later Neolithic Britain', *Cambridge Archaeological Journal*, 20: 1–15.

Thomas, J. (2012), 'Introduction: beyond the mundane?', in Anderson-Whymark and Thomas (eds), *Regional Perspectives on Neolithic Pit Deposition*, 1–12.

Tipping, R., Bunting, M. J., Davies, A. L., Murray, H., Fraser, S. and McCulloch, R. (2009), 'Modelling land use around an Early Neolithic timber "hall" in north east Scotland from high spatial resolution pollen analyses', *Journal of Archaeological Science*, 36: 140–9.

Toolis, R. (2011), 'Neolithic domesticity and other prehistoric anomalies: excavations at Laigh Newton, East Ayrshire', *Scottish Archaeological Internet Reports* (= *SAIR*), 49: dx.doi.org/10.5284/1017938.

Topping, P. (1996), 'Structure and ritual in Neolithic houses', in Darvill and Thomas (eds), *Neolithic Houses in Northwest Europe and Beyond*, 157–70.

Walker, T. F. (1968), 'Easterton of Roseisle: a forgotten site in Moray', in J. Coles and D. D. A. Simpson (eds), *Studies in Ancient Europe*, Leicester: Leicester University Press, 95–115.

Whittle, A. (1996), 'Houses in context: buildings as process', in Darvill and Thomas (eds), *Neolithic Houses in Northwest Europe and Beyond*, 13–26.

Whittle, A. (2003), *The Archaeology of People: Dimensions of Neolithic Life*, London: Routledge.

Whittle, A., Healy, F. and Bayliss, A. (2011), *Gathering Time. Dating the Early Neolithic Enclosures of Southern Britain and Ireland*, Oxford: Oxbow Books, 2 vols.

Whittle, A. W. R., Keith-Lewis, M., Milles, A., Noddle, B., Rees, S. and Romans, J. C. C. (1986), *Scord of Brouster: An Early Agricultural Settlement on Shetland: Excavations 1977–1979*, Oxford: Oxford University Committee for Archaeology.

Wordsworth, J. (1991), 'Upper Cullernie (Inverness and Bona Parish), pit containing flint and pitchstone', *Discovery and Excavation in Scotland*, 1991: 41.

Wright, D. (2014), 'Wellhill Excavations 2014', unpublished SERF Project interim report, University of Glasgow.

CHAPTER 11

The Neolithic Pottery from Balfarg/ Balbirnie Revisited

Ann MacSween

> I can remember the weight and balance of a pot, and how its surface works with its volume. I can read how an edge creates tension or loses it. I can feel if it has been made at speed or with diligence. If it has warmth.
>
> I can see how it works with the objects that sit nearby. How it displaces a small part of the world around it.
>
> *The Hare with Amber Eyes: A Hidden Inheritance*,
> Edmund de Waal (2010)

I was fortunate to work with Gordon Barclay at Historic Scotland from 1999 until he left the agency in 2010. During that time I learned a great deal from Gordon through observing how he applied his detailed understanding of the Neolithic, and the archaeology of Scotland more generally, to the work of the Inspectorate, especially in relation to designations and casework. In considering what to write for his volume, I decided to review the Neolithic pottery from the excavations at Balfarg in Fife published by Gordon and Chris Russell-White in 1993. Since its publication, the Balfarg report has been often referred to by researchers with an interest in Scotland's prehistoric pottery. I hope that Gordon will enjoy this update, which demonstrates something of the contribution that the Balfarg/Balbirnie excavations made, and continue to make, to our understanding of the Neolithic of lowland Scotland, a subject that he has also contributed to through synthesis and overview (e.g., Barclay 2004).

The Balfarg/Balbirnie ceremonial complex

From 1983 to 1985 excavations of the ceremonial complex at Balfarg/ Balbirnie were undertaken by Barclay in response to development associated with the expansion of Glenrothes New Town in Fife (Figure 11.1). This was the final stage of three phases of excavation carried out over fifteen years and arranged by Historic Scotland and its predecessor departments (Barclay and Russell-White 1993: 48). In 1970–1, Balbirnie stone circle was excavated by

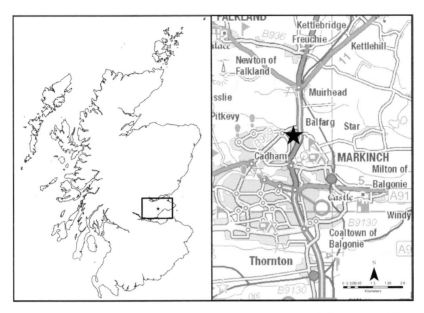

Figure 11.1 Location of Balfarg (contains Ordnance Survey data. © Crown copyright and database right 2014).

Graham Ritchie and removed to another site (Ritchie 1974), and in 1977–8 the henge at Balfarg was excavated by Roger Mercer (1981). In 1978, a previously unknown enclosure was recognised by the RCAHMS from aerial photography and named the Balfarg Riding School enclosure. This was the site excavated by Barclay, along with features in the vicinity of the enclosure, henge and stone circle (Figure 11.2).

The Balfarg Riding School excavations

Barclay's first season of excavations in the spring of 1983 concentrated on the Balfarg Riding School enclosure (henceforth BRS), and comprised a trial excavation over the ditch and part of the interior of the enclosure where post-holes were uncovered (Figure 11.2). A further season of excavation was undertaken later the same year to investigate the enclosure and its immediate surroundings. Evidence for a rectilinear timber structure was revealed within the enclosure. The area to the south and west of the enclosure was investigated further in the third phase of excavations in 1984. Forty-six small, machine-dug trenches were opened in the area and two produced archaeological features, including a pit with quantities of Grooved Ware. The fourth season, later in 1984, further examined the features uncovered in the third season and a ring-ditch/ring-cairn complex was revealed as well as a rectilinear timber structure similar to the one uncovered in the interior of the BRS

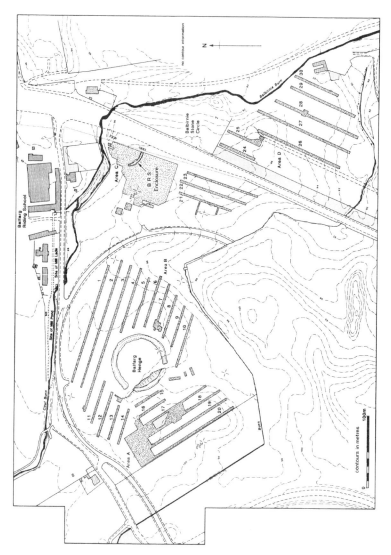

Figure 11.2 Plan showing the location of the excavation areas at Balfarg and Balfarg Riding School (from Barclay and Russell–White 1993: illus. 4, reproduced courtesy of the Society of Antiquaries of Scotland).

enclosure. The final season, in 1985, continued the work on the ring-ditch/ring-cairn and a second timber structure. In addition, extensive sampling was carried out between and around the three main foci of activity. An area of Neolithic activity and a Bronze Age cemetery were discovered to the west of the henge, and further features between the henge and the Balfarg Riding School site. (Barclay and Russell-White 1993: 50–1, and illus. 4, 50).

The pottery assemblage from Balfarg Riding School

Trevor Cowie and Audrey Henshall reported on the pottery from the 1983 and 1985 excavations at BRS and defined three broad groups of Neolithic pottery (Cowie and Henshall 1993: 57):

- Earlier Neolithic round-based bowls: Carinated Bowls (Group 1 pottery) were found *in situ* in Area C pits F8016 and F8017, and as a residual scatter in Area A pits; and globular bowls (Group 2 pottery) were found in Area A pits, principally F2039 and F2430.
- Grooved Ware: was recovered from layers in the middle part of the fill of the BRS enclosure ditch and a small number of other contexts including the large pit F1002.
- Impressed Ware: mainly heavily abraded sherds, was limited in its distribution to the area of protected old ground surface under Cairn A.

Cowie and Henshall noted that 'In its entirety, the prehistoric pottery assemblage from Balfarg Riding School provides a major addition to the inventory of Neolithic pottery from Scotland, but much of it is frustratingly fragmentary' (1993: 57). Twenty years after publication, Balfarg remains an important assemblage for the interpretation of the ceramics of the Neolithic of Scotland. A number of key assemblages, from the east mainland of Scotland, which have been published during this period, have provided a wider context for the Balfarg assemblage.

Earlier Neolithic Carinated and globular bowls

In his analysis of the earlier Neolithic pottery from Balfarg, Cowie (1993a) identified two groups of round-based bowls from different areas of the site (Barclay and Russell-White 1993: 60).

Group 1 pottery, from Area C on the east of the site, consists of sherds from nine recognisable vessels and twenty-seven sherds not attributed to a vessel. The assemblage includes a Carinated Bowl, a shouldered bowl and sherds of 'plain bowl'. All seven pits in Area C had large stones, often closely packed, in the upper layers of the fill. Four contained charcoal-stained soils and/or burnt bone fragments. This was interpreted as the result of a complex of activities, including the digging of pits and their backfilling, and one

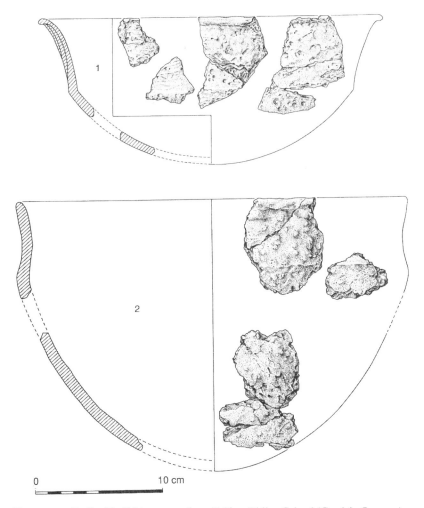

Figure 11.3 Earlier Neolithic pottery from Balfarg Riding School (Cowie's Group 1)
(after Barclay and Russell-White 1993: 67; reproduced courtesy of the Society of
Antiquaries of Scotland).

pit (F8016) was noted as having sherds from three vessels which had been
deposited carefully and deliberately (Cowie 1993a: 65).

Group 2 pottery, found only in Area A, was recovered in and around pits
located across the summit of a low ridge. The sherds attributed to Group
2 are from heavy, globular bowls and miscellaneous vessels. A number of
Group 1 sherds were also recovered from this area (Figure 11.3). Fifteen
pits in Area A contained sherds of Group 2 pottery, often associated with
charcoal or charcoal-stained soil. One of these, F2430, had large quantities
of sherds representing a minimum of twelve vessels, including one vessel

which was virtually complete, as well as burnt material (Barclay and Russell-White 1993: 63). Fourteen features around the pits with the Group 2 pottery were undatable.

The radiocarbon dates for Balfarg put the use of the Early Neolithic round-based bowls at between 3700 and 3400 cal. BC (Dalland 1993: 161). Cowie (1993a: 65) suggested that the Group 1 and Group 2 assemblages at Balfarg may be chronologically distinct, although the radiocarbon dating evidence was not conclusive. He noted a difference in both fabric and form between the two assemblages, with the Group 1 sherds including a number of finer-walled vessels, often finely gritted and with a good surface finish. While this type of pottery is often referred to as in the Grimston/Lyles Hill tradition, Cowie suggested that the Balfarg round-based pottery was best described simply as being in the 'plain bowl style', because of the heterogeneity and fragmentary nature of the group. Apart from the pottery included in the pits, which he took to represent the primary discard of artefacts, he concluded that because of its fragmentary condition and dispersed distribution the assemblage was best interpreted as a residual scatter of pottery associated with the earliest Neolithic activity on the site (Cowie 1993a: 66).

Cowie suggested that the Group 2 pottery, a range of heavy bowl forms in coarse fabrics (Figure 11.4), represents a local ceramic development, a stage in the development of the thick-rimmed heavy bowls that are a characteristic element of Impressed Ware assemblages of the later Neolithic, their thick rims providing a platform for the distinctive decoration of this type of pottery. He noted that, like the Group 1 vessels, the Group 2 vessels were undecorated, but that some of them may have had lugs (Cowie 1993a: 69). In addition, while these vessels have similarities with the plain bowl styles of the earlier Neolithic, the fabric is much coarser and more like the fabrics of the pottery of the later Neolithic (*ibid.*: 71, 75). Cowie concluded that the differences between the Group 1 and Group 2 pottery are so great that they are 'not readily explained as a reflection of functional differences within a single ceramic repertoire' (*ibid.*: 69).

In his overview of the context of Early Neolithic round-based bowls in the excavation report, Barclay (1993: 168) suggested that some of the Early Neolithic pits at Balfarg that contained sherds of round-based bowls displayed characteristics which might imply a more complex function than 'the unelaborated disposal of domestic rubbish'. He noted, for example, that the deposition in one of the pits in Area A (F2430) gave the distinct impression that the pit had been lined with slabs of pottery from a number of vessels. Barclay (1993: 167) was careful not to overplay the ritual aspect of the deposition, however, agreeing with Richards and Thomas (1984) and Whittle (1988) that ritual is an indivisible part of ordinary life with domestic ritual actions at one end of the spectrum and more formal public rituals at the other.

Update on the round-based Early Neolithic pottery

Since the publication of the Balfarg/Balbirnie excavations many more assemblages of round-based Neolithic pottery have been recovered and published allowing progress to be made in our understanding of Scotland's earliest pottery. Much of the work in synthesising this data has been carried out by Alison Sheridan, who has noted similarities in this Traditional Carinated Bowl pottery throughout much of Britain and Ireland. To explain its widespread distribution, she argues convincingly for the rapid spread of Traditional Carinated Bowl pottery across Britain and Ireland (Sheridan 2007: 468). She notes that the predominance of carinated forms within these assemblages, the rim types, wall thickness (high incidence of thin-walled vessels) and surface treatment (frequency of burnishing) are features which vary little over the wide geographical area where this type of pottery is found (Sheridan 2009: 91). All these characteristics indicate a well-established tradition of pottery manufacture, and because of this Sheridan (2007: 442) suggests that the distribution of Traditional Carinated Bowl pottery represents the arrival of small farming groups from the Continent, communities which became established in Britain and Ireland between 3950/3900 and 3800 cal. BC and are associated in some areas with the building of timber halls, smaller wooden houses, long barrows, mortuary enclosures and cursus monuments (Sheridan 2007: 453). This narrative has, however, been challenged by others (e.g., Whittle *et al.* 2011).

The debate about how to interpret the contents of pits dating to the Early Neolithic continues with an expanded body of data but no firm conclusions. Barclay (2001: 81; and Chapter 9, this volume) noted that in interpreting the contents of pits, care should be taken not to see all those containing sherds and other material as being the result of deliberate selection and deposition, and suggested that a distinction should be drawn between pits with contents that may indicate deliberate selection and those that could represent material that was accidentally incorporated. While a precautionary approach when interpreting the contents of a pit or deposit is generally the norm, in some cases the explanation of deliberate deposition seems not unreasonable. Recently published examples include Kintore, Aberdeenshire, Pit 25, where ten vessels were present with rim sherds and body sherds represented for seven of the vessels and only rim sherds for three vessels, possibly indicating the deliberate inclusion of rim sherds for each vessel represented in the pit. In another of the Kintore pits, P35, between one and four sherds from thirty-seven vessels seem to have been used to line the pit (Cook and Dunbar 2008: 61–3, 66; MacSween 2008: 180). At Eweford West, in East Lothian, the fill of one of the larger pits (025) was found to contain numerous sherds from seven pots in the Carinated Bowl tradition (Lelong and MacGregor 2008: 20). Each pot had been broken before deposition and sherds representing a small part of each vessel were placed in the pit.

More recently, Brophy and Noble (2012: 63) have emphasised that it is likely that Neolithic pits, whatever they contain, are somewhere on a spectrum between ceremonial and mundane. The dramatic increase in the number of assemblages from Neolithic pits available for study has highlighted the wide variation in depositional practices from region to region, site to site, and even one area of a site to another, and Brophy (2006: 22–5) has stressed the need to include the use of pits in our narratives of daily life in the Neolithic. There is evidence, for example, that some pits were recut and more pottery added at a later date (e.g., MacSween 2008: 180). Depending on the length of time between the digging of a pit and its recutting, it is possible that it would have been necessary for the pit to be marked in some way, perhaps by a cairn or a post-marker (Thomas 2012: 9). This requires a shift from thinking about pits as filled-in holes left to grass over without trace, to thinking of them as very much enduring features in the landscape.

One of the largest assemblages of Traditional Carinated round-based bowls, published shortly after Balfarg, is that from the excavation of Neolithic artefact scatters at Biggar Common in South Lanarkshire (Johnston 1997; Sheridan 1997). In her discussion of the assemblage, Sheridan (1997: 218–20) proposed using the term 'Modified Carinated Bowl pottery' to refer to the local and regional adaptations which followed soon after the introduction of Traditional Carinated Bowl pottery to an area. In the north-east of Scotland, for example, the extensive use of fluting, the occasional use of lugs and a preference for relatively shallow bowl forms define this modified phase, which Sheridan has suggested may, in some cases, have followed within a few generations of the first appearance of Traditional Carinated Bowl pottery (Sheridan 2009: 92–3).

From the available evidence it is likely that Traditional Carinated Bowls continued in use throughout the first half of the fourth millennium cal. BC (Sheridan 1997: 219–20). A number of later dates, including those from Forest Road, Kintore, Aberdeenshire (Cook and Dunbar 2008; dates summarised in MacSween 2008) and from Carwood Hill, Biggar Common (Johnston 1997; dates summarised in Sheridan 1997: 219), raise the possibility that they continued in use during much of the fourth millennium cal. BC, at least in some areas of Scotland, and in Ireland similarly late dates have been noted (summarised in Sheridan 1995: 18). Parker Pearson (2003: 12) has argued that round-based bowls were designed for sharing food (liquids could have been drunk directly from them), while the later Neolithic flat-based Grooved Ware vessels were more likely to have been used for storage, so even if changes in fashion encouraged the adoption of new types of vessels, the function attached to round-based bowls may, in some areas, have led to their retention alongside the new vessel types.

So how has the material recovered in the last twenty years changed our interpretation of the round-based Early Neolithic pottery from Balfarg? Arguably, while the distinctive Traditional Carinated Bowl assemblages of the Early Neolithic are relatively straightforward to identify and describe, the terminology and categorisation of other Early Neolithic assemblages are less so. An important question that remains to be addressed in relation to Balfarg is what the two groups of Early Neolithic pottery on the site represent. As noted above, the Balfarg assemblage has a Traditional Carinated Bowl assemblage (Group 1) and a much coarser assemblage of round-based vessels (Group 2), with radiocarbon dates placing both groups in the period 3700–3400 BC (Dalland 1993: 161).

Gibson (2010: 65) has recently referred to the Balfarg Riding School Group 2 pottery as a 'Modified Carinated Bowl' assemblage. It may, however, be more helpful to reserve the term 'modified' for pottery like the fluted Carinated Bowl assemblages of the north-east which include the assemblage from Boghead (Henshall 1984). It appears to be a 'true' modification of an established tradition of Carinated Bowl pottery-making by relatively minor adaptation, in this case by adding fluting. In the case of the Balfarg assemblage, the Group 2 pottery, as Cowie (1993a) noted in the excavation report, is quite different from the Carinated Bowl pottery and, rather than resulting from modification of a tradition of manufacturing Carinated Bowls, it is equally possible that the Group 2 vessels represent a stage in the development of a separate tradition of pottery-making which gradually assimilated elements of the established Carinated Bowl tradition.

If the Traditional Carinated Bowl pottery represents the introduction of pottery into Britain and Ireland by groups well practised in pottery manufacture, it is not unreasonable to suppose that a parallel tradition of pottery-making developed fairly early on. Some communities keen to adopt the technology and the functional advantages of pottery may have had no need for the refinements of the Carinated Bowl assemblages such as the fine burnishing and the thin walls, or may indeed have lacked the skills to produce pottery of this quality, resulting in the production of a more utilitarian product.

In addition, the prominence of Traditional Carinated Bowl pottery in the archaeological record of the Early Neolithic may owe something to its associated depositional practices, with much of this pottery deriving from pits. Assuming that the surface discard of refuse, including poorly-fired ceramics, was the norm for some communities, this may have led to under-representation of the ceramics of these communities in the archaeological record, as low-fired ceramics exposed to the elements will leave little trace. The non-Traditional Carinated Bowl component of Scotland's Early Neolithic ceramics, as represented by the Group 2 assemblage at Balfarg, requires a depth of analysis similar to that applied by Sheridan to the Traditional Carinated Bowls in order to better define what, undoubtedly, is a complex picture of local and regional diversification. The work carried out by Cowie (1993b) summarising the Neolithic pottery of eastern and central Scotland provides a good starting point.

Grooved Ware

The Grooved Ware from Barclay's excavations at Balfarg Riding School (Figure 11.5) was associated with two sub-rectangular timber structures from Area C. Both structures had a boundary defined by post-holes with more post-holes within (Barclay and Russell-White 1993: 76), and it was concluded that these were unroofed enclosures, perhaps connected with ritual activity (Barclay 1993: 178) and that the Grooved Ware was connected with ritual practices associated with the end of the use of the sites. However, the nature, role and form of this pair of structures remain contested (Brophy 2007).

The boundary of Structure 1 consisted of lines of post-holes which seem to have supported a continuous barrier measuring internally approximately 17 m × 8.5 m. Inside this barrier were sixteen pits, also identified as post-holes. Sherds of Grooved Ware were found in two of these (F1111, one sherd from each of two vessels; F1121, one sherd) and during cleaning of the surface of a third (F1104/1131, sherds from one vessel) (Barclay and Russell-White 1993: 77). Structure 2 was similar in layout to Structure 1 and, although one end of it was more eroded, it seems to have defined an internal space of similar size. Over the southern part of the structure (*ibid*.: 84)

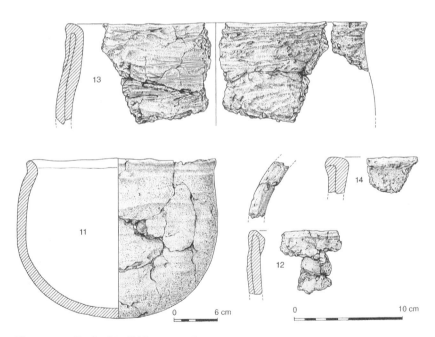

Figure 11.4 Earlier Neolithic pottery from Balfarg Riding School (Cowie's Group 2) (after Barclay and Russell-White 1993: 70; reproduced courtesy of the Society of Antiquaries of Scotland).

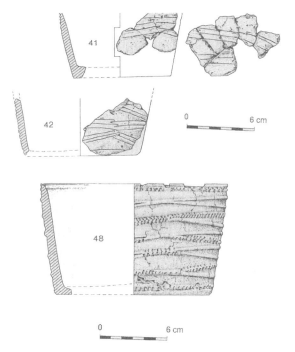

Figure 11.5 Grooved Ware from Balfarg Riding School (after Barclay and Russell-White 1993: 96, Nos 41, 42; 97, No. 48; reproduced courtesy of the Society of Antiquaries of Scotland).

was a layer obscuring the post-holes which contained substantial sherds of three vessels and interpreted as being deposited towards the end of the use of the structure. Other sherds of Grooved Ware from this structure were again from secondary contexts (F7023, parts of two vessels; F021, one sherd; F7054, fragments of one vessel). It was concluded that the Grooved Ware pottery was associated with the last use of these two structures (*ibid.*: 88).

Grooved Ware was also recovered from the Balfarg Riding School enclosure ditch (the lower middle infill levels) and from five isolated pits outside the enclosure (Barclay and Russell-White 1993). Richards (1993: 192), in discussing the context of deposition of the Grooved Ware sherds on the site, proposed that the material from the pits and the ditch could represent the disposal of 'ritually charged' material from activities being carried out at Structures 1 and 2 and at the enclosure and henge.

The total number of vessels represented within the assemblage from Barclay's excavations at Balfarg Riding School was estimated by Henshall (1993: 94) as forty-three. She noted that there was a wide range of sizes which could be divided into two main groups, small to medium, and large to very large. The vessels represented were a mixture of small tub-shaped vessels and larger bucket-shaped vessels. A small number of vessels had impressions that indicated that they had been formed in a basket (McLellan 1993: 108). Sandy fabrics as well as coarser fabrics with rock inclusions were represented.

Decoration was with incised lines, from fine lines to narrow and wide grooves, and cordons were also used. Some of the cordons were themselves decorated, by edging with small incisions, and occasionally this technique was used to push the cordon from the upper side, and then from the lower side, to produce a wavy line in false relief. Circular depressions were formed by impressing the fingertip or a circular tool into the surface of the vessel. The use of cord impression was noted only once. The incised lines and cordons on some of the smaller vessels were arranged as all-over zoneless decoration, in parallel lines or forming chevrons, sometimes joined to adjacent chevrons with short ribs of clay. On the larger vessels decoration was generally restricted to the upper portion, forming a band below the rim. Henshall (1993: 99) noted that while there were differences in the areas of the vessels that were decorated, there were many similarities between the decoration on the small vessels and on the large vessels. Almost all vessels were decorated in the interior with a single or double line or groove around the vessel just below the rim. The rims were plain or tapered and some had scalloped decoration protruding above the lip.

When the Grooved Ware from Balfarg was analysed, the accepted stylistic scheme was that of Wainwright and Longworth (1971), who identified four Grooved Ware sub-styles: Woodlands, Clacton, Durrington Walls and Rinyo. Woodlands was characterised by flat-based bucket-shaped vessels and small open bowls with converging decorative cordons; Clacton by straight-sided vessels decorated mainly with incised grooves; Durrington Walls by bucket- and barrel-shaped vessels with incised and applied decoration; and Rinyo by a variety of plastic decoration and decorative rim forms.

In her discussion of the Balfarg Riding School assemblage, Henshall (1993: 106) compared it with pottery from a number of sites from the north of Scotland to the south of England. The distribution of Grooved Ware sites in Scotland was at that time, however, very scattered. Although there was comparable material from Orkney and Lewis, the distribution more locally to Balfarg was sparse, with only a few sites known in the south-east of Scotland. Henshall (1993: 104–6) noted that the Grooved Ware from Balfarg Riding School fitted easily within the Woodlands sub-style, and also drew attention to the close similarities between the Balfarg Riding School assemblage and some of the southern English sites, including the type site of Woodlands near Woodhenge in Wiltshire. In discussing the Woodlands distribution, she concluded that while Grooved Ware was first defined and studied in the south of England, and then found at a number of sites in northern England, it tended to be assumed that the pottery had spread to the north from the south, but she urged caution as the few available dates indicated that the reverse might be the case. She listed a number of sites in Scotland that had produced pottery in the Woodlands style, including Tentsmuir in Fife (Longworth 1967: 75–8) and Knappers in West Dunbartonshire (Ritchie and Adamson 1981: 187–8). In terms of context, Henshall (1993: 108) noted that the Woodlands style of Grooved Ware in Scotland was recovered almost exclusively from pits, generally interpreted as domestic in nature, as well as from surface scatters or re-deposited material.

In addition to the Grooved Ware from Barclay's excavations at Balfarg Riding School, Grooved Ware was recovered from Ritchie's excavations at Balbirnie stone circle (Ritchie 1974) and Mercer's excavations at Balfarg henge (Mercer 1981; and see Figure 11.6). The Grooved Ware from Balbirnie was published as two small sherds with incised decoration in two directions (Ritchie 1974: 15, 18–20), although in their discussion of the Grooved Ware from Balfarg henge, Henshall and Mercer (1981: 132–3) noted that when compared in detail with the assemblage from that site, it was possible that a number of other sherds from Balbirnie could be classed as Grooved Ware. They also noted that the Balfarg henge assemblage did not fit neatly into any of the four styles defined by Wainwright and Longworth (1971: 236–43). The elaborate tight all-over linear plastic decoration that characterises the Balfarg Riding School assemblage is not a feature of the Balfarg henge assemblage, which is defined by the use of incision and jabbed decoration to form incised chevrons, incised parallel lines and infilled shapes (Henshall 1993: 102–4). In comparing the pottery from Barclay's excavations at Balfarg Riding School with Mercer's (1981) Grooved Ware from Balfarg henge, Henshall (1993: 102) noted that the 'differences are such that it is clear that the two assemblages are distinct'.

Update on Grooved Ware

Since the publication of Balfarg Riding School, Wainwright's and Longworth's four sub-styles have been reassessed by Paul Garwood (1999), who has suggested that Woodlands and Clacton may in fact be one sub-style, with Woodlands possibly a later development of the Clacton style. Garwood also suggested that, at least in England, most assemblages can be characterised as in either Clacton–Woodlands or Durrington Walls styles.

The use of the southern Grooved Ware styles to categorise the pottery from Scotland was questioned shortly after Balfarg's publication (MacSween 1995), but from the material recovered since then it has become clear that some assemblages, particularly along the east coast, can be attributed broadly to either Clacton–Woodlands or Durrington Walls (MacSween 2007: 371). It has been argued elsewhere that the Rinyo style, for example, as represented in the heavy plastic decoration of the assemblages from Skara

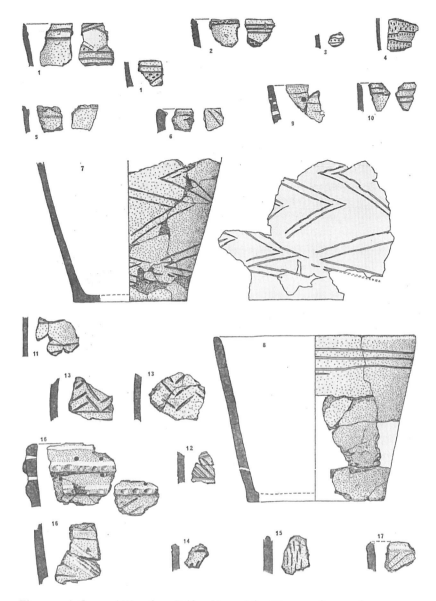

Figure 11.6 Grooved Ware from Balfarg Henge (after Mercer 1981: 130, fig. 43; reproduced courtesy of the Society of Antiquaries of Scotland).

Brae and the later Neolithic phase at Pool, may represent local development of Grooved Ware within Orkney (MacSween forthcoming).

The available dates for Grooved Ware from the east coast of mainland Scotland were recently summarised, using only dates derived from charcoal from short-lived species recovered from the same contexts as the pottery (MacSween 2007: 373–5). Dates for the southern mainland sites are slightly later than those for the Northern Isles, with dates falling in the first half of the third millennium cal. BC, preceding the generally accepted date of 2500 cal. BC for the beginnings of Beaker use in Britain (MacSween 2007: 375). A subsequent review of the available dates for Grooved Ware from Scotland took account of twenty new AMS radiocarbon determinations on human bone from the Neolithic chambered tomb at Quanterness, Orkney, and concluded that Grooved Ware emerged as a novel pottery tradition in Orkney possibly as early as 3300/3200 cal. BC (Schulting *et al.* 2010). In their discussion, these authors drew attention to the striking similarities between the Quanterness vessels and those from Balfarg henge. While the radiocarbon dates presently available suggest that the initial spread of incised Grooved Ware was from the north of Scotland, it is probable that during the subsequent development of regional styles, the pottery was adapted and adopted in many geographical directions, and it is possible that the Balfarg Riding School communities were using at least some designs that developed further south.

When the excavations at Balfarg/Balbirnie were published, the Grooved Ware phase of activity at the site of the stone circle at Balbirnie was dated to *c.* 3000–2500 cal. BC. Recent reinterpretation by Gibson (2010: 73) using additional radiocarbon dates associates the Balbirnie Grooved Ware with the construction of the stone circle, dating to the thirty-first–twenty-ninth centuries cal. BC, which he suggested predated the Balfarg circles by between 100 and 500 hundred years. He proposed that at least one timber circle was erected at Balfarg henge between 2900 and 2500 cal. BC, with the erection of at least one stone circle by around 2500 cal. BC. In the case of Balfarg henge, Gibson put forward the idea that the Grooved Ware was associated with a period of pyro-ritual activity broadly datable to the end of the third millennium based on the evidence from a layer (V2) to the north-west of Timber Circle A, in the post-holes of Circle A and from a pit (Gibson 2010: 67). He interpreted the Grooved Ware in the post-holes as deriving from earlier activity. Given the similarities in decoration between the Balbirnie Grooved Ware and that from Balfarg henge, the possibility of a similarly early date for the Grooved Ware from Balfarg henge must remain open.

Gibson also argued that at Balfarg and elsewhere, the construction of henges may post-date the Grooved Ware-associated later Neolithic, and that rather than representing the primary monument, henges may be the last monumental element, constructed to enclose an area that had been used for ritual practice for a considerable period (cf. Barclay 2005; and see Chapter 7, this volume). Gibson has hypothesised that this could account for the fact that the bank of a henge is external to the ditch so that the bank does not encroach on the 'sacred space' (Gibson 2010: 71). This reassessment accords with the view that the southward spread of Grooved Ware was fairly rapid (MacSween 2007) and that it was probably associated with the creation of timber and stone circles (Sheridan 2004).

Assemblages of incised Grooved Ware, like the pottery from Balbirnie and Balfarg henge, have been recovered from sites including, Quanterness (Renfrew 1979), the Stones of Stenness (Ritchie 1976) and Barnhouse (Richards 2005) (see comparison in Gibson 2010: 31, illus. 20), all on Orkney, and the west coast of Scotland, for example, the assemblage from Machrie Moor, Arran (Haggarty 1991: 66, illus. 6) as well as from sites in Ireland (e.g., Sheridan 1995: 16, fig. 2.5). Sheridan (2004) drew attention to a distinctive scatter of Grooved Ware finds associated with circles of timber or stone along the western fringe of Scotland and Ireland possibly a result of links with Orkney shortly after 3000 cal. BC. It is thus possible that two phases of Grooved Ware-associated activity are represented, an earlier one at Balfarg henge and Balbirnie, and a slightly later phase represented at Balfarg Riding School by the classic Woodlands style vessels.

When the Balfarg Riding School excavations were published, the lack of Grooved Ware in the north-east was striking, leading a few years later to the suggestion that this may be a real absence, with other media, such as carved stone balls, perhaps taking the place of Grooved Ware in the life of its Neolithic inhabitants (Cowie and MacSween 1999). In Scotland, over the last twenty years, however, there has been a major increase in the number of assemblages available for study, largely due to the increase in sites excavated as a requirement of development. Brophy (2006: 11), for example, has noted that between 1985 and 2004 at least 153 excavations in Scotland were carried out on known Neolithic sites or revealed Neolithic traces in a secure context. The data resulting from this work has considerably advanced our understanding of the Neolithic of mainland Scotland. The fact that these sites were excavated in response to development need rather than primarily for research has led to the exploration of a diverse range of sites, many of which may not have been an obvious choice for research excavation (Phillips and Bradley 2004; Brophy 2006). A result of this work has been the extension of the distribution of Grooved Ware into the north-east. For instance, a single sherd of Grooved Ware has been found at Fourdafourie (Murray 2003), right at the north-east tip of Aberdeenshire, while excavations in advance of development at Kintore near Aberdeen produced sherds from fifteen vessels (Cook and Dunbar 2008; MacSween 2008: 181–7). It is now apparent that Balfarg shares elements of its pottery assemblage with other sites in the east of Scotland, including Kintore (Cook and Dunbar 2008; MacSween 2008), Dubton Farm, Brechin (Cameron 2002; MacSween 2002) and Redcastle in Angus (Alexander 2005; MacSween 2005: 45–6).

Thomas (2010: 12) has considered what the widespread use of similar pottery styles means, and has suggested that the Grooved Ware assemblages may have represented a community that existed across time and space, from the north to the south of Britain. The possibility of using Grooved Ware to identify regional and local identity in the Neolithic has also been considered (MacSween forthcoming). Balfarg's geographic location makes it a key site when considering the connections between north and south along the east coast of the British mainland as represented by its Grooved Ware assemblage.

Impressed Ware

The third type of Neolithic pottery found at Balfarg was Impressed Ware, of which there were ninety-five sherds, most recovered from the old ground surface between Ring-Cairn A and Cairn B and possibly from domestic rubbish spread as manure (Cowie 1993c: 122) (Figure 11.7). Most of the sherds were from vessels with expanded rims which provided a focus for the impressed decoration that gives this type of pottery its name. Upright vessels and more open bowls are represented as well as a shouldered bowl. Decoration was by jabbing with a pointed implement to form an oval shape, the creation of a groove by joining up a series of short stabs, texturing with fingernail impressions, incising lines, the creation of lines by impressing a twisted cord, and 'maggot' impressions using whipped cord and rows of dots, possibly created by impressing a comb into the surface. As stated above, most of the decoration is on the rims: lines of impressed cord around the circumference of the vessel, or impressed cord or incised lines across it, with decoration also below the rim in some cases. From what can be made out, on the body of the vessel's decoration is either parallel lines or panels or a more general texturing with shorter impressions, for example, fingernail or maggot impressions. Cowie (1993c: 125) compared the Balfarg assemblage to assemblages from coastal dune sites, including Luce Sands (Galloway), Hedderwick (East Lothian) and Tentsmuir (Fife). In the discussion, Cowie (*ibid.*: 126) noted that there were very few dates for this type of pottery in Scotland and that while the excavator (Gordon Barclay) had 'kept an open mind' regarding the possibility that the pottery could have been as early as the first half of the third millennium in radiocarbon years, the few dates available favoured the second half of the third millennium.

Update on Impressed Ware

When the Balfarg report was published, Cowie referred to the impressed pottery as 'Later Neolithic Impressed Wares', noting that Scottish Impressed Wares (McInnes 1969) and 'later Neolithic decorated wares' (Kinnes 1985) had been used as descriptors for this material previously. The term

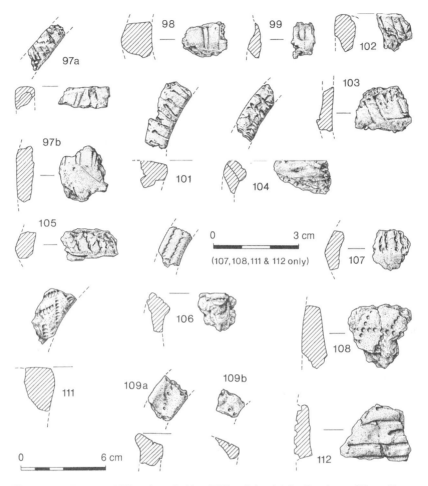

Figure 11.7 Impressed Ware from Balfarg Riding School (after Barclay and Russell-White 1993: 124; reproduced courtesy of the Society of Antiquaries of Scotland).

'Impressed Ware' is now generally supported to cover all groups of this pottery (Gibson 2002: 81).

As with round-based bowls, the most noticeable change in our understanding of the Impressed Ware of Scotland relates to its dating. It is only recently that a large enough body of dating evidence relating to Impressed Ware has accumulated to make its analysis worthwhile. Sheridan (1997) in her discussion of the dates from Biggar Common, South Lanarkshire, raised the possibility of dates in the mid- to late fourth millennium for Impressed Ware. Two similarly early dates from Meldon Bridge in the Scottish Borders had previously been dismissed as unreliable by the excavator (Burgess 1976), but determinations including a date of 3500–2920 cal. BC (Beta-73951) for pottery from Blairhall Burn, Dumfries and Galloway (Strachan *et al.* 1998) and a date of 3639–3374 cal. BC (GU-9094) from Dubton Farm, Brechin, Angus, for a pit containing Impressed Ware (Cameron 2002; MacSween 2002) gave Sheridan's suggestion of dates in the second half of the fourth millennium more weight and it now seems likely that in Scotland Impressed Ware was in use from as early as the thirty-sixth century cal. BC (MacSween 2007: fig. 33.4) as had previously been suggested for Impressed Ware use in England (Gibson and Kinnes 1997).

Ongoing analysis of the available radiocarbon dates using Bayesian modelling indicates that it is difficult to argue for dates later than the thirtieth century BC for Impressed Ware in either Scotland or England (Gibson 2010: 66). The earliest dates for Impressed Wares on mainland Scotland thus precede those for Grooved Ware. Although there are no dates for contexts with Impressed Wares from Balfarg Riding School, Gibson suggests that a date in the second half of the fourth millennium BC is probable from comparison with the rather small number of available radiocarbon dates from Scotland. If this is accepted, the phase of use of Impressed Wares at Balfarg Riding School is more likely to have preceded the period of use of Grooved Ware (*ibid.*) than succeeded it, and so Impressed Ware rather than Grooved Ware is likely to have been associated with the second phase of activity on the site, comprising the construction and use of the timber structures (Gibson 2010: 66).

Meaningful regional groups of Impressed Wares have not been identified and it appears that the observation made by McInnes (1969) still holds today, namely, that the preferred forms and decorative styles vary from one site to another. Some regional traits have been suggested, for example, the use of impressed decoration to form heavy rustication favoured in the west of Scotland (MacSween 2001). As for the origins of the Scottish Impressed Wares, the possibility that a north-eastern style of Impressed Wares evolved out of earlier Neolithic pottery was advanced by Henshall (1983) and then taken further by Cowie (1993b: 18), who noted that impressed decoration may have developed into the use of incised stab-and-drag decoration.

In the Balfarg Riding School report, Cowie (1993a: 69) suggested that the heavily tempered Early Neolithic round-based bowls, of which the Balfarg Group 2 vessels are examples, may lie behind the development of the thick-rimmed vessels that are a major element of the Impressed Wares. Since then, the use of impressed decoration on the rim and the upper portion of round-based vessels has been noted in a number of assemblages from the north-east, giving credence to Cowie's suggestion of a link between the round-based vessels and the types of decorative common to the Impressed Wares. Examples of vessels which demonstrate these decorative traits include a classic Unstan bowl from Spurryhillock near Stonehaven, Aberdeenshire

(Cowie 1997) and a vessel from Kinbeachie in the Black Isle, just north of Inverness, on which the impressed decoration is restricted to its upper portion (Barclay *et al.* 2001: 78).

These recent finds have demonstrated that within Scotland an earlier tradition of pottery existed which shares aspects of its morphology and decoration with Impressed Wares (MacSween 2007: 368) and its identification adds weight to the argument that Impressed Ware styles developed locally. While in England pottery with impressed decoration is usually found in funerary contexts, this is not the case in Scotland where, if not found as domestic rubbish unrelated to particular features, Impressed Ware is most commonly found in pits (MacSween 2007: 370).

Conclusion

This brief ceramics-based overview has highlighted the continued importance of the Balfarg excavations in interpretations of the Neolithic of lowland Scotland. Over the past twenty years a vast amount of data has become available, often from developer-funded archaeological investigations. Much of this data is from relatively small-scale excavation and while its value is occasionally questioned on a site-by-site basis, its contribution to the construction of a fuller picture of the Neolithic of lowland Scotland is not in doubt. A recent overview, for example, led Brophy and Noble (2012: 74) to conclude that locations considered suitable for pit digging followed different trajectories, with some being abandoned after their initial use, some returned to and used again, and others, like Balfarg, developed into monumental locations and complexes (see also Chapters 7 and 9, this volume). While much of the data that will improve our understanding of the Neolithic of lowland Scotland will doubtless continue to be obtained through small-scale fieldwork, the importance of large-scale excavations to test evolving models is obvious. We also need to continue to prioritise synthesis, review and reinterpretation, building on the lead that Gordon Barclay provided in his many overviews of the Neolithic.

Bibliography

Alexander, D. (1997), 'Excavations of pits containing decorated Neolithic pottery and early lithic material of possible Mesolithic date at Spurryhillock, Stonehaven, Aberdeenshire', *Proceedings of the Society of Antiquaries of Scotland*, 127: 17–27.

Alexander, D. (2005), 'Redcastle, Lunan Bay, Angus: the excavation of an Iron Age timber-lined souterrain and a Pictish barrow cemetery', *Proceedings of the Society of Antiquaries of Scotland*, 135: 41–118.

Anderson-Whymark, H. and Thomas, J. (eds) (2012), *Regional Perspectives on Neolithic Pit Deposition: Beyond the Mundane*, Oxford: Oxbow Books.

Barclay, G. J. (1993), 'The interpretation of the structures', in Barclay and Russell-White, *Proceedings of the Society of Antiquaries of Scotland*, 123: 175–82.

Barclay, G. J. (2001), 'Neolithic enclosures in Scotland', in T. Darvill and J. Thomas (eds), *Neolithic Enclosures in Atlantic Northwest Europe*, Oxford: Oxbow Books, 144–54.

Barclay, G. J. (2004), '"Scotland cannot have been an inviting country for agricultural settlement": a history of the Neolithic of Scotland', in G. J. Barclay and I. A. G. Shepherd (eds), *Scotland in Ancient Europe. The Neolithic and Early Bronze Age of Scotland in their European Context*, Edinburgh: Society of Antiquaries of Scotland, 31–44.

Barclay, G. J. (2005), 'The "henge" and "hengiform" in Scotland', in V. Cummings and A. Pannett (eds), *Set in Stone. New Approaches to Neolithic Monuments in Scotland*, Oxford: Oxbow Books, 81–94.

Barclay, G. J. and Russell-White, C. J. (1993), 'Excavations in the ceremonial complex of the fourth to second millennium BC at Balfarg/Balbirnie, Glenrothes, Fife', *Proceedings of the Society of Antiquaries of Scotland*, 123: 43–210.

Barclay, G. J., Russell-White, C. J. and Tavener, P. N. (1993), 'Description and Interpretation', in Barclay and Russell-White, *Proceedings of the Society of Antiquaries of Scotland*, 123: 57–76.

Barclay, G. J., Carter, S. P., Dalland, M. M., Hastie, M., Holden, T. G., MacSween, A. and Wickham-Jones, C. R. (2001), 'A possible Neolithic settlement at Kinbeachie, Black Isle, Highland', *Proceedings of the Society of Antiquaries of Scotland*, 131: 57–85.

Brophy, K. (2006), 'Rethinking Scotland's Neolithic: combining circumstance with context', *Proceedings of the Society of Antiquaries of Scotland*, 136: 7–46.

Brophy, K. (2007), 'From big houses to cult houses: Early Neolithic timber halls in Scotland', *Proceedings of the Prehistoric Society*, 73: 75–96.

Brophy, K. and Noble, G. (2012), 'Within and beyond pits: deposition in lowland Neolithic Scotland', in Anderson-Whymark and Thomas (eds), *Regional Perspectives on Neolithic Pit Deposition*, 63–76.

Burl, H. A. W. (1984), 'Report on the excavation of a Neolithic mound at Boghead, Speymouth Forest, Fochabers, Moray, 1972 and 1974', *Proceedings of the Society of Antiquaries of Scotland*, 114: 35–73.

Burgess, C. (1976), 'Meldon Bridge: a Neolithic defended promontory complex near Peebles', in C. Burgess and R. Miket (eds), *Settlement and Economy in the Third and Second Millennia BC*, Oxford: British Archaeological Reports, 151–79.

Cameron, K. (2002), 'The excavation of Neolithic pits and Iron Age souterrains at Dubton Farm, Brechin, Angus', *Tayside and Fife Archaeological Journal*, 8: 19–76.

Cleal, R. and MacSween, A. (eds) (1999), *Grooved Ware in Britain and Ireland*, Oxford: Oxbow Books.

Cook, M. and Dunbar, L. (eds) (2008), *Rituals, Roundhouses and Romans: Excavations at Kintore, Aberdeenshire, 2000–2006, vol. 1: Forest Road*, Edinburgh: Scottish Trust for Archaeological Research.

Cowie, T. G. (1993a), 'Plain Neolithic pottery', in Barclay and Russell-White, *Proceedings of the Society of Antiquaries of Scotland*, 123: 65–76.

Cowie, T. G. (1993b), 'A survey of the Neolithic pottery of eastern and central Scotland', *Proceedings of the Society of Antiquaries of Scotland*, 123: 13–41.

Cowie, T. G. (1993c), 'Later Neolithic Impressed Ware', in Barclay and Russell-White, *Proceedings of the Society of Antiquaries of Scotland*, 123: 121–26.

Cowie, T. G. (1997), 'The Neolithic pottery sherds', in Alexander, *Proceedings of the Society of Antiquaries of Scotland*, 127: 22–4.

Cowie, T. G. and Henshall, A. S. (1993), 'The prehistoric pottery: an introduction to the reports', in Barclay and Russell-White, *Proceedings of the Society of Antiquaries of Scotland*, 123: 56–7.

Cowie, T. G. and MacSween, A. (1999), 'Grooved Ware from Scotland: a review', in Cleal and MacSween (eds), *Grooved Ware in Britain and Ireland*, 48–56.

Dalland, M. (1993), 'The calibration of the radiocarbon dates', in Barclay and Russell-White, *Proceedings of the Society of Antiquaries of Scotland*, 123: 161–2.

de Waal, E. (2010), *The Hare with the Amber Eyes: A Hidden Inheritance*, London: Chatto & Windus.

Garwood, P. (1999), 'Grooved Ware in southern Britain: chronology and interpretation', in Cleal and MacSween (eds), *Grooved Ware in Britain and Ireland*, 145–76.

Gibson, A. (2002), *The Prehistoric Pottery of Britain and Ireland*, Stroud: Tempus.

Gibson, A. (2010), 'Dating Balbirnie: recent radiocarbon dates from the stone circle and cairn at Balbirnie, Fife, and a review of its place in the overall Balfarg/Balbirnie site sequence', *Proceedings of the Society of Antiquaries of Scotland*, 140: 51–77.

Gibson, A. M. and Kinnes, I. A. (1997), 'On the urns of a dilemma: radiocarbon and the Peterborough problem', *Oxford Journal of Archaeology*, 16: 65–72.

Haggarty, A. (1991), 'Machrie Moor, Arran: recent excavations at two stone circles', *Proceedings of the Society of Antiquaries of Scotland*, 121: 51–94.

Henshall, A. S. (1983), 'The Neolithic pottery from Easterton of Roseisle, Moray', in A. O'Connor and D. V. Clarke (eds), *From the Stone Age to the Forty-Five. Studies Presented to R. B. K. Stevenson*, Edinburgh: John Donald, 19–44.

Henshall, A. S. (1984), 'Appendix 1: the pottery from Boghead, Fochabers, Moray', in Burl, *Proceedings of the Society of Antiquaries of Scotland*, 114: 59–66.

Henshall, A. S. (1993), 'The Grooved Ware: vessels P41–82', in Barclay and Russell-White, *Proceedings of the Society of Antiquaries of Scotland*, 123: 94–110.

Henshall, A. S. and Mercer, R. (1981), 'Report on the pottery from Balfarg, Fife', in Mercer, *Proceedings of the Society of Antiquaries of Scotland*, 111: 128–33.

Johnston, D. A. (1997), 'Biggar Common, 1987–93: an early prehistoric funerary and domestic landscape in Clydesdale, South Lanarkshire', *Proceedings of the Society of Antiquaries of Scotland*, 127: 185–254.

Kinnes, I. A. (1985), 'Circumstance not context: the Neolithic of Scotland as seen from outside', *Proceedings of the Society of Antiquaries of Scotland*, 115: 15–57.

Kinnes, I. and Varndell, G. (eds) (1995), *Unbaked Urns of Rudely Shape: Essays on British and Irish Pottery for Ian Longworth*, Oxford: Oxbow Books.

Lelong, O. and MacGregor, G. (2008), *The Lands of Ancient Lothian*, Edinburgh: Society of Antiquaries of Scotland.

Longworth, I. H. (1967), 'Further discoveries at Brackmont Mill, Brackmont Farm and Tentsmuir, Fife', *Proceedings of the Society of Antiquaries of Scotland*, 99: 60–92.

MacSween, A (1995), 'Grooved Ware from Scotland: aspects of decoration', in Kinnes and Varndell (eds), *Unbaked Urns of Rudely Shape*, 41–8.

MacSween, A. (2001) 'Scottish Neolithic Impressed Wares', in Barclay *et al.*, *Proceedings of the Society of Antiquaries of Scotland*, 131: 76–9.

MacSween, A. (2002), 'Pottery report', in Cameron, *Tayside and Fife Archaeological Journal*, 8: 34–42.

MacSween, A. (2005), 'Neolithic pottery', in Alexander, *Proceedings of the Society of Antiquaries of Scotland*, 135: 45–6.

MacSween, A. (2007), 'The Meldon Bridge period: the pottery from south and east Scotland twenty years on', in C. Burgess, P. Topping and F. Lynch (eds), *Beyond Stonehenge: Essays on the Bronze Age in Honour of Colin Burgess*, Oxford: Oxbow Books, 367–76.

MacSween, A. (2008) 'The prehistoric pottery', in Cook and Dunbar (eds), *Rituals, Roundhouses and Romans*, 173–89.

MacSween, A. (forthcoming), 'Changing regional and local identities in the later Neolithic of Scotland as reflected in the ceramic record', in L. D. Campbell, D. Wright and N. Hall (eds), *Roots of Nationhood: The Archaeology and History of Scotland*, London: Springer.

McInnes, I. J. (1969), 'A Scottish Neolithic pottery sequence', *Scottish Archaeological Forum*, 1: 19–30.

McLellan, V. J. (1993), 'Basketry and textile impressions on the Grooved Ware', in Barclay and Russell-White, *Proceedings of the Society of Antiquaries of Scotland*, 123: 108.

Mercer, R. J. (1981), 'The excavation of a Late Neolithic henge-type enclosure at Balfarg, Markinch, Fife, Scotland, 1977–78', *Proceedings of the Society of Antiquaries of Scotland*, 111: 63–171.

Murray, J. C. (2003), 'Fordafourie, Rathen, Fraserburgh (Fraserburgh parish), evaluation', *Discovery Excavation in Scotland*, n.s., 4: 4, 18.

Parker Pearson, M. (ed.) (2003), *Food, Culture and Identity in the Neolithic and Early Bronze Age*, Oxford: Archaeopress.

Phillips, T. and Bradley, R. (2004), 'Developer-funded fieldwork in Scotland, 1990–2003: an overview of the prehistoric evidence', *Proceedings of the Society of Antiquaries of Scotland*, 134: 17–51.

Renfrew, C. (ed.) (1979), *Investigations in Orkney*, London: Thames & Hudson.

Richards, C. (1993), 'Contextual analysis of the Grooved Ware at Balfarg', in

Barclay and Russell-White, *Proceedings of the Society of Antiquaries of Scotland*, 123: 185–92.

Richards, C. (2005), *Dwelling Among the Monuments: Excavations at Barnhouse and Maeshowe*, Cambridge: McDonald Institute.

Richards, C. C. and Thomas, J. S. (1984), 'Ritual activity and structured deposition in later Neolithic Wessex', in R. Bradley and J. Gardiner (eds), *Neolithic Studies: A Review of Some Current Research*, Oxford: British Archaeological Reports, 189–218.

Ritchie, J. N. G. (1974), 'Excavation of the stone circle and cairn at Balbirnie, Fife', *Archaeological Journal*, 131: 1–32.

Ritchie, J. N. G. (1976), 'The Stones of Stenness, Orkney', *Proceedings of the Society of Antiquaries of Scotland*, 107: 1–60.

Ritchie, J. N. G. and Adamson, H. C. (1981), 'Knappers, Dunbartonshire: a reassessment', *Proceedings of the Society of Antiquaries of Scotland*, 111: 197–204.

Schulting, R., Sheridan, A., Crozier, R. and Murphy, E. (2010), 'Revisiting Quanterness: new AMS dates and stable isotope data from an Orcadian chamber tomb', *Proceedings of the Society of Antiquaries of Scotland*, 140: 1–50.

Sheridan, J. A. (1995), 'Irish Neolithic pottery: the story in 1995', in Kinnes and Varndell (eds), *Unbaked Urns of Rudely Shape*, 3–21.

Sheridan, A. (1997), 'Pottery', in Johnston, *Proceedings of the Society of Antiquaries of Scotland*, 127: 202–23.

Sheridan, A. (2004), 'Going round in circles? Understanding the Irish Grooved Ware "complex" in its wider context', in J. Bradley, J. Coles, E. Grogan, B. Raftery and H. Roche (eds), *From Megaliths to Metal: Essays in Honour of George Eogan*, Oxford: Oxbow Books, 25–36.

Sheridan, J. A. (2007), 'From Picardie to Pickering and Pencraig Hill? New information on the "Carinated Bowl Neolithic" in Northern Britain', in A. Whittle and V. Cummings (eds), *Going Over: The Mesolithic–Neolithic Transition in North-West Europe*, Oxford: Oxford University Press, 441–92.

Sheridan, J. A. (2009), 'The pottery', in H. K. Murray, J. C. Murray and S. Fraser (eds), *A Tale of the Unknown Unknowns: A Mesolithic Pit Alignment and a Neolithic Timber Hall at Warren Field, Crathes, Aberdeenshire*, Oxford: Oxbow Books, 81–93.

Strachan, R., Ralston, I. and Finlayson, B. (1998), 'Neolithic and later prehistoric structures at an early medieval metalworking at Blairhall Burn, Amisfield, Dumfriesshire', *Proceedings of the Society of Antiquaries of Scotland*, 128: 55–94.

Thomas, J. (2010), 'The Return of the Rinyo–Clacton folk? The cultural significance of the Grooved Ware complex in later Neolithic Britain', *Cambridge Archaeological Journal*, 20: 1–15.

Thomas, J. (2012), 'Introduction: beyond the mundane?', in Anderson-Whymark and Thomas (eds), *Regional Perspectives on Neolithic Pit Deposition*, 1–12.

Wainwright, G. J., with Longworth, I. H. (1971), *Durrington Walls: Excavations 1966–1968*, London: Thames & Hudson.

Whittle, A. W. R. (1988), *Problems in Neolithic Archaeology*, Cambridge: Cambridge University Press.

Whittle, A. W. R., Healy, F. and Bayliss, A. (2011), *Gathering Time: Dating the Early Neolithic Enclosures of Britain and Ireland*, Oxford: Oxbow Books, 2 vols.

CHAPTER 12

Pursuing the Penumbral: The Deposition of Beaker Pottery at Neolithic and Ceremonial Monuments in Chalcolithic and Early Bronze Age Scotland

Neil Wilkin

Introduction

Beaker pottery has been recovered from a surprisingly large proportion of excavated Scottish Neolithic monuments. Among the approaches taken by those attempting to explain this phenomenon, two are of particular relevance. First, the notion of a newly arrived people or ideology appropriating or staking claims to the 'ancestral' monuments of the indigenous past (e.g., A. Shepherd 1994: 270–1, 283; Armit 1996: 94–5); a claim supported, to some extent, by typological observations (I. Shepherd 1986: 9–10; Morton 1990). Second, more recent, interpretive approaches that are exploring the role of memory and the appropriation of older sites in the (re)construction of social relations and identities (e.g., Jones 2003, 2010; cf. Bradley 2002: 82–111; Hingley 2009). While the former approach provides a coherent – albeit at times somewhat reductive – narrative, it is based on a now outdated understanding of the absolute chronological and typo-chronological sequence of Beaker pottery. Post-processual accounts have recognised the ways in which existing monuments were incorporated into contemporary symbolic schema and the techniques by which identity and remembrance were constructed. They have, however, tended to be suspicious of more traditional approaches to comparing and analysing the data, thereby overlooking detailed chronology of depositional practices and variations in the morphology and decoration of the associated Beaker assemblages that are central to the more contextual approach advocated in this chapter (cf. Hodder and Hutson 2003: 180–3). It will be argued that the significance of depositing Beakers at pre-existing ceremonial monuments changed through time and in relation to contemporary grave good traditions and funerary practices in different regions.

In pursuing a more contextual approach, this chapter has three principal sections. First, analysis of Beaker completeness, decoration, morphology and chronology is presented. Second, Beaker deposition at monuments is reviewed in terms of its nature, location and sequence. In the third section, the resulting patterns are reviewed in order to understand the changing nature of Beaker deposition and what it reveals both about inter-regional connections and the variable ways in which Beakers were combined with more local, enduring and ancient, megalithic and non-megalithic monument traditions. It is worth noting at this early stage that I use the term 'Neolithic and ceremonial monuments' as shorthand for the monuments considered in this study, although differentiation by monument types is made apparent in the analysis at various points and in the Appendix below.

Dataset and distribution

The most authoritative account of Beaker pottery from Neolithic chambered tombs in Scotland remains Audrey Henshall's landmark study of Scottish chambered tombs (1963, 1972, *in passim*, esp. 105–7, 187–91; cf. Henshall and Ritchie 2001, 76–9), while Morton's (1990) unpublished doctoral study addressed the occurrence of Beakers at British henge monuments. An updated overview of the available evidence extended to all recognised pre-existing monument types in Scotland, most of which can be firmly dated to the Neolithic period, is presented in the Appendix. Recumbent Stone Circles have been included in the analysis, although recent dates obtained for Tomnaverie, Aberdeenshire (Appendix, No. 57) by Richard Bradley (2005) indicates a Chalcolithic or Early Bronze Age date for the construction of at least some examples of this type of monument, now supported by a recent dating programme for Hillhead, Tarland, Aberdeenshire (Bradley and Clarke n.d.; R. Bradley pers. comm.; *contra* Curtis and Wilkin 2012: 241–4). A similar point could be made regarding some of the smaller and less well-understood stone circles, henge and henge-like monuments considered below. However, the ceremonial – rather than purely funerary – use of these varied monuments, coupled with the observation that their architecture recalls already ancient Neolithic, megalithic traditions means that they can usefully be considered in the context of pre-existing ceremonial monuments at which Beaker pottery was deposited. The primary focus of this study is therefore Neolithic and Beaker period ceremonial (non-funerary) monuments.

Beakers have now been recovered from over sixty monuments that fit these criteria (Table 12.1, Figure 12.1). This is a significant number: greater, for instance, than the total number of Beaker burials in the archaeologically rich regions, such as east-central Scotland, and rivalling the 'heartland' regions of Aberdeenshire for overall number of vessels represented (cf. I. Shepherd 1986), although many are very fragmentary and from disturbed contexts. It serves to underline the need to re-adjust the disproportionate attention given to the study of Beaker pottery *per se* and Beaker funerary practices. However, it is important not to over-privilege the occurrence of Beakers at pre-existing monuments as a consequence: they also occur

Table 12.1 Number of sites with Beaker vessels arranged by monument type (number of Beaker vessels is not available for all sites, see Appendix for details).

Site type	No. of sites	No. of vessels	Av. No. of vessels per site
Chambered Cairn & Long Cairn	32	87	2.75
Non-megalithic Long Mound	4	17	4.25
Non-megalithic Round Mound	5	17	3.4
Recumbent Stone Circle	4	7	1.75
Stone Circle/Cairns	2	3	1.5
Henge & related monuments	7	38	5.5
Other	4	4	1

in a number of other contexts, including pits and surface scatters, which, although not fully addressed in this contribution, are likely to be under-represented due to their ephemeral nature and judging from Irish Beaker deposition (Carlin 2011), revealed in part by the recent spate of developer-funded excavations there. Connections between some of these non-funerary contexts are discussed below, and future discoveries are likely to further illuminate the similarities and differences between them.

The composition of the dataset has changed considerably since the early 1970s, when almost all recorded sites were chambered tombs. Around twenty sites relevant to my study have been excavated in the intervening decades, and sixteen of these have been non-megalithic. This change has interpretative implications as several of the non-megalithic monuments lack enduring, accessible architecture and may not have been associated with funerary practices, either in their primary use or in later appropriations.

It is important to stress that many of the Neolithic monuments under study were constructed centuries prior to the deposition of Beaker pottery at them (cf. Sheridan 2007a, 2010). Traditionally it was assumed that the use of many monuments for Neolithic communal burial could have been fol-lowed shortly or directly by the adoption of Beaker practices (e.g., Piggott and Powell 1949: 124; Ritchie 1973: 45–6), and therefore this sequence required no special explanation in terms of the political and socio-cultural conditions that initiated a return to depositional practices at these sites after a potentially significant hiatus. The assumption of continuity was perhaps exacerbated by the geographical occurrence of many of these finds: on the northern and western edges of Beaker distributions. There has been a ten-dency to see the Beaker phenomenon as spreading from south to north and east to west (e.g., Crichton-Mitchell 1934: 160; Gibson 1984: 91; Bayliss *et al.* 2007), an assumption that has been questioned by recent discoveries and early dates from western Scotland (Sheridan 2007b: 96–8; Sheridan 2008) and the absence of considerable numbers of Beaker burials in some regions of eastern Scotland (Curtis and Wilkin 2012). The significance of deposition

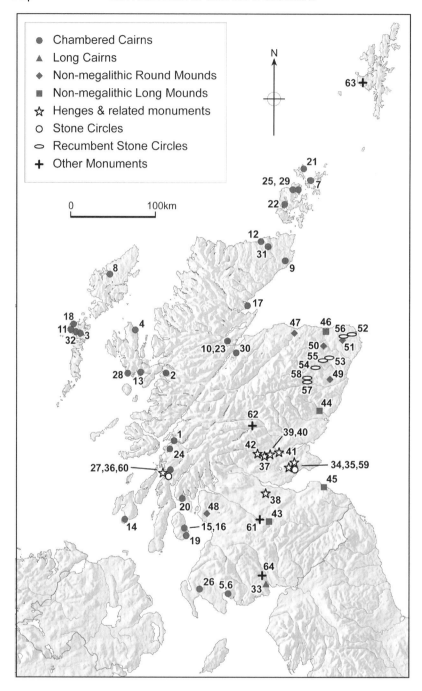

Figure 12.1 Distribution of Neolithic and Chalcolithic/Early Bronze Age ceremonial monument types producing Beaker pottery in Scotland (see Appendix for details).

at pre-existing monuments has rarely been explored without recourse to these traditional, evolutionary approaches.

In terms of overall distribution, deposits at non-megalithic monuments are largely from the eastern lowlands, while deposits from chambered tombs – unsurprising given the distribution of this monument type (Henshall and Ritchie 2001: fig. 4) – are from the Moray Firth region and the west coast, including the Western and Northern Isles (Figure 12.1). This distribution can also be related to the general differential uptake of Beaker short cist burial and to the importance of regionality and long-standing cultural and cosmological principles across Scotland during the later third millennium cal. BC (Jones 2003, 2010; Wilkin 2009; Curtis and Wilkin 2012).

The chronology of Beaker deposits from Neolithic and ceremonial monuments

Although the number of radiocarbon dates for Beaker short cists has increased sharply in the last decade (Sheridan 2007b; Curtis *et al.* 2007; Wilkin *et al.* 2009), the number of dated non-funerary contexts remains relatively small. Five sites have produced recent, relevant, high-quality radiocarbon dates (Appendix: Nos 1, 35, 45.1–4, 55, 64). Perhaps most significantly, the dates from Eweford, East Lothian, are not particularly early (i.e., post-2200 cal. BC) despite the presence of Low-Carinated profiles and All Over Cord (AOC) decoration: features commonly of Chalcolithic date when associated with funerary practices (Needham 2005: 183–8). This suggests that these deposits occurred while short cist burials, incorporating very different Beakers, were simultaneously taking place nearby (see dates in Sheridan 2007b). Indeed, there is a growing body of evidence for the chronological and contextual variability of AOC vessels, including some Low-Carinated examples (*ibid.*: 105), although processes of curation or rediscovery cannot be ruled out.

Several points emerge from improvements in typo-chronology: the burial from Biggar Common, South Lanarkshire (Appendix: No. 43) is likely to date to the Chalcolithic on comparison with Dutch Beaker burials (Sheridan 2008: 253), as may some of the (few) Short-Necked vessels (e.g., Appendix: No. 38.2, 46; cf. Sheridan 2007b; Curtis and Wilkin 2012). The date from Achnacreebeag, Argyll and Bute, accords with English and Welsh Long Necked Beakers dating firmly to the Early Bronze Age (Needham 2005: 195–8), with similar decorative motifs (bar-chevrons: Clarke's (1970) motif group 4, nos 32–3) and hints at Irish Sea connections with regions further to the south. Other Long-Necked vessels are also likely to date to *c.* 2200–1900 cal. BC (Appendix: Nos 13, 24, 28, 36, 38.1), while Weak-Carinated and Beaker/Food Vessel hybrids (Appendix: Nos 42.1, 44, 50) are likely to date slightly later in the sequence (i.e., from the twenty-first century cal. BC).

The significance of these dates for understanding the sequence of depositional practices at monuments will be outlined in the course of this chapter.

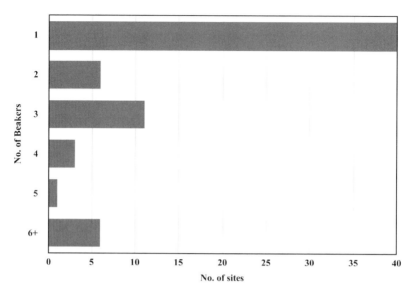

Figure 12.2 The frequency of numbers of Beakers found at monuments of all
categories in Scotland.

At present, it can be noted that they do not sit within a narrow date range
nor are they particularly early. Mismatches between typology and chronology (most notably reported in Kinnes *et al.* 1991) have been viewed by
many researchers as evidence for the ineffectiveness of existing typological
schemes. It is increasingly clear that we have only recently obtained anywhere near the number of high-quality radiocarbon dates required to convincingly critique and construct typo-chronological schemes (cf. Brindley
2007). In doing so, context as much as chronology will be important in
defining reliable and meaningful typo-chronologies (I. Shepherd, in Kinnes
et al. 1991: 72–3; Needham 2005: 174). For instance, it will be argued
that the distinction between Long-Necked (angular-necked) vessels and
Low-Carinated and more 'S'-Profiled vessels (non-angular) can be meaningfully related to chronological and contextual factors (i.e., association with
funerary and non-funerary practices). Conclusions such as this can be drawn
from detailed analysis of a range of traits.

Analysis of Beaker pottery from Neolithic and
ceremonial monuments

Number, size and completeness of Beakers

The number of recovered Beaker vessels varies between single examples to up to twelve vessels from Geirisclett chambered cairn, North Uist

(Appendix: No. 18), and probably in excess of twenty-eight vessels from Balfarg Riding School, Fife (Appendix: No. 34), in various degrees of completeness (Figure 12.2; and see Chapter 11, this volume). The presence of single vessels may put one in mind of funerary contexts and in nine cases they represent whole vessels accompanying burials, but a high proportion of sites were associated with either a handful of sherds or three or more Beakers and this appears to reflect different (and possibly more prolonged) depositional practices than so-called closed Beaker burial deposits. The proportions of vessels are also notable: several assemblages (e.g., Appendix: Nos 13, 27–8, 34.1–4, 40.1–4) include vessels that are substantially taller than the average height of Scottish short cist Beakers (approximately 165 mm, based on a sample of fifty-six complete or restored vessels from north-east Scotland), suggesting that at least some were drawn from a different range of vessels and possibly reflecting functional differences (cf. Clarke 1970: 59), a point further discussed below in relation to the recurrence of cordoned necks and the character of depositional practices.

The vast majority of the Beakers from Neolithic and ceremonial monuments (over 70 per cent) were less than a quarter complete, often considerably less so, including those excavated in recent years to modern standards (e.g., Appendix: Nos 18, 45, 57, 58). Almost all of the complete vessels were recovered from burials inserted into monuments, with the exception of Hill of Foulzie long cairn, Aberdeenshire (Appendix: No. 46), where the depositional context is unclear. Several of these vessels are late Beakers, suggesting a chronological dimension to the presence of Beaker burials at pre-existing, ceremonial sites.

The sherds recovered from pits close to the long mound at Eweford West, East Lothian (Appendix: No. 45; Sheridan 2007c) appear to decrease in size and increase in degree of abrasion relative to their proximity to the monument. The pre-pit depositional activity at this site was apparently complex, but relatively unabraded sherds were deposited in one pit, some distance from the monument (Appendix: No. 45). Similarly, many of the sherds from the Balfarg Riding School assemblage (Appendix: No. 34.1–4) were abraded and burnt at some stage after their initial firing (Cowie 1993: 1B:13–1C7), as were several deposits from chambered tombs (e.g., Henshall 1963: 110, 216; 1972: 414). These observations appear to relate to complex (pre-)depositional practices (cf. Garrow 2006: 119–38, 152–3). Beaker pottery at monuments may have been left with the intention that it was visible and accessible, sometimes for later depositional events but equally to be carried away or added to from 'domestic' middens. In other words, while later disturbance may account for displacement, for instance, within the chambers of tombs, other processes, including the removal of sherds or the selective deposition of vessels that were already fragmentary, appear to have taken place.

Table 12.2 The number of cases of particular decorative techniques being found in combination with one or more others on Beakers from site assemblages (X = number uncertain; see Appendix 1 for further details).

Appendix No./Site name	Incision	Undecor.	AOComb	AOC	Shell	Complex comb	Stab/ jab	Other
6: Cairnholy II	–	–	2	2	–	–	1	–
17: Embo	–	–	1	1	–	1	–	–
22: Howe	–	–	–	–	1	–	–	1
23: Kilcoy South	–	–	2	4	–	–	1	–
24: Kilmore	3	–	1	–	–	1	–	1
25: Knowe of Yarso	3	–	–	–	–	–	–	–
27: Nether Largie	–	–	2	1	–	2	–	–
38.1: Cairnpapple	–	1	–	–	–	1	1	–
40: Forteviot, henge 2	–	X	X	X	–	–	–	–
34: Balfarg Riding School	–	X	X	X	–	–	–	–
41: Moncrieffe	–	–	–	1	–	1	–	–
47: Boghead	1	1	–	1	–	–	–	–
50: Midtown of Pitglassie	1	1	–	1	–	–	–	1
43: Biggar Common	–	1	1	1	–	–	–	–
45.1: Eweford West	–	–	1	1	–	–	–	2
45.2: Eweford West	2	1	–	–	–	–	–	–
45.3: Eweford West	–	1	1	–	–	–	–	–
45.4: Eweford West	–	1	–	–	–	1	–	–
57: Tomnaverie	1	–	–	–	–	2	–	–
1: *Achnacreebeag*	4	1	–	–	–	–	–	1
3: Barpa Langass	2	1	–	–	–	–	–	–
4: Cadha Riach	2	1	–	–	–	–	–	–
11: Clettravel	6	–	–	–	2	–	–	–
12: Cnoc Na H–Uiseig	–	–	–	1	–	–	1	1
18: Geirisclett	3	4	1	3	–	–	–	–
19: Giant's Graves	1	–	–	–	–	1	–	1
20: Glecknabae	1	1	1	–	–	–	–	1

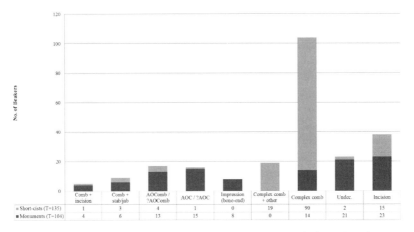

	Comb + incision	Comb + stab/jab	AOComb / ?AOComb	AOC / ?AOC	Impression (bone-end)	Complex comb + other	Complex comb	Undec.	Incision
◼ Short-cists (T=135)	1	3	4	1	0	19	90	2	15
◼ Monuments (T=104)	4	6	13	15	8	0	14	21	23

Figure 12.3 Histogram illustrating differences in decorative techniques found on Beakers from Neolithic and Chalcolithic/Early Bronze Age monuments and Beaker short cist burials from eastern Scotland. (NB: only techniques found on five or more Beakers are included.)

Decorative techniques on Beakers from monuments and funerary contexts

The decorative techniques used on Beakers from Neolithic and ceremonial monuments are relatively simple and standardised: featuring all-over decoration without complex motifs and relatively large or entirely undecorated surfaces, and similar combinations within assemblages (Table 12.2). They therefore contrast strongly with the decoration of the more complete funerary Beakers from short cist burials; a study of examples from eastern Scotland provides a useful comparative study (personal dataset). Beakers with complex, toothcomb-impressed motifs (termed 'complex' comb hereafter), frequently organised in linear zones (i.e., Clarke's motif groups 2–5 (1970: 425–8) and basic style zones a–e (*ibid.*: 12)), feature among the assemblages of only approximately 13 per cent of the Neolithic and ceremonial monuments associated with Beaker pottery. By contrast, 'complex' comb occurs on approximately 81 per cent of the Beakers from short cists (Figure 12.3). The significance of this contrast can only be fully understood with reference to morphology and chronology, discussed below. However, it is notable that the degree of completeness is matched by decorative complexity. Beakers with 'complex' comb motifs were deposited whole in burials to be visible to mourners during the limited time-scale of the funeral (cf. Thomas 1991) when their form and decoration as well as other prescribed (possibly secretive) information were conveyed; for instance, the particular gender-specific alignment and posture of the body (A. Shepherd 1989, 2012). No provision was made for the integrity of vessels from monuments and their frequent all-over decoration means that they continued to be easily readable despite the fragmentary state in which they were deposited. Beakers scattered or deposited in fragments may have provided effective markers of the presence of Beaker-using groups, perhaps to a wider audience (cf. Sharples 2009) or as part of less individualistic rituals, and this may help to account for why AOC and AOComb decorated Beakers were considered appropriate for deposition at the sites under study.

The combination of decorative techniques within assemblages of two or more vessels is notable, suggesting a broad division between assemblages with vessels that were undecorated, but also featured vessels decorated by incision, AOC or AOComb; and assemblages featuring vessels of both AOC and AOComb as well as stab/jab impression or 'complex' comb. This apparent divide appears to relate to regional preferences: with sites from the Inner and Outer Hebrides associated with the former and the east-central lowlands and Moray Firth region associated with the latter. As intimated above, these differences, between lowland Scotland and the Hebrides, also relate to the differential adoption of Beaker funerary practices and suggest the existence of complex 'blends' of practices, with regional and contextual dimensions that require further attention (cf. Wilkin 2011).

The combination of decorative and morphological properties may have been significant in both funerary and non-funerary practices. For instance, there are contrasts between incised and 'complex' comb decoration on the multiple vessels from burials containing both adults and children/infants in the north-east of Scotland. Examples of this include Cruden, Aberdeenshire (Kenworthy 1977); Dunnottar, Aberdeenshire (Kirk and McKenzie 1955); and Balblair, Highland (Hanley and Sheridan 1994). These differences may have been used in the expression and negotiation of identities within the funerary context. In the case of the monuments under study, the pit deposits at the non-megalithic mounded monuments at Eweford West (Appendix: No. 45) and Boghead, Aberdeenshire (Appendix: No. 47) contained vessels with a range of decorative techniques, forms and sizes. A similar combination occurs in a pit deposit from Elginhaugh, Midlothian, where a single, very large, rusticated and cordoned Beaker was used to line the base of a pit into which a fill containing sherds of at least four, finer, mostly AOC-decorated vessels and cereal grains was deposited (MacGregor, in Hanson 2007: 22–5, 516–22). In this context, differences may not relate to interpersonal differences, but rather to different vessels serving different functional roles within ritual and everyday practices (e.g., serving, eating and drinking; cf. Rojo-Guerra et al. 2006: 253–62, fig. 9).

The evidence for completeness and abrasion reviewed above suggests that in many cases vessels were not deposited directly into pits, but rather may have lain exposed for some time or were deposited in fragments. The practice of making Beakers may be considered in terms of distinct levels of access and control. In contrast to burials, surface and chamber deposits could have been revisited and explored, and may therefore have served to consolidate and maintain the homogeneity of the non-fine ware components of the tradition. The study of decorative techniques thus reveals differences between funerary and non-funerary deposition. A contrast can be proposed between bounded, single burials with whole 'complex' comb vessels and fragmentary, more generically decorated vessels involved in more functional and communal events at pre-existing works of communal labour, a point that can be further explored with reference to morphology and chronology.

Morphology of Beakers from monuments and funerary contexts

The distinction between neck and body is particularly important in identifying morphological variability among British Beakers. As Needham has noted (2005: 198), the distinction between angular and 'S'-Profile necks was within the control of Beaker producers and provides a useful marker of intentional variation. In the case of Beakers from monuments, attempts to analyse this relationship has unfortunately been hampered by the high frequency of fragmentation. Nevertheless, the vessels that can be reconstructed indicate that vessels with distinct angles between neck and body (e.g., Needham's (2005) Short-Necked and Long-Necked types, and Beakers with elongated necks) were considerably less common than non-angular necked vessels (e.g., Needham's (2005) Low-Carinated and 'S'-Profile types) at the monuments under study compared with short cists (just 28 per cent compared with 72 per cent; Figure 12.4). This impression is reinforced by the fact that thirteen of the vessels that cannot be reconstructed probably carry AOC decoration and are therefore unlikely to be from angular-necked vessels, compared with only four carrying complex, banded comb decoration, which are likely to derive from necked vessels. In notable contrast, Beakers from short cists in eastern Scotland are mostly of the angular-necked variety (approximately 70 per cent of vessels; Figure 12.4). Furthermore, twenty-four of thirty-eight (63 per cent) of the Beakers with non-angular necks from short cists are not decorated with 'complex' comb, but instead feature other techniques, frequently incision. There is, therefore, a notable difference in the morphology of Beakers from these respective contexts and this extends to an additional feature of form that provides evidence for functional differences: the presence of cordoned necks.

Cordons applied to the necks of vessels are a feature of around a quarter of the assemblages from Neolithic and ceremonial monuments. They are associated with vessels with non-angular profiles (just under half of which have cordons) and primarily feature incision, AOC and AOComb decoration. Cordons also appear selectively on the necks of funerary Beakers; Clarke (1970: 53) interpreted them as features of domestic ware, used to secure an organic cover and they are relatively common among non-angular

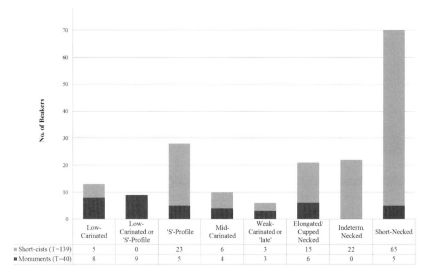

	Low-Carinated	Low-Carinated or 'S'-Profile	'S'-Profile	Mid-Carinated	Weak-Carinated or 'late'	Elongated/Cupped Necked	Indeterm. Necked	Short-Necked
■ Short-cists (T=139)	5	0	23	6	3	15	22	65
■ Monuments (T=40)	8	9	5	4	3	6	0	5

Figure 12.4 Histogram illustrating differences in Beaker typology from Neolithic and Chalcolithic/Early Bronze Age monuments and Beaker short cist burials from eastern Scotland. (NB: only types with five or more examples are included. Seventy-five vessels from monuments are too fragmentary to allow identification of form. Key: Carin: Carinated; Cup: Cupped; Neck: Necked.)

AOC vessels from sand-dune scatters, interpreted as the results of domestic activity (McInnes 1964: 54–6; Clarke 1970: no. 1808, fig. 52; Gibson 1982: 410–11). Clarke also noted that vessels with cordons could be considerably larger than other AOC vessels (1970: 52), and suggested that their size also related to their function as storage vessels. However, the set of diminutive cordoned vessels deposited at Glecknabae, Argyll and Bute, chambered cairn suggest that this does not fully explain the occurrence of cordons. The cordoned vessels from Balbirnie stone circle, Fife (Appendix: No. 59), and another from a burial at Kirkcaldy in Fife (Clarke 1970: no. 1014), were in direct association with rich grave goods of jet and bronze. Indeed, when cordons occur on angular-necked/'complex' comb vessels they are frequently associated with the richest burials with elements of the Beaker archery package (Shepherd, in Ralston 1996: 145), and this may indicate something of their symbolic as well as their functional significance. Rather than focusing on the function of the cordon we should consider its presence in terms of selection from a wider assemblage of available vessels and the ideological significance of that choice. The functional character of the Beakers noted above was perhaps required for the more communal character of the rituals in which they were deposited; if so, this suggests a degree of coherence between rituals carried out at the sites under study.

In summary, the decorative technique and morphology of Beakers from ceremonial monuments and short cist burials have been shown to differ in notable ways. This comment may seem unremarkable, but it has rarely been made and its implications have not been addressed outwith evolutionary cultural–historical models based on the transition from Neolithic communal practices to Beaker single burial and Beaker ideology and culture. It has been argued that Beakers from Neolithic monuments do not belong to a particular, early phase and include fragments (often from assemblages of three or more) from non-angular necked vessels, with all-over decoration, often with cordons, which may have had different, perhaps less individualistic or personal, significance than those from funerary contexts. The presence of cordons in a considerable proportion of the assemblages may relate to the functional use of vessels deposited at monuments – also indicated by their size. The association of cordons with, on the one hand funerary Beakers from monuments, and on the other with rich grave goods however suggests we should consider their ideological significance.

The character of Beaker deposition at Neolithic and ceremonial monuments

Beaker deposition occurs in three principal suites of contexts: chamber and blocking deposits, secondary burials, and earth-cut features (pits, ditches and post-holes) (Table 12.3).

Table 12.3 Beaker from Neolithic and Chalcolithic/Early Bronze Age monuments arranged by type of deposit. (Note: Several types of deposits are associated with some monuments: the number of monuments in each sample is shown in parenthesis; see Table 12.1 for abbreviations.)

Type of deposit (No. of sites)	CT & LC (33)	NM (9)	LM/RM	H (9)	RSC (7)	SC/C (2)	O (4)	TOTAL (64)
Pit deposit	–	5		1	1	–	1	8
Ditch fill	–	–		4	–	–	–	4
Postholes	–	–		6	–	–	1	7
Scatter	–	1		–	3	–	1	5
Cairn material	–	–		–	–	1	1	2
Chamber fill	24	–		–	–	–	–	24
Chamber 'blocking'	4	–		–	–	–	–	4
Secondary burial	8	3		6	1	2	–	20
Disturbed/redeposited	2	1		2	–	1	–	6
Uncertain/other	1	3		1	1	–	–	6

Chamber and blocking deposits

Chambered tombs make up around a half of the sites considered in this study, and Beakers were deposited in the chambers in the majority of cases (Table 12.3). The practices associated with these deposits are difficult to reconstruct as many tombs have been disturbed and few have been excavated to modern standards. In several cases, Beaker pottery appears to have been associated with the blocking of the chamber (Appendix: Nos 1, 5, 24, 27, 28, 32). Perhaps due to the impoverished chronological framework and the disproportionate attention given to burial, Beaker pottery from Neolithic chambered tombs has traditionally been associated with the wider transformation of communal to individual burial practices (e.g., Henshall 1972: 191; Armit 1996: 95). But it is too simplistic to associate this practice with Beaker users without clear stratigraphic or dating evidence, and some blocking events clearly took place during the Neolithic. The sealing of the tomb at Papa Westray, Orkney (Appendix: No. 21) took place during the Late Neolithic and was associated with Grooved Ware pottery (Ritchie 2009: 34). In the case of Achnacreebeag, Argyll and Bute, Kilmore, Argyll and Bute, and Rubh' An Dunain, Highland, the blocking was associated with deposits of human remains and may have formed part of funerary practices (Appendix: Nos 1, 24, 28). In two cases (Achnacreebeag and Kilmore) this involved cremated bone and not short cist or formal single burial. As noted above, the Achnacreebeag Beakers are of Early Bronze Age date, post-dating the earliest Beaker burials in western Scotland by a considerable margin (cf. Henshall 1972: 191). We cannot easily associate the blocking of all chambered tombs with the arrival of new ideas and individual burial practices as if the practice occurred uniformly or naturally across Britain.

An approach that does not over-generalise the evidence, but is also sensitive to what unites these deposits is required. Although the sealing of chamber passages with material may exaggerate the relative importance of Beaker pottery compared with earlier and later ceramics (Armit 1996: 95), blocking would not have physically prevented later excavation of the chambers or deposition at or around chambered tombs; yet this type of (especially non-funerary) deposit is rare. Indeed, we may recall that, of all Neolithic and Bronze Age ceramics, Beakers were among the most highly decorated and were most closely associated with a formalised set of rules regarding how they should be deposited. In this context even non-funerary vessels may have required careful deposition and the chambers of ancient tombs may have provided suitable settings. Beaker pottery and associated paraphernalia (e.g., barbed-and-tanged arrowheads and stone wristguards) have also been discovered within Irish Neolithic court and passage tombs on a relatively regular basis (Carlin 2011). Although disturbance and lack of sealed deposits prevents a clear picture regarding how the artefacts were deposited (*ibid.*), it raises the possibility of a connection between Beaker practices in east-central and western Scotland and Ireland, one that is further demonstrated during the Early Bronze Age, for instance, through Food Vessel pottery and bronze dagger burials (e.g., Cressey and Sheridan 2003: 80; Curtis and Wilkin 2012: 246–8). The significance of this connection in the context of the systems that emerged around early bronze metalwork from the twenty-second century is further discussed below.

Secondary burials

There are eight definite or possible burials from chambered tombs, of which four are associated with typo-chronologically late vessels, with Long necks and/or bar-chevron motifs that, as noted above, are likely to date to after the twenty-second century cal. BC (Appendix: Nos 1, 13, 15, 28). The exception to this is the Tall Mid-Carinated Beaker from Nether Largie South, Argyll and Bute (Appendix: No. 27), excavated by Greenwell who assumed it was associated with human remains from a nearby, disturbed cist within the chamber (Greenwell 1866: 345). However, Henshall (1972: 82) casts doubt on the association and Greenwell is unlikely to have been familiar with non-funerary uses of Beaker pottery. For Piggott and Powell (1949: 109, 120), the presence of Beaker sherds on the paving of the antechamber of Cairnholy I, Dumfries and Galloway, was also sufficient evidence to claim that Beaker burial had taken place. More recently, similar claims have been made about the Beakers from Calanais and Geirisclett, both in the Western Isles, despite the lack of clear evidence for their original association (Appendix: Nos 8, 18).

In short, although Beakers were associated with funerary practices at chambered tombs, the evidence is limited and unsubstantiated. Furthermore, the form and decoration of vessels deposited in several of the chambered tombs where burial is inferred rather than demonstrated are similar (with non-angular profiles and AOC/Comb) to vessels deposited in non-funerary contexts at non-megalithic monuments, including henge enclosures, where there has been less opportunity for post-depositional disturbance.

Several burials were made at henge monuments, and the associated Beakers appear to date to after the twenty-second century cal. BC, including Long-Necked, Handled and Beaker-Food Vessel hybrid vessels, as well as perhaps the intentional re-deposition of Beaker sherds with Food Vessel burials (Appendix: Nos 17, 40.4). The probable Beaker cremation burial from within Old Rayne recumbent stone circle, Aberdeenshire (Appendix: No. 54) is also not especially early (2210–1950 cal. BC at 95.4 per cent probability; 3690±45 BP (GrA-23982)). Several burials are also recorded from non-megalithic long mounds and these, including a Beaker Food Vessel from Dalladies long barrow, Aberdeenshire (Appendix: No. 44) and Eweford West long barrow, where sherds of three different vessels were interpreted as having been disturbed and re-deposited with a cremation burial (MacGregor and Stuart 2007: 114). The radiocarbon date from this burial is, again, not particularly early (3725 ± 35 BP (SUERC-5309); 2280–2020 cal. BC at 95.4 per cent probability). Burial at Neolithic and primarily ceremonial monuments therefore appears to have occurred generally *after* the twenty-second century BC.

The burial inserted into the Neolithic long mound on Biggar Common, is, however, likely to be notably earlier (Appendix: No. 43) and is comparable with the early dating burial at Upper Largie, Kilmartin (Cook *et al.* 2010) in being associated with an important pre-existing ceremonial landscape. The implications of the chronological dislocation of these episodes of funerary practice discussed above, positioned at either end of the Beaker period, are further discussed below.

Pits, ditches and post-holes

Beakers deposited in pits are relatively rare, accounting for under 10 per cent of all deposits at pre-existing and ceremonial monuments (Table 12.3, Figure 12.5), with half of this number from a single site, Eweford West

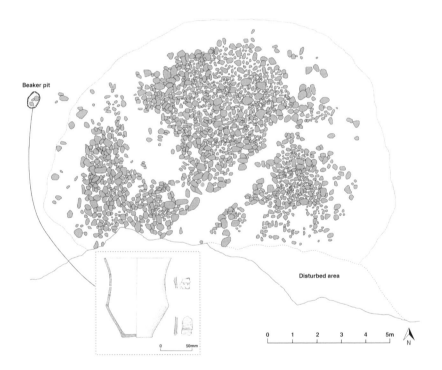

Figure 12.5 Beaker deposit at the non-megalithic round cairn at Boghead, Fochabers (Appendix: No. 47) (after Burl 1984: figs 2 and 11).

(Appendix: No. 45). This may indicate a reluctance to dig into monuments or to deposit Beakers in pits outwith funerary practices. Perhaps surprisingly, recovery from pre-existing earth-cut features (ditch fills and the upper fills of post-holes) is just as common as from pit deposits. At Balfarg Riding School enclosure a very large assemblage of primarily AOC vessels was recovered, mostly from the upper fills of the enclosure ditch but also from several other features, including the upper fills of a post-hole (Appendix: Nos 34.1–4). The excavators argued that the location of the Beaker sherds was fortuitous, and that their survival was because the surrounding surface had been destroyed by modern ploughing, although they note that this material may have been cleared into the extant hollow of the ditch (Barclay and Russell-White 1993: 127). At Forteviot henge 2, a comparable pattern of deposition was recorded: relatively large and fresh sherds of AOC Beaker were recovered from the lower ditch fills, possibly from a vessel smashed *in situ* (Brophy and Noble 2012). Other, similar, sherds were recovered from the upper fills of several post-holes (Appendix: Nos 40.2–4). These appear to represent intentional deposits, and the absence of evidence for disturbance to the upper fills suggests that they may have been intentionally placed (*ibid.*). Beaker sherds were also recovered from the hollow of a rotted post at North Mains henge (Appendix: No. 42.2).

Morton (1990: 368–70) identified the practice of re-using and re-cutting ditches and post-holes for the deposition of Beaker pottery at Scottish and English henge monuments. This observation supports the notion that people were either reluctant to cut into ancient (perhaps sacred) ground or were unconcerned with making their presence known through the act of pit cutting and filling. As noted above, on the rare occasions that Beakers were deposited in new pits, they were rarely whole pots, but rather included fragmentary vessels that varied in size and decoration, reflecting selective and/or complex pre-depositional behaviour.

In discussing attitudes to deposition at Beaker settlement sites in the Western Isles, Sharples (2009) suggests that Beaker pottery was intentionally scattered on machair soils in order to enculturate and control soil stability as part of the expansive ideology of Beaker people. The argument is strengthened by the absence of similar deposits of ceramics from earlier or later horizons at these sites (*ibid.*: 156). The evidence reviewed above indicating fragmentary and generally secondary deposition of Beaker sherds in negative features, can be matched by non-funerary Beaker practices in other regions (e.g., Garrow 2006: 119–38; Carlin 2011: 88–90). The surface scattering of broken vessels identified by Sharples is perhaps the product of a wider attitude to Beaker pre-depositional and depositional practices that resulted in them relatively rarely being interred either intact or in newly cut pits. The stone-lined short cists of northern Beaker burials may reflect an understanding that complete Beakers, as much as the associated bodies, required suitable containment and ritual circumstance if they were to be deposited intact below the soil.

In summarising this section it is useful to recall Ritchie's (1973: 45–6) suggestion that the deposition of Beakers at chambered tombs occurred in three contexts: during collective burial, during 'filling and blocking' of the chamber and afterwards, as secondary deposits. It was argued above that the evidence for collective burial with Beakers is in fact limited and that the notion that the blocking of chambered tombs was directly associated with Beaker pottery is also difficult to demonstrate. Recent discoveries, and the consistency in the decoration, form and completeness of the ceramics noted in the preceding sections instead suggest that Beaker deposition was the culmination of more complex non-funerary practices than Ritchie allowed in the case of material associated with chambered cairns. These practices were surrounded by certain prescriptions regarding where and how this pottery could be deposited. Although such deposits remain difficult to interpret, they provide an opportunity to explore the similarities and differences in the deposition of Beaker pottery across space and time. Secondary burials formed an important component of activity at older monuments, but apparently only early and late in the Beaker period.

Discussion: regional, chronological and contextual factors

On the basis of the preceding analysis, three types of chronologically specific Beaker ceramic deposits at Neolithic and contemporary ceremonial monuments can be proposed:

Chalcolithic funerary practices

Occasional burials with Low-Carinated Beakers at or close to Neolithic monuments of various types have been identified (Biggar Common (Appendix: No. 42); Upper Largie, Kilmartin; Courthill, Ayrshire (Appendix: No. 47)). It is possible that the burial from the ring-cairn at Sundayswells, Aberdeenshire (Coles 1906: 312–13) should be included in this category. Another burial, from Newmill, near Bankfoot, Perth and Kinross, was associated with a contemporary Continental-style ring-ditch and earth-cut grave, but was seemingly not related to pre-existing monuments (Watkins and Shepherd 1981). The burial with a Low-Carinated vessel and early isotopic date from Sorisdale, Coll, was cut through a midden deposit (associated with undecorated Beaker sherds) and was closely associated with a curvilinear stone setting, similar in form to Beaker houses in the Outer Hebrides (Ritchie and Crawford 1978; Sheridan 2007b: 109).

While the funerary architecture and Beakers from the burial at Upper Largie have close Continental parallels (Sheridan 2008; Cook *et al.* 2010:

197–8), the burial from Biggar Common shared a Neolithic long mound with a Late Neolithic burial with a stone Seamer-type axehead (Sheridan 1992: 205–6), the long-standing relevance of which may have been echoed in the unusual inclusion of a polished stone axehead in the Beaker grave assemblage (Johnston 1997: 242). There is, therefore, some evidence for indigenous input and negotiation in the adoption of the earliest Beaker burial practices and their landscape settings. The association may have given Beaker practices and practitioners a degree of continuity and gravitas. These practices are in contrast to later Beaker short cist burials with a new range of Beakers which were seemingly placed in locations not marked by earlier monument construction of other discernible activities.

Chalcolithic / Early Bronze Age non-funerary deposits

It was argued above that the evidence for Beaker burial at Neolithic monuments has been over-stated, perhaps due to assumptions regarding continuity and chronology, and to biases of discovery. Fragments of Beakers appear to have been deposited after complex pre-depositional activities that may have included storage and domestic activities during the Chalcolithic and Early Bronze Age, even as Beakers of other varieties (many with angular necks and complex/banded toothcomb decoration) were being placed in contemporary non-monumentalised short cist burials (from the twenty-third century cal. BC).

The recent discovery of AOC sherds from Low-Carinated or 'S'-Profiled vessels from primary fills at Forteviot henge 2 (Brophy and Noble 2012) suggests a connection between classes of monument and material culture that are usually seen as distinct cultural markers. The similarity of deposits at Balfarg Riding School and in or near several other henge-like monuments in east-central Scotland (Belhie, Moncrieffe, Lundin Farm; Appendix: Nos 37, 41, 62) indicate the existence of regionally specific understandings of how and where Beaker pottery could be used and deposited, and the continued relevance of already ancient ceremonial 'hubs' during the Chalcolithic and Early Bronze Age.

Thus, pre-existing and ceremonial monuments may have provided suitable contexts for local communities to engage with Beaker pottery (and associated ideas and ideology), while also communing with the continued significance of their own, regionally specific identities (cf. Carlin 2011; Carlin and Brück 2012). They provided one of a range of contexts (including pits and surface scatters) at which it was appropriate to deposit Beaker pottery given the genuine novelty of these finely made and highly ornate ceramics and their close association with formalised and ritualised practices in other spheres, most notably in funerary practices.

The shared features of form and decoration, identified in the above analysis, indicate the transfer of ritual knowledge through inter-regional relations in a comparable way to the northern British, east coast Beaker burial network that connected regions such as Aberdeenshire, East Lothian and eastern Yorkshire through shared funerary practices (body posture and alignment) and angular-necked, elaborately toothcomb decorated Beakers (A. Shepherd 1989, 2012; Wilkin 2011). Both may have involved Beaker practices in the expression of distinct networks of social/cultural relations and distinct interpretations of what Beaker pottery meant. It is possible that the more uniform decorative styles and functional features (especially cordons) of Beakers from communally constructed monuments relates to a more ceremonial and less individualistic ideology than expressed in funerary practices.

It is notable that the twenty-second century cal. BC marked the introduction of tin–bronze in Scotland, from sources in Ireland (Needham 2004), and ceremonial monuments may have become important in controlling redistribution, a claim supported by the distribution of flat-riveted bronze dagger burials (Curtis and Wilkin 2012: 247–9). The evidence discussed above highlights a shared tradition of Beaker deposition at pre-existing and recent monuments that linked Ireland, the Moray Firth region, east-central and western Scotland. This may be a further manifestation of synchronisation and exchange between Scotland and Ireland in terms of both material resources and funerary practices during the Early Bronze Age (Cressey and Sheridan 2003: 80; Needham 2004; cf. Brindley 2007: 332–5, fig. 153).

Early Bronze Age funerary practices

The introduction of a new range of Beaker vessels in funerary contexts (late or Weak-Carinated) is closely associated with the re-use of existing ceremonial monuments and the construction of related cairns and barrows from the twenty-second century cal. BC (Bradley 2000; Wilkin 2009: 110–21; cf. Garwood 2007). It has been argued that dense clusters of Beaker short cist burials with angular-necked vessels in certain regions of Scotland (most notably Aberdeenshire and East Lothian) represented a privileged inter-regional network of shared ritual practices that extended beyond Scotland (cf. A. Shepherd 1989, 2012). It is notable that the exclusion of east-central Scotland and much of western Scotland from this network was followed by considerable numbers of late Beaker, bronze dagger, jet ornament and Food Vessel burials in contemporary use in these regions, sometimes within the same complex cemeteries during the Early Bronze Age. Recent radiocarbon dates appear to demonstrate that the henge earthworks at North Mains were constructed at broadly the same time as just such a cemetery was developing within the henge (Barclay 2005: 86–8). The adoption of single burial practices during the Early Bronze Age did not, therefore, represent a break with the construction and relevance of ceremonial monuments in these regions. Furthermore, the above analysis suggests that several design features of

Beakers deposited at Neolithic and ceremonial monuments in the course of non-funerary practices were retained by these late Beakers: the absence of angular necks and complex comb motifs and the presence of cordons. The ongoing occurrence or absence of such traits may represent the continuity of a tradition distinct from the angular-necked fine-ware, but with its roots in the Chalcolithic.

Thus, regionally and contextually specific manifestations of the Beaker phenomenon appear to have existed within Scotland. We can consider not only how Beaker burials united regions, but also the role of Beaker practices in uniting *and* differentiating regions through a fuller range of depositional practices than usually considered. In this way, Beaker practices can be situated in the development of inter-regional networks and systems, which may have required regions to share material culture while retaining a distinct identity and role within those networks. As noted, Beaker practices may have particular relevance for understanding why and how the bronze Migdale–Marnoch metalwork system developed in Scotland from the twenty-second century cal. BC (cf. Cowie 1988; Needham 2004). The way in which different regions used Beakers in practices may also have involved varied but complementary ways of expressing remembrance and identity.

Memory, enduring principles and regional identity

I think painting is a duality ... I believe that art is recording; I think it's reporting. And I think that in abstract art, as there's no report, there's nothing other than the aesthetic of the painter and his few sensations. There's never any tension in it. (Francis Bacon, interviewed by Sylvester (1975: 58–60))

An important distinction is made by Rowlands (1993) regarding the way memory is constructed in terms of practices of 'inscription' and 'incorporation' (cf. Garwood 2007: 46–8). In the case of the former, memory is created by enduring material culture, while in the latter it is created by its destruction and removal from view and access. In the same vein, Jones (2003, 2010) has contrasted the seemingly flat Beaker short cist burials from Aberdeenshire with the (probably slightly later) monumentalised burials of Argyll, notably in Kilmartin Glen, and suggested that different mnemonic practices were involved. While interment in a short cist involved enacted practices consisting of the selection of a highly formalised and repetitive body posture, as well as choices of alignments and grave-good packages (A. Shepherd 1989, 2012), all of which were no longer visible after these practices were completed, upstanding monuments remained as physical reminders, and were thus cues for remembering and later activities (Jones 2010: 81–2).

But practices of inscription and incorporation are not always mutually exclusive and can occur at the same site, within the same burial event

(Jones 2003: 82; Garwood 2007: 47). This appears to be true for Beakers at Neolithic and ceremonial monuments; while there is evidence for their deposition in fragments after complex pre-depositional practices and of deposition in accessible chambers. There was also, of course, the continued physical presence of monuments themselves. Indeed, we may go further and suggest that the combination of the two principles was a characteristic feature of the Beaker phenomenon across Scotland, albeit in different 'blends'. For instance, the Beaker short cist burials of Aberdeenshire were incorporative, as described above, but the seemingly contemporary recumbent stone circles of Aberdeenshire involved architectural arrangements that were the product of more open, inscriptive undertakings, erecting megaliths, reproduced hundreds of times across Aberdeenshire. In east-central Scotland, the preference for particular, fixed ceremonial landscapes such as Forteviot may help to explain the relative paucity of Beaker short cist burials. The secretive and exclusive character of Beaker cists was instead provided here by access to, and knowledge of, the relict features and monuments within its boundaries; the more 'transportable' inscripted aspect by the fragmentary, complex pre-depositional practices involving Beaker sherds. Beakers were therefore deposited in different ways in these two regions, which nonetheless shared important features, involving the balancing of old and new practices using monuments with Neolithic precedence, and new, more ephemeral, but highly visible depositional practices to construct identities that were particular to the socio-political preferences and inherited traditions and landscapes of communities in Aberdeenshire and east-central Scotland.

In conclusion, this contribution has attempted to make sense of the available evidence of sometimes small and often fragmentary assemblages of Beaker pottery from Neolithic and ceremonial monuments of a range of different dates and types. While burials are set to be a major source of high quality insights for the foreseeable future, we should aim to identify and explore the non-funerary dimensions of the Chalcolithic and Early Bronze Age. Indeed, it is too simplistic to see the depositional practices of particular regions as having existed within a vacuum. Beaker pottery and practices can be related to the trajectory of regions prior to and after their first adoption – albeit in different ways due to the input and agency of communities – particularly in reference to the production of bronze metalwork and the inherited landscapes and monuments of particular regions of Scotland.

To arrive at these conclusions, this chapter began with a relatively empirical, analytical approach compared with recent, broadly post-processual, accounts that have been concerned with the workings of memory in the sequences of construction and deposition at monuments and funerary contexts in Scotland (e.g., Bradley 2002: 82–111; Jones 2003, 2010). The reasons for this were not polemical. Nor do I believe that the approach taken has ensured that my interpretations are any more convincing; in fact, it has come to some of the same conclusions. However, the reasoning that lay behind the deposition of Beaker pottery at pre-existing monuments is not something I feel comfortable in interpreting based on a particular theoretical approach or narrative theme, especially given the variations in ceramic morphology, decoration, chronology and geography involved. It follows that a more data-led approach may provide a more enduring foundation for future developments and reinterpretations (cf. Barclay 1999: 43; Garwood 2007: 48–9).

Indeed, the opening quotation of this section, Francis Bacon's perspective on abstract art, serves as a reminder that the balance between 'soft' and 'hard' elements is debated in many disciplines and can result in productive tensions. These make up what Gabriel Josipovici (1999) has described as the important balance between the suspicion of critical theory and trust in the practical and tangible: 'trust in the material, trust in our abilities, trust in the act of making itself' (ibid.: 3). The balancing of these elements is relevant to archaeological writing and to understanding the negotiations associated with the adoption and use of Beaker pottery alike. The blending of old and new traditions of material culture, incorporated and inscripted ways of remembering, and pre-existing cosmological principles, all of which varied across Scotland during the third millennium cal. BC, nonetheless seem to speak of a productive penumbra.

Appendix:
Beaker pottery from Neolithic and ceremonial monuments in Scotland

This appendix presents a list of monuments associated with Beaker pottery arranged alphabetically by monument type. An attempt has been made to provide as complete a corpus as possible, but this list is not exhaustive; a more comprehensive study of this material is required. Beaker typology is presented after Needham's (2005) classification, with some modifications: 'late' has been added to some 'S-Profile' and 'Weak-Carinated' groupings, given the results of recent dating programmes (e.g., Sheridan 2007c; Curtis et al. 2007; Wilkin et al. 2009; Curtis and Wilkin 2012). The term 'necked' is used where the vessel is too incomplete to allow for a more comprehensive identification.

Key to abbreviations of Beaker typology and decoration: AOC: All-Over-Cord; AOComb: All-Over-Comb; LC: Low-Carinated; LN: Long-Necked; N: Necked; MC: Mid-Carinated; SN: Short-Necked; SP: 'S'-Profile; WC or 'late': Weak-Carinated or 'late'.

No.	Site name(s), grave/ feature	Details of Beaker pottery
	NGR RCAHMS number/ Canmore ID	(Number of vessels; decoration; typology; completeness (1: approx. 100%; 2: approx. 75%; 3: approx. 50%; 4: approx. 25% or less); estimated height (EH), estimated base diameter (EBD) and estimated diameter (ERD) when available)

Chambered cairns

1	Achnacreebeag, Argyll and Bute *NM 9296 3639* NM93NW 4/ 23253	1. Cord (complex: horizontal lines and herringbone); three fragments, some surfaces slightly eroded; completeness: 4 (Ritchie, No. 5). 2. Incision (chevron motif) and impression (?round-toothed comb); approx. five sherds; MC; completeness: 4; RD: 155 mm (max.) (Ritchie, No. 6). 3. Incision; four fragments; completeness: 4 (Ritchie, No. 7). 4. Incision (including bar-chevron); SP; approx. ten small fragments; completeness: 3–4 (Ritchie, No. 8). 5. Undecorated; single sherd, eroded inner surface; completeness: 4 (Ritchie, No. 9). 6. Incision (horizontal herringbone); completeness: ?
2	Balvraid, Glenelg, Highland *NG 84524 16627* NG81NW 9/ 11800	Undecorated; SP or MC; completeness: ?
3	Barpa Langass, North Uist, Western Isles *NF 8376 6573* NF86NW 6/ 10236	1. Incision; three wall sherds and sherd of basal angle (possibly same Beaker) (Henshall, No. 2). 2. Incision; basal angle (Henshall, No. 3). 3. ?undecorated; sherd of basal angle (Henshall, No. 4).
4	Cadha Riach, (or Garraford), Skye, Highland *NG 4955 6757* NG46NE 12/ 11342	1. Incision; five sherds; completeness: 4. 2. Undecorated; one rim sherd, sixteen body sherds; completeness: ?
5	Cairnholy I, Dumfries and Galloway *NX 51820 54045* NX55SW 1/ 63705	1. Comb (?AOComb); eight sherds probably all from one vessel, apparently abraded; completeness: 4.
6	Cairnholy II, Dumfries and Galloway *NX 51760 53890* NX55SW 2/ 63716	1. Comb (?AOComb); 'numerous' sherds, with cordon below rim; completeness: ? 2. Cord (including inside rim, ?AOC); sherds, no further details; completeness: ? 3. Cord (?AOC); five sherds, including rim sherd with heavy cordon on neck; completeness: ?

Details	References

i. Site and deposit type
ii. Depositional context
iii. Comments

i. Neolithic chambered cairn. Associated with blocking of 'passage grave'; ?burial.
ii. Beaker sherds from (second) phase during which the chamber and passage were filled with stones and earth and included sherds of vessels (1–5), flints, cannel coal/shale disc beads and cremated bone. Ritchie suggests these represent a single ritual act as they were found throughout the filling of the chamber. Sherds of vessel (6) were found a short distance to the S, amongst the cairn material.
iii. Cremated bone from blocking of passage grave dated: 3660 ± 40 BP (GrA-26543).

References: Ritchie 1973; Sheridan 2007a

i. Neolithic chambered cairn. Chamber.
ii. Details of deposition are unclear. Some 'lignite' beads also recovered but their context is uncertain.
iii. –

References: Cormack 1964: 30; Henshall 1972: 558–9, INV 51; Henshall and Ritchie 2001: 76–9, *passim*

i. Neolithic chambered cairn (Hebridean group, round cairn). Chamber?
ii. From spoilheap of unrecorded excavation of chamber. Barbed-and-tanged arrowhead also recovered.
iii. –

References: Clarke 1970: 1670F; Henshall 1972: 500–3, UST6

i. Neolithic chambered cairn. Chamber.
ii. Beaker sherds from south side of the chamber.
iii. –

References: Close-Brooks and Ritchie 1978; Armit 1996: 94–5

i. Neolithic chambered cairn (Clyde type). Chamber.
ii. Beaker sherds from paving in antechamber. Sherds of Peterborough Ware apparently lay on the floor of the chamber.
iii. –

References: Piggott and Powell 1949; Clarke 1970: 1694F; Henshall 1972: 438–41, KRK2

i. Neolithic chambered cairn (Clyde type). Chamber.
ii. Seemingly undisturbed deposit of approx. 110 small sherds of at least six different Beakers (1–6) from paving in SW corner of antechamber.
iii. –

References: Piggott and Powell 1949: pl. XXXI; Clarke 1970: 1695F, 1696F, 1696.1F; 1696.2F; Henshall 1972: 442–4, KRK3

No.	Site name(s), grave/ feature	Details of Beaker pottery
		4. Comb (encircling lines and chevron ?AOComb), single sherd; completeness: ?
		5. Comb (?AOComb), sherds; completeness: ?
		6. Impression (stab/jab = Clarke's fingernail impression); three sherds; completeness: ?
7	Calf of Eday Long, Eday, Orkney Islands	1. Incision (faint diagonal lines); worn sherd from basal angle of vessel. Davidson and Henshall, No. 20.
	HY 5786 3861 HY53NE 18/ 3151	
8	Callanish (Calanais), Lewis, Western Isles	No details
	NB 21300 33017 NB23SW 1/ 4156	
9	Camster Round, Wick, Highland	1. Henshall (1972: 188) suggests undecorated Beaker sherd; completeness: 4 (see comments for query over identification).
	ND 2608 4403 ND24SE 16/ 8693	
10	Carn Glas, Mains of Kilcoy, Highland	1. Comb (complex); seven sherds; completeness: 4.
	NH 5784 5206 NH55SE 6/ 12837	
11	Tigh Chloiche, South Clettrava, North Uist, Western Isles	1. Shell impression (including verticals, horizontals and chevrons); ?MC; completeness: 2?
		2. Cardium impression (horizontal and herringbone; twelve sherds.
		3. Incision (horizontal) and comb; two wall sherds.
	NF 7516 7101 NF77SE 14/ 10081	4. Incision (horizontal); eleven sherds.
		5. Incision two sherds.
		6. Incision (horizontal, chevron and herringbone), twenty sherds.
		7. Incision; wall sherd, may be from a Beaker.
		8. Incision; wall sherd, may be from a Beaker.
		(Vessels (1–8) are Henshall, Nos 25–32.)
12	Cnoc Na H'Uiseig, (Lower Dounreay), Caithness, Highland	1. Stabs/jabs in groups of three; two sherds, including rim; completeness: 4; RD: 90 mm.
		2. Cord (AOC?); fragments; completeness: 4.
	NC 9969 6772 NC96NE 6/ 7300	3. Stab/jab horizontal rows and comb (chevron motif); completeness: 4. (Davidson and Henshall 1991: Nos 2–4).

Details	References

i. Neolithic chambered cairn. Chamber.
ii. From larger chamber, no further details.
iii. –

Henshall 1963: 188–93;
Davidson and Henshall
1989: 107–9, ORK 8

i. Near Neolithic chambered cairn within stone circle. Cleared contents of
cairn?
ii. Deposit possibly associated with clearing out of chamber.
iii. –

Ashmore 2002; Dunwell,
Johnson and Armit 2003:
16–19

i. Neolithic chambered cairn. Unknown.
ii. –
iii. NB: Davidson's and Henshall's (1991) comment that the Beaker was
'misidentified' by Henshall (1972). The site may therefore not qualify for
inclusion in the corpus and future study is required to check and verify
the identification.

Henshall 1972: 188;
Davidson and Henshall
1991: 102–4

i. Neolithic chambered cairn. (Orkney–Cromarty type). Chamber.
ii. Beaker from innermost compartment of chamber where an approx.
5 cm layer of sand overlay a clay floor. Sand layer disturbed by modern
sheep burial, but within it were discrete deposits of vessel (1) and small
sherds of a thick walled (approx. 25 mm), rusticated vessel, as well as a
leaf-shaped arrowhead associated with traces of a shaft.
iii. –

Woodham and Woodham
1959: 102–5; Henshall 1963:
255, 342–3; Clarke 1970: no.
1753, fig. 96; 1757F; 1758F;
1759F; Henshall and Ritchie
2001: 143–6

i. Neolithic chambered cairn (Clyde type). Chamber.
ii. Sherds (some from the same vessels) were split across several
compartments of the chamber (see Scott 1935; Henshall 1972: 511, for
details).
iii. –

Scott 1935; Clarke 1970: no.
1668F; Henshall 1972: 309,
506–11, UST12

i. Neolithic chambered cairn (Orkney–Cromarty type). Chamber; ?burial.
ii. Sherds of vessels (1–2) in association with perforated ox phalange,
animal bone sandstone axe (?whetstone) and Neolithic pottery, and were
found near a crouched inhumation burial in chamber, but the exact
relationship is not recorded. Henshall suggests that they were associated
with the skeleton. Sherds of vessel (3) found in various parts of the

Edwards 1929; Henshall
1963: 280–1; Clarke 1970:
nos 1611–1612.1; Davidson
and Henshall 1991: 124–6,
CAT 38

No.	Site name(s), grave/ feature	Details of Beaker pottery
13	Cnocan Nan Cobhar, Kilmarie, Skye, Highland *NG 5526 1734* NG51NE 7/ 11434	1. Incision, chevron and rhombus motifs; LN; completeness: 1: H: 200–210 mm; RD: 165 mm.
14	Cragabus, Kildalton and Oa, Islay, Argyll and Bute *NR 3292 4518* NR34NW 6/ 37609	1. Cord (AOC?); five small sherds; completeness: ? (Henshall, No. 2).
15	Dunan Beag (Blairmore), Kilbride, Arran, North Ayrshire *NS 0267 3299* NS03SW 8/ 40203	1. Incision; MC with Food Vessel decorative traits; completeness: ? (Henshall, No. 3).
16	Dunan Mor (Blairmore), Kilbride, Arran, North Ayrshire *NS 0280 3315* NS03SW 7/ 40202	1. Comb (chevron) (?complex) wall and base sherds from same vessel?; completeness: 4 (Henshall, No. 1).
17	Embo, Dornoch, Highland *NH 8177 9265* NH89SW 9/ 15376	1. Comb (complex); five sherds, of ?SP or ?LC vessel; completeness: 4. 2. Horizontal comb (?AOComb), circular toothed comb; sherd with cordon to ?neck; completeness: 4 (from a large vessel). 3. AOC?; several sherds, of ?SP or ?LC vessel; completeness: 4.
18	Geirisclett, North Uist, Western Isles *NF 7684 7520* NF77NE 15/ 10033	Erskine Beveridge excavations: 1. Horizontal cord and circular impressions; seven sherds from vessel with cordon, probably from below neck; completeness: ? (Henshall, No. 2).

Details	References

chamber including within a NNE–SSW aligned secondary long cist containing an inhumation burial.
iii. –

i. Neolithic ?chambered cairn. Burial.
ii. Beaker from secondary short cist (orientated NE–SW) near the top of the mound. Beaker and cremation burial from SW end of cist.
iii. –

Callander 1928; Henshall 1972:482–3, SKY 4; Clarke 1970: no. 1672, fig. 968

i. Neolithic chambered cairn (Clyde type). Chamber.
ii. Beaker sherds from near the bottom of the middle compartment of the chamber.
iii. Also from compartment were sherds of 'hard dark ware, without ornament' and flint flakes. Unburnt human bone and burnt bone from nearby compartment.

Bryce 1902: 110–11; Clarke 1970: nos. 1541F, 1541.1F; Henshall 1972: 433–4, ILY 3

i. Neolithic chambered cairn. Chamber; ?burial.
ii. From South chamber.
iii. Sections of a 'jet'-like spacer plate necklace from same chamber, as well as two crouched adult inhumations. Their relationship to vessel and necklace is not reported.

Bryce 1909: 343–50; Henshall 1972: 375–7, ARN 7; Clarke 1970: 1600F

i. Neolithic chambered cairn. Chamber.
ii. Beaker sherds from soil layer on floor of N and central compartments of the South chamber.
iii. –

Bryce 1909: 350–6; Henshall 1972: 377–8, ARN 8

i. Neolithic chambered cairn (Orkney–Cromarty type). Chamber.
ii. Sherds of vessel (1) found in disturbed and undisturbed sand in southern chamber (I) of the monument. A short cist (containing a Food Vessel and jet-like beads) had been constructed within the chamber and one sherd of vessel (1) may have derived from inside the cist, while the remainder was in sandy layers up to the level of the cist capstone, along with many human and animal bones. The cist had seemingly been cut into this layer of sand. Sherd of vessel (2) from disturbed sand in southern chamber (I) appears to pre-date the construction of a cist in this chamber. Sherds of vessel (3) (rim and base) from short cist containing two babies (new-born infant and older baby), sherds of Food Vessel and speck of bronze, inserted into chambered tomb. Sherds of vessel (3) were later reinterpreted by Henshall and Ritchie as intrusive, unintentionally redeposited material.
iii. Passage to the southern chamber (I) had been blocked with stones.

Henshall and Taylor 1957; Henshall and Wallace 1963; Henshall 1972: 582–4, SUT 63; Henshall and Ritchie 1995: 135–40

i. Neolithic chambered cairn (Clyde type). Chamber; ?burial.
ii. The exact context of the Beaker sherds recovered by Beveridge during clearing out part of the (previously disturbed) tomb is not known. During excavations in 1996–7, deposit 005 within the chamber (a gritty clay

Clarke 1970: no. 1669F; Henshall 1972: 515–17, UST 18; Dunwell et al. 2003

No.	Site name(s), grave/ feature	Details of Beaker pottery
		2. Incision (chevrons and horizontal lines); single sherd; completeness: 4 (Henshall, No. 3).
		3. Incision (chevron and herringbone); two sherds, probably from same vessel; completeness: 4? (Henshall, No. 4).
		4.? Johnson (in Dunwell *et al.* 2003: 18) suggests fourth vessel with 'stacked chevron motif' similar to (2–3).
		Dunwell *et al.* 2003 excavations:
		5. Incision; single sherd with chevron motif; completeness: 4 (Dunwell *et al.* B1).
		6. Cord (?AOC); single sherd; completeness: 4 (Dunwell *et al.* B2).
		7. Cord (?AOC); three sherds; completeness: 4 (Dunwell *et al.* B3).
		8. Cord (?AOC); two joining rim sherds with internal decoration; completeness: 4 RD: 180 mm (Dunwell *et al.* B4).
		9. Undecorated; four rim sherds; completeness: 4 (Dunwell *et al.* B5).
		10. Undecorated; single rim sherd; completeness: 4 (Dunwell *et al.* B6).
		11. Undecorated; single rim sherd; completeness: 4 (Dunwell *et al.* B7).
		12. Undecorated; base sherd; completeness: 4 (Dunwell *et al.* B8).
19	Giant's Graves, Kilbride, Arran, North Ayrshire *NS 04300 24670* NS02SW 2/ 40122	1. Comb (chevron) (?complex); rim sherd; completeness: 4 (Henshall, No. 4). 2. Comb (Unknown type) ; single sherd; completeness: 4 (Henshall, No. 5). 3. Undecorated; basal angle; completeness: 4 (Henshall, No. 7).
20	Glecknabae, Bute, Argyll and Bute *NS 00745 68263* NS06NW 8/ 40371	1. Fingernail impression; SP with cordon to neck; completeness: ?; EH: 89 mm; ERD: 76 mm; EBD: 64 mm (miniature vessel) (Henshall, No. 5). 2. AOComb; SP or LC with cordon to neck; completeness: ?; EH: 71 mm; ERD: 58 mm; EBD: 50 mm (miniature vessel) (Henshall, No. 6). 3. Undecorated; SP or LC; completeness: ?; EBD: 64 mm (miniature vessel) (Henshall, No. 7). 4 . Incision (horizontal lines) and undecorated small wall sherds; completeness: ? (Henshall, No. 9).
21	Holm of Papa Westray North, Papa Westray, Orkney Islands *HY 5091 5183* HY55SW 1/ 3242	1. Cardium impression; three wall sherds; completeness: 4 (Henshall 2009: No. 11).
22	Howe, Stromness, Orkney Islands *HY 2759 1092* HY21SE 41/ 1731	1. Cockle shell impression; neck and body sherds of N?; completeness: 4. 2. Comb (unknown type); two very small sherds; completeness: 4.

Details	References

overlying the lower fills) was particularly rich in Beaker pottery (Dunwell *et al.* 2003: illus. 9), but had been thoroughly mixed. Johnson (in Dunwell *et al.* 2003: 18) suggests the degree of sherd abrasion and spread between compartments were due to the subsequent disturbance of deposits.

iii. Residues evident on many of the sherds recovered in 1996–7.

i. Neolithic chambered cairn. Chamber?

ii. Sherds of vessels (1–3) from sieving of soil excavated from chamber.

iii. –

Bryce 1903: 44–54; Henshall, 1972: 383–5, ARN 11; Clarke 1970: 1601F, 1602F

i. Neolithic chambered cairn. Chamber.

ii. Vessels (1–3) from floor of NW chamber. No. 4 from NW chamber. Chamber contained charcoal, cremated bones and unburnt bones above the floor, on which were sherds of Beaker.

iii. Short cist with inhumation burial also inserted into monument (at southern end).

Bryce 1904: 37, 52; Henshall 1972: 411–14, BUT 4; Clarke 1970: 1603F, 1604F

i. Neolithic chambered cairn. External to cairn.

ii. Beaker sherds from outside the cairn itself, associated with limpet shells. Ritchie (2009: 34) suggests final sealing of the tomb was associated with Grooved Ware pottery.

iii. –

Sheridan 2007c: 122; Ritchie 2009

i. Neolithic chambered cairn (Maeshowe type). Disturbed.

ii. Four sherds found in disturbed contexts from area in front of the Neolithic chambered cairn.

iii. Vessel (1) had internal deposits of carbonised material.

Ross 1994: 238–9, illus. 139; A. Shepherd 1994: 283

No.	Site name(s), grave/ feature	Details of Beaker pottery
23	Kilcoy South, Killearnan, Highland (Kilcoy West; Kilcoy V) *NH 5701 5160* NH55SE 3/ 12834	1. AOComb; LC with neck cordon; completeness: 1 (Henshall, No. 1). 2. Cord (?AOC); fragment probably of SP or LC with cordon; completeness: 4 (missing base) (Henshall, Nos 2–3). 3. Cord (?AOC); fragment probably of SP or LC with cordon; completeness: 4 (Henshall, No.4). 4. Cord (?AOC); fragment probably of LC with double cordon; completeness: 4 (Henshall, No.5). 5. Cord (?AOC); double cordon; completeness: 3–4 (Henshall, No. 6). 6. Comb (AOComb?); ?necked with cordon visible at inflection between body and putative neck; completeness: 2 (Henshall, No.7). 7. Stab/jab (triangular) impressions; giant Beaker with cordon; completeness: 4 (Henshall, No. 8).
24	Kilmore, Dalineun (Loch Nell South), Kilmore and Kilbride, Argyll and Bute *NM 8799 2670* NM82NE 8/ 22934	1. Cord (AOC?); six body sherds; completeness: 4 (Ritchie, No.2). 2. Comb (complex); LN, twelve sherds; completeness: 3–4; H: approx. 160 mm RD: approx. 160 mm (Ritchie, No. 3). 3. Comb and jab; LN; completeness: 3–4; RD: approx. 144 mm (Ritchie, No. 4).
25	Knowe of Yarso, Rousay, Orkney Islands *HY 4048 2795* HY42NW 1/ 2623	1. Incision (horizontal, diagonal lines); wall sherds, 'surface much worn' (Henshall, No. 1). 2. Incision (chevrons) probably from a Beaker; wall sherds (Henshall, No. 3). 3. Incision; five sherds of basal angle and wall of possible Beaker (Henshall suggests 'Food Vessel').
26	Mid Gleniron I, New Luce, Dumfries and Galloway *NX 1877 6093* NX16SE 27/ 61608	1. Very small sherd (18.5 mm × 95 mm), comb (horizontal lines –?AOComb); completeness: 4.
27	Nether Largie South, Kilmartin, Argyll and Bute *NR 828 979* NR89NW 2/	1. Incision and comb (complex); LC or MC; H: approx. 220 mm; RD: 165 mm; completeness: 3 (Kinnes and Longworth UN 137, 2). 2. Comb (complex); twenty-five sherds (Kinnes and Longworth UN 137, 3). 3. Cord (?AOC); two sherds (including rim); completeness: 4 (Kinnes and Longworth's UN 137, 4). 4. Comb (horizontal) and unknown impression; rim sherd with cordon to neck; completeness: 4 (Kinnes and Longworth UN 137, 5). 5. Comb (?AOComb); single sherd; completeness: 4 (Kinnes and Longworth UN 137, 6).

Details	References
i. Neolithic chambered cairn (Orkney–Cromarty type). Chamber. ii. Beakers (1–5 and 7) from secondary deposit in centre of third compartment of the chamber above an oval deposit of charcoal and burnt bone, separated by layer of clean sand. iii. Fragments of same vessels supposedly found at entrance to fourth compartment. Vessel (6) from deposit found high up in silt just outside the entrance to the fourth compartment and seemingly higher than the other Beaker sherds.	Woodham 1956: 23–4; Woodham and Woodham 1957: 32–3; Henshall 1963: 348–9, ROS 24; Clarke 1970: 59, nos 1750–1756, fig. 126; Henshall and Ritchie 2001: 153–7
i. Neolithic chambered cairn (Clyde type). Chamber and associated with blocking. ii. Sherds of vessels (1 and 3) found within the undisturbed layer of the innermost compartment of the chamber. Fragments of vessel (2) found in both this undisturbed layer and among the stones blocking the chamber. Also in the blocking of stones were cremated bone fragments. iii. Irish-style Food Vessel Bowl and cremated bone recovered from a cist ('massive cist'/'cist 2') inserted into the cairn.	Ritchie 1974a; Henshall 1972: 316, ARG 3
i. Neolithic chambered cairn. Chamber. ?burial. ii. Sherds of vessels (1–2) from the lowest level in the chamber. Sherds of vessel (3) in close contact with a skull in inner compartment. Not clear whether this was an intentional association. iii. Barbed-and-tanged arrowhead and Food Vessel sherds also from chamber.	Callander and Grant 1935; Henshall 1963: 215–18; Clarke 1970: no. 1734F; Davidson and Henshall 1989: 138–40, ORK 32
i. Neolithic chambered cairn (Clyde type). Chamber. ii. From Northern chamber which had been robbed. In the lower fill, which appears to have been disturbed, Beaker sherd (1) was recovered at the base of the western orthostat (stone 16). iii. –	Corcoran 1969
i. Neolithic chambered cairn (Clyde type). ?burial in chamber. ii. Greenwell suggests that a small cist in SE corner of the rear compartment of the chamber had been rifled and that unburnt bones and Beaker sherds had been scattered. iii. –	Greenwell 1866; Henshall 1972: 335–40, ARG 23; Kinnes and Longworth 1985: UN 137, 2–6; Clarke 1970: no. 1551, fig. 232

No.	Site name(s), grave/ feature	Details of Beaker pottery
28	Rubh / Rudh' An Dunain, Bracadale, Skye, Highland *NG 3934 1636* NG31NE 2/ 11022	1. Comb (complex) and horizontal rilling; LN; completeness: 3–4; H: 198 mm; RD: approx. 191 mm (Henshall, No. 3).
29	Taversoe Tuick, Rousay, Orkney Islands *HY 4257 2761* HY42NW 2/ 2634	1. Undecorated; non-angular neck (MC or SP) vessel; completeness: 4; RD: approx. 114 mm (Henshall, No. 29) 'Beaker-like vessel', the base re-burnt after breaking.
30	Tomfat Plantation, Daviot and Dunlichity, Highland *NH 6780 3742* NH63NE 5/ 13152	1. Undecorated; six wall sherds, probably Beaker (Henshall and Ritchie, No. 1).
31	Tulach an t-Sionnaich, Halkirk, Highland *ND 0704 6192* ND06SE 10/ 7901	1. Rilling and stab/jab; two neck neck/rim sherds, probably from the same vessel; completeness: 4; RD: 115 mm (Henshall, No. 3).
32	Unival (Leacach An Tigh Chloiche), North Uist, Western Isles *NF 80033 66859* NF86NW 4/ 10234	1. Undecorated; SP or LC; completeness: ?4 (Henshall, No. 15).

Long cairns

No.	Site name(s), grave/ feature	Details of Beaker pottery
33	Lochhill, New Abbey, Dumfries and Galloway *NX 9688 6507* NX96NE 24/ 65428	1. Sherds belonging to one vessel which Masters describes as belonging to Clarke's (1970) Late Northern British group.

NB: Gregory (2002: 47, 48) notes that the long cairn at Slewcairn, Colvend and Southwick, Dumfries and Galloway, produced sherds of Beaker pottery, but no published reference is to be found in Masters' (published) interim reports (1973, 1974, 1975, 1981) and the site has not been included.

Details	References
i. Neolithic chambered cairn. burial? in chamber; blocking of chamber.	Scott 1932; Clarke 1970: no. 1675, fig. 730;
ii. Sherds of vessel (1) scattered in NW corner of the chamber in 'Beaker stratum', a layer extending approx. 30–90 cm above the chamber floor, consisting of brown earth and fallen stone and clearly distinct from the underlying 'Neolithic stratum'. Beaker, human remains (of four individuals), quartz and rounded pumice came from this layer.	Henshall 1972: 147–8, 485–8, SKY 7; Armit 1996: 95
iii. –	
i. Neolithic chambered cairn. Outside door of upper chamber.	Henshall 1963: 234–8, ORK 49; Davidson and Henshall 1989:160–3
ii. –	
iii. –	
i. Neolithic chambered cairn. Chamber.	Henshall and Ritchie 2001: 232–3, INV 52
ii. Probable Beaker sherds (1) from on or near floor of chamber.	
iii. –	
i. Neolithic chambered cairn. Chamber.	Corcoran 1967; Henshall 1972: 550–2, CAT 58; Davidson and Henshall 1991: 146–9
ii. Sherds of vessel (1) from immediately north of the northern orthostat of the chamber, found in the upper, disturbed levels of the chamber area at the level of collapsed roofing. Corcoran suggests that, 'as the bulk of the burial deposit in the chamber was undisturbed below the level of collapsed corbelling, it is possible that the Beaker sherds post-date the final use of the chamber' (1967: 17).	
iii. –	
i. Neolithic chambered cairn. Chamber; blocking of the chamber.	Scott 1948; Clarke 1970: no. 1671; Henshall 1972: 529–34, UST 34, Armit 1996: 95
ii. Sherds of vessel (1) were found '15 inches [c. 380 mm] above the floor, and separated from the highest Neolithic pot by 3 inches [c. 76 mm] of accumulated deposit' and was 'stratigraphically the latest [vessel] in the tomb' (Scott 1948: 23).	
iii. The vessel (1) may have been associated with a flat axe/adze shaped pumice pendant.	
i. Neolithic long cairn. Stones near the top of the cairn.	Masters 1973; Henshall 1972: 547, KRK 14
ii. Sherds of one Beaker vessel (1) were found mixed with stones near the top of the cairn, approximately mid-way along its central axis.	
iii. Forecourt of the monument blocked.	

No.	Site name(s), grave/ feature	Details of Beaker pottery

Henge monuments and related enclosures

34.1	Balfarg Riding School, Markinch, Fife *NO 28488 03137* NO20SE 20/ 29959	Assemblage represents a substantial proportion of four vessels and smaller portions of a minimum of twenty-one others, mostly of AOC vessels, but AOComb and ?undecorated vessels also represented, vessels have a range of sizes and profiles; ?SP or ?LC: completeness: 4.
34.2	Balfarg Riding School, Markinch, Fife *NO 28488 03137* NO20SE 20/ 29959	See entry for 34.1.
34.3	Balfarg Riding School, Markinch, Fife *NO 28488 03137* NO20SE 20/ 29959	See entry for 34.1.
34.4	Balfarg Riding School, Markinch, Fife *NO 28488 03137* NO20SE 20/ 29959	See entry for 34.1.
35	Balfarg, Markinch, Fife, P50, feature XI *NO 28198 03123* NO20SE 5/ 29990	1. Incision; Handled Beaker with cordon; completeness: 1; H: 136 mm; RD: approx. 136 mm.
36	Ballymeanoch henge, Kilmichael Glassary, Argyll and Bute *NR 833 962* NR89NW 18/ 39458	1. Comb (complex); LN; H: survives to 160; RD: 176; completeness: 3.

Details	References

i. Neolithic enclosure. Ditch.
ii. Relatively high in enclosure ditch deposits with sherds from same vessels found in contexts outwith ditch (see Cowie, in Barclay and Russell-White 1993 for details). 450 sherds, representing a minimum of twenty-five vessels, but maximum numbers substantially higher (Cowie's P115–16, 118–19, 121–3, 125, 128–30, 134–7, 142–6, 149–51, 153). In addition fragments of seven vessels are found in ditch and other contexts associated with enclosure (P117, 120–7, 131, 139, 148). Sherds from seven vessels found only outside the ditch (Cowie's P124, 133, 138, 140–1, 147, 152).
iii. A number of sherds show evidence for scorching and abrasion.

References: Barclay and Russell-White 1993: 92, 183, 196–7; Cowie, in Barclay and Russell-White 1993: 126–9

i. Neolithic enclosure. Ring-cairn/Cairn B area.
ii. See entry for 34.1.
iii. –

References: Barclay and Russell-White 1993:, 92, 183, 196–7; Cowie, in Barclay and Russell-White 1993: 126–9

i. Neolithic enclosure. F8020.
ii. See entry for 34.1.
iii. –

References: Barclay and Russell-White 1993: 92, 183, 196–7; Cowie, in Barclay and Russell-White 1993: 126–9

i. Neolithic enclosure. F8021.
ii. See entry for 34.1.
iii. –

References: Barclay and Russell-White 1993: 92, 183, 196–7; Cowie, in Barclay and Russell-White 1993: 126–9

i. Henge. Burial.
ii. Earth-cut grave with massive stone capstone, orientated approximately NE–SW, positioned at centre of henge enclosure. Young adult (14–18 years) on right-hand side facing E. Beaker (1) upright in front of the face and chest. The mouth of the Beaker was (?partially) covered by a 'thin slab of laminar stone'.
iii. Just to the north of the Beaker was a 'small knife of fine black flint', in 'extremely fresh and unabraded condition' (Mercer 1981: 72–9). Human bone (unburnt) from burial dated: 3605 ±37 BP (OxA-13215).

References: Mercer 1981: 72–9; Sheridan 2007c: 114; Brindley 2007: 300–1

i. Henge. Burial.
ii. Beaker (1) from cist approx. 3 m NNE from centre of henge monument. Cist with 'the teeth of apparently three persons' (Greenwell 1869: 349). Greenwell also suggests that 'the cover had been previously removed, when the [Beaker] was broken, and a considerable portion of it taken away' (*ibid.*).
iii. –

References: Greenwell 1866: 348–9; Clarke 1970: no. 1530, fig. 711; Kinnes and Longworth 1985: UN 134

No.	Site name(s), grave/ feature	Details of Beaker pottery
37	Belhie, Auchterarder, Perth and Kinross	No details.
	NN 9774 1610 NN91NE 18/ 25964	
38.1	Cairnpapple, Torphichen, West Lothian, 'North Grave'	1. Comb (complex); LN; completeness: 1 (Clarke, No. 1791). 2. Undecorated; completeness: 4. 3. Impression (bone-end); LN; completeness: 1 (Clarke, No.1792).
	NS 9872 7173 NS97SE 16/ 47919	
38.2	Cairnpapple, Torphichen, West Lothian, near stone- hole 8	1. Comb (complex); SN (with very short-neck); completeness: 4.
	NS 9872 7173 NS97SE 16/ 47919	
38.3	Cairnpapple, Torphichen, West Lothian, henge ditch	1. Single undecorated sherd; completeness: 4.
	NS 9872 7173 NS97SE 16/ 47919	
38.4	Cairnpapple, Torphichen, West Lothian, pit complex	1. Two undecorated sherds; completeness: 4.
	NS 9872 7173 NS97SE 16/ 47919	
39	Forteviot, Perth and Kinross, henge monument 1, ditch	1. Noted as AOC, but looked like comb when seen in August 2010; completeness: 4; analysis in prep.
	NO 05264 16928 NO01NE 33/ 26565	
40.1	Forteviot, Perth and Kinross, henge monument 2, ditch [6010]	Thirty-nine sherds: twenty-eight AOC, eleven undecorated; SP or LC; analysis in prep.
	NO 05264 16928 NO01NE 33/ 26565	

Details	References
i. 'Henge'/ 'minihenge'. Pit. ii. Beaker sherds from the pit alignment in front of 'minihenge'. iii. –	Ralston 1988: 27; I. Ralston pers. comm.
i. Henge. Secondary burial. ii. Rock-cut, grave (orientated E–W) with monolith at one end and oval setting (3 m × 2.7 m) surrounding it. Probable cairn covering it. Piggott's Phase II.3 and Barclay's Phase 3b. iii. Human bone poorly preserved, but teeth at E end. Grave goods included wooden artefacts: possible 'mask' and 'club' and ?lid with Beaker (1), which was at W end, near centre of monolith, together with fragment of base and lower wall from a second Beaker (2). Second complete Beaker (3) from NE corner of grave.	Piggott 1950; Clarke 1970: nos 1791–2, 1793 F, figs 569–70; Barclay 1999: 30–4
i. Henge. Secondary burial. ii. Rock-cut burial (f. 1.12 m × 0.61 m) positioned near rock-cut grave near stone-hole 8, orientated NE–SW. Beaker crushed on its side at N corner, base towards the W end. No surviving human remains (probably due to acidic soils). iii. Size of burial suggests child burial or cenotaph.	Piggott 1950: figs 5–6; Clarke 1970: no. 1790, fig. 333; Barclay 1999: 30–4
i. Henge. Ditch. ii. Single abraded sherd from upper silts of ditch. iii. –	Piggott 1950; Barclay 1999: 29–32
i. Henge. Pit. ii. Two undecorated Beaker sherds from near base of NW pit of 'pit complex', a feature that may have been associated with the use of the henge monument in earlier phases and quarrying for material of the 'North Grave' Beaker burial. iii. –	Piggott 1950: 83, fig. 5; Barclay 1999: 32
i. Henge. Ditch. ii. Sherds from lower fill of ditch terminal. iii. Final excavation report in prep.	Brophy and Noble 2008
i. 'Henge'. Ditch. ii. Sherds from lower fill of ditch terminal. Excavators interpret as intentional deposition of smashed vessel. iii. Final excavation report in prep.	Brophy and Noble 2010

No.	Site name(s), grave/ feature	Details of Beaker pottery
40.2	Forteviot, Perth and Kinross, henge monument 2, posthole [6027] *NO 05264 16928* *NO01NE 33/ 26565*	Forty-eight sherds, thirty-seven AOC, eleven undecorated sherds; SP or LC; analysis in prep.
40.3	Forteviot, Perth and Kinross, henge monument 2, posthole [6012] *NO 05264 16928* *NO01NE 33/ 26565*	Six sherds, three AOC, two AOComb, one undecorated sherd; SP or LC; analysis in prep.
40.3	Forteviot, Perth and Kinross, henge monument 2, posthole [6073] *NO 05264 16928* *NO01NE 33/ 26565*	1. Single AOComb sherd.
40.4	Forteviot, Perth and Kinross, henge monument 2, Food Vessel cremation burial *NO 05264 16928* *NO01NE 33/ 26565*	1. Single AOComb sherd from cremation burial.
41	Moncrieffe, Perth and Kinross *NO 1328 1933* *NO11NW 11/ 28012*	1–2. Two/three sherds representing two vessels: AOC? and comb (?complex); completeness: ?
42.1	North Mains, Strathallan, Perth and Kinross, Burial F *NN 9285 1625* *NN91NW 18/ 26006*	1. Incision; WC or Beaker/Food Vessel hybrid; completeness: 1; H: ?; RD: ?
42.2	North Mains, Strathallan, Perth and Kinross, pits A/7 and A/8 *NN 9285 1625* *NN91NW 18/ 26006*	1. Incision; fourteen sherds possibly from a single vessel; completeness: 4.

Details	References
i. 'Henge'. In upper fill of post-hole within monument. ii. Excavators interpret as intentional deposition in hollow left by post/post-hole. iii. Final excavation report in prep.	Brophy and Noble 2010
i. Henge. In upper fill of posthole within monument. ii. Excavators interpret as intentional deposition in hollow left by post/post-hole. iii. Final excavation report in prep.	Brophy and Noble 2010
i. Henge. In fill of post-hole within monument. ii. Excavators interpret as intentional deposition in hollow left by post/post-hole. iii. Final excavation report in prep.	Brophy and Noble 2010
i. Henge. ?Residual in funerary context. ii. Site report in prep. Sherd mixed with cremation burial besides Food Vessel Bowl. iii. Final excavation report in prep.	Brophy and Noble 2010
i. Henge (single entrance). Residual? ii. One sherd from NW quadrant of henge ditch – others from 0.2 m beneath 'recumbent' stone between two monoliths. iii. –	Stewart 1987
i. Henge. Burial. ii. Cremation burial of adult male in E half of cist orientated NNE–SSW. ii. Two burnt flakes found with cremation deposit and an unburnt flake beside the vessel (1).	Barclay 1983; Cowie, in Barclay 1983: 155–63
i. Henge. Post-hole. ii. In topmost fill of hollow left by two rotted posts. Decorated with bar–chevron motif with alternating filled triangles similar to Beaker from burial F. iii. A number of sherds showed evidence of burning and abrasion.	Barclay 1983; Cowie, in Barclay 1983: 155–63

No.	Site name(s), grave/ feature	Details of Beaker pottery

Non-megalithic long mounds

43	Biggar Common, Biggar, South Lanarkshire, Cairn 2, Eastern burial *NT 0033 3882* NT03NW 80/ 72629	1. Comb (?AOComb: variant? encircling lines and reserved areas); LC; completeness: 1. 2. Undecorated; Bowl: cf. LC Beakers below carination; completeness: 1. 3. Cord (?AOC: variant? encircling lines) to upper half. SN (miniature vessel); completeness: 1.
44	Dalladies, Fettercairn, Aberdeenshire *NO 6276 6737* NO66NW 27/ 35955	1. Incision, horizontal lines and lozenges; WC or Beaker/Food Vessel hybrid (with cordon); completeness: approx. 2–3.
45.1	Eweford West, East Lothian, Pit 3 [028] *NT 6637 7737* NT67NE 474/ 257432	1. AOComb (round toothed comb); LC with neck cordon; completeness: 4 (H: 195 mm; RD: approx. 120 mm). 2. Comb and jab/stab impressions (encircling); SP with neck cordon; H: approx. 140–145 mm; RD: approx. 100–110 mm; completeness: 4. 3. Comb and incision; unusual globular Beaker bowl with cordon on neck; completeness: 4; H: approx. 147 mm; RD: approx. 170 mm. 4. AOC; LC; H: approx. 200 mm; RD: N/A; completeness: 4.
45.2	Eweford West, East Lothian, Pit 148 *NT 6637 7737* NT67NE 474/ 257432	1. Incision; SP with neck cordon; completeness: 4 ; H: approx. 290 mm; RD: approx. 180 mm. 2. Incision; three small sherds, reconstruction not possible; completeness: 4; H: ?; RD: ? 3. Undecorated; two small sherds, reconstruction not possible; completeness: 4; H: ?; RD: ?
45.3	Eweford West, East Lothian, Pit 164 *NT 6637 7737* NT67NE 474/ 257432	1. Comb (chevron and horizontal: ?AOComb); single body sherd; completeness: 4 (H: N/A; RD: N/A). 2. Undecorated; single sherd from juncture of wall and base; completeness 4 (H: ?; RD: ?).
45.4	Eweford West, East Lothian, Pit 175 *NT 6637 7737* NT67NE 474/ 257432	1. Incision; four sherds; completeness: 4.
45.5	Eweford West, East Lothian, mound material *NT 6637 7737* NT67NE 474/ 257432	1. Comb (?complex); single sherd; completeness: 4. 2. Undecorated; two sherds; completeness: 4.

Details	References

i. Neolithic non-megalithic earthen long mound. Burial?
ii. Burial cut into eastern end of primary mound. Shallow (E–W aligned) grave-pit surrounded by kerb of boulders. Grave good assemblage included: Beaker (1), polished stone axe, small flint scraper and quartzite pebble. A chert flake, possible quartz core and agate pebble were found under the Beaker. Pit was covered by cairn with Beaker sherds (2) mixed with cairn material. Sherds of third Beaker (3) scattered on surface of the cairn.
iii. –

Johnston 1997; Sheridan 1992; Sheridan 2008: 253

i. Neolithic non-megalithic long barrow. Cist burial.
ii. Short-cist burial orientated E–W, on crest of long barrow. Cist contained a cremation burial, sherds of Beaker (1) and burnt plank of wood. The Beaker contained a group of worked flints and a small water-worn pebble'.
iii. –

Piggott 1974; Shepherd 1986: 35

i. In vicinity of Neolithic non-megalithic long mound. Pit.
ii. Pit deposit 200 m E of Neolithic long mound. Fragments of four different Beakers in pit with charcoal and a few burnt cereal grains (including barley).
iii. The sherds of vessels (1–4) were not heavily abraded. Date obtained from carbonised barley grain (SUERC-5299; 3775 ± 35 BP).

MacGregor and Stuart 2007: 88–90, fig. 4.20; Sheridan 2007c: 116–17

i. In quarry scoop for Neolithic non-megalithic long mound. Burial.
ii. Sherds of vessels (1–3) in pit with cremation burial of two adult males. Sherds of vessels (1–2) were abraded; vessel (3) sherds were slightly abraded.
iii. Excavators suggest sherds were disturbed and ?re-interred with cremation burial. Nearby cremation burials associated with Collared Urns. Date obtained from carbonised barley grain: 3725 ± 35 BP (SUERC-5309).

MacGregor and Stuart 2007: 114, fig. 4.21; Sheridan 2007c: 116–17

i. In quarry scoop for Neolithic non-megalithic long mound. Pit.
ii. Sherds of vessels (1–2) in pit dug into material of Neolithic mound. Pit also contained approx. 25,000 burnt cereal grains, mainly barley with some emmer wheat, charcoal, chert core, two flint chips and a burnt fragment of a bifacially worked point.
iii. Sherds (1–2) abraded. Date obtained from carbonised cereal grain: 3650 ± 35 BP (SUERC-5316).

MacGregor and Stuart 2007, 89, figs. 4.13. 5.3; Sheridan 2007c, 116–17

i. Near to (approx. 8 m) Neolithic non-megalithic long mound. Pit.
ii. Sherds of Beaker (1) in pit with approx. 9,000 grains of burnt cereal, mostly of naked barley, with some emmer and bread wheat.
iii. Sherds abraded. Date obtained from carbonised cereal grain: 3680 ± 40 BP (SUERC-5317).

MacGregor and Stuart 2007: 90, figs 4.13. 5.3; Sheridan 2007c: 116–17

i. Neolithic non-megalithic long mound. Surface scatter?
ii. From upper cairn material. Sherds (1–2) heavily abraded.
iii. Sheridan (2007c: 116–17) lists vessel (2) as 'possible' Beaker sherd.

MacGregor and Stuart 2007: 90–1; Sheridan 2007c: 116–17

No.	Site name(s), grave/ feature	Details of Beaker pottery
46	Hill of Foulzie, King Edward, Aberdeenshire NJ75NW 6/ 19244	1. Comb (complex); SN; completeness: 1 (neck lost after discovery); H: approx. 128 mm; RD: approx. 83 mm.

Non-megalithic round mounds

47	Boghead, Fochabers, Moray *NJ 3594 5922* NJ35NE 5/ 16878	1. Undecorated; LC; completeness: 2; H: approx. 250 mm (Burl, No. 44). 2. AOC; unknown form; completeness: 3–4 (Burl, No. 45). 3. Incision; unknown form with cordon (presumably on neck); completeness: 3–4 (Burl, No. 46).
48	Courthill, Dalry, Ayrshire *NS 2924 4958* NS24NE 3/ 40989	1. Comb (complex); TMC or LC with cordon to neck; completeness: 1.
49	East Finnercy, Dunecht, Aberdeenshire *NJ 7647 0429* NJ70SE 3/ 18549	Beaker AOC sherd discussed by Atkinson (1962), but was probably not from this site. Data from this site has, therefore, not been included in the analysis.
50	Midtown of Pitglassie, Auchterless, Aberdeenshire *NJ 7023 4352* NJ74SW 12/ 19198	1. Undecorated; rim sherd; completeness: 4 (Shepherd, ASH 15). 2. AOC?; three sherds; completeness: 4 (Shepherd, ASH 16). 3. Cord and grooving; two sherds; completeness: 4 (Shepherd, ASH 17). 4. Incision; WC; completeness: 3–4 (Shepherd, ASH 18).
51	Powsode (Pow Sod), Cairn No. 2, Aberdeenshire [Atherb] *NJ 925 499* NJ94NW 25/ 20617	1. AOC; no further details.

Recumbent stone circles

52	Berrybrae, Lonmay, Aberdeenshire *NK 0275 5716* NK05NW 2/ 21099	1. Incision; lost?

Details	References
i. Possible Neolithic two-part non-megalithic mound (long cairn altered by addition of a round cairn). Uncertain. ii. Unaccompanied Beaker (1) 3 m to N of Food Vessel Urn burial within round mound. At least three Food Vessel Urns, one Food Vessel Urn or Food Vessel and two short-cists, one with an unaccompanied inhumation. Possible that Beaker derived from one of these cists. iii. –	Cowie 1978: 104–5, fig. 13; Henshall 1963: 394–5; Clarke 1970: 511, no. 1455, fig 668; Shepherd 1986: 27, illus. 20
i. Neolithic non-megalithic round cairn. Pit deposit. ii. Pit located 2 m WNW from edge of round mound. Pit (0.7 m × 0.7 m and 0.6 m deep) with flat stones over the mouth and a uniform earth filling containing sherds of vessels (1–3). iii. Probably too small to be a burial pit and Beaker assemblage is not characteristic of local funerary practices.	Burl 1984; Sheridan 2010: 30–6
i. Neolithic non-megalithic round cairn? Pit filled with stones – possible burial. ii. Pit approx. 1.5 m long × 90 cm, and approx. 1 m below the original surface, filled with stones. Beaker in fragments at base. iii. –	Cochran-Patrick 1874: 281–5; Clarke 1970: no. 1558, fig. 231; Sheridan 2010: 47–9
i. Neolithic non-megalithic round cairn. Uncertain association. ii. – iii. –	Atkinson 1962: 18–19; Leivers *et al.* 2000: 183–95; Sheridan 2010: 42–4
i. Neolithic non-megalithic round cairn. Disturbed central area. ii. Beaker sherds (1–4) recovered from disturbed contexts. iii. Sherds of 1 and 2 may be from the same vessel.	Donations 1969; Shepherd 1996
i. Non-megalithic round cairn. Uncertain context. ii. Vessel (1) found crushed on its side, no further details. iii. –	Milne 1892; Clarke 1970: no. 1428F; Sheridan 2010: 37–41
i. Recumbent stone circle. Clay-filled pit in bank. ii. Beaker (1) associated with charcoal in a clay-filled pit in stony bank of the stone circle. iii. Concentration of quartz from monument, other (unidentified) sherds recovered.	Burl 1975: 7; 1976: 7; 1977: 4–5

No.	Site name(s), grave/ feature	Details of Beaker pottery
53	Loanhead of Daviot, Daviot, Aberdeenshire *NJ 7477 2885* NJ72NW 1/ 18789	Small sherds of Beaker (including cord/?AOC). Seventeen sherds photographed in Kilbride-Jones (1935). Clarke (1970) lists three vessels: one AOC and two indet.
54	Old Keig, Keig, Aberdeenshire *NJ 5965 1939* NJ51NE 2/ 17530	Several 'minute' sherds of Beaker and probable Beaker fabric. The most confident identification is of a sherd carrying comb decoration (herringbone motif).
55	Old Rayne, Rayne, Aberdeenshire *Alternative names:* Candle Hill; Tap O'Mast *NJ 6798 2798* NJ62NE 1/ 18081	1. Probable Beaker, sherds now lost.
56	Strichen, Strichen, Aberdeenshire *NJ 93674 54479* NJ95SW 2/ 20754	Three sherds – presumed lost.
57	Tomnaverie, Coull, Aberdeenshire *NJ 4865 0349* NJ40SE 1/ 17006	1. Comb (complex); two conjoining sherds; completeness: 4 (sherds 365 and 420). 2. Comb (?complex); two sherds missing external surface in places; completeness: 4 (sherds 369 and 393). 3. Incision; single rim sherd; completeness: 4 (sherd 421).
58	Hillhead, Tarland *No details, report in prep.*	1. Sherd from old land surface (same fabric as No. 2) found during excavation. 2. Sherds from outside ring cairn found during fieldwalking.

Stone circles/cairns

59.1	Balbirnie, Markinch, Fife, ?cist 5	1. Incision (double lozenge motif) and stab/jab; SP with cordon to neck; completeness: 4; H: 185 mm; RD: 172 mm.

Details	References
i. Recumbent stone circle. Surface scatter or residual.	Kilbride-Jones 1935; Clarke
ii. Sherds from various locations around the circle, including beneath the	1970: 1467F; 1468F; 1469F
recumbent stone.	
iii. –	
i. Recumbent stone circle. Surface scatter or residual.	Childe 1933, 1934; Clarke
ii. On gravel layer within inner limit of bank (Childe 1933: fig. 1). Sherds	1970: 1479F
found in a concentrated area inside inner limit of the bank, one sherd with	
herring-bone pattern created by comb.	
iii. Some or all of the sherds appear to have been abraded.	
i. Recumbent stone circle. Burial.	Coles 1902: 527–31;
ii. Central oblong pit (later filled by stones) aligned NE–SW with a	Sheridan 2007c: 114
number of features at base. A central pit with 'pieces of an urn of reddish	
colour' (probably Beaker (1) but now lost), a fragment of an archers wrist	
guard/bracer and cremated bone. Outside this central deposit were small	
deposits of cremated bone.	
iii. Cremated bone associated with Beaker pottery dated: 3690 ± 45 BP	
(GrA-23982).	
i. Recumbent stone circle. Surface scatter or residual.	Philips *et al.* 2006
ii. Disturbed area near F23 and outside bank of monument (Philips *et al.*	
2006, illus. 16).	
iii. Beaker sherds from disturbed bank material and outside the line of the	
original bank of the recumbent stone circle, another Beaker sherd found	
in a disturbed area on one side of a stone-lined grave placed centrally	
within the recumbent stone circle (F23).	
iii. Barbed-and-tanged arrowhead also found outside the bank of the	
recumbent stone circle.	
i. Recumbent stone circle. Surface scatter or residual.	Bradley 2005; Sheridan, in
ii. Sherds (1–3) are possibly from one vessel. Sherds found close together	Bradley 2005: 33–4
on the old ground surface at the edge of the cairn kerb.	
iii. Sherds of vessel (1) were abraded, sherds of vessel (2) were heavily	
abraded.	
i. Recumbent stone circle. Old land surface below ring cairn and outside	Bradley and Clarke n.d.
the ring cairn.	
ii. Small sherd from old land surface on which the ring-cairn had been	
constructed.	
iii. Sherds of same fabric found during fieldwalking a short distance	
outside the ring cairn, barbed and tanged arrowhead also found.	
Excavators suggest possible disturbed burial.	
i. Stone circle and cairn. ? burial.	Ritchie 1974b; Sheridan
ii. Beaker sherds from vessel (1) flattened in an angle created by two	2007c: 123, app. 7
rectangular planks of charred wood. It was also associated with a single jet	
bead, further jet beads were found within the body of the cairn and the	

No.	Site name(s), grave/ feature	Details of Beaker pottery
	NO 2850 0304 NO20SE 4/ 29980	
59.2	Balbirnie, Markinch, Fife	1. Incision (possibly abraded comb); single Beaker sherd; completeness: 4.
	NO 2850 0304 NO20SE 4/ 29980	
60	Temple Wood, Kilmartin, Argyll and Bute, Burial B	1. Incision and rilling; SN; completeness: 1; H: 177; RD: 105–110.
	NR 826 978 NR89NW 6/ 39504	
Unclassified/other		
61	Cloburn Quarry, Lanarkshire	1. Cord (?AOC); single, small, abraded wall sherd; completeness: 4.
	NS 947 415 NS94SW 37/ 47715	
62	Lundin Farm, Aberfeldy, Perth and Kinross	1. AOC; LC; completeness: ?
	NN 8806 5056 NN85SE 9/ 25727	
63	Staneydale Temple, Sandsting, Shetland Islands	1. ?AOC; three small sherds; completeness: 4.
	HU 28535 50240 HU25SE 1/ 387	
64	Curriestanes Cursus (Park Road, Maxwellton), Troqueer, Dumfries and Galloway	1. Twisted cord (horizontal lines) and fingernail impressions; twenty sherds; completeness: 4.
	NX 95990 75170 NX97NE 85/ 65621	

Details	References

disturbed fill of cist 1. No evidence of short cist/burial found, possibly destroyed during erection of the covering cairn
iii. Date from associated charred wood: 3280 ± 90 (GaK-3425) (non-AMS) adjusted to 3280 ± 270 BP by P. Ashmore. Standard deviation greater than 100 – date is not considered reliable.

i. Stone circle and cairn. Disturbed context – originally from burial? Ritchie 1974b
ii. Beaker sherd (1) from old land surface below cairn.
iii. –

i. Stone circle/cairn. Burial. Scott 1991
ii. Beaker from NNE–SSW short cist burial within kerbed cairn, approx. 2 m from Temple Wood southern circle. Associated with three barbed and tanged arrowheads and side scraper. Beaker at S end of the cist, phosphate levels indicated an inhumation, suggesting it may have been a crouched inhumation on left hand side, head to W or SW.
iii. –

i. Multi-phased monument. Residual? Lelong and Pollard 1998
ii. Beaker sherds recovered from 'red chip' (felsites) layer of site, in same layer as Food Vessel pottery.
iii. –

i. Uncertain date. Stone setting; ditched enclosure; cairn. Beaker from Stewart 1966; Longworth
cairn material. 1984: 312, no. 1986; Clarke
ii. Abrasion to sherds suggests they were not broken *in situ*. 1970: no. 1737.1
iii. –

i. Neolithic ritual structure? Post-hole. Calder 1952; Clarke 1970:
ii. Three small sherds of Beaker from upper filling of post-hole. no. 1778F
iii. –

i. Cursus monument. Pit deposit. Brann 2003
ii. Twenty sherds from fill of small truncated pit located within a cursus monument.

iii. Oak charcoal (*quercus* spp.) from fill of pit was dated 3875 ± 45 BP (AA-53171).

Bibliography

Allen, M., Gardiner, J. and Sheridan, A (eds) (2012), *Is there a British Chalcolithic? People, Place and Polity in the Later 3rd Millennium*, Oxford: Oxbow Books (= Prehistoric Society Research Paper 4).

Armit, I. (1996), *The Archaeology of Skye and the Western Isles*, Edinburgh: Edinburgh University Press.

Ashmore, P. J. (2002), *Calanais: The Standing Stones*, Edinburgh: Historic Scotland.

Atkinson, R. J. C. (1962), 'Fishermen and farmers', in S. Piggott (ed.), *The Prehistoric Peoples of Scotland*, London: Routledge & Kegan Paul, 1–38.

Ballin-Smith, B. (ed.) (1994), *Howe: Four Millennia of Orkney Prehistory. Excavations 1978–1982*, Edinburgh: Society of Antiquaries of Scotland.

Barclay, G. J. (1983), 'Sites of the third millennium BC to the first millennium AD at North Mains, Strathallan, Perthshire', *Proceedings of the Society of Antiquaries of Scotland*, 113: 122–282.

Barclay, G. J. (1999), 'Cairnpapple revisited: 1948–1988', *Proceedings of the Prehistoric Society*, 65: 17–46.

Barclay, G. J. (2005), 'The "henge" and "hengiform" in Scotland', in V. Cummings and A. Pannett (eds), *Set in Stone. New Approaches to Neolithic Monuments in Scotland*, Oxford: Oxbow Books, 81–94.

Barclay, G. J. and Russell-White, C. J. (1993), 'Excavation in the ceremonial complex of the fourth to second millennium BC at Balfarg/Balbirnie, Glenrothes, Fife', *Proceedings of the Society of Antiquaries of Scotland*, 123: 43–210.

Bayliss, A. C., McAvoy, F. and Whittle, A. (2007), 'The world recreated: radiating Silbury Hill in its monumental landscape', *Antiquity*, 81: 26–53.

Bradley, R. (2000), *The Good Stones: A New Investigation of the Clava Cairns*, Edinburgh: Society of Antiquaries of Scotland.

Bradley, R. (2002), *The Past in Prehistoric Societies*, London: Routledge.

Bradley, R. (2005), *The Moon and the Bonfire. An Investigation of Three Stone Circles in North-east Scotland*, Edinburgh: Society of Antiquaries of Scotland.

Bradley, R. and Clarke, A. (n.d.), 'Excavations at Hillhead, Tarland', unpublished interim report, University of Reading.

Brann, M. (2003), 'Curriestanes Cursus, Dumfries. Archaeological Monitoring of Cargenbridge Sewerage Scheme', unpublished interim report, Royal Commission on the Ancient and Historical Monuments of Scotland MS 1628, Edinburgh.

Brindley, A. L. (2007), *The Dating of Food Vessels and Urns in Ireland*, Galway: Department of Archaeology, National Museum of Ireland.

Brophy, K. and Noble. G. (2008), *Forteviot, Perthshire 2008: Excavations of a Henge Monument and Timber Circle*, Data Structure and Interim Report, University of Glasgow.

Brophy, K. and Noble. G. (2010), *Forteviot Multiphase Ceremonial Monument Excavation 2010*, SERF Project Data Structure and Interim Report, University of Glasgow.

Brophy, K. and Noble, G. (2012), 'Henging, mounding and blocking: the Forteviot henge group', in A. Gibson (ed.) *Enclosing the Neolithic. Recent Studies in Britain and Europe*, Oxford: British Archaeological Reports, 21–35.

Bryce, T. H. (1902), 'On the cairns of Arran: a record of exploration, with an anatomical description of the human remains discovered', *Proceedings of the Society of Antiquaries of Scotland*, 36: 110–1, 172–3.

Bryce, T. H. (1903), 'On the cairns of Arran: a record of further explorations during the season of 1902', *Proceedings of the Society of Antiquaries of Scotland*, 37: 44–52.

Bryce, T. H. (1904), 'On the cairns and tumuli of the Island of Bute. A record of explorations during the season of 1903', *Proceedings of the Society of Antiquaries of Scotland*, 38: 17–81.

Bryce, T. H. (1909), 'On the cairns of Arran, No. III. With a notice of a megalithic structure at Ardenadam, on the Holy Loch', *Proceedings of the Society of Antiquaries of Scotland*, 43: 341–50.

Burl, H. A. W. (1975), 'Buchan, recumbent stone circles', *Discovery and Excavation in Scotland*, 1975: 7.

Burl, H. A. W. (1976), 'Buchan, Berrybrae recumbent stone circle', *Discovery and Excavation in Scotland*, 1976: 6.

Burl, H. A. W. (1977), 'Berrybrae, recumbent stone circle', *Discovery and Excavation in Scotland*, 1977: 4–5.

Burl, H. A. W. (1984), 'Report on the excavation of a Neolithic mound at Boghead, Speymouth Forest, Fochabers, Moray, 1972 and 1973', *Proceedings of the Society of Antiquaries of Scotland*, 114: 35–73.

Calder, C. S. T. (1952), 'Report on the excavation of a Neolithic temple at Stanydale in the Parish of Sandsting, Shetland', *Proceedings of the Society of Antiquaries of Scotland*, 84: 185–205.

Callander, J. G. (1928), 'A Beaker from a short cist in a long cairn at Kilmarie, Skye', *Proceedings of the Society of Antiquaries of Scotland*, 62: 22–6.

Callander, J. G. and Grant, W. G. (1935), 'A long stalled cairn, the Knowe of Yarso, in Rousay, Orkney', *Proceedings of the Society of Antiquaries of Scotland*, 69: 325–51.

Carlin, N. (2011), 'Into the west: placing Beakers within their Irish contexts', in A. M. Jones and G. Kirkham (eds), *Beyond the Core: Reflections on Regionality in Prehistory*, Oxford: Oxbow Books, 87–100.

Carlin, N. and Brück, J. (2012), 'Searching for the Chalcolithic: continuity and change in the Irish final Neolithic/early Bronze Age', in Allen, Gardiner and Sheridan (eds), *Is there a British Chalcolithic?*, 193–210.

Childe, V. G. (1933), 'Trial excavations at the Old Keig Stone Circle, Aberdeenshire', *Proceedings of the Society of Antiquaries of Scotland*, 67: 37–53.

Childe, V. G. (1934), 'Final report on the excavation of the stone circle at Old Keig, Aberdeenshire', *Proceedings of the Society of Antiquaries of Scotland*, 68: 372–93.

Clarke, D. L. (1970), *Beaker Pottery in Great Britain and Ireland*, Cambridge: Cambridge University Press, 2 vols.

Close-Brooks, J. and Ritchie, J. N. G. (1978), '(iii) Beaker pottery from Skye', in

Ritchie and Crawford, *Proceedings of the Society of Antiquaries of Scotland*, 109: 99–102.

Cochran-Patrick, R. W. (1875), 'Note of some explorations in a tumulus called Court Hill, in the Parish of Dalry, and the County of Ayr', *Proceedings of the Society of Antiquaries of Scotland*, 10: 281–3.

Coles, F. R. (1902), 'Report on stone circles in Aberdeenshire (Inverurie, Eastern Parishes, and Insch Districts), with measured plans and drawings, obtained under the Gunning Fellowship', *Proceedings of the Society of Antiquaries of Scotland*, 36: 527–31.

Coles, F. R. (1906), 'Notices of standing stones, cists, and hitherto unrecorded cup and ring-marks in various localities', *Proceedings of the Society of Antiquaries of Scotland*, 40: 291–327.

Cook, M., Ellis, C. and Sheridan, A. (2010), 'Excavations at Upper Largie Quarry, Argyll & Bute, Scotland: new light on the prehistoric ritual landscape of the Kilmartin Glen', *Proceedings of the Prehistoric Society*, 75: 165–212.

Corcoran, J. X. W. P. (1967), 'The excavation of three chambered cairns at Loch Calder, Caithness', *Proceedings of the Society of Antiquaries of Scotland*, 98: 1–75.

Corcoran, J. X. W. P. (1969), 'Excavation of two chambered cairns at Mid Gleniron Farm, Glenluce, Wigtownshire', *Transactions of the Dumfriesshire and Galloway Natural History and Antiquarian Society*, 46: 29–90.

Cormack, E. A. (1964), 'Balvraid, Glen Beag', *Discovery and Excavation in Scotland*, 1964: 30.

Cormack, W. F. (1963), 'Burial site at Kirkburn, Lockerbie', *Proceedings of the Society of Antiquaries of Scotland*, 96: 107–36.

Cowie, T. G. (1978), *Bronze Age Food Vessel Urns*, Oxford: British Archaeological Reports.

Cowie, T. G. (1988), *Magic Metals: Early Metalworkers in the North-east*, Aberdeen: Anthropological Museum, University of Aberdeen.

Cowie, T. G. (1993), 'Beaker pottery: vessels P115 to 153', in Barclay and Russell-White, *Proceedings of the Society of Antiquaries of Scotland*, 123: microfiche 1:A4-04.

Cressey, M. and Sheridan, A. (2003), 'The excavation of a Bronze Age cemetery at Seafield West, near Inverness, Highland', *Proceedings of the Society of Antiquaries of Scotland*, 133: 47–84.

Crichton-Mitchell, M. E. (1934), 'A new analysis of the Early Bronze Age Beaker pottery of Scotland', *Proceedings of the Society of Antiquaries of Scotland*, 68: 132–89.

Curtis, N. G. W. and Wilkin, N. C. A. (2012), 'The regionality of Beakers and bodies in the Chalcolithic of north-east Scotland', in Allen, Gardiner and Sheridan (eds), *Is there a British Chalcolithic?* 237–56.

Curtis, N., Wilkin, N., Hutchison, M., Jay, M., Sheridan, A. and Wright, M. (2007), 'Radiocarbon dating results from the Beakers and Bodies Project', *Discovery and Excavation in Scotland*, n.s., 8: 220–1.

Davidson, J. L. and Henshall, A. S. (1989), *The Chambered Cairns of Orkney*, Edinburgh: Edinburgh University Press.

Davidson, J. L. and Henshall, A. S. (1991), *The Chambered Cairns of Caithness*, Edinburgh: Edinburgh University Press.

Donations (1969), 'Donations and purchases for the Museum, 1968–69', *Proceedings of the Society of Antiquaries of Scotland*, 101: 292.

Dunwell, A., Johnson, M. and Armit, I. (2003), 'Excavations at Geirisclett chambered cairn, North Uist , Western Isles', *Proceedings of the Society of Antiquaries of Scotland*, 133: 1–33.

Edwards, A. J. H. (1929), 'Excavations at Reay Links and at a horned cairn at Upper Dounreay, Caithness', *Proceedings of the Society of Antiquaries of Scotland*, 63: 138–50.

Garrow, D. (2006), *Pits, Settlement and Deposition during the Neolithic and Early Bronze Age in East Anglia*, Oxford: British Archaeological Reports.

Garwood, P. (2007), 'Before the hills in order stood: chronology, time and history in the interpretation of Early Bronze Age round barrows', in J. Last (ed.), *Beyond the Grave: New Perspectives on Barrows*, Oxford: Oxbow Books, 30–52.

Gibson, A. (1982), *Beaker Domestic Sites*, Oxford: British Archaeological Reports.

Gibson, A. (1984), 'Problems of Beaker ceramic assemblages: the north British material', in R. Miket and C. Burgess (eds), *Between and Beyond the Walls: Essays on the Prehistory and History of North Britain in Honour of George Jobey*, Edinburgh: John Donald, 74–96.

Greenwell, W. (1866), 'An account of excavations in cairns near Crinan', *Proceedings of the Society of Antiquaries of Scotland*, 6: 336–51.

Gregory, R. A. (2002), Prehistoric landscapes in Dumfries and Galloway, Part 2: Bronze Age landscapes', *Transactions of the Dumfriesshire and Galloway Natural History and Antiquarian Society*, 76: 45–78.

Hanley, R. and Sheridan, A. (1994), 'A Beaker cist from Balblair, near Beauly, Inverness District', *Proceedings of the Society of Antiquaries of Scotland*, 124: 129–39.

Hanson, W. S. (2007), *Elginhaugh: A Flavian Fort and its Annexe*, London: Society for the Promotion of Roman Studies.

Henshall, A. S. (1963), *The Chambered Tombs of Scotland*, Edinburgh: Edinburgh University Press, vol. 1.

Henshall, A. S. (1972), *The Chambered Tombs of Scotland*, Edinburgh: Edinburgh University Press, vol. 2.

Henshall, A. S. (2009), 'The pottery', in A. Ritchie (ed.), *On the Fringe of Neolithic Europe*, 35–8.

Henshall, A. S. and Ritchie, J. N. G. (1995), *The Chambered Cairns of Sutherland: An Inventory of the Structures and their Contents*, Edinburgh: Edinburgh University Press.

Henshall, A. S. and Ritchie, J. N. G. (2001), *The Chambered Cairns of the Central Highlands*, Edinburgh: Edinburgh University Press.

Henshall, A. S. and Taylor, H. W. Y. (1957), 'A Bronze Age burial at Embo, Sutherland', *Proceedings of the Society of Antiquaries of Scotland*, 90: 225–7.

Henshall, A. S. and Wallace, J. C. (1963), 'The excavation of a chambered cairn at Embo, Sutherland', *Proceedings of the Society of Antiquaries of Scotland*, 96: 9–36.

Hingley, R. (2009), 'Esoteric knowledge? Ancient Bronze artefacts from Iron Age contexts', *Proceedings of the Prehistoric Society*, 75: 143–65.

Hodder, I. and Hutson, S. (2003), *Reading the Past: Current Approaches to Interpretation in Archaeology*, 3rd edn, Cambridge: Cambridge University Press.

Johnston, D. A. (1997), 'Biggar Common, 1987–93: an early prehistoric funerary and domestic landscape in Clydesdale, South Lanarkshire', *Proceedings of the Society of Antiquaries of Scotland*, 127: 185–253.

Jones, A. M. (2003), 'Technologies of remembrance: memory, materiality and identity in Early Bronze Age Scotland', in H. Williams (ed.), *Archaeologies of Remembrance: Death and Memory in Past Societies*, New York: Kluwer Academic/Plenum, 65–88.

Jones, A. M. (2010), 'Layers of meaning: concealment, containment, memory and secrecy in the British Early Bronze Age', in D. Borić (ed.), *Archaeology and Memory*, Oxford: Oxbow Books, 105–120.

Josipovici, G. (1999), *On Trust, Art and the Temptations of Suspicion*, New Haven, CT and London: Yale University Press.

Kenworthy, J. B. (1977), 'A reconsideration of the "Ardiffery" finds, Cruden, Aberdeenshire', *Proceedings of the Society of Antiquaries of Scotland*, 108: 80–93.

Kilbride-Jones, H. E. (1935), 'An account of the excavation of the stone circle at Loanhead of Daviot, and of the standing stones of Cullerlie, Echt, both in Aberdeenshire, on behalf of HM Office of Works', *Proceedings of the Society of Antiquaries of Scotland*, 69: 169–214.

Kinnes, I. A. and Longworth, I. H. (1985), *Catalogue of the Excavated Prehistoric and Romano-British Material in the Greenwell Collection*, London: British Museum.

Kinnes, I. A., Gibson, A. M., Ambers, J., Bowman, S., Leese, M. and Boast, R. (1991), 'Radiocarbon dating and British Beakers: the British Museum programme', *Scottish Archaeological Review*, 8: 35–68.

Kirk, W. and McKenzie, J. (1955), 'Three Bronze Age cist burials in NE Scotland', *Proceedings of the Society of Antiquaries of Scotland*, 88: 1–14.

Leivers, M., Roberts, J. and Peterson, R. (2000), 'The cairn at East Finnercy, Dunecht, Aberdeenshire', *Proceedings of the Society of Antiquaries of Scotland*, 130: 183–95.

Lelong, O. and Pollard, T. (1998), 'Excavation of a Bronze Age ring cairn at Cloburn Quarry, Cairngryffe Hill, Lanarkshire', *Proceedings of the Society of Antiquaries of Scotland*, 128: 105–42.

Longworth, I. H. (1984), *Collared Urns of the Bronze Age in Great Britain and Ireland*, Cambridge: Cambridge University Press.

MacGregor, G. and Stuart, E. (2007), 'Everything in its place: excavations at Eweford West, Overhailes, Pencraig Wood and Eweford Cottages', in O. Lelong and

G. MacGregor (eds), *The Lands of Ancient Lothian. Interpreting the Archaeology of the A1*, Edinburgh: Society of Antiquaries of Scotland, 69–98.

Masters, L. (1971), 'The Lochhill long cairn', *Antiquity*, 47: 96–100.

Masters, L. (1973), 'Colvend and Southwick, Slewcairn, unchambered long cairn', *Discovery and Excavation in Scotland*, 1973: 31.

Masters, L. (1974), 'Colvend and Southwick, Slewcairn, unchambered long cairn', *Discovery and Excavation in Scotland*, 1974: 43–4.

Masters, L. (1975), 'Colvend and Southwick, Slewcairn, unchambered long cairn', *Discovery and Excavation in Scotland*, 1975: 27–8.

Masters, L. (1981), 'Chambered tombs and Non-megalithic barrows in Britain', in J. D. Evans, B. Cunliffe, and C. Renfrew (eds), *Antiquity and Man. Essays in Honour of Glyn Daniel*, London: Thames & Hudson, 161–76.

Mercer, R. (1981), 'The excavation of a Late Neolithic henge-type enclosure at Balfarg, Markinch, Fife, Scotland, 1977–78', *Proceedings of the Society of Antiquaries of Scotland*, 111: 63–171.

McInnes, I. J. (1964), 'The Neolithic and Early Bronze Age pottery from Luce Sands, Wigtownshire', *Proceedings of the Society of Antiquaries of Scotland*, 97: 40–81.

Milne, J. (1892), 'Traces of early man in Buchan', *Transactions of the Buchan Field Club*, 2: 101–8.

Morton, A. E. W. (1990), 'Beakers and Pre-existing Monuments: Aspects of Ritual in Neolithic and Bronze Age Britain', unpublished PhD thesis, University of Edinburgh.

Needham, S. (2004), 'Migdale–Marnoch: sunburst of Scottish metallurgy', in I. A. G. Shepherd and G. J. Barclay (eds), *Scotland in Ancient Europe: The Neolithic and Early Bronze Age of Scotland in their European Context*, Edinburgh: Society of Antiquaries of Scotland, 217–45.

Needham, S. (2005), 'Transforming Beaker culture in north-west Europe: processes of fusion and fission', *Proceedings of the Prehistoric Society*, 71: 171–217.

Phillips, T., Hampshire-Monk, I. and Abramson, P. (2006), 'The excavation and reconstruction of the recumbent stone circle at Strichen, Aberdeenshire, 1979–82', *Proceedings of the Society of Antiquaries of Scotland*, 136: 111–34.

Piggott, S. (1950), 'The excavations at Cairnpapple Hill, West Lothian, 1947–8', *Proceedings of the Society of Antiquaries of Scotland*, 82: 68–123

Piggott, S. (1974), 'Excavation of the Dalladies long barrow, Fettercairn, Kincardineshire', *Proceedings of the Society of Antiquaries of Scotland*, 104: 23–47.

Piggott, S. and Powell, T. G. E. (1949), 'The excavation of three Neolithic chambered tombs in Galloway, 1949', *Proceedings of the Society of Antiquaries of Scotland*, 83: 103–61.

Ralston, I. B. M. (1988), 'Belhie (Auchterarder parish) enclosed cremation cemetery, minihenge and other cropmarked features', *Discovery and Excavation in Scotland*, 1988: 27.

Ralston, I. B. M. (1996), 'Four short cists from north-east Scotland and Easter Ross', *Proceedings of the Society of Antiquaries of Scotland*, 126: 121–55.

Ritchie, A. (ed.) (2009), *On the Fringe of Neolithic Europe: Excavation of a Chambered Cairn on the Holm of Papa Westray, Orkney*, Edinburgh: Society of Antiquaries of Scotland.

Ritchie, J. N. G. (1973), 'Excavation of the chambered cairn at Achnacreebeag', *Proceedings of the Society of Antiquaries of Scotland*, 102: 31–55.

Ritchie, J. N. G. (1974a), 'Excavation of a chambered cairn at Dalineun, Lorn, Argyll', *Proceedings of the Society of Antiquaries of Scotland*, 104: 48–62, pls 9–10

Ritchie, J. N. G. (1974b), 'Excavation of the stone circle and cairn at Balbirnie, Fife', *Archaeological Journal*, 131: 1–32.

Ritchie, J. N. G. and Crawford, J. (1978), 'Recent work on Coll and Skye: (i) Excavations at Sorisdale and Killunaig, Coll; (ii) Notes on prehistoric and later artefacts from Coll; (iii) Beaker pottery from Skye', *Proceedings of the Society of Antiquaries of Scotland*, 109: 75–82.

Rojo-Guerra, M. Á., Garrido-Pena, R., García-Martínez-de-Lagrán, Í., Juan-Treserras, J. and Matamala, J. C. (2006), 'Beer and bell Beakers: drinking rituals in Copper Age inner Iberia', *Proceedings of the Prehistoric* Society, 72: 243–65.

Ross, A. (1994) 'Pottery report', in Ballin-Smith (ed.), *Howe: Four Millennia of Orkney Prehistory*, 236–57.

Rowlands, M. (1993), 'The role of memory in the transmission of culture', *World Archaeology*, 25: 141–51.

Scott, J. G. (1991), 'The stone circles at Temple Wood, Kilmartin, Argyll', *Glasgow Archaeological Journal*, 15: 53–124.

Scott, W. L. (1932), 'Rudh' an Dunain chambered cairn, Skye', *Proceedings of the Society of Antiquaries of Scotland*, 66: 183–213

Scott, W. L. (1935), 'The chambered cairn of Clettraval, North Uist', *Proceedings of the Society of Antiquaries of Scotland*, 69: 480–536.

Scott, W. L. (1948), The chamber tomb of Unival, North Uist', *Proceedings of the Society of Antiquaries of Scotland*, 82: 1–49.

Sharples, N. (2009), 'Beaker settlement in the Western Isles', in M. J. Allen, N. Sharples and T. O'Connor (eds), *Land and People. Papers in Honour of John G. Evans*, Oxford: Oxbow Books/Prehistoric Society, 147–58.

Shepherd, A. N. (1989), 'A note on the orientation of Beaker burials in north-east Scotland', in M. K. Greig, C. Greig, A. N. Shepherd and I. A. G. Shepherd, 'A beaker cist from Chapleden, Tore of Troup, Aberdour, Banff and Buchan District, with a note on the orientation of Beaker burials in north-east Scotland', *Proceedings of the Prehistoric Society*, 119: 79–80.

Shepherd, A. (1994), 'Howe: a review of the sequence', in Ballin-Smith (ed.), *Howe: Four Millennia of Orkney Prehistory*, 267–92.

Shepherd, A. (1996), 'A Neolithic ring-mound at Midtown of Pitglassie, Auchterless, Aberdeenshire', *Proceedings of the Society of Antiquaries of Scotland*, 126: 17–51

Shepherd, A. N. (2012), 'Stepping out together: men, women and their Beakers in time and space', in Allen, Gardiner and Sheridan (eds), *Is there a British Chalcolithic?*, 257–80.

Shepherd, I. A. G. (1986), *Powerful Pots: Beakers in North-east Prehistory*, Aberdeen: Anthropological Museum, University of Aberdeen.

Sheridan, J. A. (1992), 'Scottish stone axeheads: some new work and recent discoveries', in N. M. Sharples and J. A. Sheridan (eds), *Vessels for the Ancestors: Essays on the Neolithic of Britain and Ireland in Honour of Audrey Henshall*, Edinburgh: Edinburgh University Press, 194–212.

Sheridan, J. A. (2007a), 'From Picardie to Pickering and Pencraig Hill? New information on the "Carinated Bowl Neolithic" in northern Britain', in A. W. R. Whittle and V. Cummings (eds), *Going Over: The Mesolithic–Neolithic Transition in North-west Europe*, Oxford: British Academy, 441–92.

Sheridan, J. A. (2007b), 'Scottish Beaker dates: the good, the bad and the ugly', in M. Larsson and M. Parker Pearson (eds), *From Stonehenge to the Baltic. Living with Cultural Diversity in the Third Millennium* BC, Oxford: British Archaeological Reports, 91–123.

Sheridan, J. A. (2007c), 'Beaker Pottery from Eweford', Archive Report for O. Lelong and G. MacGregor (eds), *The Lands of Ancient Lothian. Interpreting the Archaeology of the A1*. Edinburgh: Society of Antiquaries of Scotland (archived).

Sheridan, J. A. (2008), 'Upper Largie and Dutch–Scottish connections during the Beaker period', in H. Fokkens, B. Y. Coles, A. L. van Gijn, J. P. Kleijne, H. H. Ponjee and C. G. Slappendel (eds), *Between Foraging and Farming. An Extended Broad Spectrum of Papers presented to Leendert Louwe Kooijmans*, Leiden: Leiden University, 247–60. (= Analecta Praehistorica Leidensia, 40).

Sheridan, A. (2010), 'Scotland's Neolithic non-megalithic round mounds: new dates, problems and potential', in J. Leary, T. Darvill and D. Field (eds), *Round Mounds and Monumentality in the British Neolithic and Beyond*, Oxford: Oxbow Books, 28–52.

Stewart, M. E. C. (1966), 'The excavation of a setting of standing stones at Lundin Farm near Aberfeldy, Perthshire', *Proceedings of the Society of Antiquaries of Scotland*, 98: 126–42.

Stewart, M .E. C. (1987), 'The excavation of a henge, stone circles and metal-working area at Moncrieffe, Perthshire', *Proceedings of the Society of Antiquaries of Scotland*, 115: 125–50.

Sylvester, D. (1975), *The Brutality of Fact. Interviews with Francis Bacon*, London: Thames & Hudson.

Thomas, J. (1991), 'Reading the body: Beaker funerary practice in Britain', in P. Garwood, F. Jennings, R. Skeates and J. Toms (eds), *Sacred and Profane: Proceedings of a Conference on Archaeology, Ritual and Religion, Oxford, 1989*, 33–42 (= Oxford University Committee for Archaeology Monograph 32).

Watkins, T. and Shepherd, I. A. G. (1981), 'A beaker burial at Newmill, near Bankfoot, Perthshire', *Proceedings of the Society of Antiquaries of Scotland*, 110: 32–41

Wilkin, N. C. A. (2009), 'Regional Narratives of the Early Bronze Age. A Contextual and Evidence-led Approach to the Funerary Practices of East-central Scotland', unpublished MPhil thesis, Institute of Archaeology and Antiquity, University of Birmingham.

Wilkin, N. (2011), 'Grave-goods, contexts and interpretation: towards regional narratives of Early Bronze Age Scotland', *Scottish Archaeological Journal*, 33: 21–37.

Wilkin, N., Curtis, N., Hutchison, M. and Wright, M. (2009), 'Further radiocarbon dating results from the Beakers and Bodies Project', *Discovery and Excavation in Scotland*, n.s., 10: 216–18.

Woodham, A. A. (1956), 'Kilcoy West', *Discovery and Excavation in Scotland*, 1956: 23–4.

Woodham, A. A. and Woodham, M. F. (1959), 'The excavation of a chambered cairn at Kilcoy, Ross-shire', *Proceedings of the Society of Antiquaries of Scotland*, 90: 102–15.

Woodham, 'Dr' and Woodham, A. A. (1957), 'Kilcoy West', *Discovery and Excavation in Scotland*, 1957: 32–3.

Index